D1112882

AMERICAN PASTIMES

AMERICAN
PASTIMES

THE VERY BEST

of **RED SMITH**

EDITED AND WITH AN INTRODUCTION BY **DANIEL OKRENT**
AFTERWORD BY **TERENCE SMITH**

A SPECIAL PUBLICATION OF THE LIBRARY OF AMERICA

Distributed to the trade in the United States
by Penguin Group (USA) Inc.
and in Canada by Penguin Books Canada Ltd.

Book design by David Bullen.

Library of Congress Control Number: 2013930950
ISBN 978–1–59853–217–3

First Printing

Printed in the United States of America

Contents

FISHING FOR BASS

SPORTS IN THE SEVENTIES

BASEBALL 1962-1981

Introduction

Red All Over

In 1987, shortly after his peers named him "Sportswriter of the Year" for the fifth time, Frank Deford attempted to confront the ambiguity lurking in those four words. In the introduction to a collection of his work, he declared he had finally "resolved the issue with myself: that I am a writer, and incidentally I write mostly about sports, and what is important is to write well, the topic be damned." But being named the best sportswriter nonetheless provoked the title Deford chose for his collection: *The World's Tallest Midget*.

I believe Deford would not object to the assertion that Red Smith was taller still. I also believe Smith was tall enough to stand shoulder-to-shoulder with the finest prose artists in twentieth-century American literature. He never wrote a book. His work appeared in 800-word increments in daily newspapers. When circumstances demanded it, he would address matters serious enough to merit the attention of those who didn't care about sports, but that was only rarely. For half a century American sports fans were granted the privilege of reading his crystalline sentences four, six, for a period seven times a week. If a surprising number of people who couldn't tell the difference between a left hook and a left tackle were familiar with the purity of his prose, it was likely because there was someone else at the breakfast table reading choice selections aloud. Consider your encounter with this collection a proxy for that breakfast table. If you intend to underline appealing phrases, sentences, and paragraphs for later recitation, arm yourself with a fistful of pens. It will keep you busy.

Walter Wellesley Smith, born in 1905, emerged from Green Bay, Wisconsin, via the University of Notre Dame, where an instructor taught him that a sentence should be "so definite that it would cast a shadow." He wanted to be a newspaperman, but writing about sports wasn't a particular goal. In his first job, he chased fire trucks for the *Milwaukee Sentinel*. A year later, in 1928, he moved to the copy desk of *The St. Louis Star*, where he wrote headlines, deleted commas, and mended split infinitives. He started covering sports only because there was an opening, and the managing editor needed a body.

Smith began to shape his style in St. Louis. It was an era when the stars of the sportswriting profession were Grantland Rice, who celebrated what came to be known as the "Golden Age of Sports," and Westbrook Pegler, whose more cynical description was the "Golden Age of Nonsense." Early on, Smith found a voice neither florid like Rice's nor sulfurous like Pegler's but closer in its sidelong, raised-eyebrow gaze to another of his sportswriter heroes, Damon Runyon. Unlike Pegler, who soon brought his acerbity to political commentary, or Runyon, who migrated to fiction, Smith emulated his friend Rice's path, if not his prose. For the next fifty-four years, until the end of his life, Red Smith wrote about sports.

He started to make a reputation extending beyond the readership of his own paper only when he moved to *The Philadelphia Record*, in 1936. According to his excellent biographer, Ira Berkow (upon whom anyone writing about Red Smith's career can lean confidently, and must lean frequently), he signed on with the *Record* for two reasons: a five-dollar-a-week raise and, crucially, proximity to New York.

In Philadelphia Walter W. Smith began using his nickname in his byline, and if you read the *Record* there was no way of avoiding him. He was in the paper every day during the baseball season. When the season ended (for the Phillies and the Athletics, that was always on the early side) he stepped directly into college football, basketball, minor-league hockey, or whatever else his editors required, producing as many as ten articles a week, plus a Sunday column. Boxing and horse racing were both year-round engagements, and when other opportunities arose, he seized them. In Mexico City, where the A's conducted spring training in 1937, he interviewed the exiled Leon Trotsky (headline: "Red Smith Talks to Red Trotsky"). The column he'd been writing on Sundays became a daily fixture in 1939.

Six years later, New York called. Around the time Smith arrived in town, the writers who gathered at the circular bar at Toots Shor's on West 51st Street functioned as a command-and-control center that determined the nation's sense of sports. Eight daily papers battled for the attention of the city's millions, and the town's most ambitious sports editors believed their turf reached across the entire country. Or at least across half of it; televised sports didn't yet exist, and as far as most sportswriters and fans were concerned neither did Los Angeles, nor any other place west or south of the most distant outpost of the big time, St. Louis.

The man who brought Smith to New York was Stanley Woodward, the celebrated sports editor of the *Herald Tribune*, whose appetite for talent was voracious. (A Woodward rival once said "Holy smokes! These guys will be hiring Thomas A. Edison to turn off the lights!") For a sportswriter, the *Trib* was the top rung. It had nearly the prestige of the *Times*, but without the stultifying formality the *Times*'s editors imposed on its sports pages.

Woodward had been following Smith's work for years, clipping the best of it for a thickening file. "He obviously was writing too much [in Philadelphia], probably 500,000 words a year," Woodward would recall, "but he made it all good and much of it excellent. Some of his columns were afterthoughts, conjured up out of thin air, written perhaps between innings of a ball game or between races. However, they were never dull and it was easy to see what a man like this could do if relieved of the heavy burden he was carrying." At the *Trib*, he would be asked to write just one story a day—by modern standards, a killing pace. "He reacted amazingly," Woodward wrote. "From the start his product was brilliant." In his editor's view, and soon enough in the view of Smith's colleagues and competitors, at the *Trib* Smith became "the greatest of all sports writers, by which I mean that he is better than all the ancients as well as the moderns."

Shortly after Smith's arrival in New York, Woodward sent a fistful of *Trib* sportswriters to cover the World Series, but gave Smith no
specific assignment. When Smith asked him what he was supposed
to do, Woodward told him to "write about the smell of cabbage in the
hallway." In other words, keep your senses open and alert, and you'll
find something that no one else is paying attention to.

This couldn't have been a revelation to Smith—he'd been doing
just that for years—but he liked the sound of it, and for the rest of his
career quoted Woodward frequently. An intense focus on the sideshow
to the main event was essential to Smith's craft. Not the roaring cars
hurtling around the Indianapolis Speedway, but the faces and clothing
and refreshment choices of the crowd in the infield. Not the punch
that knocked out the champion, but the look in his eyes as he struggled
to rise from the canvas.

Over the next twenty-two years his *Herald Tribune* column, "Views
of Sport," propelled him to national renown. In 1950, *Time* saluted
him in an article headlined "Red from Green Bay." Eight years later,
his face decorated the cover of *Newsweek*, above the words "Star of
the Press Box." Edward R. Murrow brought a CBS crew to his house in
Connecticut—they had to erect a transmission tower in the backyard—
for a live broadcast of *Person to Person*. He assumed permanent occu-
pancy at Table Number 1 at Shor's. His column was syndicated to more
than 100 newspapers across the country. It reached across the Atlantic as well: In *Across the River and into the Trees* Ernest Hemingway
describes his protagonist, Richard Cantwell, sitting in Venice with
a glass of Valpolicella and a copy of the international edition of the
Herald Tribune, reading a Smith column. This was a small, writerly
detail, of the kind that may seem inconsequential but in fact tells the
reader a great deal. In this case, it helped define Cantwell, and simultaneously signified the stature Smith had achieved.

In some ways, columnists during the heart of the Red Smith Era had
it easier than beat writers. They could pick their sports and their shots.
Compelled to write about nothing in particular, they could write about

anything at all. And they weren't burdened with having to provide
the tick-tocky play-by-play of the run that crossed the plate in the
fourth, the touchdown that put the visiting team ahead, the putt that
rimmed the cup on 14. There was no need for a columnist to quote
the vacuous "We'll take 'em one day at a time" of the defeated pitcher,
the obligatory "I just saw my pitch and hit it" of the guy who knocked
in the winning run. The men on the beat could do that.

But the columnists' freedom was a diluted virtue; it meant they had
to search for another way to say what everyone who'd read the beat
guy's article already knew—and to say it in a way that was not only
insightful but fresh. No one did this as well as Smith, whose loathing
for clichés was almost pathological. The feedback loop of broadcasters
and sportswriters parading and parroting the same bromides "is worse
than a vicious circle," he wrote in 1949. "It is a noose." Most days, he
was the last man in the press box, crumpling up page after page of false
starts, discarding strained metaphors, struggling to dodge the ancient
banalities that infest so much sportswriting—in a word, struggling to
write like Red Smith.

In the late afternoon or early evening of October 3, 1951, Smith
wrote what is, to me, the platonic ideal of a column about a major
sports event. This was, of course, the day that Bobby Thomson's ninth-
inning home run lifted the National League pennant from the pocket of
the Brooklyn Dodgers. By the time the *Herald Tribune* landed on door-
steps the following morning, there could not have been an English-
speaking New Yorker (and very few non-English speakers) who did not
know what had happened the previous afternoon in upper Manhattan.
About half the way into the piece, Smith begins to give some of the
details of the game before stopping in mid-recitation to ask, "What's
the use?"

Smith's loss for words led him to turn the piece inside out and
create as fine a lead as any sportswriter has ever committed to paper.
It's reprinted here on page 76, but it's worth looking at those first few

sentences independent of the paragraphs that follow. More than sixty years later, it feels as immediate, and as definitive, as it must have on the day it was published. Listen:

"Now it is done. Now the story ends. And there is no way to tell it. The art of fiction is dead. Reality has strangled invention. Only the utterly impossible, the inexpressibly fantastic, can ever be plausible again."

There's no better way to murder great prose than to subject it to close analysis. But, to me, these few sentences reveal some essential aspects of Smith's matchless technique.

1. *The simple string of declarative sentences*—sentences, as his Notre Dame instructor would have said, that "cast a shadow." There is no preening syntax here (which might explain why Hemingway admired him so much). The first five sentences—four words, four words, eight words, six words, four words—establish a rhythm that launches the last one.

2. *The absence of distraction.* Someone with a better eye than mine might find more examples than I did, but I couldn't locate in the present collection more than a dozen semicolons. Dashes, ellipses, parentheticals, and all the other prosy hems and haws we lesser writers depend upon are scarce. The water-treading transitions we use to get from one idea to the next ("Of course . . . ," "Indeed . . . ," "And then . . .") are even rarer. In a Red Smith column, links with the sentences that precede and follow one another arise from logic, not tired idiom. It is an extremely difficult rhetorical strategy to execute, requiring both agility and control.

3. *Rhetorical invention*—for instance, "The art of fiction is dead." Killing off fiction because of a baseball game is ingenious, amusing, and audacious. With very few exceptions, Smith's metaphors, similes, and other devices are as sharp as . . . well, I'd better not go there.

Let them speak for themselves. Here, from another column, is the end of a brutal championship fight: "In the closing seconds you couldn't have scraped the winner off the loser with a putty knife." Or this, from a piece on Knute Rockne: "Rock was a stocky man of slightly less than medium height who gave the impression that instead of dressing he just stood in a room and let clothes drop on him."

4. *Verbs as emphasizers*. We're all taught to use strong verbs, but Smith could summon verbs so powerful they rendered adjectives unnecessary: "Reality has strangled invention." One could say this brilliant little sentence merely repeats the one that precedes it. But extraordinary events deserve extraordinary emphasis, and it is very difficult to imagine a verb as strong as "strangled," which is the fulcrum of the entire paragraph.

These were not the only elements of Smith's technique. Among the others: heightened irony (a line drive that "performed an appendectomy" on a third baseman); a somewhat facile but nonetheless endearing self-deprecation (describing himself: "a seedy amateur with watery eyes behind glittering glasses, a retiring chin, a hole in his frowzy haircut, and a good deal of dandruff on his shoulders"); and what the political columnist James J. Kilpatrick called his "wonderfully funny, pool ball sense of humor; he could play caroms and cushions before hitting his target." Fans at a wintry Harvard-Yale game were "wrapped thickly in the skins of dead animals." In the 1946 World Series, as the Cardinals' Enos Slaughter sped home with the winning run, Boston shortstop Johnny Pesky didn't pause before throwing to the catcher; he "stood morosely studying Ford Frick's signature on the ball." Like Mark Twain, Smith let his humor shine through the unfolding narrative, never pausing to snicker at his own jokes. Of the hundreds and hundreds of caroming pool shots he executed over his long career, my favorite is the rueful one he wrote after Richard M. Nixon announced the lineup for his own personal all-star team. "When you regard him as a sportswriter," Smith wrote, "you can't help feeling that he really ought to go back to being President of the United States. That's a dreadful, difficult line to write."

I don't mean to suggest that Smith's capacity for invention was limitless. No one could possibly write 10,000 columns over the course of a career and not repeat himself. In this collection, I stumbled across one image that he twice pulled out of his kitbag: a boxer "being separated from his intellect" and, twenty-three years later, a football player who is "knocked loose from his intellect."

If you're going to reuse an image every twenty-three years, it might as well be as good as that one.

From *Red*, by Ira Berkow: "There's nothing to writing. All you do is sit down at the typewriter and open a vein."—Red Smith

On a plaque in the courtyard of the Poynter Institute, St. Petersburg, Florida: "Writing is easy. All you do is sit down at the typewriter and open a vein."—Red Smith

From *The New York Times*, when Smith won the Pulitzer Prize for commentary: "All you have to do is sit down and open a vein and bleed it out, drop by drop."—Red Smith

To my knowledge, Smith's most frequently quoted words never appeared in print below his byline, which may explain why so many different versions have been circulating around the journalism business for decades. But in interviews about the way he practiced his profession, he never failed to make a distinction between the work a writer does before he sits down to write, which he loved, and the act of writing itself, which he claimed to loathe.

In addition to those opened veins, his comments on the act of writing invoked lashes and chains. He called his home office the Torture Chamber. Asked how long it took him to write a column, he would come back with his own question: "How much time do I have?" He joked about the difficulty of the task, but he didn't complain. Writing, he said, "is the price I have to pay for this lovely job."

He struck a nice metaphor for his view of that job in the title of one of his collections: *Strawberries in the Wintertime*. For a man as congenial, as informal, and as compulsively energetic as Smith, the raffish world of fight promoters, ballplayers, racetrack touts, and other sportswriters was his own moveable feast. Before the big leagues reached the west coast in 1957, the sports world traveled by train. Three-week road trips to Cleveland and Chicago and St. Louis created a touring fraternity. Spring training provided a sunny group vacation punctuated by daytime ballgames and nighttime revels. "I don't want to be a millionaire," said Smith's counterpart at the New York *Journal-American*, columnist Bill Corum. "I just want to live like one."

As much as he liked the life, or disliked the writing, Smith loved the reporting—noting the smell of the cabbage in the hallway, but also digging deeply into the personalities of the people he wrote about. He enjoyed the company of athletes more than managers, managers more than owners, owners more than commissioners. "Bowie Kuhn doesn't tell you anything," he said when Kuhn ruled baseball, "so I don't know whether he lies or not."

For Smith, an interview was a conversation, less question-and-answer exercise than bantering dialogue, and never made formal or self-conscious by the intrusion of pen, steno pad, or tape recorder. He never took notes. "In contrast to the modern sportswriters who can't live without tape recorders," Miami Dolphins coach Don Shula once said, "Red Smith wrote accurately from memory." From each conversation he would preserve the salient quotes, the sound of a voice, the revealing facial expression—all the elements needed to fashion a full character.

His favorite spectator sports were baseball, boxing, and thoroughbred racing. Back when college football was largely an honest expression of amateurism, he was charmed by its ambience and engaged by its boisterous drama. Fishing—the only sport he participated in—induced a particularly ruminative quality in his prose. In his fishing columns, Smith exhaled. They're his most personal pieces, written in a tranquility that the spectator sports rarely afforded him. If most sports page readers had no interest in the sport itself, they could still be captured by the prose. Captured, and transported as well, as I am each time I read this perfect little sentence, from 1950: "A pair of loons flew overhead, taking their time."

Smith didn't much care for hockey, and he detested basketball. "I like the sports that write well," he told an interviewer in 1950. "Baseball writes itself. It's two out and the bases are loaded and—well, you've got a situation right there. In basketball, some big goon throws the ball up and it either goes in or it doesn't." He called basketball and hockey "up-and-down sports," or "back-and-forth sports." Baseball and boxing were all unfolding narrative; hockey and basketball depended on the brief, explosive moment. In Smith's lexicon, James Naismith hadn't invented basketball, he "perpetrated" it. In the same piece he acknowledged that "this is written by one who would rather drink a Bronx cocktail than speak well of basketball." Even so, he could find inspiration during the game at hand, in one instance settling his attention on a giant center who "plucked rebounds off the backboard like currants off a bush."

Auto racing charmed him even less. Two pieces in this collection reveal a nearly moralistic unease with the sport. In the first, "Rendezvous with Danger," on page 126, Smith displays an uncharacteristically snobbish distaste for the fans at the "gigantic, grimy lawn party" that gathers around the Indianapolis 500, "where the infield crowds fight for position near the turns because the turns [offer] the likeliest opportunity to see a man untidily killed." Twelve years later, in "Greaseniks" (page 367), he's equally sour. "They kill spectators at Le Mans, they kill little girls at Watkins Glen," he wrote, and at Sebring "guys said, 'Gee what a shame.'"

The violence of boxing, on the other hand, was essential to a sport he loved deeply. It would be a close contest with the ballpark, the trout stream, and the backstretch of a thoroughbred track, but you get the sense that Smith found his greatest professional joy at ringside for a championship match. Next best would be a training camp, a neighborhood fight club, the dressing room of a defeated contender. He loved the fights, and the fighters, and the trainers, and even a few of the promoters who got rich from the exertions and pains of the men in the ring.

In 1962, when middleweight Benny Paret died at the fists of Emile Griffith ("Death of a Welterweight," page 361), Smith made an effort to look head-on at the potentially fatal violence that lurked in the wings at every prizefight. First he dilates on the appeal of boxing, "the most

basic and natural and uncomplicated of athletic competitions, and—
at its best—one of the purest." Still, he doesn't object to "those who
sincerely regard it as a vicious business that should have no place in
a civilized society." What he doesn't like are the hypocrites. "Some of
the fakers now sobbing publicly over Paret have waxed ecstatic over a
Ray Robinson or Joe Louis," he wrote. "It must be comforting to have
it both ways." And then he skitters away into a wonderful and entirely
tangential story about the trainer Ray Arcel.

I think Smith veered off course in this piece because he just couldn't
deal with the paradox that straddled both his distaste for violence and
the thrill he found in hand-to-hand combat. When writing about
boxing, he generally confined his outrage to the honesty of a fighter's
performance. Apart from his rare pieces about political subjects
(Muhammad Ali's suspension for avoiding the Vietnam draft, the
denial of rights to ballplayers in the years before free agency, the gross
and repeated moral failures of the International Olympic Committee), I don't think Smith ever summoned moral outrage equal to his
condemnation of Jersey Joe Walcott's mendacious rematch with Rocky
Marciano in 1953 ("Cheap at Half the Price," page 215).

A few years earlier, Smith had praised Walcott as man and as fighter,
someone whose valor in the ring "earned the reward he is sure to get—a
rich outdoor return match next summer, which will bring financial
security for him and his six children." But in the Marciano fight, Walcott made no visible effort. To Smith, this was a capital crime. He often
referred to the sports pages as the "toy department" or the "play pen,"
but this good-natured belittling of the importance of sports vanished
when he perceived a professional athlete giving a dishonest performance. "Walcott was guaranteed a quarter of a million dollars for this
night's work," he wrote after the Marciano fight. "If its finish guarantees his departure from boxing, the price was not too great."

The self-deprecation Smith deployed to endear himself to his
readers, which also gave him the stage for some of his best jokes, wasn't
entirely false. He knew he was an exceptionally lucky man to have

found so gratifying a professional life. But he rarely dropped the aw-shucks pose. "I flinch whenever I see the word 'literature' used in the same sentence with my name," he once said. "I'm just a bum trying to make a living running a typewriter."

This was disingenuous. So was another of his floor-pawing tropes: "I'm just a working stiff, trying to write better than I can." But maga-zine covers and network television profiles do not accrue to the weary "bum trying to make a living." He knew precisely how good he was. When his exact contemporary, *New York Times* columnist Arthur Daley, became the first sports columnist to win the Pulitzer Prize in 1956, Smith didn't hide his peevishness. His friend Shirley Povich, of the *Washington Post*, told Ira Berkow that the Pulitzer committee's nod to the excellence of all of Daley's columns led Smith to scowl, "Name one!"

But the greatest insult Smith suffered in his long career jolted him in 1967, with the folding of the *Trib*'s successor, the *World-Journal-Tribune*. Smith continued to write five columns a week for syndication, but he had no New York outlet. "It's like writing my piece every day," he said, "and flushing it down the toilet."

Fourteen months passed before his column finally found a New York home. For the next three years, a sportswriter so well known that he'd even been satirized in a *New Yorker* cartoon (wife to hus-band, watching a TV quiz show: "If you know all the answers, Mr. Red Smith, why don't you try to get on?") saw his column appear in *Women's Wear Daily* under a heading he couldn't possibly have chosen himself: "Sportif."

In 1971, *The New York Times* brought him in from the cold.

I remember the delight sports fans and Smith fans shared when he joined the *Times*. He was, immediately and obviously, the best writer in the paper. Concerned at first that the *Times* might be too sober for his light touch, he soon seemed to be at least partly responsible for the loosening of constraints throughout the paper. The *Times* had always venerated accuracy, thoroughness, and reportorial enterprise. With Red Smith in its pages, it seemed to begin to pay more attention to the words as well. In 1976, he finally won his own Pulitzer, in the category of Commentary. The imposing list of others who won the Commentary prize during that decade included George F. Will, David Broder, and William Safire.

For eleven years, Smith's column appeared in the *Times* four days a week. He wrote more energetically about the NFL than he had before, but mostly he remained attached to boxing, baseball, and the ponies. He had a lot to say about Ali—first crankily negative, later largely positive—but also about Secretariat and Henry Aaron and Reggie Jackson and Seattle Slew. Memorial columns eulogizing men he had known in his long career appeared more frequently. So did ambling, loose-limbed pieces connecting the sporting present to the sporting past.

On January 11, 1982, the headline above Smith's column read "Write Less—and Better?" (see page 527). In the second sentence, Smith announces that he is cutting back to three columns a week. Then he goes about his digressive way, recalling the Philadelphia years when he wrote seven times a week, which leads to an anecdote set at Arlington Park in Chicago, eventually careening back to Philadelphia, which in turn yields a lovely anecdote about Sonny Liston. Almost as if catching his breath, he stops to report that the two questions he is most often asked are, "Of all those you have met, who was the best athlete?" and "Which one did you like best?" This had an oddly valedictory ring to it, as did the very last line: "Some day there would be another Joe DiMaggio."

That was the last sentence Red Smith wrote. He died four days later, having traveled something like 8,000,000 words from Green Bay.

Daniel Okrent, January 2013, New York City

Prologue

My Press-Box Memoirs

In a time when college football commanded more newspaper space than it does today, Frank Graham and I accompanied the Navy team to Cleveland for a game with Notre Dame. Frank was writing a column in the *New York Journal-American* and I was on the *Herald Tribune* and we traveled together so often that guys around the racetracks knew us as an entry, 1 and 1A. On this assignment we were lodged in the boathouse at Annapolis for a night or so, then went with the team to Washington where a special train waited.

Chances are there are sportswriters today who have never been on a railroad train, let alone a special. They'll never know what they missed. We didn't think of the era of the streamliner as the age of leisure, yet the Navy's train found time to stop in suburban Silver Spring to pick up Francis Stann of the *Washington Star*. Even that early in the trip, the level of Gemütlichkeit in the club car was rising.

Dinner was followed by innocent amusements such as drinking whiskey and playing charades with officers and their wives. This was followed by drinking whiskey. After that it was a simple matter of survival of the fittest. By three A.M. the club car was deserted except for the great Navy pilot Killer Kane; Jerry Flynn, civilian director of sports information at Annapolis; 1 and 1A; and the dining-car steward who was doubling as bartender.

When a porter appeared with a third summons from Mrs. Kane, the Killer defected. About an hour later Jerry Flynn glanced at his watch. "Wow!" he said. "Time to knock it off." As he got to his feet, Frank Graham regarded him thoughtfully. During World War II, Jerry had been a lieutenant aboard the carrier *Enterprise* where he claimed to have won distinction as the greatest coward in the Pacific.

"Now I know what happened to the Navy at Pearl Harbor," Frank said softly. "Sitting ducks, asleep in their beds."

Jerry set his jaw and sat down. "A little less water this time, if you please," he told the steward.

Shortly after daylight the steward got some of the dining-car crew out of bed. They came up with scrambled eggs and bacon, hot toast and coffee. By the time that was consumed, the train was on the outskirts of Cleveland. It was a dirty November morning. Frank Graham sat at the window watching traffic stream toward the city.

"Look at the suckers going to work," he said.

That is what I remember first when someone asks what it has been like pounding the sports beat all these years. "Underpaid and over-privileged," Jim Roach of *The New York Times* said of our kind. There were jobs that paid less than ours. Here and there there may have been an individual who had more laughs. But I cannot believe there ever was another group that had so little money and so much fun at the same time.

Of all the privileges I have enjoyed, the greatest was to go around for a few years as one of a threesome with Frank Graham and Grantland Rice. Make no mistake about Granny: He was a giant. Some of his stuff seems like immature gushing today, but he was exactly right for his time and if he had lived in another time he would have been right for that one.

"Take care of Grant," Kate Rice urged when we set off for the 1950 World Series. "He's been down with pneumonia and shouldn't even be working."

It is not easy to take care of a genius with pneumonia who goes off to Philadelphia in October without a topcoat. For the first game we commandeered a raincoat for him from a rookie writer, but he was pretty blue about the gills before that day ended, so the next day we talked him into staying in the rooms the three of us shared in the Bellevue Stratford. He could watch the game on television and file from there.

He protested that he didn't know how to work a TV set, which was true enough. He could swing a golf club or punch a typewriter but he couldn't change a tire and he never did learn to tune in a radio. Frank set the dial at the World Series channel. "If you want it louder, Granny," he said, "turn this to the right. Softer, turn it left."

"Great," Granny said. "I'll be fine."

"Want to bet?" Frank asked when we were outside.

After the game I stayed to work in the press box, but Frank caught a taxi with Bill Corum, whom he invited up for a drink. As they neared the suite they heard voices.

"Granny must have company," Bill said.

"No," Frank said.

They found Granny sitting in semidarkness watching something for kids—Howdy Doody or an animated cartoon. "Geez, they have some terrible programs on this thing," he said. He didn't know how to turn the thing off, and he was too polite to walk away.

Another chapter in Granny's Philadelphia story was written in 1952 when Rocky Marciano won the heavyweight championship of the world there from Jersey Joe Walcott. We had all been in town for days when Granny arrived on the afternoon of the fight wearing a big patch over one eye.

"Never mind, Granny," said Morris McLemore of Miami, "you'll whip him next time around."

"I'm not sure I can," Granny said. "He was a hotel." He had been in Washington for a golf tournament, had slipped on a loose rug and cracked his head open.

At a cocktail party before the fight, Granny got half a skinful of martinis. Then in the stadium when Marciano won by a knockout, the ring was stormed by Rocky's townsmen from Brockton, Massachusetts, who had bet their lives on him. They surged over the press rows in waves, walking on typewriters, trampling ears. At the crest of the flood I saw Granny pecking away at his portable, apparently unaware of the hobnails over his bandaged head.

It was hours past midnight when the last of us got back to the hotel. Gerry Hern of Boston came up with a jug. We woke Granny, who got up

and put on a raincoat in lieu of a dressing gown. It must have been four
o'clock before the jug was empty and Frank Graham, Granny's roommate, said he had changed his mind about catching the nine o'clock
train for New York. At eight A.M. Frank woke to see Granny bathed,
shaved, and breakfasted. "See you in New York," Granny said.

The rest of us made it downstairs about noon. We talked about Marciano, knocked flat in the first round, blinded around the sixth and
seventh, punched and punished through twelve rounds yet still strong
enough to take his man out with a single shot in the thirteenth.

"You think Rocky is tough?" said Jimmy Cannon. "How about that
old bastard with the hole in his head?"

Jimmy Cannon. He may have had more natural talent than anybody
else who ever covered sports. He could make words behave for him as
they would not behave for others. Never willing to settle for less than
a masterpiece, he overwrote outrageously. "When Jimmy Cannon sets
out to write a piece to end writing," Ernest Hemingway said, "he's
going to leave writing dead on the floor."

In my estimation the finest all-round sportswriter of my time was
Frank Graham. He wouldn't stir you to laughter as John Lardner, Joe
Palmer, and Westbrook Pegler could, he was no minstrel like Grantland Rice, John Kieran, or Damon Runyon, and he didn't swing a meat-
ax the way Dan Parker and Stanley Woodward did, but for putting the
reader on the scene he had no peer. He probably did not originate the
conversation-piece column, but he did it so well it became his own,
although it was imitated everywhere.

When Joe Vila died and Frank was invited to take over his column in
the *New York Sun*, he told himself: "My job is to invite the reader into
places where his ticket does not admit him—the dugout and dressing
room and jockeys' quarters and fight camp—and let him see how the
athletes act and hear what they say." With his eye for detail, his marvelous ear and extraordinary memory, he did that better than any before
or after him.

Frank was gentle and generous and considerate—"psychopathically
polite," his friend Bob Kelley said—but too honest to pull a punch. Bob

Meusel, the outfielder, was surly and uncommunicative until his waning days with the Yankees, when he mellowed. "He is learning to say hello," Frank wrote, "when it's time to say good-bye."

That gift of saying a lot in a few words is a quality that distinguished Garry Schumacher. Before he quit the *Journal-American* for the baseball Giants, Garry's stories were models of economical exposition. So was his speech, enriched by a Brooklyn accent and the terminology of sports. A history buff, he summed up the Napoleonic campaigns orally: "Napoleon could've taken Moscow, but the bum had no bench." About the Confederate forces in the War Between the States: "Real good club; couldn't win on the road."

When I was a boy, it never crossed my mind that I might someday cover sports for a living, but I revered good writers. One of my earliest heroes was Ring Lardner. He had left the newspaper business before I got into it, and I met him just once. I was covering the St. Louis Cardinals of 1930 when they won the pennant with a closing rush. Just before the start of a doubleheader in Philadelphia I heard the voice of Stu Boggs, the Western Union chief, at the press-box entrance: "Well! It looks like old times!" Stu ushered a tall, hollow-eyed man to a seat beside me. I shivered with pleasure.

Less than a year earlier, the Philadelphia Athletics had mauled the Chicago Cubs in the World Series. The papers had made much of Connie Mack's strategy in the opening game, when he passed over his aces, Lefty Grove and George Earnshaw, and started the aging Howard Ehmke, who had pitched only fifty-five innings that season and had not worked at all in many weeks. Crafty old Connie, the analysts wrote, had caught the Cubs by surprise and before they could regain their balance Ehmke set a World Series record of thirteen strikeouts.

It is indeed a fact that Connie caught his own players by surprise. "Are you gonna start *him?*" Al Simmons, the left fielder, demanded incredulously when Ehmke began to warm up.

"If it's all right with you, Al," Connie said, and Simmons buttoned his lip. But were Joe McCarthy and his Cubs caught by surprise?

"I talked to McCarthy about the World Series late last summer,"

Lardner said. "He told me: 'We're not worried about Grove and Earn-shaw. We can hit speed. But there's one guy on that club. . . .' He used a very vulgar expression. He said, 'He's what I call a shit pitcher. That's Howard Ehmke, and he's the guy we're going to see in the Series.'"

We chatted through two ballgames, but I have no idea what else we talked about. I don't know, I may have been a little numb. I do know that years later when Ring Lardner's son John began writing about sports I resented him. Here, I felt, was a punk upstart being funny like his old man. It took me a while to discover that John was a bona fide original in his own right, at least as witty as his old man, and a delight-ful companion. He wrote the best lead I ever read:

"Stanley Ketchel was twenty-four years old when he was fatally shot in the back by the common-law husband of the lady who was cooking his breakfast."

Mention of Ketchel recalls little Francis Albertanti, sportswriter and publicist, who loved to tell of an evening in the Toy Bulldog, a watering hole at Eighth Avenue and Forty-ninth Street ostensibly operated by Mickey Walker. A patron was slobbering over Walker.

"Mickey, you're the greatest middleweight ever pulled on a glove, don't let anybody kid you. Pound for pound, you could be the greatest fighter in any division. . . ."

"Ever see Ketchel?" Albertanti asked.

"Ketchel! I seen Ketchel plenty times. Eight, a dozen fights at least."

"How would Mick here do with Ketchel?"

The drunk wheeled on Mickey, snarling.

"Walker, you bum! You couldn't whip one side of Ketchel the best day you ever saw!"

Frank Graham had a standing offer to bet that any time three or more sportswriters get together, the name of Harry Grayson must come up inside ten minutes. Somebody called Harry "the sportswriter from Mars," but actually he was out of the Pacific Northwest by way of San Francisco. Once settled in the East, he subscribed to Bugs Baer's dictum that when you leave New York, everything else is Bridgeport.

Harry was sports editor of Newspaper Enterprise Association.

Because the main office was in Cleveland, he was required to make his headquarters there for some years. One day, with a blizzard howling in off Lake Erie, he was plodding up Euclid Avenue leaning into the wind. A car pulled over to the curb.

"Hey, Mac," the driver called, "how do I get out of town?"

"Silly son of a bitch," Harry said, not breaking stride. "Think if I knew I'd still be here?"

Wherever Harry went, his presence was known. On Calumet Farm at Lexington, Kentucky, grooms paraded horses out for display to a pack of visiting newspapermen and their hosts. At this time Calumet was cleaning up on the racetrack, sweeping the big stakes with the progeny of Bull Lea, then the prepotent sire in American racing. Never noted as a stayer when he was on the track, Bull Lea fathered horses that could run all day.

One after another, Calumet's big horses were shown and duly admired. Last came the boss horse in all his magnificence, head high, coat shimmering in the sunshine. A cathedral silence descended. Kentuckians fought back the impulse to genuflect. Then the pear-shaped tones of Harry Grayson:

"Still a no-good, quittin' son of a bitch for my money! Plenty of times I bet on him and the pig stopped at the top of the stretch."

In addition to this charming quality of candor, Harry had staying power. In his view, if a party was worth holding at all, it ought to last several days. On one such occasion when merriment began to flag he submitted several proposals for picking up the pace, but his companions begged off. One had a prior commitment to take his wife to the theater. Another said there were guests coming for dinner and he had promised to be home. A third pleaded pressing domestic responsibilities.

Harry was disgusted. "What've we got around here?" he said. "A lotta goddamn wife-lovers?"

If this reminiscence has a slightly alcoholic flavor, that is because a lot of alcohol was consumed over the years and the days and the nights. There was also a lot of work. Always a bleeder at the typewriter, I was sometimes self-conscious about being last out of the press box. If I wasn't the last, I seldom got better than a dead heat with Allison Danzig of *The New York Times*, or Westbrook Pegler, another bleeder. Those two weren't much comfort. I knew Danzig's story would be twice as long as mine and Pegler's twice as good.

The only truly fine writer I knew who gave the appearance of writing without pain was Joe Palmer, who did horse racing for the *Herald Tribune*. He was a touch typist who could produce a thousand joyously readable words in what seemed hardly more time than a stenographer would need for a letter of the same length. However, that was during the season when he did one column a week in addition to his routine racing coverage. He had had a week to construct the whole thing in his wonderfully organized mind. For that matter, he could also do square root in his head or quote from *Beowulf* in original Anglo-Saxon.

His quicksilver mind intimidated and delighted me. One night we were having a drink after attending an amateur boxing card in the recreation hall maintained for backstretch workers in Saratoga. Joe was telling a story about cockfighting and, just to rouse him, I said something disapproving. What, he demanded, was wrong with chicken fighting?

"It's cruel," I said, "inhuman."

"Inhuman?" he said. "Of course it's inhuman! And that stuff we were watching tonight—that's unchicken!"

"Isn't he out of Nashville?" F. Ambrose Clark once asked me. "Son of a Palmer from Nashville, Tennessee, who had that good colt in the Futurity about 1912?" Uncle Brose of Cooperstown, Westbury, and Aiken, South Carolina, looked like a cutout from an old English hunting print.

No, I told him, Joe was the son of a photographer in Georgetown, Kentucky, and the first in his family, as far as I knew, to have any connection with racing. A film had come over Uncle Brose's eyes and I knew I had lost my audience but I rattled on, remarking that Joe was not only my neighbor but that he was also my best friend.

"Oh," Brose said vaguely, "do you live there, too?" He may have meant Georgetown or Nashville or, for all I know, Cooperstown or Aiken. When I said no, we lived in Malverne, Long Island, he was startled.

"Not in the winter, too!" he said.

But to get back to the drinking set, it was alcohol that brought a riposte from Tom Meany one night in a World Series press headquarters. Tom didn't consume the booze, an old friend of his did, a friend whose affection for Tom grew with every swallow. He stayed at Tom's side all evening, contributing little to the wisdom of the ages. At long last Tom got up to leave.

"Just a minute till I finish this drink," his friend said. "I'll drive you home."

"You already have," Tom said, and stalked out.

Another Tom of beloved memory, Tom O'Reilly, had some fairly memorable bouts with the sauce before giving it up. During one binge he was gathered up by his friend Jack Kelly, father of Princess Grace of Monaco, and stowed in a monastery to recuperate. "Geez," said a friend when that news reached the racetrack, "I hope it ain't one of them monasteries where the monks jump on grapes. That O'Reilly'll have 'em all broke down in two days."

O'Reilly and Meany, Joe Palmer, Harry Grayson, Bill Heinz, Granny Rice, Garry Schumacher, Stanley Woodward, John Lardner, Jimmy Cannon—there were so many friends and now there are few. "You hafta remember," Casey Stengel says, "a lot of guys my age are dead." Remembering, I somehow always come back to Frank Graham.

A cop flagged us down between Richmond and Petersburg, Virginia, where great big signs warned of a speed limit of fifty miles an hour.

"Mr. Smith," the cop said, after inspecting my operator license, "can you read?"

"The son of a bitch can't even write," said my friend the passenger.

October 1975

★ BASEBALL 1934–1951 ★

Dizzy Dean's Day

Cards Trounce Reds for National League Pennant

Sᴛ. Lᴏᴜɪs, Mᴏ., *September 30, 1934*
T HROUGH THE murk of cigarette smoke and liniment fumes in the Cardinals' clubhouse a radio announcer babbled into a microphone.

"And now," he read with fine spontaneity from a typewritten sheet prepared hours in advance, "and now let's have a word from the Man of the Hour, Manager Frank Frisch."

The Man of the Hour shuffled forward. He had started changing clothes. His shirttail hung limply over bare thighs. The Man of the Hour's pants had slipped down and they dragged about his ankles. You could have planted petunias in the loam on his face. The Man of the Hour looked as though he had spent his hour in somebody's coal mine.

Beside him, already scrubbed and combed and natty in civilian clothes, awaiting his turn to confide to a nationwide audience that "the Cardinals are the greatest team I ever played with and I sure am glad we won the champeenship today and I sure hope we can win the World Series from Detroit," stood Dizzy Dean, destiny's child.

There was a conscious air of grandeur about the man. He seemed perfectly aware of and not at all surprised at the fact that just outside the clubhouse five thousand persons were pressing against police lines, waiting to catch a glimpse of him, perhaps even to touch the hem of his garment.

He couldn't have known that in that crowd one woman was weeping into the silver fox fur collar of her black cloth coat, sobbing, "I'm so happy! I can't stand it!" She was Mrs. Dizzy Dean.

All afternoon Dizzy Dean had seemed surrounded by an aura of greatness. A crowd of 37,402 persons jammed Sportsman's Park to see the game that would decide the National League pennant race. To this reporter it did not appear that they had come to see the Cardinals win the championship. Rather, they were there to see Dizzy come to glory.

It was Dean's ballgame. He, more than anyone else, had kept the Cardinals in the pennant race throughout the summer. He had won two games in the last five days to help bring the Red Birds to the top of the league. Here, with the championship apparently hinging upon the outcome of this game, was his chance to add the brightest jewel to his crown, and at the same time to achieve the personal triumph of becoming the first National League pitcher since 1917 to win thirty games in a season.

And it was Dizzy's crowd. Although the game was a box office "natural," it is doubtful that, had it not been announced that Dean would pitch, fans would have been thronged before the Dodier Street gate when the doors were opened at 9:30 A.M. They were, and from then until game time they came in increasing numbers. Eventually, some had to be turned away from lack of space.

Packed in the aisles, standing on the ramps and clinging to the grandstand girders, the fans followed Dizzy with their eyes, cheered his every move.

They whooped when he rubbed resin on his hands. They yowled when he fired a strike past a batter. They stood and yelled when he lounged to the plate, trailing his bat in the dust. And when, in the seventh inning, with the game already won by eight runs, he hit a meaningless single, the roar that thundered from the stands was as though he had accomplished the twelve labors of Hercules.

The fact was, the fans were hungry for drama, and that was the one ingredient lacking. With such a stage setting as that crowd provided, with such a buildup as the National League race, with such a hero as Dizzy, Mr. Cecil B. DeMille would have ordered things better.

He would have had the New York Giants beat Brooklyn and thus make a victory essential to the Cards' pennant prospects. He would have had Cincinnati leading St. Louis until the eighth inning, when a rally would have put the Red Birds one run ahead. Then Mr. DeMille would have sent ex–St. Louis Hero Jim Bottomley, now one of the enemy, to bat against Hero Dean, with Cincinnati runners on every base. And he would have had Dizzy pour across three blinding strikes to win the ballgame.

In the real game there was no suspense. Cincinnati tried, but the Cards couldn't be stopped. They just up and won the game, 9–0, and the pennant, and to blazes with drama.

Still, drama is where you find it. The crowd seemed to find it in the gawky frame of Mr. Dean, and in the figures on the scoreboard which showed Brooklyn slowly overhauling the Giants in their game in the east.

Dean was warming up in front of the Cardinal dugout when the first-inning score of the New York–Brooklyn game was posted, showing four runs for the Giants and none for the Dodgers. As an apprehensive "Oooooh!" from the fans greeted the score, Dizzy glanced toward the scoreboard. Watching through field glasses, this reporter saw his eyes narrow slightly. That was all. A moment later he strolled to the plate, entirely at ease, to accept a diamond ring donated by his admirers.

Then the game started, and for a few minutes the customers' attention was diverted from their hero by the exploits of some of his mates.

In the first inning Ernie Orsatti, chasing a low drive to right center by Mark Koenig, raced far to his left, dived forward, somersaulted, and came up with the ball. To everyone except the fans in the right-field seats it seemed a miraculous catch. The spectators closest to the play were sure they saw Orsatti drop the ball and recover it while his back was toward the plate. But everyone screamed approbation.

Magnificent plays, one after another, whipped the stands into a turmoil of pleasure. In Cincinnati's second inning, after Bottomley had singled, Leo Durocher scooted far to his right to nail a grounder by Pool and, in one astonishingly swift motion, he pivoted and whipped the ball to Frisch for a force-out of Bottomley.

Again in the fourth inning, there was a play that brought the fans whooping to their feet. This time Frisch scooped up a bounder from Pool's bat and beat Koenig to second base, Durocher hurdling Frisch's prostrate body in order to avoid ruining the play. A few minutes earlier Frisch had brought gasps and cheers from the stands by stretching an ordinary single into a two-base hit, reaching second only by the grace of a breakneck headfirst slide.

Play by play, inning by inning, the crowd was growing noisier, more jubilant. Cheer followed exultant cheer on almost every play.

Meanwhile the Cards were piling up a lead. Meanwhile, too, Brooklyn was chiseling runs off New York's lead, and the scoreboard became a magnet for all eyes. When Brooklyn scored two runs in the eighth inning to tie the Giants, announcer Kelley didn't wait for the scoreboard to flash the news. He shouted it through his megaphone, and as fans in each succeeding section of seats heard his words, waves of applause echoed through the stands.

Shadows were stretching across the field when Cincinnati came to bat in the ninth inning. The National League season was within minutes of its end. The scoreboard long since had registered the final tallies for all other games. Only the tied battle in New York and the contest on this field remained unfinished.

Dean lounged to the pitching mound. The man was completing his third game in six days. He was within three putouts of his second shutout in those six days. He didn't seem tired. He hardly seemed interested. He was magnificently in his element, completely at ease in the knowledge that every eye was on him.

The first two Cincinnati batters made hits. Dizzy was pitching to Adam Comorosky when a wild yell from the stands caused him to glance at the scoreboard. The Dodgers had scored three runs in the tenth. New York's score for the inning had not been posted.

Seen through field glasses, Dean's face was expressionless. He walked Comorosky. The bases were filled with no one out. Was Dizzy tiring, or was he deliberately setting the stage for the perfect melodramatic finish?

The scoreboard boy hung up a zero for the Giants. The pennant belonged to the Cardinals. Most pitchers would have said, "the hell with it," and taken the course of least resistance, leaving it to the fielders to make the putouts.

But this was Dean's ballgame. Seen through a haze of fluttering paper, cushions, and torn scorecards, he seemed to grow taller. He fanned Clyde Manion. A low roar rumbled through the stands. The fans saw what was coming. Dizzy was going to handle the last three batters himself.

Methodically, unhurriedly, he rifled three blinding strikes past pinch hitter Petoskey. Was that a faint grin on Dizzy's face? The roar from the stands had become rolling thunder. The outfielders foresaw what was coming. They started in from their positions as Dizzy began pitching to Sparky Adams.

They were almost on the field when Adams, in hopeless desperation, swung at a pitch too fast for him to judge. His bat just tipped the ball, sending it straight upward in a wobbly, puny foul fly to DeLancey.

Dean didn't laugh. He didn't shout or caper. The man who has been at times a gross clown was in this greatest moment a figure of quiet dignity. Surrounded by his players he walked slowly to the dugout, a mad, exultant thunder drumming in his ears.

It Wasn't the Hits

Whose Color Compares with Resplendent Ruth's?

PHILADELPHIA, PA., *October 2, 1938*

THIS MORNING'S sermon was to have been devoted to explaining the game of baseball to Dave Walsh, who, unless I am misinformed, held Abner Doubleday's coat that fateful day in Cooperstown.

Mr. Walsh and a number of other literary Reveres have been clattering pell-mell over the rhetorical cobblestones of late, shouting "Up! Up! Heavy, heavy, heavy hangs over the Yankees' heads."

My colleague—which is a Sunday word for boss—is perturbed more than somewhat by the rapidity with which the Yanks, after gathering the league championships to their bosoms, assumed a position so spectacularly horizontal as to make them practically indistinguishable from the Phils.

He fears the recumbent posture will become habitual and permanent; that when the Yankees try to bestir themselves from lethargy they will find themselves unequal to it, partly because they will have lost the knack and partly because by that time the Cubs will be astride their stomachs, industriously beating their brains out.

In short, Mr. Walsh, along with Mr. C. Mack and others who give evidence of knowing whereof they speak, warn Joe McCarthy that his players may in spite of themselves loaf on him in October as they did in September. And Jimmy Walker should sue me for that.

Until I changed my mind about the text of this lecture, I planned to point out that the Yanks have faced this situation before and mastered it along with the opposition. They lost five out of six shortly after collaring last year's pennant. Late in the season they performed the death-defying, awe-inspiring feat of curtsying thrice before the Athletics on two occasions. They lost three in a row here and three in another row in New York.

Still, it is my recollection they did tolerably in the World Series. If I am wrong Bill Terry can set me straight.

For the point is, those Yanks are money players. They know when to relax and when and how to bear down. They have the pitcher of the year in Red Ruffing. In Lefty Gomez they have a man who never has lost a World Series game. And they all swing a moderately effective cudgel when the blue chips are on the baize.

No, I wouldn't begrudge the Yankees their little breathing spell. Rather, I'd hazard a guess that only one thing may prevent them from thumping the breath out of Chicago. That's the chance that the Cubs, after the race they have run, will be all out of breath in the first place.

All this and more I intended to write. So, looking for some big words to borrow, I thumbed through the paper to the brains department— the page festooned by Heywood Broun, Charley Fisher, Jay Franklin, and Eleanor Roosevelt. And there Charley Fisher suggested a topic that seemed much more interesting.

Charley wonders why a nation which went daft when Babe Ruth set a record of sixty home runs should look coldly down its nose at the possibility that Hank Greenberg will break the record. Remembering the hysteria of 1927, he can't understand the calm of 1938.

Well, for one thing, this isn't the first time Ruth's mark has been threatened. Hack Wilson came close in 1930, Jimmie Foxx closer in 1932. Hardly a July passes without at least one statistician pointing out that Joe Broadrear is seven days and four homers ahead of Ruth's pace of like date. It has come to be an old story; many threaten but none makes it stick.

And even if someone did, it wouldn't matter. Because the someone wouldn't be, couldn't be Ruth. Charley touched on this when he said Ruth had color and Greenberg hasn't. And what, he asked, is color?

Charley, I don't know. But it has something to do with a fat, ungainly, and aging man waddling around in left field in Chicago in 1932, stooping to pick up elderly lemons and discouraged legumes showered on him from the stands and brazenly, cheerfully playing catch with the hostile crowd. Greenberg would have ignored the flora and gone quietly and conscientiously about his business.

It has something to do with a man standing at the plate in the same World Series, signaling which pitch he would hit, pointing to the spot in the remote bleachers where he would hit it, and parking it there. To Greenberg that would be florid exhibitionism, repugnant to his nature.

It has something to do with a mature man so much a kid in spirit that he could deliberately exile himself from the world he loved because his boss wouldn't let him go to a party. For Ruth, you remember, quit the Braves and baseball in a huff when his employer refused to give him a day off to go down and see the *Normandie* dock.

It has something to do with his squat homeliness, his overwhelming good nature, his buoyant friendliness, his vocabulary that would make a mule-skinner pale with awe, his immeasurable, boundless vanity. Strangely, there's nothing offensive about his conceit. No more than about the conceit of a small boy who, turning somersaults with play-mates, repeatedly shrieks, "Look at me! Watch how I do it!"

Look, Charley, I can't explain it. But it wouldn't matter greatly if Greenberg hit one hundred home runs. Because it wasn't homers we were cheering back in 1927. Lord knows we're juvenile and naïve over here in the boys' department. But we don't go completely batty over a record in a book.

It wasn't the hits. It was the man who was making 'em.

A Toast to
Coach Wagner

Benswanger Honors the Pirate Who Made Him

T H E B I G man sat in the far end of the club car talking with several
KANSAS CITY, MO., *April 1, 1940*
ballplayers and slowly sipping a beer.

He wasn't a tall man, especially, but thickset, big all over. Big head,
its white thatch close-cropped; heavy, ruddy face; great ruddy horn
of a nose. Thick chest and shoulders, thick waist, heavy and solid all
the way down to the ridiculously bowed legs. In his prodigious hand,
which could hold three baseballs as the ordinary man might hold three
plums, the amber glass was lost, swallowed up.

In the other end of the car, Bill Benswanger, president of the Pittsburgh Pirates, was telling a story, pausing now and then to glance
down the aisle where the big man sat. A queerly sentimental little
story to be coming from such a plain, unsentimental-seeming man.

It had to do with a small boy who used to go to the ballgames in
Pittsburgh back in the early years of the century. A small boy named
Bill Benswanger, who worshipped a square-rigged Dutch idol named
Johannes Peter Wagner.

The boy would beg seventy-five cents from his mother for a grandstand seat but he wouldn't sit in the grandstand. He'd spread the money
over three games, spending a quarter a day to sit in the bleachers. The
left-field bleachers, where he could get a closeup view of Honus Wagner's broad-beamed stern.

Young Bill hardly ever saw his hero's face except from a distance when the Pittsburgh shortstop was at bat. Mostly he just sat and watched him from the rear, day after day, summer after summer.

You know how kids are. To young Bill Benswanger there never was anybody else, never could be anybody else like Honus Wagner. Had they met face to face on the street the kid might not have recognized his hero. But from the bleachers he knew everything about him—the look of the barrel-stave legs; the broad, powerful slope of hunched shoulders and sturdy back; the way those huge hands gobbled up ground balls, smothered pop flies; the queer, buckity stride of the man rounding the bases.

Bill knew, better than he knew his lessons, the year-by-year batting and fielding averages of Wagner. As time went on he came to know how, when the Federal League started and players all through organized ball were jumping for the juicy contracts offered in the new league, Wagner said no, the hell with the money, he'd stick with the Pirates. And how the Pirates' owner, Barney Dreyfuss, swore he'd never forget the man's loyalty.

"All that," Benswanger said, telling the story, "was a long time ago. And then—"

Well, then it was 1931 and lovable, excitable, comical, generous Barney Dreyfuss was dead—and his son-in-law, Bill Benswanger, was president of the Pirates. It was winter and Benswanger was alone in his office when there was a rap on the door and a middle-aged couple entered.

The man was big all over. Not tall, especially, but thickset and big. Big nose. Big chest and shoulders. Prodigious hands that fumbled a little timidly with the hat he held. He twisted the hat brim, standing silent while his wife did the talking.

"Mr. Benswanger," she said, "Honus needs a job."

President Benswanger sat looking at them across his polished desk. Do you know the thoughts that were in his mind, the shiver that prickled his spine, the lump that formed in his throat, as he sat there studying his idol, front view? If you don't you never will, for there's no expressing that sort of thing in words. Kids grow up and leave their childhood behind them and forget a lot, but there are some things they can't ever forget.

But there wasn't much Benswanger could say. George Gibson was manager of the Pirates and he'd just hired his own coaching staff and there was no immediate opening for a scout. Perhaps some sort of work with the groundkeeper—

"No," Mrs. Wagner said. "That would kill him. Let him just do something where he can wear a uniform again. Anything. He'd be happy then."

Well, the president would see what could be done. He'd have to get in touch with Gibson first because he was not under any circumstances going to interfere with the manager's authority. Honus could understand how that was. But if they'd drop back in a day or so, perhaps something could be arranged.

Gibson was off somewhere on a hunting trip, Western Union reported the next day, and there was no forwarding address. Just have to wait until he got home.

Benswanger waited. Every day the couple came to the office asking for news. Every day Honus just sat there, fumbling with his hat, letting Mrs. Wagner do the talking. It was ten days before a reply came from Gibson.

"Of course," the wire read. "Glad to have him."

In the club car Benswanger finished his story and glanced down the aisle where the big man sat.

"That's all," he said simply. "That's why we've always carried three coaches since 1931, and always will."

Winning by Striking Out

Owen's Mitt Betrays Dodgers as Yanks Take Game 4

IT COULD happen only in Brooklyn. Nowhere else in this broad, untidy universe, not in Bedlam nor in Babel nor in the remotest psychopathic ward nor the sleaziest padded cell could The Thing be.

Only in the ancestral home of the Dodgers which knew the goofy glories of Babe Herman could a man win a World Series game by striking out.

Only on the banks of the chuckling Gowanus, where the dizzy-days of Uncle Wilbert Robinson still are fresh and dear in memory, could a team fling away its chance for the championship of the world by making four outs in the last inning.

It shouldn't happen to a MacPhail!

As Robert W. Service certainly did not say it:

> *Oh, them Brooklyn Wights have seen strange sights.*
> *But the strangest they ever did see,*
> *Today was revealed in Ebbets Field*
> *When Owen fumbled strike three!*

Among all the Yankee fans in the gathering of 33,813 who watched the fourth game of the World Series, only one was smiling when Tommy Henrich faced Hugh Casey in the ninth inning with two out, nobody on base, the Dodgers in front by one run, and a count of three balls and two strikes on the hitter.

That one gay New Yorker was Jim Farley, whose pink bald head gleamed in a box behind the Dodger dugout. He sat there just laughing and laughing—because he hadn't bought the Yankees, after all.

Then The Thing happened.

Henrich swung at a waist-high pitch over the inside corner. He missed. So did catcher Mickey Owen. Henrich ran to first. Owen ran after the ball but stopped at the grandstand screen.

That was Mickey's biggest mistake. He should have kept right on running all the way back home to Springfield, Missouri.

That way he wouldn't have been around to see and suffer when Joe DiMaggio singled, Charlie Keller doubled, Bill Dickey walked, Joe Gordon doubled, and the Dodgers went down in horrendous defeat, 7 to 4.

Out of the rooftop press box in that awful instant came one long, agonized groan. It was the death cry of hundreds of thousands of unwritten words, the expiring moan of countless stories which were to have been composed in tribute to Casey.

For just as Owen has taken his place among the Merkles and Snod-grasses and Zimmermans and all the other famous goats of baseball, so now Casey belongs with the immortal suckers of all time.

The All-American fall guy of this series—round, earnest Casey—was only one pitch short of complete redemption for his sins of yesterday.

Remember that it was he whom the Yankees battered for the winning hits in the third game of the series. It was he whom Larry MacPhail castigated for failing, in MacPhail's judgment, to warm up properly before relieving Fred Fitzsimmons yesterday.

Now he was making all his critics eat their words. He was making a holy show of the experts who snorted last night that he was a chump and a fathead to dream that he could throw his fast stuff past the Yankees.

He was throwing it past them, one pitch after another, making a hollow mockery of the vaunted Yankee power as each superb inning telescoped into the one before.

No one ever stepped more cheerfully onto a hotter spot than did Casey when he walked in to relieve Johnny Allen in the fifth inning. The Yankees were leading, 3 to 2, had the bases filled with two out, and the hitting star of the series, Joe Gordon, was at bat.

Casey made Gordon fly to Jim Wasdell for the final putout, and from there on he fought down the Yankees at every turn.

He made Red Rolfe pop up after Johnny Sturm singled with two out in the sixth. He breezed through the seventh despite a disheartening break when DiMaggio got a single on a puny ground ball that the Dodgers swore was foul.

Leo Durocher said enough short, indelicate words to Umpire Larry Goetz on that decision to unnerve completely anyone within earshot. But Casey, determined to hear no evil and pitch no evil, shut his ears and shut out the Yanks.

In the clutch, the great Keller popped up. The ever-dangerous Dickey could get nothing better than a puerile tap to the mound.

So it went, and as Casey drew ever closer to victory the curious creatures that are indigenous to Flatbush came crawling out of the woodwork. They did weird little dances in the aisles and shouted and stamped and rattled cowbells aloft and quacked derisively on little reedy horns.

Their mouths were open, their breath was indrawn for the last, exultant yell—and then The Thing happened.

Far into this night of horror, historians pored over the records, coming up at last with a World Series precedent for "The Thing."

It happened in the first game of the 1907 series between the Cubs and Detroit, when the Tigers went into the ninth inning leading, 3 to 1. With two out and two strikes against pinch hitter Del Howard, Detroit's Wild Bill Donovan called catcher Charley Schmidt to the mound for a conference.

"Hold your glove over the corner," Donovan said, "and I'll curve a strike into it."

He did, but Schmidt dropped the strike, Howard reached base, and the Cubs went on to tie the score. The game ended in darkness, still tied after twelve innings, and the Cubs took over the next four contests in a row.

That's about all, except that it should be said the experts certainly knew their onions when they raved about the Yankee power. It was the most powerful strikeout of all time.

Big Man for His Size

Shortstop "Bunny" Griffiths Is a Major Minor Leaguer

YORK, PA., *October 22, 1943*

JOHNNY GRIFFITHS is a compact Irishman, slightly larger than a growler of beer, with the sort of Irish face that discourages levity about personal matters, such as his age, for instance.

He doesn't kid about that the way Sammy Gray, the old pitcher, used to do. When Sam got to be thirty he took a shine to that age and kept it, year after year. One night a long time ago he and Alvin Crowder were arguing.

"I've seen thirty summers," Gray insisted.

"And," Crowder prodded him, "how many winters?"

A slow, sly grin cracked Sam's weather-beaten features.

"Daown home in Texas," he chuckled triumphantly, "we don't have any winters."

Well, anyhow, when Johnny Griffiths tells you he's thirty-eight you may suspect that he, like most ballplayers, is giving himself a fast count on birthdays but you don't mention it. Because it doesn't really make any difference.

He was young enough this summer to play every inning of every game, and at shortstop, too, which is the toughest position of all for a guy whose legs are beginning to crack. And when a guy can do that he doesn't have to worry about what the calendar may say. Johnny doesn't have to worry; he's already signed for next year.

John "Bunny" Griffiths has been a professional baseball player for nineteen years, yet it is quite possible you never heard of him. He never got up to the big leagues for so much as a day.

You need only to see him to know the reason for that. He stands five-foot-six and in his youth his best playing weight was 126.

Generally speaking, baseball is a gruesome career for a fellow who can't hope to reach the top. It's a dead-end street. Night games followed by long bus jumps. Cheap hotels and boarding houses and one-armed hash houses.

Johnny doesn't mind, though. If there's such a thing as a successful minor league ballplayer, he's it. He's been all around and winters he's always come back home to work in a Camden machine shop and he doesn't figure anybody owes him anything, or vice versa.

He's playing manager of the White Roses, a figure of importance in town, a shortstop of repute throughout the Inter-State League. In York he even rates as a youngster, for that's the team that has two pitchers whose ages total one hundred years—Lefty George, fifty-seven, and Dutch Schesler, forty-three.

He doesn't hold it against the scouts because they ignore the little guys. But he thinks this policy causes them to overlook some pretty good bets.

"These big guys," he says, "you're always reading about how they're laid up with charley-horses and sprains and pulled muscles. Now me, I've never had a charley-horse in my life."

He's had, in fact, only one baseball injury that caused him any concern. It was suffered early in the 1942 season when he was playing manager at Rome, N.Y.

"I got around to third on a play and I had a kid coaching there who was a little slow with his signs. I rounded the bag and had to dive back, head first. I made it, but the third baseman went up in the air on the play and he came down, wham, right on the back of my neck.

"Next day I couldn't turn my head. What was worse, I couldn't begin to lift my right arm. The club president was a doctor and he started giving me diathermy treatments. The neck just kept getting stiffer.

"It drives me nuts to sit on the bench. But the boss was swell about it, told me to take my time. I kept doctoring. No results. One guy took X-ray pictures of my shoulder. They showed nothing. Another guy told me I'd thrown my arm out. That made me mad, because I knew it happened on that play at third.

"Finally, just before the Fourth of July, I told the boss I was going into the lineup, no matter what. I played a doubleheader but I had to throw underhand. A few days later they called me into the front office and told me they had bad news for me.

"I said, 'You got no news for me. I told you two weeks ago I couldn't play.' So I came home. It was the first time I'd been home in July since 1924. That was kind of nice, but my neck still wouldn't turn. So finally my wife's brother, who's a doctor, had some pictures made."

It wasn't much. Just a cracked vertebra. A broken neck. And the sonofagun's playing again, as though nothing ever happened.

Spit Is a Horrid Word

Detroit's Tommy Bridges Eyes 200th Win

LAKELAND, FLA., *February 20, 1946*

TOMMY BRIDGES, a former sergeant in the Army who formerly was a former pitcher, became an active pitcher and a former coach of the Detroit Tigers today. On the theory that life begins at forty for the proprietor of a good curveball, Bridges voluntarily abandoned a career of teaching young Tigers how to pitch and resumed his old profession of teaching American League batters a thing or two.

Tommy is a wry-necked, thin-featured old gentleman about as big as thirty cents' worth of liver, who has had batters chasing after his jagged hooks for fifteen seasons. He is probably the most warmly esteemed character who ever hung his lingerie in a Briggs Stadium locker. While he was away in the Army last summer and younger Tigers were battling for a pennant, Detroit fans chose him as their number-one pin-up boy in a popularity contest and festooned him with war bonds, an order for a new automobile, and assorted gewgaws.

Setting out on his sixteenth season with the only major league club he ever worked for, he signed as a coach, but today asked to be restored to the active players' list.

"I want to win two hundred games," he said after the Tigers' first pass at muscle-bending here. "I figure I'm a cinch to do it."

He has scored 193 victories for Detroit, counting the one accomplished after the Army let him go last August, and is the only logical candidate for the 200 Club in the American League this year.

"He'll work once a week and give the hitters plenty of trouble," Bridges' manager, Steve O'Neill, said.

"I asked to be signed as a coach," Bridges explained. "The Detroit club has been so good to me all these years that I wanted to quit before I became a loser. And it looked to me as though I might be a loser. I couldn't do much good last summer. Trouble was, I came back with only about thirty days of the season left and I couldn't convince myself there was time enough left to get anywhere. As a matter of fact, there wasn't time enough. You just haven't got it when you come out of service.

"But this year it's different. With plenty of time to get ready, I'm starting out feeling a lot different. I know now I can win in this league. I know it because I've been working at Bob Feller's baseball school in Tampa, and I can tell from the way I feel that I'm going to be ready again. I like the idea of coaching, but there's time enough for that later. As long as I can win, I want to keep pitching."

Bridges' fame is based chiefly on his curve, but that isn't necessarily his best pitch. Not, at least, if you accept a yarn the Detroit catcher Paul Richards spins.

As Richards tells it, Tommy was working against the Washington Senators one day, struggling to protect a one-run lead with runners on base and the menacing Stan Spence at bat.

Richards crouched and flashed a sign for a curve, but Bridges shook his head. Richards gave the sign for a fastball and again Tommy shook him off. Paul tried the change-of-pace signal, but Bridges was cold to the suggestion.

"Well," Richards thought, "the only thing left is the spitter."

He got set for that, and it came. A honey.

"Strike one," said Bill Summers.

They went through the routine again. Curveball sign. A head-shake. Fastball sign. No go. The change. Not this time. Again Richards got ready for the bucking spitter. Again it came, fluttering even more sharply this time. Again Spence took the pitch.

"Strike two," Summers said.

This time Richards didn't bother with a sign. He just got ready, and the pitch whistled in, jumping and ducking.

"Strike three," Summers yelled.

Spence flung his bat away and screamed protests. They looked like spitters to him. His manager, Ossie Bluege, dashed out to second the motion. After a long argument a delegation composed of Summers, Bluege, Spence, and Richards advanced upon the mound.

"Tommy," Summers said, "these gentlemen say you've been throwing spitters."

"Why, Mr. Summers," he said, "don't you know the spitter has been outlawed for years? How would I ever learn to throw one?"

Defeated, Summers and his complaining witnesses started back toward the plate. As they departed, Bridges cupped his glove to his mouth and addressed the umpire in a stage whisper.

"Hey Bill," he said softly. Summers halted and turned. "Wasn't that last one a sweetheart, though?"

Plagiarists from
the Polo Grounds

Giants Steal from Dodgers' Playbook in Ebbets Field Opener

★　　★　　★

BROOKLYN, N.Y., *April 19, 1946*

THE DODGERS should sue. What happened in Ebbets Field yesterday had the Brooklyn copyright stamped all over it. It was redolent of Flatbush. It fairly smoked with the rich, aromatic, pungent, pervading bouquet of the Gowanus. But the perpetrators were Giants, low, skulking plagiarists from the Polo Grounds.

One customer and one center fielder caught batted balls with their profiles; the Dodgers stole five bases, including home plate, four of them in one inning; a Brooklyn base runner was ruled out on an interference play without a murmur of protest from stands, field, or dugout; a Giant runner went gamboling dreamily around the bases on an infield pop and got himself doubled off the bag by 180 feet; Ernie (Wingfoot) Lombardi laid down a bunt and had it beaten easily when it rolled foul, then he outsped an infield single. Through it all, a lone trumpeter played a brassy paean of joy, and toward the end a male quartet made with the tonsils under the stands.

Neighbors, summer is back in Brooklyn.

It was opening day in Ebbets Field, but not just an ordinary opening day, assuming any ballgame in Brooklyn can be ordinary. This was a Dodgers-Giants opener, which is like crepe suzette for breakfast, or, a circus opening with the tigers uncaged.

As you came up out of the subway, and later when you turned into McKeever Place, cops grabbed you and demanded, "Got a ticket, bud?"

Later it developed that the crowd of 31,825 was somewhat less than capacity, suggesting that the law was there not to turn away loiterers but to mooch an extra ticket for Mayor William O'Dwyer.

That pillar of horse-race society, New York's first gentleman of the turf, occupied a box seat beside the Dodgers' dugout. This couldn't have happened in the day of Commissioner Landis, who tolerated no union between baseball and the horsey set.

Bill-O stood up with his hat on and brandished a baseball aloft in his right fist while flash bulbs blazed. Then he stood up with his hat off, revealing an almost unnecessarily wide part of his coiffure and brandished the ball some more. Then he threw the ball, a weak little blooper that plopped almost unnoticed on the turf.

By this time the band was parading to the flagpole, flanked by enough military to occupy Formosa. The players didn't march, having had enough of that these last four years.

On the first play of the game, the Giants' Bill Rigney stretched a single, sliding into second just as the ball arrived. "Safe," said George Magerkurth, a large umpire. From the stands came the poignant, haunting, melodious mating call of the Greenpoint jungle.

"You," Billy Herman advised Mr. Magerkurth, with simple dignity, "are a short word of Anglo-Saxon origin."

"And," said Pee Wee Reese, more in sorrow than in anger, "a blind, bug-eyed one into the bargain."

"Now," Mr. Magerkurth mused, "I know I'm in Brooklyn." Some of Mr. Magerkurth's fondest memories concern Brooklyn. It was there a customer leaped from the stands a few years ago, a small customer in a large rage, who clambered aboard Mr. Magerkurth's wishbone and struck him with repeated blows.

No such indelicacies marred this lawn party, however. The utmost in punctilio was observed as each side was retired scoreless for two innings. The Giants' Harry Feldman was a no-hit pitcher for this space, and his success was seized upon as evidence by those who contend Mel Ott (benched with a gimpy leg) is a better manager in the dugout than in the field.

"See," they argued, "how much more effectively Mel thinks sitting down."

At that point the Dodgers scored five runs on five hits, including a triple by Billy Herman, who first bounced a foul off a patron's nose. It was time for a statement by Ott regarding Feldman.

"Ugh!" Ott said, putting it in a nutshell. In came Mike Budnick, to be succeeded soon by Jack Brewer. Brewer was the pitcher when a ground ball hit by Reese caromed off Babe Young's features in center for a triple and Brooklyn's sixth run.

Jack was still pitching in the fifth. That was the inning when Pete Reiser walked, stole second, ran to third as Lombardi's throw bounced into the outfield, then stole home; when Gene Hermanski walked and stole second; when Carl Furillo singled Hermanski home, and stole second. The thefts were committed against Brewer, not Lombardi.

With one out and two on base in the sixth, Buddy Kerr bunted and was thrown out. Walker Cooper then batted for Brewer.

"What kind of strategy is that?" a witness demanded. "Bunting when they're eight runs behind!"

"I think," a man said, "Ott feared a double play. Wanted to be sure to get a pinch hitter up there, so he wouldn't have to look at Brewer again before June."

It's All Genuine,
Although Synthetic

Brooklyn's Red Barber Talks a Great Game

St. Louis, Mo., *August 28, 1946*

To the average Dodger fan who can't get out to Ebbets Field to see a ballgame, the next best thing is to tune in on Red Barber. That's what the Dodger fan thinks and he's wrong. Next to seeing a ballgame, the best thing is to sit in the studio with Mr. Barber and watch and listen as he takes the skeletonized report of a game coming over the telegraph wire and wraps up the bare bones with flubdub and pads it out and feeds it to the customers so it sounds as though he, and they, were seeing the plays.

"This is just a business," Mr. Barber explained before the wire opened for the third game of Brooklyn's series in St. Louis. "We don't try to fake it. We have the telegraph sounder right in here near the microphone where it can be heard because we don't try to kid the listeners that this is anything but a telegraphed report.

"From spring training on, Connie Desmond and I are studying the mannerisms of the players in the National League and memorizing them so that when we do a game like this we can visualize them on the field. For instance, I remember how Ed Stanky stands at the plate, how he crouches lower and lower when he's trying for a base on balls. So when I describe it over the air I'm not faking. I know he's doing that."

For a "reconstructed" game a telegraph operator in the studio copies the wire report on a typewriter. Barber stands beside him talking into a microphone which is hung over one of those thingummies that orators use to support their notes and elbows. Because this is radio, the thingummy is painted robin's egg blue. Although Barber sits down in his booth at Ebbets Field, he prefers to stand in the airless studio because sitting makes him loggy.

At his elbow, propped up on a sort of music rack, are the lineups of the two teams with the current batting average of each player. John Paddock, a left-handed statistician who is a cousin of the great sprinter Charley Paddock, keeps the averages up to the minute, writing in a new figure after each new time at bat. He doesn't do the arithmetic himself but uses a "Ready Reckoner," one of those little books that show at a glance what a man is hitting when he has 104 hits for 396 times at bat. A passionate Dodger fan, Paddock daren't talk during a broadcast but roots for his guys with ardent gestures.

Here's the way Barber builds up a play:

The telegraph types: "Reiser up—bats left."

"And here's Pete Reiser," says Red. "Hitting .283, 106 base hits. He's having a tough year, fighting that bad shoulder. Dickson will pitch very carefully to him. Reiser up, square stance, he's one of those square-built guys, not very tall. Strength is not necessarily dependent upon height. The Cards are playing this fellow a step in because of his speed.". . .

All this time there's been nothing over the wire except the bare fact that Reiser is up. The rest all comes out of Barber's memory and knowledge, filling the gap until the typewriter adds: "B 1 OS (Ball one, outside)." . . . "Dickson comes down," Barber says, "and misses the plate. Ball one, outside." . . . Or "S 1 C (Strike one, called)." . . . "Dickson comes in with one," Barber says, "and Reiser is caught lookin'. Strike one, called."

The telegrapher writes: "H. Walker up—bunt, foul—hit—Walker singled to right."

Barber says, "Harry Walker, who's always nervous and pickin' at that cap of his, has to have it sittin' just right. He cuts at the first pitch and tries to bunt it, fouls it off. One strike. Melton working very deliberately. That's his custom, you know. Walker, with that two-toned bat of his—swings on it, bloops a single to right, turns first, and stops as his brother Dixie fields the ball."

The Cardinals get Harry Walker and Stan Musial on the bases, and Barber reminds his listeners that they're there: "Walker and Musial takin' a lead off first and second. They both of 'em can run like scalded cats, you know."

It infuriates the announcer when a friend remarks after a broadcast, "What were you doing reporting all those pick-off throws to first base. Trying to fill in?"

It infuriates him, because he doesn't add a pitch or play that doesn't happen. He merely embroiders each play with words. He can't read Morse code and doesn't want to learn because he doesn't want to know too soon how the next play is coming out. "If you know in advance what's happening, you're no longer a broadcaster," he says. "You're a dramatic artist." Ordinarily, he waits until the telegrapher finishes a sentence before he announces the play.

Once, however, he got himself trapped. The Dodgers had Stanky on first with the tying run, and the operator wrote: "Stanky was picked off first, Dickson to Musial." . . .

At that point Barber said, putting a lift of excitement into his voice, because after all, he's a Brooklyn fan: "Dickson wheels, throws, and Stanky is picked off."

"But," the operator wrote, and went on to report how Stanky, trapped off the bag, fled toward second, jockeyed, retreated, and finally regained first base safely. Barber had a hell of a time talking fast enough to fill in until he could get the play straight on the air.

There were a couple of excusable errors when Barber or Desmond, reading over the telegrapher's shoulder, mistook a swing for a called strike, or vice versa. Generally, though, the broadcast was painstakingly accurate, including only the telegraphed facts and the "color" provided by the announcer.

Silvertooth Mike
Is Right Again

González Opens Door for Slaughter's Mad Dash

St. Louis, Mo., *October 16, 1946*

O LD SILVERTOOTH MIKE GONZÁLEZ, the Cuban with the smile like Cartier's window, replied to the Amalgamated Brotherhood of Grandstand Coaches today and his answer was worth $1,200 to every Cardinal. Which is better than they could do on a quiz program.

Because Mike was right when he had to be, the Cardinals are baseball champions of the world for the sixth time. Because Old Silvertooth had the wit to see a chance and the gambler's gall to take it, Harry Brecheen rode out of Sportsman's Park on his playmates' shoulders, the first pitcher in twenty-six years to win three games in a World Series. Because of Mike's $40,000 decision, Joe Cronin walked alone through the crowd that poured out from the stands staring at his shoes as though trying to memorize them.

Old Silvertooth is the Cardinals' third-base coach, and the grandstand brotherhood has been second-guessing him ever since this series began away back there in the good old days. He should have sent Country Slaughter home when he tripled in the first game. He should have held up Whitey Kurowski and Joe Garagiola in the fourth game. And so on.

Mike paid no attention. He just flashed his metallic grin and stuck to his knitting out there on the white line, watching the play and shouting his orders: "You go. He stay. Come on, Slats, you can do." And then today the big question was asked, and Mike had the answer.

It was in the eighth inning with the score tied, two out, Slaughter on first base and Harry Walker at the plate. Walker hit a long drive that slanted out to the left of Leon Culberson in center field, and Slaughter took off.

If the ball had got by Culberson, as seemed likely, there'd have been nothing to it. But it bounced high on the hard, knobby earth and leaped into Culberson's glove before Slaughter was far past second. Johnny Pesky, in shallow center field to take the relay, caught Culberson's throw just about the instant Slaughter came charging into third.

You'd have called it a fantastic notion that even the fleet Slaughter could score. Walker was so far short of second base a quick play there would have retired him for the third out. But González never hesitated. He was waving Slaughter on from the moment Enos turned for third. Slaughter wheeled sharply at the corner and fled for home.

Pesky, still out behind second, stood morosely studying Ford Frick's signature on the ball. His interest was natural, for the ball he's accustomed to play with is signed by Will Harridge. At length he turned dreamily, gave a small start of astonishment when he saw Slaughter halfway home, and threw in sudden panic.

The throw was weak. Roy Partee, the catcher, had to take a step or so from the plate and as he caught the ball Slaughter slid in behind him.

Chances are the run that got the bully's share of the swag for St. Louis might never have scored if Dom DiMaggio hadn't doubled home two runs to tie the score for Boston in the top half of the eighth. DiMaggio was injured running out the hit and had to leave the game. It is unlikely González would have dared challenge Dom's squirrel-rifle arm if he'd been playing center instead of Culberson.

Anyhow, that was the payoff in one of the most exciting World Series games ever played. Ten minutes later, witnesses were comparing it with the seventh game of the 1926 series, which Grover Alexander saved for the Cardinals when he relieved Jesse Haines and struck out Tony Lazzeri with the bases filled.

There was some similarity, too, for this one was saved by the relief pitching of bandy-legged little Breechen, called to the aid of his friend, Murry Dickson.

Possibly because they're little squirts in a game populated mostly

by big, sweaty, muscular lumps of gristle, Breechen and Dickson
have been pals as long as they've played for the Cardinals. They room
together, eat together, sit up nights talking baseball together, and after
the season they team up on hunting and fishing junkets.

So when Rip Russell singled and George Metkovich doubled at the
start of the eighth for the fourth and fifth Boston hits off Dickson,
Murry dumped a large load of grief on his friend. Dickson walked alone
to the dugout, his head down, and the crowd made with a Comanche
yell when Breechen started in from the bullpen.

Breechen, a nine-inning pitcher on Sunday, rarely is at his best with
less than four days' rest but don't waste your winter trying to sell the
Red Sox that idea. He was almost good enough to put out the fire right
away, for he struck out Wally Moses and got Pesky on a fly so short that
Russell didn't dare run even against Slaughter's gimpy arm. But then
DiMaggio doubled on a three-and-one pitch, putting the question up
to Slaughter, Walker, and Old Silvertooth.

At the end the Cardinals hoisted Breechen to their shoulders but
other players, clamoring to get near him, reached up and hauled him
down like a goal post. As they disappeared from the field, Cronin came
out of the first-base dugout and pushed slowly through the crowd. Now
and then a man hurrying past reached out to tap his big shoulders. Joe
didn't lift his head.

The Big Train, Westbound

Walter Perry Johnson, 1887–1946

WALTER JOHNSON, one of the most beloved of baseball players and perhaps the greatest of all pitchers, was buried today beside the grave of his wife in a little country cemetery. A funeral procession three blocks long wound through the thickets of Maryland to Rockville Cemetery after services in the National (Episcopal) Cathedral, which contains the crypt of an ardent Johnson fan, Woodrow Wilson.

"Big Barney's" casket was carried by eight of the men who were his comrades when he whipped the Giants in the deciding game of the 1924 World Series—Ossie Bluege, present manager of the club; Nick Altrock, now a coach; Muddy Ruel, new manager of the Browns; Joe Judge and Roger Peckinpaugh, who served with Bucky Harris and Bluege in Washington's finest infield; Sam Rice, outfielder; Tom Zachary, pitcher; and Mike Martin, who was the club trainer throughout Walter's twenty years with the Senators. All are graying or balding or both.

Bucky Harris, present manager of the Yankees, who was the "boy wonder" leader of the 1924 Senators, was an honorary pallbearer. So were Clark Griffith, president of the club; Edward Eynon, secretary; Clyde Milan, who roomed with Johnson for fourteen seasons; Jack Bentley, the Giant pitcher who lost that final World Series game; E. Lawrence Phillips, the Griffith Stadium announcer in megaphone days; Bill McGowan, dean of American League umpires; Spencer

Abbott, scout and manager of Washington farm teams; Jim Shaw, a colleague of Johnson's on the pitching staff; and Lu Blue, former first baseman for Detroit and St. Louis. George Weiss, Yankee farm administrator, came down from New York, and Dick Nallin, a former American League umpire, from his farm near Frederick, Maryland.

"How he could pitch!" a man said. "How many bases on balls would you say he allowed in 1913 when he won thirty-six and lost seven games? Well, he had forty-three decisions that year and he walked thirty-eight men. In Hal Newhouser's best year, when he won twenty-nine, he walked one hundred and two."

"The best pitching I ever saw," Altrock said, "was in Detroit. The Tigers filled the bases on two boots and a walk with none out. Three left-hand hitters, Cobb, Veach, and Crawford, came up. Walter struck 'em out on nine pitches."

"That wasn't his best pitching," Griff said. "Neither was his game in the '24 Series or the time he beat New York three times in four days. The best of all was in 1912 against the Athletics with Eddie Collins, Home Run Baker, and the rest of that one-hundred-thousand-dollar infield. We'd been feuding with the A's all season and while we were fighting, the Red Sox slipped in and won the pennant.

"We had a three-game series in Philadelphia to close the season and the team that won the odd game would take second place. Jim Shaw over there started the series, the first game of a doubleheader, and led, 3 to 0, until the seventh. Then the A's tied the score and Johnson came in. He shut 'em out until the nineteenth, when his catcher got hurt. We put in Rippey Williams, who always wanted to catch Johnson, and the first pitch got by him and clipped Billy Evans, the umpire, on the ear. Billy clapped a hand to his ear and it came away bloody.

"'You're not gonna get me killed,' he told Williams. And he called the game on account of darkness, although it was only about four-thirty. Next day another doubleheader was scheduled and the same thing happened. Walter had to come in again with the score 3 to 3 after seven innings. This time it went to the twenty-first before we won, 4 to 3. So he worked twenty-six innings against the greatest team of its time without allowing a run."

Johnson's eighty-year-old mother; his sons, Walter, Jr., and Edward and William; and his daughter, Barbara, were among the mourners. The simple services were conducted before a congregation of several hundred, mostly of middle age or older who packed one nave in the vast cathedral. Earlier in the day there had been a stream of visitors to the funeral home in suburban Bethesda, a few blocks from the house Johnson occupied until he moved to a Montgomery County farm.

These former neighbors stood in knots outside the funeral home, dropping in singly or in pairs, then lingering to talk of the plain, gentle man who is dead. A Montgomery County trooper came in alone and knelt before the casket. Walter was a member of the county commission, the only Republican. At each election, the voters would name four Democrats and Johnson.

"That woman," Griffith said, nodding, "was his nurse. She took care of him like a baby, and when she knew he couldn't get well she resigned. She couldn't bear to stay."

"See that man?" Griff said. "As long as Walter could eat anything, he took a quart of ice cream all the way out to the farm every day."

"Did you ever see such a guy for eating ice cream?" Bucky Harris said. "He hardly ever smoked or drank, except once in a while he'd take a few puffs out of a cigar, looking as awkward about it as a girl.

"What a sweet guy! My first year as manager I was young and I didn't know how some of the older players might take to me. We took the pitchers to Hot Springs for early training and Walter was the bellwether, setting an example that made 'em all work.

"You know, he pitched fifty-six consecutive scoreless innings for me. The last six innings of the streak he had St. Louis shut out, but then we scored six runs and I said to myself, 'Good night, here it goes.' I knew he'd coast on that lead, and I'd advertised him in Detroit, where we were going next, and Cobb had been promising to score on him and I knew we'd get a crowd up there.

"Sure enough, he threw a nothing ball to Ken Williams, who hit a triple. Joe Gedeon tripped Williams at second, fell on him, hollered for the ball, and tagged him. But Billy Evans sent Williams on to third for interference, and he scored on a fly."

"Cobb," somebody said, "once confessed that if he hadn't been so sure of Walter's control and didn't know how careful Walter was not to hit anybody Ty couldn't have batted .100 against him. As it was Ty knew he could take a toehold."

Another said, "Henry Edwards once told me he asked Walter if he'd ever used a spitter. Walter said just once. It almost got away from him and he never tried it again for fear he'd kill somebody."

"When we had squad games in training camp with Walter pitching," Bluege said, "practically everybody that was supposed to hit against him would suddenly get sick or hurt."

Another said, "Remember the time Ruel and Milan were hurrying to a show with him and some fan spoke to him and held 'em up half an hour? They kept signaling him to break away and when he finally did they gave him hell. He said he was sorry, but the fan was a fellow who grew up in Kansas and knew his sister well and he didn't want to be rude.

"Milan said, 'I didn't know you had a sister.'

"'I haven't,' Walter said. 'But he was a nice feller!'"

Next to Godliness

Cookie Swings for Fence, Ruins Bevens' No-Hitter

BROOKLYN, N.Y., *October 3, 1947*

THE GAME has been over for half an hour now, and still a knot of worshippers stands clustered, as around a shrine, out in right field adoring the spot on the wall which Cookie Lavagetto's line drive smote. It was enough to get a new contract for Happy Chandler. Things were never like this when Judge Landis was in.

Happy has just left his box. For twenty minutes crowds clamored around him, pushing, elbowing, shouting hoarsely for the autograph they snooted after the first three World Series games. Unable to get to Lavagetto, they were unwilling to depart altogether empty-handed. Being second choice to Cookie, Happy now occupies the loftiest position he has yet enjoyed in baseball. In Brooklyn, next to Lavagetto is next to godliness.

At the risk of shattering this gazette's reputation for probity, readers are asked to believe these things happened in Ebbets Field:

After 136 pitches, Floyd Bevens, of the Yankees, had the only no-hit ballgame ever played in a World Series. But he threw 137 and lost, 3 to 2.

With two out in the ninth inning, a preposterously untidy box score showed one run for the Dodgers, no hits, ten bases on balls, seven men left on base, and two more aboard waiting to be left. There still are two out in the ninth.

Hugh Casey, who lost two World Series games on successive days in 1941, now is the only pitcher in the world who has won two on successive days. One pitch beat him in 1941, a third strike on Tommy

Henrich, which Mickey Owen didn't catch. This time he threw only
one pitch, a strike to Tommy Henrich, and this time he caught the ball
himself for a double play.

Harry Taylor, who has had a sore arm half the summer, threw eleven
pitches in the first inning, allowed two hits and a run, and fled with
the bases filled and none out. Hal Gregg, who has had nothing at all
this summer—not even so much as a sore arm—came in to throw five
pitches and retired the side. Thereafter Gregg was a four-hit pitcher
until nudged aside for a pinch hitter in the seventh.

In the first inning George Stirnweiss rushed behind second base
and stole a hit from Pee Wee Reese. In the third Johnny Lindell caught
Jackie Robinson's foul fly like Doc Blanchard hitting the Notre Dame
line and came to his feet unbruised. In the fourth Joe DiMaggio caught
Gene Hermanski's monstrous drive like a well-fed banquet guest picking his teeth and broke down as he did so. Seems he merely twisted an
ankle, though, and wasn't damaged.

Immediately after that play—and this must be the least credible of
the day's wonders—the Dodger Simp-Phony band serenaded Happy
Chandler. The man who threw out the first manager for Brooklyn this
year did not applaud.

In the seventh inning two Simp-Phony bandsmen dressed in motley
did a tap dance on the roof of the Yankees' dugout. This amused the
commissioner, who has never openly opposed clowning.

In the eighth Hermanski smashed a drive to the scoreboard. Henrich backed against the board and leaped either four or fourteen feet
into the air. He stayed aloft so long he looked like an empty uniform
hanging in its locker. When he came down he had the ball.

In the ninth Lindell pressed his stem against the left-field fence
and caught a smash by Bruce Edwards. Jake Pitler, coaching for the
Dodgers at first base, flung his hands aloft and his cap to the ground.

And finally Bucky Harris, who has managed major league teams in
Washington, Detroit, Boston, Philadelphia, and New York, violated all
ten commandments of the dugout by ordering Bevens to walk Peter
Reiser and put the winning run on base.

Lavagetto, who is slightly less experienced than Harris, then demonstrated why this maneuver is forbidden in the managers' guild.

Cookie hit the fence. A character named Al Gionfriddo ran home. Running, he turned and beckoned frantically to a character named Eddie Miksis. Eddie Miksis ran home.

Dodgers pummeled Lavagetto. Gionfriddo and Miksis pummeled each other. Cops pummeled Lavagetto. Ushers pummeled Lavagetto. Ushers pummeled each other. Three soda butchers in white ran onto the field and threw forward passes with their white caps. In the tangle Bevens could not be seen.

The unhappiest man in Brooklyn is sitting up here now in the far end of the press box. The "v" on his typewriter is broken. He can't write either Lavagetto or Bevens.

Pitching Takes Brains

Al Schacht Picks His All-Screwball Lineup

"**M**Y ALL-STAR all-screwball team," Al Schacht said, "starts with Art
Shires on first base—no, that's wrong. It starts with Moe Berg behind
the plate. Berg is a kind of nut, you know. He's an educated mental
case. An educated catcher, which is the worst kind. Then there's
Smead Jolley in the outfield. Did I ever tell you about Smeadie in Boston? Don't answer.

"Smeadie was playing left field when there was a hill in Fenway
Park. A sort of incline up to the left-field wall—Duffy's Hill they called
it, for Duffy Lewis. Every time Smeadie started up after a fly he'd trip
and fall on his face and finally they got him out mornings and had him
practice running up the hill after fungoes.

"Well, Washington comes to town and somebody says: 'Smeadie,
how you going to manage Duffy's Hill today?' Smeadie says: 'Don't
worry about me, guinea'—he called everybody 'guinea'—'Don't worry
about me, I got it mastered.' Well, the first ball hit out there is one by
Joe Cronin that looks like it might be caught if Smeadie can make the
hill.

"Jolley turns and dashes up the hill and wheels with his back pressed
against the fence. Then he sees he has overrun the ball, so he starts
down. One step and, oops, here he goes flat on his kisser, the ball hits
him on the head, Cronin slides into third base, and Smeadie is out of
the ballgame.

"Well, he's sitting there on the bench rubbing the knot on his head and cussing. 'A lot of smart guineas on this nine,' he says. 'Ten days you spend teaching me how to go up the hill and there ain't a guinea in the crowd with the brains to teach me how to come down.'

"The next day they decide to make a catcher out of him. He's a great big guy, you know, that can hit. That's all he can do. So he's behind the plate and the first batter up is Joe Judge. Smeadie ain't caught a pitch yet in a major league game, but Joe turns to him and says: 'Smeadie, how do you like this catching racket?'

"'Well, Joe,' Smeadie says, 'I'll tell you. Out there in the outfield you're all alone by yourself, but here you got conversation.' With that, there's a pitch and Judge hits a high foul straight up in the air.

"Now, Smeadie was getting a little bald and his wife was always telling him to wear a tight cap. 'When your cap flies off, Smeadie,' she'd tell him, 'you look like an old man.' He used to wear a cap so tight he'd have to wrench it off like this in the clubhouse.

"When this foul went up, Smeadie yanked off his mask, and of course the cap came off, too. Smeadie thought of his bald spot. He claps his mitt over the top of his head and turns to the stands. 'I got it, Mary!' he yells. Then he turns to the third baseman and hollers: 'Okay, guinea, it's all yours!'

"The next day he was in the minors."

"My all-screwball team," said a man at the luncheon table, "would start with the pitcher."

"What do you mean?" Mr. Schacht demanded. "Pitching takes brains. Strategy. Lemme tell you about when I was in the International League. We're playing a doubleheader in Baltimore and between games I play a screwy golf game with a fungo stick and one of those ten-cent baseballs we called Rockets. It's just like a regular baseball only it's sawdust. When I finish the act I stick the Rocket in my hip pocket.

"Sixth inning of the second game our pitcher is getting belted and Chief Bender sends me into the game. Three men on bases. Seems like there's always three on when I'm pitching.

"In those days you could discolor the ball with licorice or tobacco juice. As I walk in, I'm reaching back in my pocket for my licorice and I feel the Rocket. 'Oh-oh,' I say, 'oh-oh.' I stick the Rocket in my glove and, when I'm on the mound, I turn my back to the crowd and slip the real ball into my shirt.

"Joe Boley's the first hitter. I lay one in for him and he tees off with everything he's got. Fffzzzz, it goes in a little pop fly to the shortstop. One out. Len Stiles is next, and he tees off. Phzzzzz, another pop fly. Two out. The third guy is big Rube Parnham, which I can always beat him because I talk to him and get his goat. This time, though, I'm busy massaging that Rocket back into shape, because it's pretty lopsided. Finally I lay one in and he swings and it goes spiraling up over my head. It's just the shape of this hard roll here. I wave everybody away and make the catch myself. Three out.

"But now I can't leave the Rocket on the mound and I can't get the real ball, which has worked around here to the back of my shirt. So I carried the Rocket into the dugout, but before I could get the real ball out, Bill McGowan, the umpire, starts hollering and I got to roll the Rocket out to him. It goes skipping and hopping out across the grass.

"Of course, there's a terrific howl, and after a lot of argument I say: 'Well, all right. I confess I tricked the Rube, but I got Boley and Stiles legitimate.' I figure I'm going to get fined anyway, and I might as well get away with something.

"So McGowan rules it an illegal pitch to Parnham, and I take the real ball out of my shirt and go out to pitch to the Rube again. I get two strikes on him, and then I start working on him. I reach into my shirt, and the crowd starts yelling: 'Watch him!' and McGowan comes storming out to me. 'You just live your life, and leave me live mine,' I tell him. 'See, here's the ball, and it's okay.' So he goes back, and I throw one more to the Rube right up here under his chin, and he strikes out.

"Well, he's so mad he comes howling out to the mound, and I say: 'Here's the ball; look at it.' And I toss it to him. He grabs the ball and whirls and throws it clean out of the park, and McGowan fines him twenty-five dollars.

"See what I mean," Mr. Schacht asked, "about pitching strategy?"

Young Old Master

Joe DiMaggio at 34

BROOKLYN, N.Y., *January 8, 1948*

AFTER THE Yankees chewed up the Dodgers in the second game of the World Series, Joe DiMaggio relaxed in the home club's gleaming tile boudoir and deposed at length in defense of Pete Reiser, the Brooklyn center fielder, who had narrowly escaped being smitten upon the isthmus rhombencephali that day by sundry fly balls.

The moving, mottled background of faces and shirt collars and orchids, Joe said, made a fly almost invisible until it had cleared the top deck. The tricky, slanting shadows of an October afternoon created a problem involving calculus, metaphysics, and social hygiene when it came to judging a line drive. The roar of the crowd disguised the crack of bat against ball. And so on.

Our Mr. Robert Cooke, listening respectfully as one should to the greatest living authority on the subject, nevertheless stared curiously at DiMaggio. He was thinking that not only Reiser but also J. DiMaggio had played that same center field on that same afternoon, and there were no knots on Joe's slick coiffure.

"How about you, Joe?" Bob asked. "Do those same factors handicap you out there?"

DiMaggio permitted himself one of his shy, toothy smiles.

"Don't start worrying about the old boy after all these years," he said.

He didn't say "the old master." That's a phrase for others to use. But it would be difficult to define more aptly than Joe did the difference between this unmitigated pro and all the others, good, bad, and ordinary, who also play in major league outfields.

There is a line that has been quoted so often the name of its originator has been lost. But whoever said it first was merely reacting impulsively to a particular play and not trying to coin a *mot* when he ejaculated: 'The sonofagun! Ten years I've been watching him, and he hasn't had a hard chance yet!"

It may be that Joe is not, ranked on his defensive skill alone, the finest center fielder of his time. Possibly Terry Moore was his equal playing the hitter, getting the jump on the ball, judging a fly, covering ground, and squeezing the ball once he touched it.

Joe himself has declared that his kid brother, Dominic, is a better fielder than he. Which always recalls the occasion when the Red Sox were playing the Yanks and Dom fled across the county line to grab a drive by Joe that no one but a DiMaggio could have reached. And the late Sid Mercer, shading his thoughtful eyes under a hard straw hat, remarked to the press box at large: "Joe should sue his old man on that one."

Joe hasn't been the greatest hitter that baseball has known, either. He'll not match Ty Cobb's lifetime average, he'll never threaten Babe Ruth's home-run record, nor will he ever grip the imagination of the crowds as the Babe did. Or even as Babe Herman did. That explains why the contract that he signed the other day calls for an estimated $65,000 instead of the $80,000 that Ruth got. If he were not such a matchless craftsman he might be a more spectacular player. And so, perhaps, more colorful. And so more highly rewarded.

But you don't rate a great ballplayer according to his separate, special talents. You must rank him off the sum total of his component parts, and on this basis there has not been, during Joe's big league existence, a rival close to him. None other in his time has combined such savvy and fielding and hitting and throwing—Tom Laird, who was writing sports in San Francisco when Joe was growing up, always insisted that a sore arm "ruined" DiMaggio's throwing in his first season with the Yankees—and such temperament and such base running.

Because he does so many other things so well and makes no specialty of stealing, DiMaggio rarely has received full credit for his work on the bases. But travel with a second-division club in the league for a few seasons and count the times when DiMaggio, representing the tying or winning run, whips you by coming home on the unforeseen gamble and either beats the play or knocks the catcher into the dugout.

Ask American League catchers about him, or National Leaguers like Ernie Lombardi. Big Lom will remember who it was who ran home from first base in the last game of the 1939 World Series while Ernie lay threshing in the dust behind the plate and Bucky Walters stood bemused on the mound.

These are the reasons why DiMaggio, excelled by Ted Williams in all offensive statistics and reputedly Ted's inferior in crowd appeal and financial standing, still won the writers' accolade as the American League's most valuable in 1947.

It wasn't the first time Williams earned this award with his bat and lost it with his disposition. As a matter of fact, if all other factors were equal save only the question of character, Joe never would lose out to any player. The guy who came out of San Francisco as a shy lone wolf, suspicious of Easterners and of Eastern writers, today is the top guy in any sports gathering in any town. The real champ.

They Let George Do It

"Large Jarge" Magerkurth Hangs Up His Blue Serge

NEW YORK, N.Y., *January 27, 1948*

A CLIENT protests that George Magerkurth's retirement after nineteen years as a National League umpire received insufficient attention from the press. He is right. Razing the Empire State Building would be no more noteworthy, nor a much bigger project, than divesting the old Maje of his shiny blue suit, and permitting him to pass unsung was an inexcusable oversight. Apologies and reparations are in order.

The Major's withdrawal leaves a large hole smack in the middle of the baseball scene. A hole six feet three inches high, to be exact, and approximately four feet wide. Turning his broad back on the diamond, Large Jarge joins the doughty company of Bill Klem, Tim Hurst, Silk O'Loughlin, and the rest, but he leaves baseball the poorer. Still with us are the articulate Beans Reardon, the light-hearted Red Jones, and the matchless Bill McGowan, who can buckle a swash with any man alive, but they are exceptions in a profession that is chiefly distinguished today for a slick and colorless efficiency.

There never was anything slick about Large Jarge. No mincing mediator he. His was the noble tradition of those who would fight at the drop of an Anglo-Saxon expletive, and the National League has a dossier a yard long to prove it.

George Magerkurth probably was the only umpire for whom fans voluntarily passed the hat and collected one hundred dollars to pay off another fan whose heckling had elicited from Maje the following rejoinder: "Did you call me a thief?" Boff!

He must have been the only umpire who, when struck on the leg by a flying pop bottle, retrieved the glassware and heaved it straight back into the stands, winging the original thrower in the shoulder. That was in Reading, Pennsylvania.

He was certainly the only one in this witness's experience who seemed to relish a row more than the heroes filing a protest and who, when set upon by a pack of snapping players, would charge back at them and keep the argument going after they were ready to give up.

What Maje may have lacked in diplomacy he made up for in a quality that Dick Nallin, the old American League umpire, defined some years before Large Jarge's day. Ban Johnson demanded a report from Nallin describing how he had arrived at a certain decision on a play that happened behind his back. Dick telegraphed a single line of explanation:

"The animal instinct of an umpire."

Yup, Maje had plenty of that, but he wouldn't have chosen the telegraph as the means of communicating the intelligence to his boss. He was suspicious of Mr. Morse's invention because of a small, unhappy experience in his youth. This was during his service in the International League, where, he used to boast, he batted 1.000 as a rookie—"four riots in my first four days."

He and Billy Webb, manager of Buffalo, discussed a decision under the stands after one game and both emerged from the debate cut and bleeding and under arrest. Next day's game was under-umpired because Maje didn't show up. This called for explanation because, if John Conway Toole, president of the league, had meant to suspend the umpire he would have assigned a substitute.

Well, it seemed Maje had received a wire from Toole reading: "Send full report of trouble with Webb along with Umpire Jones' report Stop Work today."

"So," Maje said, "I stopped work."

It is characteristic of Maje that his apprenticeship was served mostly in professional football and professional boxing. He played little baseball. He grew up in sports with the conviction that the best and most natural retort to make to an adversary was a punch in the snoot, and that conviction was at the root of most of the difficulties he periodically experienced.

Thus, when Ivy Griffin addressed him in coarse fashion during a ballgame in Indianapolis, he visited the player's hotel room that evening, thumped him to a pulp, got himself pinched, and was flung out of the American Association.

When Giant players disputed Lee Ballanfant's decision that a borderline fly which Harry Craft, of the Reds, hit into the Polo Grounds stands was a home run, Maje naturally bought into the rumpus. It wasn't his argument, but he was shouting loudest of all, and sputtering somewhat as he orated. A fine spray moistened the face of Billy Jurges, the Giants' shortstop.

Jurges, nettled, spat into Maje's broad features and swung a punch. Maje spat back and punched back. Both he and Jurges were suspended.

When Maje called a balk on Hugh Casey in an important game, Casey delivered his next three pitches so hard and so high as to suggest that it was his purpose to dust off the umpire. Magerkurth demurred in a fashion that brought Leo Durocher out on the run with a remarkable request.

"I want you," said the dandiest little umpire-intimidator of his time, "to stop intimidating my ballplayers."

Probably the portrait of Maje that fans remember most clearly showed him on his back in Ebbets Field with a customer half his size astride his bosom, expressing disapproval of a decision with his knuckles. It pained Maje deeply to appear in the newspapers in so undignified a posture.

He is enormously forgiving, however. His critic, who was on parole, got sent back to pokey as a result of the affair, and when he finally got out, Large Jarge declined to press assault charges.

"I," said Maje with great indulgence and monstrous non sequitur, "am the father of a boy myself."

Jim Crow's Playmates

Branch Rickey vs. the Color Line

NEW YORK, N.Y., *February 19, 1948*

A CURIOUS sort of hullabaloo has been aroused by Branch Rickey's disclosure that when he went into the ring against Jim Crow, he found fifteen major league club owners working in Jim's corner. It is strange that the news should stir excitement, for surely it couldn't have come as a surprise to anyone.

At the time Rickey signed Jackie Robinson for Montreal, anybody who knew anything about baseball was aware that a Jim Crow law did exist in the game, although baseball men never had the courage to put it in writing. And after Robinson was signed, open opposition to his presence continued until publication of the news stories which killed the projected player strike against him last summer.

Well, no matter. A year ago Rickey was weaving and ducking and bobbing in an effort to elude people who wanted to have him stuffed and mounted as a prime specimen of tolerance. He insisted he was not interested in Robinson as a black man or a member of an underprivileged race and that his purpose in signing Jackie was not, as described in Arthur Mann's song, to "triumph over prejudice and the excess profits tax."

"I want ballplayers," he said. "I don't care if they're purple or green and have hair all over them and arms that reach down to their ankles, just so they can beat the whey out of the Cardinals and win a World Series."

That was his story, and it was as good as any except for the technicality that it wasn't true. Here is the truth.

In 1903, when Rickey was baseball coach at Michigan, he had a Negro named Charley Thomas on the squad. The first trip the boy made was to South Bend, Indiana, where the hotel management declined to let him register. Rickey blamed himself later for not having had the foresight to brief the kid in advance, preparing him for such experiences.

Rickey and the team captain were sharing a suite. When Branch learned of Thomas' difficulties, he hurried down and asked whether the management would let Thomas move into the suite. This was agreed, provided Thomas didn't register, and all three retired to their quarters.

Upstairs Rickey and the captain got to talking. Thomas sat on the edge of Rickey's bed with his head low, so that his face was concealed. When Branch tried to draw him into the conversation, the boy lifted his head. He was crying. He was wringing his hands between his knees, twisting the fingers as though trying to pull the skin off.

"It's these," the kid said, lifting his hands.

Rickey didn't understand.

"They're black," the kid said. "It's my skin," the kid said. "If it wasn't for my skin, I wouldn't be any different from anybody."

"My hands," the kid said. "They're black. If they were only white!"

Rickey said: "Tommy, the day will come when they won't have to be white." That was forty-five years ago. It was forty-three years before Rickey found the right time and the right place and the right guy in Jackie Robinson. In those years Rickey has gone a lot of places and done a lot of things and been pictured in many lights. He may be all the things they have called him—a rush of wind in an empty room, a glib horse-trader, a specious orator, a coon-shouting revivalist. He has been described, in purest Brooklynese and with faithful accuracy, as a "man of many facets—all turned on."

It remains a simple matter of fact that he has not forgotten Charley Thomas. He has kept up with Charley Thomas, knows where he is today and what he is doing and how he is doing. Charley's doing all right, by the way.

In the circumstances, it was not hard to believe Rickey yesterday when he described his feelings at the major league meeting where fifteen club owners approved a report stating that the employment of a Negro in professional baseball was jeopardizing their investment.

"I was," he said, "deeply disturbed."

The Babe

George Herman Ruth, Jr., 1895–1948

T̲H̲E̲ ̲S̲T̲O̲R̲Y̲ made page one of the *Ocean Times* immediately below
the bulletin about the Kremlin conversations. The headline read
"Death of Baseball Idol," and the dispatch announced that "Babe Ruth,
baseball's beloved homerun king, died in his sleep last night. The fifty-
three-year-old famed Sultan of Swat died after a week-end rally that
had raised the fading hopes of his legions of admirers. The end came
swiftly."

ABOARD M.V. BRITANNIC, *August 18, 1948*

Even in midocean, news like that arrives punctually. It was news,
too, in Japan and Pakistan and Johannesburg and Canberra. There are
a great many places on this earth where baseball is not played, but
very few indeed where the name of Babe Ruth was unknown. Which
could be, if you liked, a way of saying how much bigger the man was
than the game.

The end came swiftly, the dispatch said. Not swiftly enough. Not
without years of unceasing, remorseless pain. Not so suddenly as to
take anyone by surprise. Not anyone at all. "I haven't much farther to
go," the Babe told his friend Frank Stevens in the hospital last winter,
"but I'm not going to die in here. I'm going to get out and have some
fun first."

The betting was against him on that, but he did get out as he said
he would. How much fun he had only he could have said. It didn't
look like fun being convoyed around Florida, where he'd had, in his
time, some fun that really was fun. You'd encounter him in Miami
and Tampa and St. Petersburg and Clearwater at the spring training

games or maybe at a dinner, always with a squad of cops fending off the autograph hounds and a horde of junior executives chuffing and scurrying like tugboats around a liner.

There always seemed to be junior executives around him in those last few months. In Florida he had some sort of business tie-up with a motor company and later, back home, there was a great fuss about the launching of his autobiography into the market, and after that came the screening of the book in Hollywood. Seemed as though everyone had an idea how to make some more money, but there wasn't much time and it had to be hurry, hurry, hurry.

Always there was a pain that never went away. He was so dreadfully sick even to the layman's eye. There was a sadness even in the jauntiness of his tan cap and camel's-hair polo coat. Still, probably it was better than the hospital, and maybe he did have some fun of a sort.

There was a day at a ballgame in St. Pete's Al Lang Stadium, the shiny new playground on the site of old Waterfront Park where Babe and the other Yankees used to tee off in the spring. Somebody asked him about the old days in St. Pete. He pointed to the weathered facade of the Gulf Coast Inn, which, when the old park was up, had stood an everlasting distance beyond the outfield wall. He remembered, he said in the husk of voice he had left, how he'd really got his *adjectival* shoulders into a swing and had knocked the *indelicacy* ball against the *Anglo-Saxon* hotel out there.

"Gee!" the other said. "Quite a belt!"

"Yeah," Babe said, "and don't forget the *adjectival* park was a block back this way then."

His eyes gleamed with something like pleasure. Some of the old joie de vivre remained, all right. But the end didn't come swiftly, really. The Yankees of Ruth's day who have gone, they didn't get many breaks at the end. There was the Babe with his intractable pain these last several years. There was Lou Gehrig dying by inches and knowing it and facing it. There was Tony Lazzeri alone in the dark when the finish came. Little Miller Huggins was luckier. He went tragically, but suddenly.

Now that Babe is gone, what's to be said that hasn't been said?

Nothing, when you come down to it. Just that he was Babe Ruth. Which tells it all, for there never was another and never will be. Probably he was the greatest ballplayer who ever lived, Ty Cobb and Honus Wagner and the rest notwithstanding.

It's a typically shabby trick on history's part that, as time goes by, he will be remembered merely for his home runs. He was also, remember, a genuinely great pitcher, a genuinely great outfielder, a genuinely great competitor, a truly great personality.

Merely by being part of the game, he wrought lasting changes in its strategy, its financial standards, its social position, and the public conception of it. Somebody else will come along to hit sixty home runs, probably very soon. That won't make somebody else a second Babe Ruth. Never another like him.

They Played It
by Radio

Red Sox Make Playoffs But DiMaggio Makes Them Work

I T WAS a day when malice lay over everything, thick as mustard on a frankfurter, and you could reach out and feel it like something tangible. The Yankees, killed off by the Red Sox yesterday, were out here in Fenway Park to gouge back an eye for the one they had lost, and the Red Sox, inspired by the loftiest sort of cupidity, wanted that World Series money so badly they could taste it.

The 31,354 specimens penned in the park had a sort of shine on their faces, the sweatily eager look that a bullfight crowd wears when the bull is five runs ahead of the matador in the ninth inning.

It was the third inning and the Red Sox, who had been two runs behind, had scored three times and had two runners on the bases, with one out and Bill Goodman at bat. Chuck Dressen, the Yankees' opulent coach, was out in the middle of the diamond talking to Bob Porterfield, the rookie pitcher, and the crowd started to scream.

At first, the notion was that the customers were only trying to work on Porterfield, hoping to shake the kid's unnatural poise. But there was a different sort of note in the crowd's voice. People behind the Boston dugout were standing and cupping hands to mouths and shouting things to the players, and after a little while it was apparent what was happening.

There were portable radios in the stands and the customers had just heard about that third inning in Cleveland. The word had reached the press box. The Tigers had a run home and the bases filled with one out. Then another flash came: "Wakefield doubled."

You should have seen that crowd. Everybody was on his feet, and everybody was screaming, but the ballplayers acted as though they hadn't heard anything. Goodman singled, driving in Boston's fourth run.

The crowd made a fair fuss about that, but that was nothing. The small, unseen man who lives in the scoreboard swung a panel open and took down the number of the Cleveland pitcher and put up another. He took down 19 and put up 26, which meant that Bob Feller had been replaced by Sam Zoldak.

You should have heard that crowd. They weren't watching the Red Sox, who were scoring another run just then on a force-out by Birdie Tebbetts. They were watching the scoreboard, where the figure 5 went up for Detroit. That was a mistake, and a moment later the sign was changed and the number 4 was posted, the real Detroit score for the third inning.

Now the third inning was over up here. The Red Sox were in front, 5 to 2, and out in Cleveland the Tigers were leading, 4 to 0. Everybody knew Hal Newhouser was pitching for Detroit. Everybody knew that if Boston could stay ahead, there would be a tie for the American League pennant. Nobody thought for a moment that Newhouser would blow a four-run lead.

Of course he didn't. And of course the Red Sox won, setting up the first playoff the American League has had. But it wasn't easy. The Yankees have a guy named Joe DiMaggio. Sometimes a fellow gets a little tired of writing about DiMaggio; a fellow thinks, "there must be some other ballplayer in the world worth mentioning." But there isn't really, not worth mentioning in the same breath with Joe DiMaggio.

That guy, DiMaggio, had hit a double in the first inning and driven in New York's first run. He had grounded out in the third, but in the fifth Phil Rizzuto singled. Bobby Brown doubled Rizzuto to third, and then Joe came up. There were two runs on the bases and DiMaggio was the tying run at the plate.

First base was open. Up in the press box, people said, "I don't care how wrong it is to put the tying run on base. They have got to put this guy on."

But Joe McCarthy didn't. Heaven knows, the Red Sox manager is aware of what DiMaggio can do. The champ did it often enough for McCarthy when they were together on the Yankees. But McCarthy let Joe Dobson pitch to the guy. So, naturally, the guy hit another double, slamming the ball to the left-field fence and dragging his dead left leg stiffly as he ran to second base while two runs came home.

He had now driven home three of New York's four runs. He had twice made a contest of this game. He brought the Yankees up close enough to scare the daylights out of the Red Sox, until Joe's brother Dom hit one over the wall in the sixth.

Joe went on to make four hits in five times up, in his last game of the year. When he singled in the ninth, Bucky Harris sent Steve Souchock in to run for him. Maybe Bucky wanted the guy to walk off by himself, so he could get a personal tribute from the crowd instead of just going off, unnoticed, along with eight other guys. Because Harris thinks of things like that. Or, maybe, Bucky just wanted a sound runner on first base.

Anyway, Souchock went in and DiMaggio limped off, and the crowd stood up and yelled for the guy who had done more damage to Boston than any ten other guys they could mention. He tipped his cap and disappeared into the runway leading to the clubhouse.

That's all, except for one small story. Last night, Joe and his brother Dom dined together. Joe said, "You gave us hell today, but tomorrow I'll hit my fortieth home run."

His little brother said, "I don't think you will, but I'm gonna hit my ninth."

One of them had to be right.

A Nation of Hams

America's Pastime Mugs for the Camera

Take me out to the ball game,
I want to see Quinnie work:
I like Lefty and Rube and Cy,
But it's always the umpire
Who catches my eye——

YEARS AGO they sang a song beginning like that at a party attended by Johnny Quinn, then an American League umpire. It was strictly a rib, and nobody imagined then that the day might come when the performer in blue serge could steal scenes from the player in white flannels.

But recently at a game in Brooklyn, a lady said, "I just love to watch Dascoli behind the plate. Barrymore was never like him." Obviously, the lady had been seeing games on television.

Perhaps the impression is confined to this quarter, but it is the notion here that the televising of ballgames has done more to bring back vaudeville than any other development since Nora Bayes. Or, rather, the change has been wrought by the umpires' discovery of television's possibilities.

Unless he is even blinder than practitioners of the craft are cracked down to be, an umpire must realize, the first time he sees baseball on television, that at least 80 percent of the time he occupies the featured position downstage, in the exact center of the screen. He would be less than human if this discovery did not bear fruit in his work.

With a few notable exceptions like Bill Klem, who was always keenly aware of his duty to the public, umpires used to call a strike by lifting the right arm limply and letting it drop. They signaled a ball by doing nothing whatever. Some also announced their decisions vocally, but seldom in tones that carried past the catcher.

Today, conscious of the great unseen audience, they play every decision out like the balcony scene from *Romeo and Juliet*. On a strike they gesticulate, they brandish a fist aloft, they spin about as though shot through the heart, they bellow all four parts of the quartette from *Rigoletto*. On a pitch that misses the plate, they stiffen with loathing, ostentatiously avert the gaze, and render a bit from *Götterdämmerung*.

In parlor and pub, you see the umpire today. And hear him.

The virus is infecting the fans, too. When a foul is hit into the stands, the camera usually is trained on the fan who recovers the ball. Used to be that a guy catching a foul would pocket his loot almost furtively and go on watching the game. Today he wheels toward the camera, holds his prize aloft, shouts, and makes faces.

Television is making us a nation of hams.

The voice on virtually all telecasts is that of a reconverted radio announcer. Trained up in a business where silence is the unforgivable sin, they have not yet realized fully that much of their chatter is unnecessary and downright irritating to the guy who can see for himself what's happening. Mr. Red Barber is the only one who has given welcome relief to his tonsils and these ears.

Some recent remarks which this listener could have done without included:

"Down in the bullpen, Ted Wilks, stocky little right-hander for the Cards, just in case George Munger has any more trouble or difficulty." . . . "Monte Kennedy is now in danger of walking George Munger as these two pitchers have locked horns here." . . . "We'll be T-V-talkin' to yuh."

"The old soupbone is pretty well oiled up." . . . "Munger is better than matching Kennedy's sterling performance." . . . "Ah, the levity that goes on at a ballpark!"

"There's Clyde Sukeforth, the old woodchopper from Maine, going out to the Dodger bullpen." . . . "Shortstop for the Chicubs." . . . "Four hits in toto off Banta." . . . "This boy lives in Gloucester, Mass., his wife's home town. He's from South Carolina, was married in Italy, his son was born in Tennessee, and he struck out." . . . "He's trying to etch his fourth win."

"Number 16 down there with the wood is Mickey Owen, who nipped Reese off second base in a play that proved to be the pivotal play in the first game and snuffed out a potential Dodger rally. . . ."

Soupbone . . . locked horns . . . sterling performance . . . in toto . . . with the wood . . . snuffed out. . . . They sound worse than they read. There are the ancient, blowsy clichés that were coined ever so many years ago by baseball writers with an original turn of the quill pen, were inherited and worked and worn by succeeding generations of bad sportswriters, and finally were lifted by radio guys whose reading had led them to believe this was the proper language of the game.

Corruptions like "Chicubs" are frightful enough in their own right, but at least they were coined for a purpose, by some copyreader trying to make a headline fit. They were never intended to be spoken aloud in any capacity.

What is saddest of all, young baseball writers now are borrowing from the language of radio. Today you can read, if your stomach can stand it, that there were "ducks on the pond" or that the "bases were F.O.B. (Full of Brooklyns)."

By the sacred beard of Gutenberg, it is worse than a vicious circle. It is a noose.

One Vote for
Will Harridge

A.L. President Makes Wise Call

New York, N.Y., *September 28, 1949*

IN THE eighth inning on Monday, Willie Grieve ruled Johnny Pesky safe at home on a squeeze play, and in that instant the Red Sox moved a full game ahead of the Yankees. Later—most accounts agree that it was not during the varied exchanges of opinion which ensued immediately, but under the grandstand when the game was over—Cliff Mapes, the Yankees' utility outfielder, demanded of the umpire: "How much did you have on the game?"

If this was as Grieve construed it, an accusation of dishonesty and not a clumsy, singularly tasteless attempt at a witticism, then Mapes has no claim whatever to clemency from Will Harridge, the American League president. Mapes is a comparatively recent pledge in Mr. Harridge's fraternity, but he has been around long enough to learn that big league ballplayers do not remonstrate with the umpire by suggesting that he is betting on the opposition.

Fans of half the nation at least must be rooting for the Yankees because of the gallant battle they have sustained since April. This skeleton of a team, its bones stripped bare by injuries and sickness, could ill afford the loss of even a .245 hitter at this point. Undoubtedly that is why Harridge refrained from suspending Mapes, assessing a fine instead, and demanding an apology.

Harridge ruled wisely. This pennant race should be decided on the playing field, not in the league office. The Yankees should not be made to suffer because one of their number could not or would not mind his tongue. They deserve the leniency that was shown. Mapes does not.

In fact, everybody in authority bore down heavily on the virtue of forbearance in this affair. In ordinary circumstances Ralph Houk, Joe Page, and Casey Stengel would have been drummed off the field immediately following Grieve's decision.

Any competent dramatic critic would have Houk banished for overplaying his impersonation of a homicidal maniac. Mr. Stengel bumped waistcoats with Mr. Grieve, an offense against the caste system which designates umpires as untouchables. Entering his demurrer, Page flung his glove aloft. This is by definition a gesture calculated to incite the populace to riot.

Under the rules, therefore, Mr. Grieve was clearly entitled to lift the imperious thumb, not once, but thrice. He knows Houk, however, for a hustling, combative operative who was unmistakably sincere in his conviction that the umpire had booted the play. He appreciates how Stengel has been hag-ridden by worry. He rendered unto Page the respect which that stout-hearted character has earned from everyone this season. And he was aware of the significance of his decision. So Willie kept his temper. In their moment of greatest need he declined to deprive the Yankees of the services of their manager, their matchless relief pitcher, and the only able-bodied catcher then available. He should be saluted for it, not vilified.

This is Willie Grieve's sixteenth year as an umpire, his twelfth season in the American League. He knows that almost anything may be said in the heat of a close, important contest. Houk was not wired for sound, but judging from appearances, just about everything must have been said on the field. In sixteen years any umpire must overlook a fairly wide assortment of capsule critiques offered on the spot.

He pays no attention to charges of incompetence, such as were batted around the Yankee clubhouse after the game, for he knows that if the decision had gone the other way, the Yankees would be applauding him for a "great call," and it would have been the Red Sox who'd describe him as "the worst umpire in the game."

But it is something else again when a player, especially a noncombatant, having had a couple of innings to cool off and think it over, directly challenges an umpire's integrity.

Willie Grieve needs no character witnesses. It is belaboring the obvious unmercifully to say that he is a man of uncompromising honesty. And twelve years is a long time for an incompetent to hold a job, unless the American League office is even more lenient with umpires than with pop-off outfielders.

As to the decision that set off the uproar, only an idiot would base an opinion on what he could see from the Black Hole of Calcutta that serves as a press box in Yankee Stadium. On a big day it is all anyone can do to cover a game from that slum, let alone umpire it. It is possible to say only that Grieve was on the play and called it as soon as it was completed. In his time he has had a lot of close ones. Unquestionably he has called some of them wrong. He could have been right on this one or wrong. Nobody will ever know. The photographs prove nothing.

Pesky insisted that Willie was right. Pesky is an honest little guy, but scarcely unprejudiced in this case, and anyhow the rules of baseball do not require players to tell the truth about their close ones. The Yankees, not altogether unbiased either, were just as positive that Willie was wrong.

In the excitement one point has been generally overlooked. That is, the Yankees did not lose because of an umpire's decision. They lost because they played bad baseball and booted away a three-run lead.

The Vacant Chair

Casey Stengel Paces

BRONX, N.Y., *September 24, 1950*

HALF AN hour before the people giving an automobile to Lefty McDermott threw out the first polysyllable, amplifiers outside Yankee Stadium were warning the crowds that all reserved seats were exhausted. This was erroneous. During the first game of the itsy-bitsy World Series between the Yankees and the Red Sox, the seat reserved for Casey Stengel remained unoccupied. It was Casey that got exhausted.

Before the game, the doughty field marshal of the Yankees did deign to sit down, if you can call his posture sitting. While the players warmed up he assumed a characteristic pose, in which the only part of him in contact with the bench was a spot on the back of his neck about the size of a silver dollar. Disposed thus in defiance of all natural laws, he plaited his legs into a long braid and, folding his arms, hugged himself tightly, as though wrapping himself up in himself against the afternoon's gray chill.

It was Yogi Berra who called attention to the weather. His comely features were unshaven and somebody remarked about the thick shrubbery on his jaw.

"I'm wearin' it to keep warm," Yogi explained sensibly. "I got a little cold."

Physicists were still studying this when Ed Lopat went to work on the pitching rubber. Thereafter, Marshal Stengel covered more ground than both DiMaggios. A witness watching nobody but Casey could have told pretty accurately what was happening on the field.

When Dom DiMaggio opened the first inning for Boston by cow-tailing a fraternal triple over the head of J. DiMaggio in center field, Casey clutched for support and got hold of an upright supporting the dugout roof. He stood frozen. So did Dominic as Lopat retired Johnny Pesky, Ted Williams, and Junior Stephens in order.

Nobody knew it then, but that brotherly belt of Dominic's was to be the only loud hit off Lopat all day. It was almost as loud as the boos which welcomed Sir Williams on his first time at bat in the Stadium since early July.

In the Yankees' first inning, Berra's beard hissed in the breeze as he rushed down to first base in time to beat a double-play throw which would have retired the side. Then Joe DiMaggio took one pitch for a ball and sliced a fly into the first-row seats in right field. Joe's hit traveled about 310 feet, his kid brother's approximately 450. The big guy got two runs, junior got exercise. In baseball, there is no substitute for experience and savvy.

As the ball leaped from Joe's bat, Mr. Stengel leaped from the dugout. His cap was off and he was springing about in such a whirling frenzy he looked like several Hopi Indians in a tribal sun dance. He swung his cap again and again in an encircling gesture that said: "All the way around! All the way!"

In the second inning, Bobby Doerr tied into a pitch and lashed it on a line over second base. Clean, stand-up double, one would say as it started. Joe raced in on a long angle to his left, thrust out his glove, palm up like a landlord taking a payoff under the table. The ball snuggled into the pocket.

Casey stood on the dugout step, his face blankly agape. His chin, which is fairly long in repose, touched his breastbone.

In the third inning, Joe charged into left field, reached up, and plucked a drive by Dominic out of the air. Casey shoved his paws into his hip pockets and strutted the length of the dugout, his chest out. A few minutes later he was straining across the bat rack, his jaw waggling so fast it was a mere blur. Joe Paparella, the plate umpire, had called a strike against Bill Johnson and Mr. Stengel was offering a suggestion.

Johnson walked, Phil Rizzuto doubled, and Joe DiMaggio was purposely passed, filling the bases. John Mize hooked a single into right for two runs. This flushed Yankees out of the dugout like a covey of quail, but this time Mr. Stengel indulged in no theatrics. His manner was that of a commander whose operations were proceeding precisely according to plan.

He responded similarly when Hank Bauer followed with a double good for the fifth New York run. Casey popped up the steps so he could follow the ball's flight into right field, then relaxed, planting an elbow on the dugout roof and leaning there at peace with the world.

By this time early returns were in from Cleveland and the scoreboard recorded the beginning of Detroit's ordeal out there. With the Tigers headed for defeat and Lopat breezing along on a five-run cushion, just ambling toward his fourth shutout of the season, Mr. Stengel was relatively content.

As the afternoon darkened and New York prospects brightened, he did a good deal of pacing, shouting, wigwagging, and leaping about. But his carriage was jaunty now, with just the proper touch of swagger for the manager of a club leading its league by a game and a half, with a three-game bulge on the Red Sox.

If he frowned, ever so slightly, it was in concentration, thinking of today's game.

Off the High Board

Phillies Nab First Pennant in 35 Years

THE TALLEST, steepest, swiftest, dizziest, daredevil, death-defying dive ever undertaken by a baseball team came off with a rich and fruity climax yesterday when the Phillies toppled headlong into the World Series.

For thirty-five years the Phillies struggled to win a National League pennant. For the last twelve days they battled mightily to lose one. Then in the tenth inning of the 155th game of their season, all snarled up in a strangling tie with the team that had closed eight laps on them in a fortnight, they were knocked kicking into the championship by the bat of Dick Sisler.

George Sisler, probably the greatest first baseman who ever lived, whose .400 hitting couldn't get him into a World Series, sat in Ebbets Field and saw his big son slice a three-run homer that shattered the pennant hopes of the Dodgers, whom George now serves.

Sisler's hit won the game, 4 to 1. Minutes earlier, lustrous pitching by Robin Roberts had saved it, after the Dodgers had come within a dozen feet of the victory that would have closed the season in a tie and brought Philadelphia and Brooklyn together for a playoff.

"There hasn't been such a finish," said Mr. Warren Brown, the noted Chicago author, "since sporting British officials carried Dorando over the line in the 1908 Olympic marathon."

On September 19 the Phillies had the pennant won in every sense save the mathematical one. They were seven and one half games ahead of the Boston Braves, and Brooklyn was third, nine games off the pace.

The Dodgers won fourteen of their next seventeen games, the Phillies three of their twelve. So when they showed up yesterday before Ebbets Field's largest gathering of the year, the Phils' lead was exactly one game, with one game to play.

They had neither won nor lost the championship, but they had qualified handsomely for off-season employment—substituting for the diving horse in Atlantic City.

They had also brought gold pouring in a bright yellow stream into the Brooklyn box office. Instead of leasing out their park for family picnics this weekend, the Dodgers sold 58,952 tickets for the last two games, many of them to customers who stood outside the bleacher gates all Saturday night.

By four A.M., cars were pulling into parking lots near the field. By six thirty, there were five thousand or six thousand persons in line. By one P.M., all gates were closed and nobody without a reserved-seat ticket was admitted. Cops estimated that twenty-five thousand were turned away. It was bigger than many World Series crowds in Brooklyn, and properly so, for this was bigger than a World Series game, where even the losers gather much loot. The losers of this game got the winter off.

In spite of everything, the Phillies managed a surface appearance of confidence. Before the game the Philadelphia manager, Eddie Sawyer, was asked to name his pitcher for the first playoff game today.

"That's one thing I never do," he said mildly. "Announce my pitcher for the day after the season closes."

For what seemed an interminable time, though, there was reason to doubt that the season ever would close. Big Don Newcombe was rocking back on his hind leg, waggling a big spiked shoe in the Phillies' beardless faces, and firing his service past them. They had at least one base runner in every inning after the first, but these Phils are kids still damp from the nursing bottle, and this was hard stuff Newcombe was serving.

Roberts, who passed his twenty-fifth birthday watching the Phillies lose on Saturday, was pouring an even more poisonous potion. In seven innings the only Dodger to hit him was Pee Wee Reese, who was to make three of Brooklyn's five hits and the only Dodger run.

This was the run that tied the score in the sixth inning when Pee Wee sliced a ball which got jammed in a chink on the top of the right-field wall, at the base of the screen that surmounts the wall. Ground rules specify that a ball lodging where this one did remains in play for an Oriental homer.

To say tension was growing is to abuse the mother tongue. Things reached such a pass that when a bug flew into the eye of Mike Goliat, the Phillies' second baseman, Mr. Babe Alexander, of Philadelphia, cursed. "Those Dodgers," he said, "have adopted germ warfare."

But things were practically lethargic then compared with the Brooklyn ninth, when the Dodgers put their first two batsmen on base and Duke Snider lashed what had to be the deciding hit into center field. Richie Ashburn fielded the ball on one hop, threw swiftly and superbly to the plate, and Cal Abrams, coming home with the winning run, was out by twelve fat feet.

Nobody ever saw better pitching than Roberts showed then. With runners on second and third and one out, he walked Jackie Robinson purposely to fill the bases, then reared back and just threw that thing through there. Carl Furillo popped up. Gil Hodges flied out.

Ken Heintzelman and Ken Johnson ran all the way from the bullpen to shake Roberts' hand. Eddie Sawyer patted Robin's stomach. Those were gentle hands. Sisler and Roberts felt others later.

Sawyer watched his operatives pummel this pair when their great deeds were done. Then he announced that the Phillies would take today off. Most of them to rest. Roberts and Sisler to anoint their bruises.

New Year's Baby

Mickey Mantle, Age 19, Says "Hello, New York!"

Bronx, N.Y., *April 18, 1951*

An hour and a half before the New Year dawned, Mickey Charles Mantle—he was christened Mickey, not Michael, after Mickey Cochrane, whose name is Gordon Stanley—was standing on the top step of the Yankees' dugout looking back into the stands where a kid in a bright windbreaker brandished a homemade sign fashioned from a big pasteboard carton. The sign bore a photograph of Phil Rizzuto, cut out of a program, and crude lettering read: "C'mon, Lil Phil. Let's go."

Sitting on the bench, Casey Stengel could see his newest outfielder only from the chest down. The manager grunted with surprise when he noticed that the sole of one baseball shoe had come loose and was flapping like a radio announcer's jaw. He got up and talked to the kid and came back shaking his head.

"He don't care much about the big leagues, does he," Casey said. "He's gonna play in them shoes."

"Who is he?" a visitor asked.

"Why, he's that kid of mine," said Mr. Stengel, to whom proper names are so repugnant he signs his checks with an X.

"That's Mantle?"

"Yeh. I asked him didn't he have any better shoes and he said he had a new pair, but they're a little too big."

"He's waiting for an important occasion to wear new ones," the visitor said.

Casey is not unaware of the volume of prose that was perpetrated about this nineteen-year-old during his prodigious spring training tour, when he batted .402, hit nine home runs, and knocked in thirty-one runs.

"How about his first game in a big league park?" a kibitzer said. "Saturday in Brooklyn, when he got only one single. What was wrong?"

"My writers," Mr. Stengel said, "had an off day."

Mr. Stengel told about Mantle asking him how to play the right-field wall in Ebbets Field.

"It was the first time the kid ever saw concrete," he said. "I explained how the ball hits the wall like this and bounces like this and how you take it as it comes off the wall. I told him, 'I played that wall for six years, you know.' He said, 'The hell you did!'"

"He probably thinks," Mr. Stengel said, "that I was born at the age of sixty and started managing right away."

A couple of newspapermen were talking to Bill Dickey. About Mantle, naturally.

"Gosh, I envy him," one of them said. "Nineteen years old, and starting out as a Yankee!"

"He's green," Bill said. "But he's got to be great. All that power, a switch hitter, and he runs like a striped ape. If he drags a bunt past the pitcher, he's on base. I think he's the fastest man I ever saw with the Yankees. But he's green in the outfield. He was a shortstop last year."

"Casey said that out in Phoenix he misjudged a fly and the ball stuck on his head."

"It hit him right here alongside the eye," Bill said. "He's green, and he'll be scared today."

"If anybody walks up to him now," a newspaperman said, "and asks him if he's nervous, Mantle should bust him in the eye. Golly, Bill, do you realize you were in the big league before he was born?"

"He was born in 1932," Dickey said, "and that was the year I played my first World Series."

"And I'd been covering baseball years and years," the guy said. "What's been happening to us?"

After that there was a half-hour of relentless oratory at the plate, and then Whitey Ford, the Yankees' prize rookie of last year, walked out in his soldier suit to pitch the first ball, and then the season was open and it was New Year's Day.

Mantle made the first play of the season, fielding the single by Dom DiMaggio which opened the game for the Red Sox. He broke his bat on the first pitch thrown to him and was barely thrown out by Bobby Doerr. He popped up on his second time at bat.

When he came up for the third time the Yankees were leading, 2 to 0, with none out and runners on first and third. Earlier Joe DiMaggio had started a double play with an implausible catch of a pop fly behind second, as if to tell Mantle, "This is how it's done up here, son." Now Joe, awaiting his turn at bat, called the kid aside and spoke to him.

Mantle nodded, stepped back into the box and singled a run home. Dickey, coaching at third, slapped his stern approvingly. When the kid raced home from second with his first big league run, the whole Yankee bench arose to clap hands and pat his torso. He was in the lodge.

American Indian Day

Yanks' Allie Reynolds Pitches No-Hit Pennant Clincher

BRONX, N.Y., *September 28, 1951*

AFTER ALL these years the Yankees just had to find a new way to make sure of finishing in first place. Since they got the habit in 1921 they've been in a rut, just pennant after pennant, championship after championship, season after season—eighteen times in thirty years. The dreary, weary, yawning ennui of it all!

This, though, was laying it on a little too thick. This was showboating of the most vulgar and ostentatious sort. Here it was, American Indian Day according to the *Farmer's Almanac*, and out there was the noble red man, Allie Reynolds, pitching the first game of a doubleheader, pitching the game the Yankees needed to guarantee a tie for the title, at worst.

The only no-hit pitcher ever born to the Creek nation—he won that distinction against the Cleveland Indians last July 12—was working against the Boston Red Sox, malevolent leaders of the American League batting lists and prime contenders for the pennant until a few days ago. These were the sort of guys Jimmy Dykes described to a rookie pitcher about to make his first big league start for the Athletics in Boston: "You are just like a mouse in a cage with nine big cats."

So now it was the eighth inning and the Yankees were leading, 8 to 0, and Reynolds had not allowed a hit. He came up to bat, walking through a tunnel of noise, and paused beside Phil Rizzuto, who was kneeling in the chalked circle where the next hitter waits.

"Stengel says," he told the Yankee shortstop, "that if I get away with this one I can have the rest of the season off."

This was the only time he hinted that he was going for his second no-hitter in a single season, a feat brought off only once in history and never in the American League. While pitching his no-hitter in Cleveland he had horrified Yogi Berra by mentioning it in defiance of the superstition that forbids speaking of such matters while the game is on. Afterward he got letters from fans scolding him for "tearing down baseball traditions," so this time he wasn't talking.

Now it was the ninth inning, three putouts to go. Every time he threw the ball, the crowd screamed. A pinch batter named Charlie Maxwell grounded out. Dominic DiMaggio walked. Johnny Pesky took a curve for a third strike. Ted Williams slouched up; his pale bat looked as long as he is.

Berra walked out to the mound, waddling under his catcher's armor. "Take it easy, now," he said. "What do you want to throw to him?"

"Anything," Reynolds said, and Yogi went back behind the plate to call the pitches. Rizzuto, shifted a little to the right of second base for the lopsided defense against Williams, was talking with Charlie Berry, the umpire.

"Holy cats," Phil said, "let's walk this guy and work on Vollmer."

"Naw," says Berry, courageous as a fight manager. "Allie's got good stuff. He can throw it by this fella."

"Charlie's cool," Rizzuto said later. "He's got it all figured out—and I'm fainting!"

The first pitch to Williams was a called strike. Williams hit the second straight up, a towering foul behind the plate, and Reynolds dashed in to give help if Berra should need it. A draft swept the ball back over Berra's head, and Yogi lunged backward for it, missed, and fell at Reynolds' feet. Allie tripped over him but didn't fall. Instead, the pitcher bent to help the catcher up, patted his back, spoke in his ear. Yogi didn't want to get up. He wanted to keep going down, into a hole, out of sight. The game should be over, and now, if Williams should get a hit on this second chance—

One wondered how Williams was feeling. The Red Sox weren't going to win, no matter what he did, but he was hitless for the day and he is a hitter. The crowds in Yankee Stadium always boo him, just for living. If, on this undeserved last chance, he should ruin Reynolds' no-hitter, they'd curse every breath he drew into his old age.

"Allie had Williams, two strikes and nothing," Bill Dickey said later, "and now he can work on him. So what does he do? He rams the next one right through there."

It was another strike, and again Williams lifted a foul, over in front of the Yankee dugout this time. Berra went over and Reynolds went with him. "Lots of room!" Tommy Henrich cried from the bench. ("There was about three feet of room," Tommy confessed afterward. "But it looked like a lot to me right then. If Yogi falls in the dugout, we'll catch him.")

Yogi caught the ball, and Reynolds caught Yogi. Everybody on the Yankee bench sprang out and caught the pair of them. Henrich, on the fringe of the knot, dived up onto the top of the mob, cracking heads together as he clawed toward Reynolds.

After a while things got quiet in the clubhouse. There was still one more river to cross this side of a pennant, but nobody doubted that it would be crossed, as it was within three hours. Reynolds was quietest of all, crouched in his locker, answering questions.

"Come back in about two hours," he said apologetically, "and I'll give you some better answers."

Art Patterson, of the Yankees' office, told him about the *Farmer's Almanac* designating this as American Indian Day.

"Does it say anything about Creeks?" Allie asked.

Miracle of Coogan's Bluff

Bobby Thomson's "Shot Heard 'Round the World"

NEW YORK, N.Y., *October 4, 1951*

Now it is done. Now the story ends. And there is no way to tell it. The art of fiction is dead. Reality has strangled invention. Only the utterly impossible, the inexpressibly fantastic, can ever be plausible again.

Down on the green and white and earth-brown geometry of the playing field, a drunk tries to break through the ranks of ushers marshaled along the foul lines to keep profane feet off the diamond. The ushers thrust him back and he lunges at them, struggling in the clutch of two or three men. He breaks free, and four or five tackle him. He shakes them off, bursts through the line, runs head-on into a special park cop, who brings him down with a flying tackle.

Here comes a whole platoon of ushers. They lift the man and haul him, twisting and kicking, back across the first-base line. Again he shakes loose and crashes the line. He is through. He is away, weaving out toward center field, where cheering thousands are jammed beneath the windows of the Giants' clubhouse.

At heart, our man is a Giant, too. He never gave up.

From center field comes burst upon burst of cheering. Pennants are waving, uplifted fists are brandished, hats are flying. Again and again the dark clubhouse windows blaze with the light of photographers' flash bulbs. Here comes that same drunk out of the mob, back across the green turf to the infield. Coattails flying, he runs the bases, slides into third. Nobody bothers him now.

And the story remains to be told, the story of how the Giants won the 1951 pennant in the National League. The tale of their barreling run through August and September and into October. . . . Of the final day of the season, when they won the championship and started home with it from Boston, to hear on the train how the dead, defeated Dodgers had risen from the ashes in the Philadelphia twilight. . . . Of the three-game playoff in which they won, and lost, and were losing again with one out in the ninth inning yesterday when— Oh, why bother?

Maybe this is the way to tell it: Bobby Thomson, a young Scot from Staten Island, delivered a timely hit yesterday in the ninth inning of an enjoyable game of baseball before 34,320 witnesses in the Polo Grounds. . . . Or perhaps this is better:

"Well!" said Whitey Lockman, standing on second base in the second inning of yesterday's playoff game between the Giants and Dodgers.

"Ah, there," said Bobby Thomson, pulling into the same station after hitting a ball to left field. "How've you been?"

"Fancy," Lockman said, "meeting you here!"

"Ooops!" Thomson said. "Sorry."

And the Giants' first chance for a big inning against Don Newcombe disappeared as they tagged Thomson out. Up in the press section, the voice of Willie Goodrich came over the amplifiers announcing a macabre statistic: "Thomson has now hit safely in fifteen consecutive games." Just then the floodlights were turned on, enabling the Giants to see and count their runners on each base.

It wasn't funny, though, because it seemed for so long that the Giants weren't going to get another chance like the one Thomson squandered by trying to take second base with a playmate already there. They couldn't hit Newcombe, and the Dodgers couldn't do anything wrong. Sal Maglie's most splendrous pitching would avail nothing unless New York could match the run Brooklyn had scored in the first inning.

The story was winding up, and it wasn't the happy ending that such a tale demands. Poetic justice was a phrase without meaning.

Now it was the seventh inning and Thomson was up, with runners on first and third base, none out. Pitching a shutout in Philadelphia last Saturday night, pitching again in Philadelphia on Sunday, holding the Giants scoreless this far, Newcombe had now gone twenty-one innings without allowing a run.

He threw four strikes to Thomson. Two were fouled off out of play. Then he threw a fifth. Thomson's fly scored Monte Irvin. The score was tied. It was a new ballgame.

Wait a moment, though. Here's Pee Wee Reese hitting safely in the eighth. Here's Duke Snider singling Reese to third. Here's Maglie wild-pitching a run home. Here's Andy Pafko slashing a hit through Thomson for another score. Here's Billy Cox batting still another home. Where does his hit go? Where else? Through Thomson at third.

So it was the Dodgers' ballgame, 4 to 1, and the Dodgers' pennant. So all right. Better get started and beat the crowd home. That stuff in the ninth inning? That didn't mean anything.

A single by Al Dark. A single by Don Mueller. Irvin's pop-up, Lockman's one-run double. Now the corniest possible sort of Hollywood schmaltz-stretcher-bearers plodding away with an injured Mueller between them, symbolic of the Giants themselves.

There went Newcombe and here came Ralph Branca. Who's at bat? Thomson again? He beat Branca with a home run the other day. Would Charlie Dressen order him walked, putting the winning run on base, to pitch to the dead-end kids at the bottom of the batting order? No, Branca's first pitch was a called strike.

The second pitch—well, when Thomson reached first base he turned and looked toward the left-field stands. Then he started jumping straight in the air, again and again. Then he trotted around the bases, taking his time.

Ralph Branca turned and started for the clubhouse. The number on his uniform looked huge. Thirteen.

The Real Amateur

DiMaggio Leaves the Game He Loves

O NE OF the very few very great pros of professional sports issued a statement yesterday to the press and to the public. It was the statement of an amateur, in the best sense of the word.

"When baseball is no longer fun," said Joe DiMaggio, "it is no longer a game. . . . And so, I have played my last game of ball."

That is the amateur view. It is the feeling which prevents a great commercial enterprise like baseball from ever becoming a commercial enterprise exclusively. Joe DiMaggio made a great deal of money playing baseball. Most of all, though, he played for fun, and now that it is no longer any fun, he isn't gong to play any more.

Back in the days when Babe Ruth drew $75,000 or $80,000—which was more than any other ballplayer had received before him or has received since, if you allow for inflation and taxes—it used to be said that Babe was the truest amateur in the game. That is, he played baseball because he loved baseball, and the money was a mere by-product. He would, if necessary, have played without salary or have paid for the privilege of playing.

The same has been true of Joe. The same was true of most of the others who were the best and who won the greatest rewards, including that affluent old gentleman, Ty Cobb. Through salary and investments, Cobb made a million dollars. Yet when others were playing for money, he was playing for the game's sake.

"Of all the guys I have known," Al Simmons said one time, "Cobb was the only one who played as hard after he got rich as he ever did when he was hungry." There was the true competitor talking of the true amateur.

This is a meandering way of approaching the simple, flat fact that the greatest ballplayer of our day and one of the greatest of any day quit baseball yesterday.

It was by no means unexpected. As far back as last spring, DiMaggio revealed that the thought of retirement was in his mind. He said 1951 might very possibly be his last year as a player, and when he said it the Yankee bosses were upset. They knew, of course, that the time of decision must eventually arrive, but they didn't want to believe it must come so soon.

When the World Series was over, Joe again made it clear that he wanted to give up. Again the Yankee owners stalled for time, hoping that a couple of months' rest would recharge Joe's battery and he would come to believe that there was at least one more good season left in him.

Then yesterday, when the whole town knew that a press conference had been scheduled and the irrevocable decision would be announced, the whole town was talking about it. Wherever you went yesterday in the early afternoon, the waiters and captains and cab starters were asking the same question: "What about Joe?"

It would have done Joe good to know how the waiters and captains and cab starters were talking yesterday. Not that they could have or would have helped him to make up his mind, or would have changed his mind for him once it was made up.

"It was my problem, and my decision to make," he pointed out. And, of course, it was. Had he said the word the Yankees would have handed him a contract willingly. Yes, eagerly. It was for him to say, and he realized that as he has always realized it, for all through his adult life he has been a lonely guy who had to choose his own path and walk it alone.

When he came to New York from San Francisco he was scared. He'd been fed a lot of fiction about what a hard-boiled town this was, and he believed at least part of it.

"Forget it," said his San Francisco manager, Lefty O'Doul. "It's the friendliest town in the world."

Joe found that out. If New York was hard-boiled, he soon cracked its shell. But it was a long time before he could come out of his own, this shy, silent guy.

One night he was in Toots Shor's with a crowd that included Lefty Gomez. This was years ago, when Lefty was still pitching for the Yankees. Table hoppers kept coming to say hello and try out their newest, most studiously rehearsed wisecracks, and Gomez had the quick and easy and affable retort for all of them.

Joe listened for a long time as Lefty batted the badinage about. Then he turned to the guy beside him. "I'd give a million dollars," Joe said, "if I could do that."

So he would have been pleased, although he wouldn't have shown his pleasure, to know how they were talking about him yesterday around this town. Maybe it would please him to know that they approved his decision.

They hate to see him go, but they know and understand why he decided as he did. They know he's quitting because he cannot stand mediocrity in anything, and least of all in himself. They couldn't stand it either, not in Joe. On him, it couldn't look good.

★ SPORTS IN THE FORTIES ★

Gaelic Disaster

Army Levels Notre Dame, 59 to 0

NEW YORK, N.Y., *November 11, 1944*

QUIET COUNTRY churchyards from Killarney to Kimberly gave off a strange, whirring sound this afternoon as departed Irish whirled and spun and did flipflops under the sod.

In the most horrendous Gaelic disaster since the Battle of the Boyne, the Celtic Szymanskis and Dancewiczes of Notre Dame were ravaged, routed, and demolished by Army's football team by the most garish score in history—59 to 0.

Billed as the classiest spectacle in sports, the gridiron's equivalent of the Kentucky Derby, the World Series, and the Philadelphia Assembly, it was a travesty engineered by the joint efforts of the best of all West Point's teams and one of South Bend's weakest.

Yankee Stadium's plus-capacity crowd of 74,430 witnesses—some of whom paid scalpers as much as $25 for a seat behind a steel stanchion or a backless bench built up against the rafters or a funeral-parlor chair on the sideline—watched the dreadful destruction with mixed feelings, in which numbed disbelief predominated.

It was Army's first triumph over Notre Dame since way back before the Roosevelt Administration—the Cadets' last was achieved in 1931—and if it had happened a week earlier it probably would have cost the New Deal the Irish vote.

But if it seemed a low-comedy burlesque to Notre Dame's famed "subway alumni," its reception was something else again in the left-field stands populated by the gray-coated corps of the Military Academy.

From the early moments of the opening quarter, when Army

stormed forty-four yards to its first touchdown, until the red hand of the clock completed its last revolution, these young characters whooped and gloated and screamed for more of the same.

Not one of them ever saw an Army team score against Notre Dame. (Neither did anyone else since 1938.) Now they were seeing it happen almost every time they lifted their eyes. When the score was 46 to 0 they set up a hungry chant:

"More yet! More yet! More yet!"

When the count was 58 to 0—matching the score Wisconsin made in 1904 in Notre Dame's worst previous hiding—the chorus still resounded: "We want more! We want more!"

And Army's coach, Lt. Col. Red Blaik, is not the sort to go soft and disappoint his constituents. He rushed his place-kicking specialist, Dick Walterhouse, in to convert the fifty-ninth point.

The mission briefed for unbeaten Army this day was threefold. The Cadets had to spread salve on wounds that Notre Dame has kept raw by winning twenty-two of thirty earlier engagements; they had to strike terror into the hearts of Penn, their next victims; they had to make this the first season that ever saw both Navy and Army triumphant over the Irish, and in doing so improve on the Midshipmen's 32–13 margin of victory last week.

They had what it took, and to spare. They unwrapped a backfield far more versatile than Navy's, although perhaps not quite so loaded with crushing power, in which Doug Kenna and Glenn Davis and Max Minor and Dale Hall and Felix Blanchard vied at uncorking ever more blinding speed.

They needed no help to win as they pleased. But help they got nevertheless, in job lots. Notre Dame persistently furnished aid by resorting again and again to a passing game, which was Army's most devastating weapon.

Army intercepted eight passes—Notre Dame completed only ten— and five touchdowns stemmed from these thefts, one of the interceptors scoring as he made his catch.

Two other touchdowns resulted from blazing punt runbacks, one of sixty yards by Minor, which went over the goal line, and one that took Kenna thirty-seven yards to the Notre Dame 20.

Another was accomplished by the dazzling Davis on a fifty-six-yard sprint from scrimmage. Still another was made possible by recovery of a fumbled Notre Dame lateral. And, finally, there was one built on plain power.

Thus, although the Irish were bound to lose whatever they tried, the fact is they dug their own grave deeper by insistent gambling with an air game against a defense whose members all field like the St. Louis Cardinals' Slats Marion.

Davis scored three touchdowns, Minor two, Kenna one, a pair of ends, named Ed Rafalko and Dick Pitzer, one each, and a tackle named Harold Tavzel one. Here's how:

1. Receiving Notre Dame's first punt, Army drove forty-three yards to the 1-yard line on straight T-formation plunges, plus one pass. On third down, center Frank Szymanski smashed Minor for a five-yard loss, and on fourth down Kenna missed Rafalko with a pass.

However both teams were offsides on this play, so instead of losing the ball, Army got another chance. This time Kenna fled wide around his right end as one tackler after another hurled himself against his blocking screen, and bounced off.

Kenna scored, as did all the others, standing upright and hermetically sealed away from prying hands.

Walterhouse converted from placement. He made good five times in nine chances, once from the 26-yard line after Army drew a holding penalty. Two kicks were blocked. Once the pass from center was wild, and he made a hurried, futile effort at a drop kick.

2. Almost immediately after the ensuing kickoff Kenna intercepted a pass by Frank Dancewicz and ran to Notre Dame's 26. Here, on a magnificently faked reverse to the left, Minor broke into the clear.

3. Notre Dame's next play was a pass which Blanchard leaped high to grab, coming down on the Irish 35. Kenna faded and fired a strike to Rafalko, who had slipped past Bill Chandler at the goal line.

4. Davis snatched a pass by Dancewicz from under Bob Kelly's nose

and leaped along a curling, forty-one-yard course to the 7-yard line where Dancewicz, the passer and last defender, spilled him. Then he circled his right end.

5. Catching a punt on his 43, Kenna started to his right but was trapped near the sideline by Bill O'Connor, who had fought off two blockers. Reversing his field, he dashed toward the left boundary, was eased around the corner by George Poole's cruel block, and ripped down to Notre Dame's 20. When the ball reached the 5-yard stripe, Davis slipped around end on a bootleg reverse.

6. Two minutes after the second half opened, Kenna caught a punt, darted to his right and handed the ball to Minor, who met him at top speed. Flashing sixty yards down the left sideline, Minor met only Kelly, whom Blanchard bounced aside.

7. After Pitzer grabbed a lateral muffed by Kelly, he caught a touchdown pass from Kenna.

8. Taking a direct pass from center on his 44-yard line, Davis faked a pass, tucked the ball under his arm, slanted off to the left of center and broke out of the pack, completing the trip alone.

9. Still gambling for a score with less than three minutes to go, Notre Dame tried a screen pass, with the passer in his end zone. Joe Gasparella's toss went to the astonished Tavzel, who collapsed from sheer glee. He had the foresight to collapse across the goal line.

The Lost Cause

Army, Navy, Commander in Chief

PHILADELPHIA, PA., *November 27, 1948*

A SLIGHT, four-eyed man stood teetering on tiptoe down near the 40-yard line in Municipal Stadium, his pearl-gray hat bobbing like a floating cork as he craned and twisted and strained to see over the wall of blue Navy overcoats and white Navy caps whose owners towered in front of America's Commander in Chief.

Harry Truman, of Independence, Missouri, a former haberdasher and prominent fancier of hopeless causes, was struggling to focus his lenses on the hopeless Navy football team, a team that had lost thirteen successive games and now, with fifty-eight seconds of its season remaining, stood tied with undefeated Army, champion of the East, third-ranking power of the nation, and twenty-one-point favorite in the trustworthy Minneapolis line.

Fifty Secret Service men fidgeted, watching protocol go down the drain. For safety's sake, it has been their custom to get the President clear of the crowd two minutes before an Army-Navy game ends. Hot or cold, out he goes with two minutes to play.

But Harry Truman wouldn't budge. Like the 102,580 others present at the forty-ninth meeting of service academies, he simply had to see Navy fire the last shot in its locker.

Pete Williams took a pitch-out and lost three yards. Bill Hawkins went twisting and wrestling through the line, gaining five. The clock showed thirty-three seconds left. Slats Baysinger, the quarterback, tried to sneak around end. He lost six. Navy huddled once more, rushed up to the line for one more play, but the referee stepped in, waving his arms.

The red hand of the clock stood at zero, and the best, most exhilarating, and least plausible Army-Navy game in at least twenty years was over. The score, 21 to 21, was the same as that of 1926, the year historians always mention first when they try to name the finest of all Army-Navy games.

And even if you'd seen it, it was fearfully hard to believe. While the referee tossed a coin to decide on permanent possession of the ball, Baysinger walked around the periphery of huddled players, shook hands with Army's Tom Bullock and then with Arnold Galiffa. Army's guys walked off hurriedly, but Navy's froze to attention while the midshipmen's band played "Navy Blue and Gold."

Then all the players save two departed, as civilians and noncombatant midshipmen and cadets swarmed over the field. Dave Bannerman, Navy's substitute fullback, and Ted Carson, left end, just stayed there where the deed had been done. When small boys came asking for autographs, they signed abstractedly and kept rubbering around through the crowd. Maybe they were looking for a couple of peach cakes to share an evening's liberty. But it seemed more likely they were waiting in the hope that someone would give them one more crack at Army.

The great, sunswept crowd that paid six dollars a head hadn't expected anything like this. The customers had come for the show, the spectacle, the pageant of youth that always is about as thrilling as anything in American sports. They had thought to get their money's worth out of just being there; out of seeing the magnificent parade these kids always bring off superbly before the game; out of the shiver that scampers along the spine when the colors are brought to midfield and the band plays the national anthem and the packed stands are a frozen block of color, with the bright blue-gray of the Army on one side and the shimmering white of Navy caps on the other.

They figured to get a chuckle out of the kids' musty nonsense. And of course they did. There was a Navy dreadnought that rolled around the cinder track and shot off cannon and went down in flames. There was a huge papier-mâché goat and a huge papier-mâché mule. There were signs in the Navy stands: "Gallup Picks Army" (to which the Army stands replied with a cheer: "Gallup, Gallup, Gallup!") and a sly reference to the difference between Army and Navy schedules: 'When do you play Vassar?" ("Vassar, Vassar, Vassar!") and then after the Navy scored first: "Send in Alan Ladd" (no response to this).

But nobody expected a ballgame, except the few people who bore in mind an old, old truth which the game restated dramatically. That is, that there never can be between undergraduate football teams of the same league a gap in ability too great to be bridged by spirit alone. Navy proved that beyond remotest doubt, and the guy who did most to prove it was a fellow playing on spirit and very little else. Bill Hawkins, ill a long while this season with a blood disorder that doctors call acute infectious mononucleosis, was entirely out of action for three weeks in midseason. Without preparation, he came back to play against Michigan on November 6. Then he played three minutes against Columbia and was hurt November 13. Since then he hadn't a minute of physical contact until today.

But today he was a bull, and a mad bull into the bargain. He ran the ball fourteen times and made fifty important yards. He scored two touchdowns. He backed up the line, his blocking was like a crime of passion, and he played almost all afternoon.

It wasn't exactly a football game, it was an exhibition of pure, unbridled fury on both sides for both sides persistently moved the ball against incredibly savage resistance. It was, altogether, as good a thing as could possibly happen to football.

Thirty-two Navy players got into the game, which means—if there is such a thing as justice—that the Navy added thirty-two full admirals today. For the guys down there on the field today were officer material, as ever was. It goes without saying that there are more than thirty-two full admirals in Philadelphia tonight.

The Most
Important Thing:

Yale's Band Is Two Steps Faster Than Harvard's

"GENTLEMEN," THE sainted Tad Jones is alleged to have said in the cathedral hush before a Yale-Harvard game, "you are about to play football for Yale. Never again in your lives will you do anything so important—"

America has been through two world wars, a world-wide depression, and had a couple of flings at inflation since then and yet, corny as it seems, the young Yales appeared actually to feel that T. Jones was right when today's affair with the Harvards ended.

As the last whistle blew, a great passel of Yales swarmed onto the field to hug the combatants to their bosoms and even from the press box you could see grins as broad as Kate Smith upon the soiled faces of the belligerents. There was a brief, ecstatic huddle, and then Levi Jackson, the tall, dark, and handsome fullback of the Yales, broke away from his companions and raced across the field to pump any and all Harvard hands within reach. Meanwhile, a small boy snatched the cap of G. Frank Bergin, the umpire, and fled with the official in pursuit.

The cap-snatch was brought off on Harvard's 20-yard line. The small miscreant fled to Yale's goal line on a long, clean, eighty-yard dash, circled to his right and raced back ten yards, then angled off into the crowd with the stolen haberdashery still in his possession. Mr. Bergin, puffing, gave up.

This was far and away the most spectacular play of the long, gray day. But such post-game shenanigans were no more than frosting on an extraordinarily fancy cake. The show itself was the thing, and it was the greatest thing since the invention of the wheel.

Here were two teams that had made a career of failure and had enjoyed staggering success at it. One had lost four games, the other three. Neither had beaten anyone of importance. And so, between them, they drew a crowd of 70,896, biggest gathering this holy of holies has attracted in seventeen years.

It was a hairy crowd, wrapped thickly in the skins of dead animals and festooned with derby hats, pennants, and feathers of crimson and blue. It wore the pelts of mink and beaver and raccoons. Indeed, counting the coon coats in any section of the Bowl, you could be excused for assuming Coolidge was still President. Here and there a moth took wing as some fur-bearing customer flapped his arms in an effort to keep warm. It was concluded that although the science of offensive football was advanced by every play, the entertainment set the fur industry back thirty years. There were enough crew haircuts in evidence to supply the Fuller Brush Company for the next generation.

All the appurtenances of elegance were present. The bands paraded and postured between halves according to the strictest dictates of tradition. The Harvard tootlers wore crimson jackets and ice cream pants. From the waist up they looked like a road company chorus out of *Rose Marie*. From there down, they suggested Good Humor men on holiday.

The Yales came oompah-ing onto the scene after their guests were done. Yale costumes its bandsmen to impersonate bellhops in a good but unpretentious hotel. The somber ranks of blue shifted and twitched and maneuvered, deploying into fascinating but undecipherable formations. The only one which could be spelled out from the press loft seemed to be a salute to the Reliable Jersey House. It appeared to read: "Yale minus 7."

Critics agreed the Yale band was two steps faster than Harvard's. This was approximately the difference between the two teams. Harvard passed, but Yale ran. Rather, Yale marched, driving relentlessly in short, savage bursts, chewing out yardage with a persistence which

Harvard couldn't resist. Thus Yale scored first, and was tied scarcely more than a minute later when Harold Moffie raced down from his flanker position on the right side, got behind Ferd Nadherny and made a casual catch of Jim Kenary's pass into the end zone.

Yale clawed down for another touchdown and Harvard responded with one of its own, fashioned chiefly on two plays. One was a forward pass to Chip Gannon, who faked two tacklers out of their underwear on a slick run. The other was a bolt through the middle by Paul Lazzaro on a fake pass-and-buck play which is called the bear trap because the Chicago Bears no longer use it.

So the score was tied again, but it stood to reason it wouldn't stay that way. You couldn't expect Harvard to keep on coming up with one-play touchdowns to match a team that could grind out gains as Yale was doing. Harvard finally gave Yale an unearned chance by roughing the New Haven kicker and drawing a penalty for same. This resulted in the winning touchdown. A little later, a low snapback from center loused up a Harvard punt, giving the ball to Yale for the score that made the game safe.

It was noted that the incredibly erudite Harvard coach, Dr. R. Harlow, made unique use of the free substitution rule. He would haul a guy out of the game, give him special instructions and run him back in again, all in one pause between plays. He did this with a couple of his key men just before the first half ended. The results were significant. On the next play, Yale intercepted a Harvard pass.

A Whole Troop
of Calverley

R.I. State Point Guard Thrills Crowd at Garden

NEW YORK, N.Y., *March 16, 1946*

A FEW more nights like the opening round of the National Invitation Basketball Tournament and the memory of Dr. Naismith, who perpetrated basketball, will cease to be a hissing and a byword around here. Indeed, get a few more guys like Rhode Island State's Ernie Calverley playing the game and some movie company is a cinch to do the life of Dr. Naismith, picturing him as a benefactor of the human race like Mme Curie, Alexander Graham Bell, and Al Capone.

This is written by one who would rather drink a Bronx cocktail than speak well of basketball. Yet it must be confessed that there hasn't been another sports show in years which lifted the hackles and stirred the pulse quite so thoroughly as the performance of young Calverley leading his team to an overtime conquest of Bowling Green.

Calverley is a gaunt, pale young case of malnutrition who'd probably measure up as a fairly sizable gent in your living room, but looks like a waif among the goons who clutter up the courts. He may be, as alleged, the most detached defensive player on a team whose members seem to feel there is something sordid and unclean about defensive basketball. But when he lays hand on that ball and starts moving, he is a whole troop of Calverley, including the pretty white horses. The guy is terrific, colossal, and also very good.

Throughout the fevered match with Bowling Green, he was the man who set up Rhode Island's plays, taking the ball down the court, hiding it, passing it, shooting, dribbling, feinting, weaving, running the show with almost unbelievable dexterity and poise. He played without relief through a breakneck game that had others gasping inside the first quarter-hour and once he was knocked cold as an obsolete mackerel.

Making a pass, he tripped and hit the deck with his bony shoulder-blades. As he lay there supine, the ball came back to him out of a scramble and he reached up and caught it and passed it off, and then passed out.

But despite his elegance, Bowling Green was winning the game as long as Don Otten remained in circulation. Otten is the Bowling Green center. He measures one-half inch less than seven feet from end to end and he looks and moves more like an institution than a man, with agonizing deliberation and great grinding of gears.

Joe DiMaggio would be hard pressed to throw a baseball over the top of Otten and there aren't any DiMaggios playing for Rhode Island. He loped gawkily around the joint with his mouth open and plucked rebounds off the backboard like currants off a bush, while waves of adversaries surged around him and bounced off in a sort of spray. When a teammate missed a shot he simply reached up and palmed the ball and pushed it down through the hoop.

With three minutes, twenty seconds to go he committed his fifth personal foul and was flung out. The crowd cheered and it wasn't applause; it was the rejoicing of Rhode Island fans, who figured they now had a chance.

There would have been no chance, however, without Calverley. A minute and ten seconds before the last horn, he took aim from a point near the center stripe and fired a long shot that went through the hoop as though it had eyes, squaring the match at 72–all. A moment later he was fouled and missed the throw that might have won. With ten seconds to play, Vern Dunham scored for Bowling Green, and that looked like the business. But somehow, in the scant time remaining, a Bowling Green player contrived to squeeze in another foul, giving Rhode Island the ball out of bounds at midfloor with two seconds remaining.

The ball came in to Calverley in the back court. There was no time for a pass or a play and from where he stood a field goal was impossible. So, with appalling calm, he shot a field goal. Time was up.

Over in front of the Rhode Island bench, substitutes were leaping around in a crazed sort of war dance, flinging arms aloft and shouting, and out on the floor Calverley's playmates were shouting and pummeling him and the kid had his head flung back and was laughing at the ceiling.

Well, Rhode Island scored eight fast points in the extra period and Bowling Green scored five, and with a minute and a half left Calverley set out to freeze the ball. He did a magical job, dribbling in and out and around the back, keeping an appraising eye on the enemy, passing when necessary, and then squirming loose for a return pass.

Then the game was over and there was a threshing swirl of players and spectators in a knot on the floor and Calverley was shoved out of the pack and rode off on the others' shoulders. Which was fair enough, since the others had ridden to victory on his. They rushed him out and he broke loose barely in time to get down and avoid being skulled where the exit ramp goes under the stands. They like to bashed his brains out.

Falling Off Mountains

Berkshire-Bound New Haven Line Makes
First Postwar Ski Run

NEW YORK, N.Y., *January 29, 1946*

Falling off a mountain, a pastime that has enjoyed an unaccountable growth in popularity, regained some of its prewar eminence as big business when New York's first ski train in four years ran—or, to be brutally frank, crept—to the Berkshires Sunday.

Seen from the upper-level entrance in the depressing darkness before dawn, the concourse of Grand Central Terminal was a forest of skis. The crowd surging through the train gate looked like Birnam Wood advancing upon Dunsinane. This impression was heightened by a closer view of the lethal ski poles which the attackers brandished like battle pikes. As to raiment, the opinion of observers was divided. Some, noting movie cameras in operation, concluded that this was a mob scene in an Orson Welles film of a Martian invasion. Others said no, it was just one of those "hard times" costume parties of Depression days breaking up a few years late.

The New York, New Haven & Hartford Railroad, which has a heart as big as a locomotive, operated a diner and a grill car, served sandwiches and hot coffee on the side and provided medication with choice of soda or water. It also arranged to carry the party as far from home as was reasonably possible. Sliding down a nearby hill is no fun; skiers don't feel they're getting their money's worth unless they cross several states to some remote slope. This keeps them on a warm train and out of the fresh air virtually all day.

Experts versed in such matters described the crowd as "eager, expectant, and excited." Also "gay." Ski experts can recognize eagerness in the way a resident of the Bronx sleeps sitting up.

Not all slept, however. Some laid their skis upon the backs of several seats, sort of braiding them among the ears of other passengers, and rubbed wax on their (the skis') bottoms. One outdoorsman in a checkered lumberman's shirt borrowed needle and thread and darned his mittens. During the last thirty minutes of the ride every one stood up and buckled on gear, which is somewhat heavier and more complicated than that carried by infantrymen.

At Pittsfield, Massachusetts, townspeople were waiting to see the train disgorge. As at the Bronx Zoo, there is no admission charge at the Pittsfield snow-train station.

Buses carried the merrymakers to Bousquet's Farm. Several hundred automobiles were parked there and several hundred pairs of skis were stacked against fences, their owners being inside a hut where coffee, frankfurters, and doughnuts were for sale. The New Haven's six hundred passengers also stacked their skis and hastened indoors to stand in line for coffee.

Tiring of this healthful exercise after a while, some went outdoors. Strong, motor-driven ropes of a size suitable for hanging horse thieves pulled them to the top of the mountain. In ski parlance, this maneuver is known as "going über alles."

Now came the moment for which the ski world has waited four long, war-torn years. Arriving at the crest, the athletes turned around—and slid downhill! It was a thrilling sight. There is something inexpressibly beautiful in the long, hawklike swoop of an accomplished skier performing the graceful glockenspiel and then, at the instant when he seems certain to catapult into a pack of women and children at the foot of the slope, coming to a halt in a cloud of powdered snow as he executes a perfect schlemiel.

The press delegation included a number of experts. One, a newsreel man, led photographers to the summit.

"How do we get down?" a newspaper cameraman asked.

"The easiest way," the newsreel man said, "is to break a leg. Then an ambulance comes and takes you down."

The newsreel man then strapped on his skis, started down, broke a leg, and an ambulance came and took him away.

After a while everybody came indoors again. Every cheek was ruddy with health. Eight out of every ten posterior elevations were snowy white, indicating mastery of the platzboomer technique. Breathing the invigorating tobacco smoke indoors, some skiers burst into song.

The buses came and New York's first snow special in four years loaded up and crept back home. It was unanimously voted a great day of sport, calculated to popularize basketball if anything can.

The Strongest Lady in the World

Miss Dorcas Lehman, Weightlifter

NEW YORK, N.Y., *May 22, 1947*

FOR A few hours yesterday New York wore, like an orchid in her hair, a flower of femininity named Miss Dorcas Lehman, who is the strongest lady in the world. Miss Lehman is a red-haired saloonkeeper of York, Pennsylvania, and a Dunkard—a member of one of those Pennsylvania German sects whose members paint hex marks on the barn and wear somber black sunbonnets if they are women and spade whiskers and porkpie hats if they are men. Miss Lehman, however, is a nonconformist in costume and custom. Her clothes, lips, and finger-nails have a good deal of red in them, and her hobby is letting large gentlemen jump on her stomach.

It amuses the lady to form a bridge by placing her feet on one wooden bench and her head on another, whereupon a 230-pound man sits on her abdomen and swings his feet. York, which is a nest of weightlifters, has a 132-pound Hawaiian named Emerick Ishikawa, national featherweight champion. When Dorcas is making like the Triborough Bridge, she permits little Emerick to leap upon her dia-phragm from a height of five or six feet.

"I feel good when I get through exercising," she explained cordially.

This durable vessel was accompanied here by a bald weightlifter named Bob Hoffman, proprietor of the York Barbell Company and of a stable of musclemen. They were met by appointment, and this bureau, arriving tardily, found Miss Lehman standing in the middle of the room hoisting a hundred-pound barbell aloft again and again with what appeared to be a mere flip of the wrists. Mr. Hoffman sat by, silent with admiration. This, it was to turn out, was the only moment when that adjective could be applied to him.

Dorcas was trig as a trip-hammer in a dress of soft gray with a bow at the throat, a beige jacket, red shoes, a rather frivolous hat of red and white, and harlequin spectacles with red plastic frames. She had diamonds on both brightly manicured hands. Turned out she was in town to buy contact lenses.

She weighs 160 pounds, is five feet six inches tall and comely in a strapping, healthy sort of way. To a timid question she replied readily that her age was thirty-two and smiled, adding: "Don't mind being asked; only sometimes they think I'm forty, and that burns me up."

Five years ago she weighed 210 pounds. She attended a weightlifting demonstration and was smitten with admiration for the physiques on display. So she bought a fifty-pound dumbbell and went home and started lifting it. It was some time later that she encountered Mr. Hoffman's appraising eye.

"She was already sensational," Mr. Hoffman said. "A little skinny in the chest at 149 pounds, but with a pair of legs you wouldn't see anywhere outside a show. I always say Dorcas should have been an artist's model. I call her a female John Grimek, and he has the greatest body you ever saw. You've seen pictures of these peasant women, entirely undeveloped, but perfectly proportioned? That's Dorcas. A little excess weight around the hips, but thin women often have that."

Dorcas sat looking at her hands folded in her lap.

"Stand up and show how you can make your waist smaller than your leg," Mr. Hoffman said.

Dorcas stood up, placed a palm against her stomach, and inhaled. Her abdomen receded, making a hollow over which her short ribs hung like eaves. There was no opportunity to measure for the suggested comparison.

As operator of a bar called Ted's Place, the lady has found it unnecessary to employ a bouncer.

"Dorcas doesn't like to talk about herself," said Mr. Hoffman, who makes it unnecessary, "but when they put the Big Inch pipe line through York, they brought an awful tough gang from the Southwest. They killed the bartender in the Union Hotel one night when they were cutting up. Well, one night they came to Dorcas' looking for trouble. She threw one man bodily into the street and the rest ran."

He laughed. "The other night a man she had barred tried to come in. She started around the bar and he took out and ran for his life; funniest thing I ever saw. And then the other night when a fellow took a swing at her—"

"Did he hit you?" Miss Lehman was asked.

"Tapped me on the cheek," she said. "I took off my glasses and got him outside. Gettin' ready to hit him, but he ran. Oh, well. Don't like to be hitting 'em too much. Means always having to be going down to court."

"Do you lose your temper?"

"Once in a while. If they call me names."

"And to show she is a complete woman," Mr. Hoffman said, "she has two hundred pairs of shoes, size nine and a half, lots of which she's never worn."

"I just like shoes," the lady said. "Lots of times I just stop in a store and buy four, five pairs without trying 'em on. Just give the size."

"Furthermore," Mr. Hoffman said, "she is a wonderful cook and a marvelous dancer. That's her only dissipation—dancing. She loves to eat and she's a pretty good beer-drinker."

Miss Lehman said she had no suitors, muscular or puny. "Guess I prefer to be an old maid," she said. Meanwhile Mr. Hoffman was reciting her achievements.

She can break a chain by expanding her chest. She can fit her feet into straps anchored to a wall, place a forty-pound dumbbell on each shoulder and bend backward until her head touches the floor, then straighten up. She can swing seventy-five pounds overhead eighteen times with one hand. She can lift 375 pounds of dead weight. With a bar across her shoulders and a man hanging on each end, she can support six hundred pounds. She can do a deep knee-bend with a 216-pound man and a hundred-pound barbell on her back. She can do a thousand-pound leg press—that is, lie on her back and hoist that weight with her feet.

When this recital was complete, the lady was ready to depart. Walking downstairs, she said she liked to visit New York, but hankered for York after about four days here. Said she guessed she was just a small-town girl. She smiled good-bye and strode off, shoulders squared.

Boxing's Elder Statesman

James J. Johnston, 1875–1946

NEW YORK, N.Y., *May 9, 1946*

Even when the man was seventy years old they still called him the Boy Bandit, which was a form of compliment by the reverse-English standards of the profession he dignified, because in the fist-fight dodge a talent for banditry is considered stock equipment, but youth is a coveted attribute. When the fight mob applied the nickname to James Joy Johnston they used it in envious tribute to a man who not only could be as bold and guileful a brigand as the best of them but also remain, at heart, younger than the youngest.

Actually, Jimmy Johnston died before the title he preferred for himself won public acceptance. He would have liked to be known as "boxing's elder statesman," which was the role in which he really fancied himself. It was a well-earned title, too, for there never was another ambassador who could carry the cauliflower gospel into such unlikely quarters with such unfailing grace as he. It was his pride and his delight that he could appear before the Browning and Fancy Needlework Guild of Mount Vernon, whose members obviously expected to see a man in a turtleneck sweater and checkered cap, and charm the bridgework out of their mouths.

He affected a cynical attitude ("Legitimate business," he said, "is a figure of speech") and it was said that he was unhappy in his last days because nobody hated him any longer. But as a matter of fact he was always at his best among friends, and the fight mob never has known such amiably social salons as he used to conduct in Charles' Restaurant.

That was the feedbox in the Madison Square Garden Building where Jimmy held a tea party every afternoon at four o'clock when he was the Garden promoter, gathering the mob about him and spinning yarns hour upon hour. It was the greatest school for young fight writers this town ever knew, and some who attended it for three or four years hand-running will swear Jimmy never had to repeat a story.

One of the tales concerned a day in his old office in what is now the Paramount Building when there materialized in the doorway a tremendous hunk of man who said he wanted to be a fighter.

"How did you get up here?" James demanded.

"By the elevator."

"That," snapped Mr. Johnston, "is a good way to get out."

"Which was a good enough retort," Jimmy related years later, "except that when I next saw the young man he was Jess Willard, heavyweight champion of the world."

This wasn't, of course, the only mistake he ever made. He used to tell of another time when he and Charley Harvey were partners and decided to import a phenomenal English boxer named Jem Driscoll. He and Harvey met the ship on which Driscoll was to arrive and scanned the debarking crowd without finding anyone who looked like a fighter. They were about to depart when a snaggle-toothed stranger with hideously cauliflowered ears introduced himself as Driscoll.

Knowing Driscoll's reputation as a defensive genius, Jimmy instantly tabbed this damaged derelict as an imposter. A reformed boxer himself, Jimmy took him to a gym and set out to expose the impostor by getting into the ring with him.

"I let go with one punch," Jimmy used to recall, "and landed outside the ropes. I put two or three pros in with the guy, and they haven't touched him yet. It turned out he had such wonderful reflexes he could dodge a punch by a sixteenth of an inch, and that's how he got his ears torn up."

Generally speaking, Jimmy didn't talk up the good fighters he handled, knowing their performance would speak for him. He was at his best building up a Phil Scott or a Mighty Menichelli or some other essentially peaceable citizen, and he was unrivaled in the art of transmuting a knock into a boost. Thus when his Bob Pastor ran away from Joe Louis, Jimmy boomed him from coast to coast as "Rapid Robert" and "Bicycle Bob."

A personal recollection concerns a night in Hollywood when Pastor appeared with one Turkey Thompson. There were either seven or nine knockdowns, although not that many punches, and once Pastor was floored by a left jab. This is a difficult feat in any circumstances, and even more so when you're in with a man who can't throw a left jab. After Pastor won, Jimmy was asked to explain how this knockdown came to pass.

"I was hollering at my Robert to stay down and take the full nine count," came the unhesitating answer, "and he misunderstood me to say 'fall down.' My Robert is very obedient."

Jimmy knew for years that his heart was unsound. His physician pleaded with him not to work in Pastor's corner in the second Louis fight in Detroit, and when Jimmy insisted, the doctor compromised by giving him a bottle of pills for use if the ticker misbehaved.

It was a perilously exciting bout, with Pastor down several times in the first round, then coming on to belabor Louis stoutly before succumbing in the eleventh. Jimmy had to feed the whole bottle of pills to the doctor.

The Pure in Heart

A Proper British Boxer Gets Nailed American-Style

NEW YORK, N.Y., *May 19, 1946*

IF BRUCE WOODCOCK is half as wise as he is beautiful, then he learned more during a nine-second nap in the Garden Friday night than in all his waking hours as a professional fist fighter. The "mug punch" that Tami Mauriello flung into his well-scrubbed and comely features in the fifth round was a priceless lesson in the facts of ring life, and if Brucie learned it, he will be a better and more prosperous brawler from now on. Toss him back against Mauriello two weeks hence and the chances are he would show marked improvement. That is, he probably would reach the sixth round before slipping off into the deep, dreamless slumber that comes to small children, the pure of heart, and all British heavyweights.

In his first American adventure Brucie appeared to have everything except an understanding of how cruel life can be out here in the colonies. He looked like a good boxer and a good puncher, but he was in with a fighter.

Brucie has a stand-up style, keeps his chin tucked away behind a pink shoulder, is cool and steady, and can throw a punch that hurts. But he fights like somebody who learned boxing out of a book and still believes it a manly art. The book, incidentally, wasn't the one written by the Marquess of Queensberry, whose cardinal rule was "defend yourself at all times." Woodcock would deliver a studied stroke and then step back to prepare for the next thrust and parry, and while he was waiting, Tami would club him three times, American style.

Give the young man a half-dozen bouts in this country against opponents who would teach him to crowd in and rough a man around and keep swatting all the time, and Bruce might whip anyone below the Joe Louis class, unless it should turn out that his chin was Dresden china. As to that, decision must be reserved because although it required only one punch to send him beddie-by, it was a punch that might have annulled anybody. Tami won't ever get a clearer shot at a more receptive profile.

The fifth round was the busiest, with both lads landing solidly, Mauriello painting Bruce's countenance with bloody mittens, and Woodcock's stiff counters opening a cut alongside Tami's left eye. They backed out of a flurry in mid-ring and for at least a half second Woodcock was perfectly motionless, flat-footed in a crouch. Tami's right hand traveled about eight inches. Flat on his back, Brucie lay with arms outstretched like a small boy playing dead in a game of cowboy-and-Indian.

At the count of eight he twitched and turned over and at ten—too late for anything but the autopsy—he pushed himself to his feet. His eyes were full of the wood violets of Doncaster. He borrowed a pair of legs from Eddie Joseph, the referee, for the journey to his corner.

"I just got nailed, y'know," Brucie said afterward, which was only part of the story. For y'knew right along, even when Woodcock was hitting his best line drives, that he was going to get nailed soon or late.

When it was all over, an apprentice genius in Woodcock's dressing room asked the champion of old Blighty which punch bothered him most.

"The last one," said Brucie, a clear thinker.

You Get a
Funny Feeling

Tommy Bell Preps for Sugar Ray Robinson

WORK WAS over in Ehsan's fight camp on the hilltop outside Summit, New Jersey. Tommy Bell, who will box Sugar Robinson for the vacant welterweight title tomorrow night, had done his last hitch of shadow-boxing, bag-punching, rope-skipping, and calisthenics. He was down under 146 pounds and ready for the drive to New York, where there would be a spot of road work in Central Park today, and then nothing to do but wait for the big moment of his professional life.

Visitors found him sitting in his dressing room wearing a faded bathrobe, with a towel hung in a cowl over his small, dark head. "What's this," he was asked, "about you breaking the union rules and offering to fight this guy for free?"

Stooping to unlace his shoes, Bell mumbled something, concluding: "Nobody else would fight him."

"Ernie says he's going to remember that offer after the match."

"It's an idea," said Ernie Braca, who operates Bell in partnership with Solly King. "Thanks for reminding me." Bell, slow to warm up, kept his gaze in his lap and scraped with a thumbnail at a spot on his robe.

"What did you think of Robinson after your other night with him?" he was asked. Robinson knocked him down in the last round of a close bout.

"Well, I just wish I'd of been in better shape."

"Tell 'em what you told me," Solly King said, "about his punch."

"Well," Bell said, "he was knocking out everybody, see? I figure if he hits me I'm gone, so I was extra careful. Then in the tenth he catches me coming out of my corner and hits me a right and a left hook to the chin. I didn't go down and I couldn't believe it. But then he moved back and I tried to move away and my legs kind of wouldn't work and I fell on my head. But I got up and it was a hell of a round after that. Now I just wish he'd of hit me in the first round insteadda the tenth, is all."

"Were you scared?"

"Nervous-like. I wouldn't like to say scared."

"Ever been afraid?"

"I can't see no sense to that. A man with a gun, maybe. But not a-scared of a man with just his hands."

There was a thoughtful moment and then he said: "You get a funny feeling sometimes when they play the Star-Spangled Banner. You're all warmed up and ready to fight and then they turn off the lights and you're all alone there in the dark. It gives you a chance to think."

Bell was born in Georgia, but grew up in Youngstown, Ohio, where his family moved when he was a year old. He began boxing as an amateur there.

"Did you ever work?"

"Oh, I had six-seven jobs. I give 'em all back to the man. I was in a C.C.C. camp and I got in a little trouble there over a card game and quit there."

"An ace drop out of your sleeve?"

"No, I was running the crap games, see? Couldn't nobody play except they asked me. Couple other guys start a couple games and I was knocking some heads around and one night they jumped me. Wasn't no doors on the rooms there, just barracks. One night a fella got his head bust open. He was beating up a little guy and the little guy says: 'I don't give a damn what you do to me now, just don't go to sleep tonight.' So that night I hear the front door open and the back door slam and this guy yelling with his head bust open. You could come in, crack a guy, and run out the back. Well, these guys snuck up behind me that night, so I took my blankets and slep' out in the woods the rest of the night. Next day I left.

"After that I worked for Republic Steel. I was on the ore cars, pushing the ore down a chute with a shovel. One day my foot slipped and I went down the chute with the ore. I quit that job.

"Then I was in a foundry, but it was too hard. I was a damper, shutting the clamps on the molds. One day a clamp bust and melted steel flies all directions. I run in the other direction. So after that they put me shoveling down sand, but I was too slow. It was piecework and the other guys didn't like me slowing 'em up. So I quit that job.

"One night I'm at a fight and I went on as a substitute. Forty dollars, the man said, and I gotta work a lot of days for that. I was going back in the amateurs, where I was fighting twice a week for twenty dollars, but I got in the ring and looked down and there was the commissioner. 'Hello, Tommy,' he says, so I can't fight amateur any more.

"So after that I fought pro. I was fighting in Detroit and my manager took my money and left me stranded there. Had to move around by myself awhile."

"Tell 'em about the time you fought three times in three cities in a week," King said.

"Yeh," Bell said, "Monday, Tuesday, and Friday in Pittsburgh, Detroit, and Youngstown. I win 'em all by knockouts."

"For how much money?"

"For nothing. We got $750 for the week and I was supposed to get half, so he gave me $350."

"Who did the arithmetic?"

"He did," Bell said, "and I got me another manager."

They Trut Him Good

Windy City Shoulders Graziano, a Roughneck and a Rowdy

CHICAGO, ILL., *July 17, 1947*

I T I S almost six months now since Rocky Graziano's tribal enemies, the cops, dropped a net over his untidy haircut, and the District Attorney's lawyers, overcoming their natural repugnance of publicity, had him detached from the rolls of the gainfully employed in New York State. The idea was to teach Rocky a lesson, a plan undertaken without especial success by the police, who bent nightsticks around his ears when he was growing up, by the disciplinarians he encountered in the Army, by sundry fist fighters who had engaged him on the streets and in the ring. But this time it worked. Rocky did learn a lesson. In geography. He discovered a new state called Illinois. Wherefore he is middleweight champion of the world today.

"I like Chicago," the young man said with simple, rhetorical dignity. "They trut me good."

The fact that Rocky Graziano last night possessed enough stamina and punch to take a frightful whipping from Tony Zale and knock him out—almost exactly as Zale took a whipping and knocked Rocky out last September—has nothing whatever to do with the charges brought against him before the New York Athletic Commission in February. Nevertheless, his victory must inevitably bring his case back to the attention of the commissioners. And when they look it over, may they look and think straight.

The first thing to remember is that there has not been a smidgen of proof that Graziano committed any offense save a technical violation of the commission's Rule 64, which requires a boxer to holler copper when any sinister influence makes a pass at him. There was something about a silly offer of a ridiculous bribe, which Rocky did not accept to take a dive in a fight that was not fought. Beyond this the prosecution produced nothing but sly insinuations that "we know plenty more but we're not telling."

On those grounds alone the commissioners convicted.

Almost half a year has passed. The District Attorney's men have been before a grand jury, which was certainly the place to spill such dirt as they had, and they did not get an indictment. Isn't it high time for them to come clean? Or is it too much to ask of public officeholders that they admit: "We have no case against Graziano; we never had a case; we cannot make a case; we can show no reason why he should not work for a living in this state"?

If this is not the case, then let the District Attorney prove it. If it is, then let him say so honestly. Or let Commissioner Eddie Eagan speak for him. Continued silence could mean only one thing to the public— that the entire Graziano affair was a cynical and deliberate job of sacrificing a kid to a political advertising campaign.

If all this sounds like special pleading for Graziano, who is a roughneck and a rowdy, then that's unfortunate. One would prefer that it be read as a plea for the principle that an accused man is innocent until proved guilty. In America that's supposed to apply to prize fighters as well as preachers.

Meanwhile the operators of Graziano will concern themselves with questions of the date and site of Rocky's first title defense. The identity of the challenger is not an issue. Zale has a ninety-day option on a third match with Rocky if he wishes to take it up. The notion here is that Tony would live to a happier, although perhaps less affluent, old age if he abstained from further engagements of this sort. He looked last night like a man whose best days had been left somewhere back of his thirty-third birthday. Age and punches will not improve him. However, he's a professional fist fighter and so the chances are he'll take the bout for the money he can make.

Possibly he believed along with many others that Johnny Behr, the referee, was overhasty in stopping last night's fight. But of all the protests made to this effect, Tony's were the most perfunctory. With fifty seconds of the sixth round remaining, Tony was utterly, hopelessly, defenseless. To be sure, he had been equally helpless for longer periods in the first fight, in which he was punished oftener and more severely. Yet he came on to win that one.

Perhaps, because he is the game and durable guy he is, he could have survived additional damage last night. Perhaps, too, he could have been killed. Johnny Behr was in there to exercise his best judgment, and he did, and it looked right.

So Long, Joe

Joe "The Champ" Louis Meets Mr. Ten-to-One

THE BUZZER sounded a ten-second warning before the fifteenth round, and Joe Louis, world champion, straightened on his stool, flattening his stomach with a long, deep breath. He stared out into the Garden crowd owlishly, grotesque and a little ludicrous with one eye wide and the other beaten almost shut by the punches of Jersey Joe Walcott, the 10-to-1 nobody.

The title Louis had owned for ten and a half years was up for grabs now. It was out there in mid-ring, waiting for the better man to take it. Or so, at least, it was in this book, for the score here showed seven rounds for each man with the Eagan-system points exactly even.

For several rounds the crowd had been roaring ceaselessly, almost as loudly between rounds as during them. Eighteen-thousand-odd howling and jabbering, and you knew what they were thinking. They had come and paid their money on the wild, forlorn chance that they might see the impossible happen.

Already the implausible had come to pass before their eyes. They had seen Walcott, the squat and humorless and luckless butt of a hundred bad jokes, punch with Louis, box with him, and twice knock him sprawling. They had seen a chunky old family man take the best punches of one who has been called the greatest puncher of all time. (Or so they believed, not knowing Louis had fought nine of the fourteen rounds with a damaged right hand.) They had seen Walcott, the obscure, win round after round, and some of the others were so close that many considered Walcott already so far ahead that only a knockout could save Louis. What they had seen already was far beyond belief, so it was easy for them to believe just a little bit more and imagine they could see the championship moving across the ring.

The bell rang and Louis was up and shuffling forward. He was in a hurry. He and Walcott touched gloves briefly. Then the champion went after his man—and his title.

Louis landed a jab. And another. Walcott jabbed back once and fled. Louis crowded Walcott, who backed into a corner, and the roar of the crowd swelled expectantly, foreseeing sudden destruction. But Walcott ducked away, unhit, and circled warily beyond arm's reach. There was a small, sluggish flow of blood from Louis' nose, which had started bleeding in the eleventh round.

It was plain what Walcott's purpose and instructions were. His handlers, having watched the fight with a strict and natural partiality, had assured him that he needed only to escape a knockout now and the title would surely be his. So Jersey Joe fled.

As he ran he flicked feathery lefts into the champion's face, little back-handed pit-pats that came in pairs. One, two. Pit-pat. One, two.

Now Walcott was in full flight, and the crowd was booing him. He ducked and danced and ran. He was caught and bit; he clinched and held; he ran again.

Louis drew near and jabbed twice. Louis jabbed twice again. Louis landed two more jabs as the bell rang.

It seemed a long time before Harry Balogh, the voice of purest brass, got the official ballots and stood in mid-ring, scowling over them. A regiment of cops had formed a hollow square on the ring apron and were arguing with strays who tried to climb between the ropes. Handlers clotted up in both corners, and it was difficult to see the fighters.

Louis, though, moved a half-step out in front of his gang and stood there, not looking Walcott's way, but staring straight across the ring, out into the hall, as Balogh gave his melodramatic best. The first vote was for the champion. There came a howl and then a great rumble of boos, surely the first Louis ever heard directed his way. Not a flicker of expression crossed his face.

The second ballot went to Walcott. Cheers from the gallery. No sign from Louis. The third and last was for Louis. One handler yelled and slapped his shoulder. There was nothing in Joe's bruised and furrowed face but inexpressible weariness. He looked, suddenly, like a small boy about to cry.

Somebody lifted Louis' hand, and he went out quickly. Boos followed him. For the first time it was possible to see Walcott.

Dan Florio, Jersey Joe's trainer, led him out toward mid-ring and lifted his hand. Felix Bocchicchio, one of Walcott's proprietors, clapped hands ardently, leading the crowd in applause. Walcott smiled, and the customers cheered. This touching tableau dissolved once, was put together again for pictures, and once again Bocchicchio led the applause, like the stooge in a radio studio.

So Jersey Joe, whom they called the great dark father of mediocrity, almost became the heavyweight champion of the world. In the opinion of many, not including this onlooker, he did win the title and was robbed.

That version doesn't go down here, but it was desperately close. Not even in his first match with Billy Conn had Louis been so near the brink. The man who pushed him to the crumbling edge did a good job—a smart and cool and skillful job. Perpetually moving, shifting, sidling crabwise, he kept the champion off balance and joggled his aim. When Louis jabbed, Walcott countered solidly with a looping right that he crossed over the left. Now and then he hooked hard with a left.

Beyond any possible dispute Walcott earned the reward he is sure to get—a rich outdoor return match next summer, which will bring financial security for him and his six children. Yet it remains impossible for a die-hard to believe he will win the title next time.

He did, unquestionably, make Louis look old and slow. For the first time ever the champion's age showed in public. But Walcott is older still.

Water-Fed Panther

Harry Wills Observes the Liquid Diet

ONE OF these days soon Harry Wills is going to quit eating. Everybody does, of course, sooner or later. But the old Brown Panther of New Orleans does it on purpose. Every year since 1908, he says, he has passed up all vittles for a month. Ordinarily February is the month he picks, but he has just returned home from his mother's funeral in New Orleans and hasn't got around to thinking about the fast this year.

"It's a water fast," he said yesterday. "No, it don't weaken me. Makes me stronger. Clears out the system. I guess it's a kind of a hobby with me now."

"You really don't take anything but water for a whole month, Harry?"

"Feel a little faint, maybe a spoonful of sugar. That's all. First two days I'm hungry, then that goes away. First three-four days maybe, a little dizzy. After that I feel good. I'm prob'ly two hundred and fifty pounds now. I'll drop fifty-five, sixty pounds. Once it was more'n seventy. I got the idea from Macfadden."

"Bernarr Macfadden?"

"Him. Yeh. Fella I was going around with, he got cured by it. So I took it up. No, I wasn't sick. Never been sick in my life except the flu in 1918. When I was fighting I'd go on it in February because that was the shortest month, but I've done it in every month of the year, one time or another.

"I never looked for no publicity on it, but in 1921 I'd beat Kid Norfolk in the old Garden and Jack Renault was going good then and they wanted me to fight Renault before the circus come into the Garden. So when they come up to see me I told 'em I couldn't because I was on this fast. Walter St. Denis was Tex Rickard's press agent. He sent a reporter up to see me, and that's how it all come out."

Being a panther of affluent leisure anyhow, Harry doesn't have to change his habits when he's fasting. Just keeps an eye on his Harlem properties and takes his comfort in his elegantly furnished apartment in the building he owns at 76 St. Nicholas Place. He was relaxing, as he talked, in a living room big enough to contain a concert grand piano without crowding. He wore tweeds of a brown mixture. A diamond the size of a small prune glittered on his left hand.

"How's the fight game?" he asked. "How's Joe?"

Well, everybody said both were slipping.

"Joe's hit thirty-four," he said. "He's been in the limelight eleven, twelve years, and that's an awful yoke. Always afraid to do anything or say anything or go anywhere because somebody might think wrong about you. Crowds around all the time like you're a bear in a cage. Of course Joe wants to win, but maybe he's tired. Maybe he don't care so much any more. And Joe's hit thirty-four. When you hit thirty-four, for a fighter, you're going down. Thirty-three, even. Guess that's why in the Masonics they have that thirty-third degree—because thirty-three is it."

He flung his head back and laughed, slapping a thigh.

"How old were you when you quit, Harry?"

"Mmmm, now you started me to figuring. Let's see, 1911 to 1934— I was forty-eight." (If he was forty-eight in 1934, he'd have been born in 1886.)

"Actually, or on the records?"

"My real age. Record says I was born 1892. Actually I was born 1889. My father died when I was little and my mother had to scramble a few years and then she got married again and my stepfather moved us up in the country awhile. Then we come back to New Orleans and I was getting boy-size. I skipped out from home. I come back in about six years, and after that I started fighting.

"The way it was, I'd been fighting some on ships and there was a bout in New Orleans between Johnny Tholmer, the colored champion of the South, and Nat Dewey, from Denver, Colorado. The Wonder of the West, they called him. I had my few pennies in the promotion. Well, Johnny took sick and I said I'd go in and substitute for him so's we wouldn't lose the promotion money. I beat Dewey. That's how I started. Never fought a preliminary and never fought in the amateurs. I went out to the Coast and did good there. Then I went to Cuba to see Willard and Johnson, and a fella down there got me to come to New York. Been here ever since."

"Were you ever hurt?"

"Chappie, you always hurt if you're in that ring. When you're in good shape, your blood stream carries it off and in the excitement of fighting you don't notice it. You don't exactly enjoy fighting, but it's like this. You're young and a fella you knows goes to fighting and you say: 'Hell, I can lick him.' And then you go to fighting and there's a kind of a glamour and excitement and when you get hardened to fighting you get kind of immune to punches. You don't feel 'em when they hit, maybe. But the next day, chappie, you hurt. Like out in Denver, fella in the dressing room ask Kid Broad how he feels. 'Well,' the Kid say, 'outside of a busted jaw and a cracked rib and my hands busted up, I feel all right.'"

Harry roared with laughter.

"Outside of a busted jaw and a cracked rib and his hands busted, he feels good. Kid told 'im right."

Videots

Fusari, Castellani, Dewar's & Philco

NEW YORK, N.Y., *February 20, 1949*

THE SALOON, which is less than two blocks from Madison Square Garden, has walls pretty well covered with enlarged photographs of hockey players, boxers, and ballplayers, mostly autographed. A shoulder-high partition from front to rear makes the space before the bar fairly narrow. There are booths on the other side of the partition and the television screen is on the rear wall at the end of the bar.

All the bar stools were occupied before ten P.M., and some men were standing. The fights from the Garden came on at ten. A few minutes after that, there were two solid rows of men in front of the bar, about all that the space could accommodate. Maybe six were whiskey drinkers; the rest had beer.

Somebody had said: "You ought to hear 'em in the bars when the fights are on. The arguments they have and the way they bet." This was a quiet crowd, though; the whole evening didn't produce what you could call an argument, and there was no evidence of betting.

Still, it was worthwhile getting the proper slant on a fight, for once. As every sportswriter and boxing judge and referee has learned from experience, those who see a fight from the working press rows or even from the ring itself generally see it all wrong. When mail poured in after the first Louis-Walcott bout, for instance, the most positive and vituperative letters came from the videots (generic term for television viewers) and members of the radio audience.

It can be stated flatly, therefore, without fear of successful contradiction, that the proper score of Friday night's match between Rocky Castellani and Charley Fusari was seven rounds to three in Fusari's favor. Don't pay any attention to the judges, the referee, and newspaper guys like Jess Abramson, who scored it closer. Us guys in the saloon, we know; we seen it on television!

The bar fell silent when the main event started. The two bartenders, having made sure everyone had a drink, leaned with a hand on the back bar and watched Castellani knock Fusari down. The videots only grunted at that, except for one of the whiskey men (Dewar's White Label), who was rooting softly for Fusari.

"Stay down," he muttered, "stay down," and then when Fusari got up at the count of three: "Ah, you dope." He turned to a neighbor and explained the importance of taking a full nine-count when you're floored early like that, before you get warmed up.

The people in the booths ignored the fight and went on about their own business. They were much noisier than the men on the bar side. One woman especially kept lifting a voice that was shrill with drink. "Mary, oh, Mary," she called to someone in her party. And to someone else, "Kiss me, honey."

When the first round ended, a big one for Castellani, one bartender turned to the other and said, "Hey, George, Castellani." He made a sort of thumbs-down gesture with one hand down at his hip. His meaning was obscure, but his tone and the expression in his face were cynical and knowing, much like the manner of a racetrack tout telling the tale.

The Dewar's man nodded and said, "Sure, same thing last Wednesday," whatever that meant. Between rounds the barkeeps worked leisurely. They didn't exactly hustle any customers, but when a man set down an empty glass the barkeep near him would draw another beer or, if it was a whisky glass, would say, "What was that again?" It was more an order than a question.

Fusari took control of the fight from the second round on. This was a good big television screen, but in spite of what they say, you couldn't see the fight nearly so well as from a reasonably good ringside seat. Lots of times you couldn't be sure Castellani's swings were missing, although they looked wild, and when a punch landed it was difficult to tell how much damage it did.

The announcer was a help. He didn't whoop it up and he didn't try to lead you by the nose, telling you things you could see for yourself. Every little while he'd say, "Fusari on the left, Castellani on the right," or "Fusari in light trunks, Rocky Castellani dark," to straighten out late arrivals. Because the camera did not pick up the clock, he would announce the time: "One minute to go in the fifth."

He made like an expert only twice, saying, "Castellani carries his left awfully low against a right-hand puncher like Fusari," and "In a match like this it's usually the best counterpuncher who scores." There were grunts of agreement in the bar. Mostly the announcer was wisely silent.

Nevertheless, the trade was on the alert to contradict him with jeers. Once he said left when he meant right, correcting himself quickly, and the videots hooted, "Make up your mind." When Castellani landed a good right and the announcer said it was the same sort of punch that had floored Fusari in the first round, a man growled, "Fathead, it was a left knocked 'im down."

About the fifth or sixth round a man said, "I make it only the first for Castellani." The man to his left agreed, saying, "Fella over here says it's even. Can't see it." A man on the right said, "Way I see it, he's just a flash in the first."

When the decision was announced—five, four, and one; five, three, and two; six, three, and one—there was a small mumble of dissent. "Should of been more for Fusari," a man said without heat.

The crowd thinned out swiftly. The bartenders got busy. The one named George was asked: "These fights bring the crowds in, but do they make more business?" George said a little bit, not much.

"Don't a lot of 'em come in for one beer and watch the fight?"

"Yeh," George said, and shrugged.

Somebody had a Bing Crosby record going on the juke box. Television had been switched off. The screechy woman cried, "Kiss me, honey."

Rendezvous
with Danger

Duke Nalon Wins the "500"

A INDIANAPOLIS, IND., *May 31, 1948*
FAT, jovial man is sitting on the tailboard of a small inclosed truck inside the first turn of the Indianapolis Motor Speedway. His machine is four rows back from the rail, one among thousands and thousands of cars that stand, glittering under the sun, almost as far as the eye can see across this clamorous, hideous cauldron of noise, and speed, and reeking oil. On the truck's floor is a bed of straw with tangled blankets and mussed pillows. The man says he and two friends—"three bachelors from Gary"—drove over yesterday and pulled up in line maybe half a mile outside the gate about eight o'clock last night.

"How was the sleeping in here?"

"Fine. We had a great time. Left the truck in line and went into town and drank coffee all night. The line started moving in at five this morning. Have a can of beer?"

At his feet, a metal box holds beer cans in melting ice. He has a box of crackers open at his knees, a beer in his hand, and around him are paper parcels of food.

"You're pretty well stocked. Can you see the race from the truck top?"

"Not so good. We were over by that gate a while. Couldn't see anything from there, either."

"Kind of a long drag, wasn't it, waiting all night and not seeing much now?"

"Yes, but it was worth it. Sure you won't have a beer?"

This particular area, where the infield crowds fight for position near the turn because the turns are the danger points in the annual five-hundred-mile race, offering the likeliest opportunity to see a man untidily killed, is an indescribable place, a grassy slum of gay squalor.

Here a fat woman in halter and shorts sits sunning herself on a camp stool. There a girl in slacks lies sprawled in sleep beneath a truck. The car tops are cluttered like window sills along the Third Avenue "El," covered with mattresses and blankets and seat cushions and homemade platforms supporting boxes, chairs, folding stools.

The car interiors have the homey, lived-in look of beds that haven't been made up for three days. Some have blankets or newspapers hung over windows and windshield for protection from the sun and a smidgen of privacy. The men are virtually all coatless, for it's a warmish day, and many are peeled to the waist. There's one shaving in front of his rear-view mirror. When a luggage compartment is opened, it generally reveals a washtub of iced beer.

There is a skeleton skyline of scaffolding, mostly unpainted two-by-fours set up astraddle the automobiles and supporting an observation platform perhaps fifteen feet high. Some are professional jobs of structural steel, bolted together and rising as high as twenty-five feet.

One of the tallest and certainly the most precarious looking consists of two double-length painters' ladders propped up in an inverted V. Two or three planks thrust between the upper rungs make unsteady perches against the sky.

The earth is a vast litter of crushed lunch boxes and tattered paper and beer cans and whisky bottles and banana skins and orange peels and the heels of used sandwiches and blankets and raiment and people. Over everything is the reek of burning castor oil, the incessant, nerve-shattering roar of racing motors.

This is the Indianapolis "500," a gigantic, grimy lawn party, a monstrous holiday compounded of dust and danger and noise, the world's biggest carnival midway and the closest sporting approach permitted by the Humane Society to the pastimes which once made the Roman Colosseum known as the Yankee Stadium of its day (cars are used in this entertainment because the S.P.C.A. frowns on lions).

The speedway is a rambling, ramshackle plant enclosed by two and a half miles of brick-paved track and the only space not jammed is the nine-hole golf course in the remotest part of the infield. Through binoculars from the press loft, couples can be seen reclining in comradely embrace beneath the trees on the links, but there seem to be no golfers.

It is said there are 175 thousand people here, although gates started to close half-an-hour before race time. At that morning hour the Purdue University band was on the track giving brassy evidence of the advantages of higher education. At length these embryo Sammy Kayes tied into the national anthem and followed with "Taps," just in case. Bombs went off. Rockets burst in air, making a heavy flak pattern below cruising planes. James Melton sang "Back Home in Indiana" slowly, a full four seconds off the track record.

The cars had been pushed into place, three abreast in eleven ranks. Their drivers, goggled and helmeted, looked like Buck Rogers cutouts. The flying start was a burst of thunder, a blur of colors. Since then, it has been an unceasing grind, hour after hour, making the eyeballs ache, the temples throb. Every car has a different voice, none soothing. There is a twelve-cylinder Mercedes said to have been built for Adolf Hitler; it runs with a scream like Adolf's conscience.

Now, late in the race, the favored lane near the outside, which is called "the groove," has been blackened with oil. Coming down the straightaway, the cars skitter nervously on this slick, swinging their hips like Powers models. Most of the thirteen drivers still in the race steer to the cleaner bricks inside the strip.

Duke Nalon stays in the groove, though, and is leading with only fifteen of the two hundred laps remaining. He has the fastest, most powerful brute of a car ever put on this track, but its speed requires a special fuel which gives poor mileage, and now he pulls in for refueling. The crowd gives him a yell, the first time its voice has been heard all day. The pit crew works swiftly, finishes, can't get the motor started again. The car starts once, dies, and must be pushed back to the pit for more feverish seconds. This is the day's most exciting moment.

When Nalon finally goes away, to another small cheer, Mauri Rose and Bill Holland are ahead of him. The race is over; it was lost there at the gas pump.

The Old Man Earned His Pension

No Rewrite Possible for Grandest Story in Horse Racing

SAN FERNANDO, CALIF., *March 7, 1940*

FOR THE better part of a week now, arguments have raged up and down this coast over the question of whether Seabiscuit was the best horse in the Santa Anita Handicap or just the second-best horse with the best stable connections.

Even at the moment when the red silks of Charles S. Howard were flashing under the wire and the roar of California's biggest race crowd was rolling toward the Sierra Madres, there were some onlookers—this myopic one included—who believed another horse could have won the race if his owner and rider had wanted it so.

The other horse was, of course, Kayak II, Seabiscuit's little Latin brother-in-arms in the Howard stable, who finished a fairly leisurely second, slightly more than a length behind his colleague, with Buddy Haas straightened up in the stirrups and idly watching the struggling pack up the track.

To say that Kayak could have won is to say he could have tied or broken the world record for a mile and a quarter, for the race as run was only a fragment off the best time ever made at the distance. Yet that is what they're saying, and that could very possibly be the case.

This much is so without question:

Kayak, slow to get running, was trailing the field, something like eleven lengths off the pace, as the pack wheeled around the clubhouse turn and headed into the backstretch. Running the long way around, the Argentine circled the field and pulled up almost level with the Biscuit in the homestretch.

After that Haas came up in his stirrups, glanced to right and left as though seeking possible contention for the Howard favorite, and proceeded the rest of the way in the sedate and orderly fashion of a policeman assigned to protect a $100,000 bauble from hijackers but under no circumstances to snatch it for himself.

That was the way the thing was planned and announced in advance, Howard having declared to win with the Biscuit, and that's the way virtually everyone in the crowd wanted it. So there would have been no argument of any sort had not the worshippers of Seabiscuit taken immediate and vociferous umbrage at the suggestion that their idol could have been beaten.

It was and is their contention that no horse in training, possibly no horse ever foaled, could have beaten the Old Man at a mile and a quarter last Saturday. Supporting this, they point to his time of 2.01 1-5 and argue there's no way of telling how much run may have been left in the elderly legs at the finish.

Suppose Haas had persevered on Kayak, they say. Who knows what the Biscuit might have done if challenged? Haas might have flogged the everlasting be-jeebers out of his mount and still failed to gain an inch against a Seabiscuit that felt any real need of running.

Thus they have wrangled, until in the last day or so a demand has grown for a match race some time this summer at Hollywood Park, which would be, as far as we know, the first case in history of a stable racing against itself on a winner-take-none basis.

We are not ordinarily inclined to become sentimental about a horse, but we've been frankly and unashamedly soft about the son of Hard Tack ever since he licked War Admiral at Pimlico a year and a half ago.

Thinking of the fragile forelegs that have given him trouble all his racing life, we thought after that victory that he should be retired before the inevitable breakdown. He wasn't retired and he did break down, and it was little less than a miracle that enabled trainer Tom Smith to nurse him back into condition to realize Howard's great ambition to set a money-winning record.

Now that has been done, and we're all the more convinced the Old Man has earned his pension. It could prove little to race him against Kayak again. There is hardly one chance in a thousand that both horses could be brought to the superb peak of condition they had last Saturday or that the track and weather conditions of that race could be duplicated.

So that even if they did meet again the result would not necessarily be conclusive. And the grandest story of modern racing could end with the shabbiest of all anticlimaxes, a line in the chart reading: "Seabiscuit broke down and was destroyed."

Death of
"The Iceman"

George Monroe Woolf, 1910–1946

NEW YORK, N.Y., *January 5, 1946*

THE FATAL injury of Georgie Woolf in a spill at Santa Anita Thursday is a reminder of something which race fans forget with the greatest of ease when they boo and sneer and rail at some dusty kid who has just finished out of the money astride the horse they're betting. That is, that every time one of these little guys scrambles into the saddle for a race he is literally taking his life in his hands.

Nothing could illustrate this truth with more shocking clarity than the circumstances of "The Iceman's" death. Here was one of the genuinely great riders of our time, conceded without argument to be right up there alongside Eddie Arcaro at the very top of his profession. Here was one of the most nearly perfect craftsmen alive, famed among fans and respected among jockeys for his cool skill and daring. He had ridden in every stake of importance in America and won virtually all of them at least once and it is not recalled that he ever had a serious fall from the time he was seven years old and riding his father's horses on the hayseed tracks of Alberta, Canada.

There was no jamming or interference of any sort in his last race. He had a tight hold on his mount, Please Me, and was in the clear behind the field. The horse stumbled, flinging Georgie over his head, and that was all.

It was ironic that a fellow who rarely accepted mounts in any but the major events should be killed in an ordinary $3,500 allowance race. Because he declined assignments in the minor events, some of the public got the impression that he was high hat. Now he is dead, there is no reason to conceal the fact that he wasn't physically able to ride complete cards day in and day out.

He was diabetic and didn't dare train down below 115 pounds or ride too often. A quiet little blond who took few people into his confidence, he didn't advertise what watchful care he had to exercise in order to work at all.

He would sleep most of the morning on the day of a race and shortly before saddling he would drink a Coca-Cola spiked with spirits of ammonia. His wife supervised the rigid diet he had to keep, traveling with him from their home in Arcadia, near Santa Anita, where they had invested in a restaurant in anticipation of the day when Georgie would quit the track.

Georgie Woolf was a bit of a hero in the jockey rooms, personally popular with the other riders and respected as a competitor whose tactics were fair but whose temper permitted no liberties. More than one jockey got a whip across the face for trying to rough up "The Iceman."

He came fast on the big wheel, for it was less than fifteen years ago that he first wandered into Saratoga wearing dusty jeans and a big white cowboy hat. They laughed at the "Montana cowboy" then and guyed him, until they saw him on a horse.

He'd been riding almost as soon as he could walk. His father, a rider and stagecoach driver in Montana before he settled in Cardston, Alberta, taught him racing on the backwoods tracks of southern Alberta and in 1926 the fifteen-year-old Georgie rode his first race on an organized track, a horse named Catch Me at Chinook Park, Calgary.

Once he reached the big leagues, he rode the best in the biggest and scarcely any big prize eluded him except victory in the Kentucky Derby. At Churchill Downs he never got closer than on second on Staretor in 1941.

He took his greatest personal satisfaction in winning the first $100,000 Santa Anita Handicap with Azucar, a reformed steeplechaser from Ireland. In that race Woolf drove Azucar up from fourteenth place and won by two lengths, with the beloved favorite, Equipoise, far back in seventh place.

Others, however, remember more vividly his ride on Whirlaway in the Massachusetts Handicap in 1942, when Whirlaway broke Seabiscuit's earnings record. Red Pollard, Seabiscuit's jockey, sat in the press box and watched as Woolf restrained his horse frighteningly far behind the pacemaking Rounders.

Pollard was the first to spot the flash of devil's red when Georgie began to move on the far turn. The redhead leaped to his feet, yelling "Here he comes! Here he comes, the son of a bitch!"

And there was the golden afternoon at Pimlico when, with Pollard in a hospital, Woolf got up on Seabiscuit and stole the start and the horse race from Charley Kurtsinger in the unforgettable match with War Admiral, whose owner had dictated all the conditions right down to a walk-up start.

"Didn't think I could do it, did you?" Georgie shouted when Seabiscuit broke ahead of War Admiral. "Get that whip ready, because I'm going to make you run," he said when Kurtsinger drew even with him on the backstretch.

On the stretch turn Georgie spoke once again. "Good-bye, Charley," he yelled. He didn't wait for an answer.

Love Story

First Whirl, Son of Whirlaway, Makes Debut at Keeneland

LEXINGTON, KY., *October 25, 1946*

WELL, WHIRLAWAY'S love child won a race the other day and that recalls a story which may or may not have been told here before but can, in any event, bear retelling because it is a tale of pure and lofty sentiment suitable to the ears of young and old. It is a yarn about horse-lovers in the strict sense of the term, meaning one horse that's in love with another horse, and not the sort of horse-lovers you see out at Jamaica, where affection is peddled at $2 a heartthrob, less taxes, take, and breakage.

The story starts back in the late summer of 1943 when they took Whirlaway out of racing and shipped him down to Calumet Farm outside Lexington, Kentucky, to establish his "court," as the euphemism goes.

Now, in setting up a seraglio in a style befitting a celebrity of Whirlaway's eminence, a number of amenities are involved. Among other things, there's a fertility test, but as a rule thoroughbred mares are not used for this purpose.

However, there chanced to be a thoroughbred named Mary V. living down the Versailles Pike a piece on the farm of a man named Wilson. A nature-story author would say Mary V. set her cap for Whirlaway, but that seems like giving whimsy its head and, after all, this is a journal of record. Chances are her attitude toward Whirlaway was just about that of any female for a handsome fellow who, at the age of five, had earned $561,000 and some small change. Whirlaway, you'll remember, was tall and good-looking with a clear copper complexion, a lot of swagger, and a tail of luxuriant splendor.

Anyhow, there was Whirlaway, and although it was long past the normal breeding season, Mary V. found him not unattractive. The test was a complete success and Warren Wright, squire of Calumet, was furious.

One school of thought holds that they never expected Mary V. to get in foal so late in the year and were astonished when she did. If it was a miscalculation, why, that's happened before and probably will again. Another argument is that somebody wanted to slip under the wire and get a foal by Whirlaway ahead of schedule (it wasn't planned to open the champion's court until the normal breeding season the next spring). Since it was only a test, there was no arrangement about Whirlaway's fifteen-hundred-dollar stud fee.

However it was, Wright felt he'd been jobbed. He put on a scene that lacked only wind machines and prop snowflakes to go right into *East Lynne* or *Adrift in New York*. He turned practically everyone involved, except Whirlaway himself, out into the night with orders never to darken his doorway again.

You see, Mary V.'s foal was due to be born, and was born, the following autumn, late in the year. Since the universal birthday of thoroughbreds is Jan. 1, the little guy would become a year old officially just a couple of months after his birth and all through his racing life he'd have to give away a chunk of age to others in his class. Wright feared that a runt known as Whirlaway's first get would make the stallion look bad as a sire.

Mary V. foaled a leggy son. Wright, in the best theatrical tradition, refused even to look at the colt. Somebody said he vowed he wouldn't even permit the foal to be registered, but that's unlikely because his authority didn't extend so far.

That's how things stood when Charles T. Fisher, owner of Dixiana Farm, first saw the colt. Mary V. had been a gift from Fisher to Wilson. Fisher, who makes automobile bodies, went home to Detroit to potter with chrome and plastic and upholstery samples, but he couldn't get that son of Mary V. off his mind. So back he went to Lexington and bought the colt from Wilson. Mr. Fisher has the kind of money that speaks in the same clear, clarion tone as Mr. Wright's. So matters finally were settled and the colt was registered under the name First Whirl.

Because of the age handicap, it wasn't planned to start First Whirl until he was officially three years old. But he must have shown something in training, for they put him in a race at Keeneland Wednesday. He took the lead early and ran hard through the stretch to beat back a challenge from the favorite. He didn't, like his sire, save his run for the homestretch. But he got there first. And that was like his sire.

Belmont of
the Backwoods

Sunshine Park, Between Tampa and Clearwater

ST. PETERSBURG, FLA., *May 11, 1947*

AMERICA'S NEWEST palace of pleasure and temple of chance is a rude clearing in the palmetto thickets that is aptly called Sunshine Park because the sun has steadfastly refused to shine upon it and the nearest park of consequence is Yellowstone. It is meant as a shrine to the sport of kings, but things have been a mite tough at the inaugural meeting and the owners have settled for the sport of one-eyed jacks, with maybe deuces wild once in a while.

This back-country Belmont is situated twenty-six miles from here, between Tampa and Clearwater, and when you motor over from St. Pete you find your way by incantation and sorcery. This isn't precisely as planned, either. In preparation for the opening, a factotum known locally as the Agha Cohen was sent out to post signs pointing the way along the highways and byroads. All but a handful have disappeared. The Agha Cohen says he learned that a car followed fifteen minutes after him and its occupants pulled down the signs as fast as he put 'em up. It is not known whether the strangers were motivated by enthusiasm for dog racing, the top sport hereabouts, or by the sort of simple piety which deems the horse an instrument of Satan.

In a previous incarnation, Sunshine Park operated as Tampa Downs, but the venture folded during the Depression and the plant sort of melted away. The new promoters have done such refurbishing and building as limited time and materials permitted, so that the place now looks like one of those desert hamlets you see along the Santa Fe right-of-way in Arizona. But it has a totalizer, a daily double, touts, a 37-percent average of winning favorites, forms, scratch sheets and handicappers' cards for sale at the gate, seasoned, alert racing officials, and—oh, yes—horses of a sort. Which makes it as close an approximation of paradise as an honest man has a right to expect.

It also has a feature which metropolitan tracks had to abandon when the mutuels came in—a supply of fresh air that has not already been used by four other customers. The promoters do not care deeply for this feature, because they've been taking a financial licking with small crowds and an average handle of only ninety-six thousand dollars, but to a fugitive from Aqueduct it is balm in Gilead.

Sunshine Park, in short, is the sort of place where a wanderer can have fun, where a fifteen-year-old horse can and does win, where a horseman like John Red can and does make a living. John Red, in fact, is one of the leading owners, with seven firsts and seven seconds to show for his eight-horse string, and officials think so well of him that when visitors gathered in the stewards' coop it was suggested that he be invited over from the barns.

In response to a telephone summons, he came across the weedy infield with a swift stride, a gaunt figure in blue jeans and faded army shirt. He had to ask a patrol judge for directions to the stewards' aerie, and when he reached the roof there was such a worried expression beneath his tangle of blond hair that Jim Milton, the veteran Maryland starter who is a steward at this meeting, had to laugh.

"Ever been called up by the stewards before, John?"

"No, sir. Not at any track."

"How long you been around racetracks?"

"Six years."

"How old are you?"

"Twenty-eight, twenty-nine—twenty-nine, I guess."

"And never been called up before, even when you were riding?'"

"No, sir."

"Well, that's a pretty good record."

John Red is owner, trainer, exercise boy, blacksmith, and night watchman in the stable which is his home. When he started out he was the stable jockey, too, but he doesn't ride in races now. Too busy working the horses and treating their ills; shoeing them and saddling them and cooling them out and studying the condition book for races they can win and, in his spare time, feeding them and mucking out the stalls. His youngest horse is eight and his oldest is eleven. He likes nine-year-olds best because "they're the easiest to train. Older than that, they're just as easy but can't race so often. I don't hardly ever claim a horse unless he's claimed off of me, then I try to claim him back. Mostly I leave the other fella's stock alone; everybody else wants the younger horses, so I leave 'em have 'em."

First John Red punched cows—"I rode over half of Arizona"—then he broke thoroughbreds for the Ellsworth brothers in Arizona, saved his pay and bought a stallion named Silver Static from them.

"I raced him against quarter-horses at Tucson, but the fellas who ran the track didn't like a thoroughbred beating their quarter-horses and they kept writing the conditions to bar my horse. Finally, I got in a race and win by six and they disqualified me. I got me another horse and I put him in at five-sixteenths and he was laying fourth to the stretch turn. When I moved to the outside, the other boys moved out in front of me; when I ducked in, they lugged in. Finally I went out in the middle of the track and won by a head, but they said they had no photo and they wouldn't give me the race.

"So I quit there. I went to Phoenix and Gresham, Oregon, and Seattle and Aksarben and Pascoag and Charles Town. The best horse I ever had was Whistling Boy. They claimed him off of me in Nebraska and broke him down."

"Do you like this life, John?"

"Well, it's the only place a fella can make some money and own a good horse, and I like horses. There's things about it good and things not so good. If you own all allowance horses, it's all sport, but if you got to run in claimers it's a rough go. You get a horse you like a lot claimed off of you and they abuse him—well, that's a rough go."

A Day of Beauty

Jet Pilot Wins Kentucky Derby

Louisville, Ky., *May 3, 1947*

Bullet Proof got kissed by a great beauty. Another lady, who has parlayed beauty into a great fortune, got $92,160, and an unidentified Louisville cop got a beauty of a kick in the pants from the winner of the seventy-third Kentucky Derby this gray, cool, exciting afternoon.

Jet Pilot had plowed through the drying mud pack of the Churchill Downs homestretch and thrust his unspattered chestnut countenance into the camera's eye just this far ahead of Phalanx. He'd been led into the horseshoe of geraniums in front of the tote board to get his corsage of roses, and they had delivered the swag to Mrs. Elizabeth Arden Graham, the beauty salon keeper.

Now the colt started back across the track toward the paddock, frisking and dancing in a tight little convoy of cops. Too tight a convoy, for as they reached the outside rail Jet Pilot upped with his off hind hoof and planted it firmly in the rear of one officer's lap.

This was the great moment of the day for the crowd on Colonel Matt Winn's littered lawn—a crowd that was estimated by means of the sorcery commonly used to count Derby gatherings at a hundred and fifteen thousand persons. Chances are that all of the witnesses had yearned at one time or another to boot a policeman from behind but, not being fast enough to win a Derby, had enjoyed no such privilege.

For the minority who happened to be in a position to see it, watching the race was even more fun than watching that kick-in-the-pants. It was an elegant race with a finish—closest since Bold Venture headed Brevity in 1936—that put a peaked cap of excitement on a day whose tension had been mounting hour-upon-hour since early morning.

There'd been hours and hours of preparation, an undertaking which annually involves the destruction of Kentucky's mint crop, and then came a sort of lull following the sixth race. The Derby horses came over from the barns to the paddock and the delectable Mrs. Liz Whitney went down there to see her colt, Bullet Proof, saddled.

Bullet Proof is a little bit of a horse, perhaps the smallest ever to start in a Derby, and there's no mistaking his owner's affection for him. She was a scenic bundle of furs and nervousness and emotion as she planted a consignment of kisses on the chestnut muzzle. The horse took it with what some masculine witnesses considered inordinate calm.

For a long while the massed band in the infield had been standing at attention. Now the romantic squeak of a phonograph sounded "Boots and Saddle," and a bubble of cheers broke. The bandsmen stiffened. The whole sprawling multitude seemed to draw together suddenly, like a hangman's noose.

One band played the national anthem. A platoon of stage managers stood on the track staring at their watches. Then one lifted a hand, and a huge, hybrid blend of bands made with "My Old Kentucky Home." Out of the chute beneath the stands came an outrider leading Stepfather. It seemed no more than right that this horse should be the first out. Harry Warner paid $200,000 for him so he could see his colors finish ninth in a Kentucky Derby. The sales prices of all the other starters, which weren't bred by their present owners, total $172,500.

Stepfather was followed out by his stablemate, W. L. Sickle, but then there was a longish delay and the stage managers could be seen frantically beckoning Cosmic Bomb's rider to hurry into view. Their small panic was comical, but just the same there was something about the whole picture that sent things scrambling up and down the spine.

Well, they paraded and they had to wait at the gate because Jett-Jett tossed his rider and ran away and got himself roundly jeered when he cantered back, but finally they got off and had themselves a honey of a horse race. It was marred for the chalk-eaters because Eddie Arcaro got away indifferently on the favored Phalanx—whose breeder remarked recently that the horse wasn't especially agile leaving the post—but after running last down the backstretch Phalanx put on a run at the leader that was something to see.

Jet Pilot came back to the merest flutter of applause, because a photo sign had flashed on the board and only those few in ideal positions knew he was the winner; but there was a yell when his number went up.

He was standing on the track with Eric Guerin still on his back and his trainer, Tom Smith, holding his bridle. Tom Smith almost grinned—with him that amounts to laughing like a loon—as he fondled the horse's head. They went into the floral horseshoe followed by Mrs. Graham, who shook hands with Smith, shook hands with Guerin, then stood on tiptoe to pat Jet Pilot's neck. She is not a tall lady.

There was a large dose of poetic justice here. Last year Tom Smith couldn't saddle the horses in Mrs. Graham's fragrant Maine Chance string because he'd been suspended for squirting ephedrine up an animal's snoot. Lady Lipstick put in a three-horse entry last year which was considered a kick-in, but all three finished way back there. That was just a day or so after a stable fire in Chicago destroyed virtually all of the Maine Chance two-year-olds.

Jet Pilot escaped the fire, being here at the time. It seemed only fair that this crowd should get hunk with their jinx this time. They'd been pushed around by luck more than somewhat. It was time they kicked back at something. Even a cop.

A Horse You
Had to Like

Remembering Seabiscuit

UKIAH, CALIF., *May 20, 1947*
I F THIS bureau had a prayer for use around horse parks, it would go something like this: Lead us not among bleeding hearts to whom horses are cute or sweet or adorable, and deliver us from horse-lovers. Amen.

In this case issue is not taken on the rhetorical grounds adopted by James Thurber when he observed that to him the expression "dog lover" meant one dog that was in love with another dog. Rather, the idea here is merely to get on record with an opinion that horses are animals which a guy can like and admire and have fun betting on or just watching. This is no knock at love, either.

With that established, let's talk about the death of Seabiscuit. It isn't mawkish to say there was a racehorse, a horse that gave race fans as much pleasure as any that ever lived, and one that will be remembered as long and as warmly. If someone asked you to list horses that had, apart from speed or endurance, some quality that fired the imagination and captured the regard of more people than ever saw them run, you'd have to mention Man o' War and Equipoise and Exterminator and Whirlaway and Seabiscuit. And the honest son of Hard Tack wouldn't be last.

It wasn't primarily his rags-to-riches history that won Seabiscuit his following, although reaching success from humble beginnings never dims a public figure's popularity. It wasn't the fact that he won more money than any other horse up to his time, although that hurt neither his reputation nor his owner. He wasn't a particularly handsome horse, nor especially big or graceful, and he never was altogether sound. Up to now, his get have not made him famous as his sire.

The quality he had was expressed one day by a man in the press box who said, "Look at his record. He's the Canzoneri of horses."

Look at his record and you see what the man meant. Just as Tony Canzoneri barnstormed through the fight clubs of the land taking on everyone they tossed at his head, so Seabiscuit made the rounds of most of the mile tracks between the oceans, and left track records at more than a few. Hialeah Park (his record reads), Bowie, Havre de Grace, Jamaica, Rockingham, Narragansett, Suffolk, Saratoga, Aqueduct, Agawam, Empire City, Pimlico, Belmont, Detroit, River Downs, Bay Meadows, Santa Anita, Tanforan, Laurel, Agua Caliente, Arlington, Del Mar, Hollywood.

He didn't always win, of course. Indeed, he was whipped seventeen times hand-running in allowance purses and maiden races and claimers before he won one, and that one was worth $750. Those were the days when he went unclaimed for $2,500.

It has often been written how his first owner, Ogden Mills, tossed him away from $8,500 in a private sale to Charles S. Howard. Actually, Mills did all right with him. Seabiscuit ran forty-seven times and won nine races for his breeder: His winnings and sale price brought Mills $26,965. No one could have guessed he would earn $419,265 racing for Howard.

In these days when a Shetland pony won't break out of a walk for less than $50,000, earnings are an incomplete measure of a horse's class. Seabiscuit's record of $437,730 has been surpassed by several horses. But he had to work for most of his. He often came out of a race with $25 or $50 in third or fourth money, and he had to make three runs at the Santa Anita Handicap, losing twice by a nose, before he grabbed his biggest prize of $86,650.

With the news story of his death was a photograph of Seabiscuit with Red Pollard, his regular jockey. It brought to mind several names that were associated with the horse. There was his owner, who was known as "Lucky Charley" Howard when his stable, led by Seabiscuit, was polishing off stakes like mad, making him first among money-winning owners. They haven't started running benefits for Howard yet—he was nineteenth among owners, with purses of $182,885 last year—but you don't see those red and white silks out front as often as you did, and they don't call him "Lucky Charley" any more.

There was Pollard, who certainly wasn't ever called lucky. The little redhead rode to fame on Seabiscuit but he missed the ones he wanted most. He'd been second, beaten by a nose by Rosemont, in the Santa Anita Handicap of 1937 and he was getting ready for a second shot the following year when he got busted up in a spill. Had to sit back and look on while his horse lost the same race by the same margin, this time to Stagehand.

He was just about recovered from the injury when he came East to ride Seabiscuit in New England. A gypsy horseman, a friend, asked him to work a two-year-old for him. The colt bolted and smashed Pollard's left leg. He was still laid up when Seabiscuit ran the most memorable race of all, the match with War Admiral.

Seabiscuit broke down in his next start, and Pollard went to the farm with him, put in a year helping to bring him around. They came back together in 1940, and together they finally won the $100,000 handicap. One hasn't heard much of Red since, although he was still riding a fair share of winners last year.

Then there's Tom Smith, who trained Seabiscuit. He's changed jobs, and things haven't been entirely smooth for him. Just got back this year after his suspension in that ephedrine case.

And then there was Georgie Woolf, who rode Seabiscuit in the match with War Admiral, the best horse race these eyes have seen. That was the race for which Sam Riddle, War Admiral's owner, dictated virtually all the conditions, including a walk-up start because his horse didn't like gates.

Ed Christmas was talking about Woolf recently, recalling how he used an old trick of quarter-horse racing to steal the start from Charley

Kurtsinger, who didn't have his experience of racing out on the Western plains. As they walked up to the line, Georgie kept Seabiscuit's head turned in toward War Admiral, determined that if he didn't get away alone he'd leave no room for War Admiral to dart past him. If ever a rider swiped a race, Woolf swiped that one at the start, leaping away ahead of a horse that was habitually first out of the gate.

Georgie Woolf? He's dead, too.

Derby Day, Southern Fried

The Calumet Capers—Coaltown and Citation

LOUISVILLE, KY., *May 1, 1948*

RAIN BEGAN to fall at precisely the instant Citation walked onto the track. It never amounted to much, though. Neither did the seventy-fourth Kentucky Derby. Not as a horse race, that is. As a horse race, the whole story is told by the chart, which reads: "Starts good, won handily, place easily."

It was that simple. There never was a contest, outside of the strictly intramural rivalry between Citation and his brother-in-baking-powder, Coaltown. There never was a moment when competition even threatened for the unmerciful pair from Calumet.

But for those to whom it means something just to see an exceptional horse in a spectacular setting, it was as good as a race could possibly be. For those who can taste a connoisseur's pleasure in the perfect performance, where the horse and the rider and the trainer stir all their talents together into a suave and bland blend, no treat could be more richly rewarding than this meat course in Colonel Matt Winn's phrenetic family picnic.

Citation was so very, very good, he ran his race so willingly in such tractable obedience to Eddie Arcaro's guidance, he won with such indisputable ease, that it simply must be true what they've been saying about him.

No horses could be got ready better to do a job more surely than the pair that put a double lock on Ben Jones' fourth Derby, bringing him to a level with Derby Dick Thompson, the only other trainer who ever slipped bridles onto four winners at this unbridled carnival. Nor could any rider do a more deft job than Arcaro did when he went gathering him rosebuds this cloudy afternoon. The dark, sharp-featured little guy who now is the only rider of four Derby winners, is an earnest student and a seasoned general when a big stake is up for grabs. He will study his mount in earlier races and in morning works; he will sit up nights weighing the merits of the opposition and devising the strategy to beat them; he will walk the track on the day of the race, testing the footing with his own small dogs.

In this case, everyone knew how earnestly he wanted to win, almost everyone assumed he had the best chance, but nobody could be sure what his tactics would be. He made them clear early.

Confident in his own mind that he had the best horse, he concentrated on two goals—keeping out of trouble and keeping within range of Coaltown. The moment he was clear after hustling out of the gate, he steered to the outside where he couldn't get pinched or blocked or pocketed and wouldn't have to abuse his horse to run away from trouble.

He did let Coaltown get six or eight lengths on top for a moment in the backstretch, but even then he was closest in pursuit, and the chances are he couldn't prevent it. Neither his horse nor any other was going to run all the way with Coaltown, whose time of 1:11 $^2/_5$ for six furlongs was sheer destruction in this mud.

Arcaro didn't let the lead endure a moment longer than necessary. He was telescoping the margin before he left the backstretch. He was moving resolutely on the turn. He had Coaltown collared on the last bit of bend. He straightened into the lead. He flicked Citation once between the eighth and the sixteenth poles—or so it seemed from here, although maybe he was just drawing his whip to wave it alongside Citation's jowls the rest of the way home.

He was the last one back after the field pulled up. Newbold Pierson rode back a little ahead of him aboard Coaltown and got cheered by customers who mistook his red silks for Arcaro's. When Eddie returned he was grinning like a skull and gabbing to the outrider, thirteen words to the dozen.

This was the third time he'd got up on a favorite and gone riding out after his fourth Derby. Last year he's been second on Phalanx; the year before, fourth on Lord Boswell. Before that, trying for his third victory, he'd picked Greentree's Devil Diver and lost to Greentree's Shut Out.

"For once I took the right horse," he chortled to his employer, Warren Wright, in the winner's circle today.

Wright chortled right back. His Calumet Farm now had three Derby winners, two seconds, and one third in eight starters. He also had $93,400 in first and second money out of today's turn of business. There is a grave shortage of people who are unable to chortle when surrounded by $93,400.

A Very Pious Story

The Christian Bettor: A Tale from the Track

LOUISVILLE, KY., *May 4, 1948*

A T THE Derby, Walter Haight, a well-fed horse author from Washington, told it this way.

There's this horseplayer and he can't win a bet. He's got patches in his pants from the way even odds-on favorites run up the alley when he's backing them and the slump goes on until he's utterly desperate. He's ready to listen to any advice when a friend tells him: "No wonder you don't have any luck, you don't live right. Nobody could do any good the way you live. Why, you don't even go to church. Why don't you get yourself straightened out and try to be a decent citizen and just see then if things don't get a lot better for you?"

Now, the guy has never exactly liked to bother heaven with his troubles. Isn't even sure whether they have horse racing up there and would understand his difficulties. But he's reached a state where steps simply have to be taken. So, the next day being Sunday, he does go to church and sits attentively through the whole service and joins in the hymn-singing and says "Amen" at the proper times and puts his buck on the collection plate.

All that night he lies awake waiting for a sign that things are going to get better; nothing happens. Next day he gets up and goes to the track, but this time he doesn't buy a racing form or scratch sheet or Jack Green's Card or anything. Just gets his program and sits in the stands studying the field for the first race and waiting for a sign. None comes, so he passes up the race. He waits for the second race and concentrates on the names of the horses for that one, and again there's no inspiration. So again he doesn't bet. Then, when he's looking them over for the third, something seems to tell him to bet on a horse named Number 4.

"Lord, I'll do it," he says, and he goes down and puts the last fifty dollars he'll ever be able to borrow on Number 4 to win. Then he goes back to his seat and waits until the horses come onto the track.

Number 4 is a little fractious in the parade, and the guy says, "Lord, please quiet him down. Don't let him get himself hurt." The horse settles down immediately and walks calmly into the starting gate.

"Thank you, Lord," says the guy. "Now please get him off clean. He don't have to break on top, but get him away safe without getting slammed or anything, please." The gate comes open and Number 4 is off well, close up in fifth place and saving ground going to the first turn. There he begins to move up a trifle on the rail and for an instant it looks as though he might be in close quarters.

"Let him through, Lord," the guy says. "Please make them horses open up a little for him." The horse ahead moves out just enough to let Number 4 through safely.

"Thank you, Lord," says the guy, "but let's not have no more trouble like that. Have the boy take him outside." Sure enough, as they go down the backstretch the jockey steers Number 4 outside, where he's lying fourth.

They're going to the far turn when the guy gets agitated. "Don't let that boy use up the horse," he says. "Don't let the kid get panicky, Lord. Tell him to rate the horse a while." The rider reaches down and takes a couple of wraps on the horse and keeps him running kind, just cooking on the outside around the turn.

Wheeling into the stretch, Number 4 is still lying fourth. "Now, Lord," the guy says. "Now we move. Tell that kid to go to the stick." The boy outs with his bat and, as Ted Atkinson says, he really "scouges" the horse. Number 4 lays his ears back and gets to running.

He's up to third. He closes the gap ahead and now he's lapped on the second horse and now he's at his throat latch and now he's past him.

He's moving on the leader and everything behind him is good and cooked. He closes ground stride-by-stride with the boy working on him for all he's worth and the kid up front putting his horse to a drive.

"Please, Lord," the guy says. "Let him get out in front. Give me one call on the top end, anyway."

Number 4 keeps coming. At the eighth pole he's got the leader collared. He's past him. He's got the lead by two lengths.

"Thank you, Lord," the guy says, "I'll take him from here. Come on, you son of a bitch!"

Super

Mr. Frank Keogh, Steward of Aqueduct

NEW YORK, N.Y., *September 8, 1949*

IN THE steeplechase a horse named Leche Hombre tossed his rider at the first fence and Frank Keogh, watching from the Aqueduct infield, kind of sucked in his breath.

"That's what I hate to see," he said, "a boy fall."

"You ever ride the jumpers?" he was asked.

"Not in a race," he said. "I used to school 'em."

Frank Keogh is the little guy who scrubs Aqueduct's face with such loving care that the Queens County garden spot is handsomer right now than it ever appeared before. Now track superintendent there, he used to be a jockey, as anyone might guess from his size and the weathered, crinkly look around his eyes and his large, strong hands. What you wouldn't guess is that he did his first riding wearing skirts.

"It was in a Hippodrome," he said, "riding Roman standing races around the county fairs. I can still remember how I looked with a white band around my head and a little short skirt like a toga.

"I'd been a kid growing up in Charleston, S.C., helping around a livery stable. Fellow that ran the stable took some horses for a debt and I shipped out with him to the Fort Erie track, but when we got there we found the horses had been ruled off and couldn't race. We got 'em into a freight car that night and shipped out. Before very long the man and the horses disappeared and I was stranded.

"I hit Wheeling, W. Va., where I picked up a little work galloping horses for my feed. Then I bumped into Mr. Cheek. Ever hear of him, Tom Cheek? Quite a character. Long white beard down to here. He lived to be over a hundred and he was still racing horses when he died down in Cuba.

"Well, he gave me a job galloping for him and he bought me my first pair of long pants. Things got tough that winter, though. There wasn't enough to eat. I caught on with this fellow with the Hippodrome he took around the fairs. I'd ride two horses standing up on three in a tandem, riding the rear one with two in front. He had a dozen or so greyhounds and I'd get on a horse and race the dogs. The man had nothing but thoroughbreds, and sometimes we'd race on the half-milers.

"The way it was, I just drifted around and drifted around. Finally I got out to Seattle. The man I was working for had promised to give me some mounts—I was sixteen and I'd been working with horses five years but I'd never had a mount on a regular track and never had a winner anywhere. When the meeting started, the man had another rider under contract.

"I hollered and he said he couldn't let a green boy like me ride his good horses. He owed me two or three hundred dollars so I asked for the money. He said he couldn't pay me. So there I was, sitting on the fence feeling pretty low, and along came Captain Rice.

"Captain R. R. Rice. He was another character. He had a long beard, too, white as snow. He asked me what was the trouble and I told him I was giving up. 'Come along with me,' he said, and he took me to the clerk of scales and said, 'Give this boy a license,' and next day he put on this big old bay gelding named Duellist.

"Walking out of the paddock, the horse stopped and laid his ears back. I just took my whip and tickled his ear and he started walking along again. Going to the post—the race was a mile and an eighth—he stopped again and I touched him with the whip again.

"The starter hollered, 'You crazy fool! That horse'll kill you!' but the horse broke on top and we must've won by ten lengths. Then I found out, it was supposed to be a crazy horse. Down in New Orleans he'd jumped over the fence and into the betting ring and kicked all the bookmakers' slates to pieces.

"I didn't know it, and that was the answer. Tell a boy a horse is a bad actor and he'll grab hold of him and try to jerk him around, and the horse knows the boy is scared and so he gets scared, too. I won seven straight races with Duellist and should've won the eighth but the boys ganged up and took care of me in that one. I'd been winning too much for a green boy."

Frank Keogh went on for twenty years, riding and training horses here and all over Europe. He came home when he saw war ahead, bought a couple of horses, then changed his mind.

"I couldn't get decent stable help," he said. "I can't stand seeing horses abused. If I'd tried to go on. I'd have wound up in an asylum or the electric chair."

"Life is similar for a track superintendent, eh?"

"There are plenty of headaches in this, too. Phone rings all hours of the night. Man ships in without stalls reserved, the gateman doesn't know what to do, so he calls me out of bed. Sometimes you can find stalls for a man overnight, and then the next day you can't get him out. There's one was ordered out of here last fall and he's still here with his horses. A real good stayer."

Missouri Mortician

Herman Keiser Undertakes the Masters

Augusta, Ga., *April 7, 1946*

THE TALL man with the look of a guy who has known great sorrow sat in the Augusta National Golf Club, unmoving, expressionless, not drinking or eating or saying much.

Just sitting there like a ballplayer in a hotel lobby.

"Get a load of Laughing Boy Keiser," somebody said. "And hey, look who's talking to him. That a picture, eh?"

It was Craig Wood talking to him and it was indeed a picture. For here was Herman Keiser, who looks like a Missouri mortician, sweating out the time between his finish in the Masters golf tournament and the moment when they'd say his score was good enough to win. And there, talking quietly to him, was the guy who'd done the same thing in the same place eleven years ago.

Exactly eleven years ago Wood sat in this club with a score of 282 on the board—exactly the score Keiser had tonight—and the mob was thumping his back and buying wine and shouting: "Boy, o boy! What a wedding anniversary for you, Craig, old pal!" And then just when the committee was ready to draw him a check for the first prize, Gene Sarazen shot a double-eagle 2 on the fifteenth hole and came home tied for first and the next day Gene won in a playoff.

Maybe they both remembered that as they talked, although Keiser hadn't been around in those days. At any rate, they could hear the crowd cheering for Ben Hogan as he came ripping home with his sights set on that first prize of twenty-five hundred dollars. Every cheer meant that Hogan was one stroke closer.

When he was on the seventeenth green Keiser heard that Hogan

playing behind him was three under par. Which meant they were tied and due for a playoff tomorrow. As he sat there in the club he was told Hogan needed a par-4 to preserve the tie.

"I hope," he said, "Ben shoots either a three or a five."

He's a curious guy, this newest and most obscure winner of the Masters. Ten thousand people paid five dollars apiece today expecting to see him chewed up like a sad-faced Christian flung among lions. They went clamoring and skidding up slippery slopes and trooping through sand traps and stomping across greens and every now and then they caught up with the parade and, standing tiptoe, saw Keiser's white sun visor as he straightened after hitting a ball.

But they didn't see him blow up. They caught, for their five-spot, occasional glimpses of a guy who approached and shot with sad detachment, like an undertaker approaching a job he didn't particularly fancy. He is the walkingest and waitingest and studyingest guy that ever won a major competition.

He hits a shot and then he ambles down and stares with distaste at his lie and then he walks over some nearby hill and stands gazing unhappily at the flag. Then he comes back, glares at the ball again, lifts a club from his bag and takes a few practice swings. At last he stands over the ball and shifts his feet and waggles his hips and brandishes his club threateningly, and at long length he hits his shot.

When he gets on the green he slows up. He walks from the ball to the pin. Then he walks from the pin to the ball. Then he gets behind the ball and squats and studies the line. Then he takes his putter from the bag and aims it like a rifle across the ball. Then he swings it crosswise, tilts it this way, tilts it that way, and sights across it like a painter stepping back and measuring his canvas across his brush. Then he creaks up and pokes the bloody thing into the cup.

He never varied this routine today. He never showed a real trace of nervousness. He hit his shots firmly and patted his putts deliberately. Even on the eighteenth green he gave no sign that he heard the applause which greeted him after coming out of the rough onto the carpet.

He walked up and took his time and then swung his putter, aiming for the cup twenty feet away. He gave the ball a bit of "body English" as it rolled, swinging his hips and taking two or three prowling steps to his right. The ball rolled past the cup. He tried again, deliberately, and when he missed the cup again, his tall, lank figure sagged. That meant three putts on the eighteenth. And that could mean the tournament. Even as he tapped his last putt, a cheer rattled across the hills from Hogan's gallery.

Keiser went into the club and waited. The whole gallery flocked back up the course to pick up Hogan. Ben was playing along as usual, his face expressionless, a cigarette always burning between his lips. He came up to the eighteenth green needing a par for a tie, a birdie to win. He three-putted. As the ball rolled past the cup, he straightened, shuddered a little, and looked down at the grass. Then he strode over and pushed the ball in and then they gave the prize to Keiser. Even then Herman's face was mournful.

Kings Get In Free

Olympic Torch Lights Up Wembley Stadium

LONDON, U.K., *July 29, 1948*

ENGLAND'S BIGGEST track meet in forty years opened this afternoon with a pageant of nationalism, an orgy of oratory and a paroxysm of symbolism but no running, jumping, or bulging of the biceps. The recorded casualties were a half-dozen Boy Scouts and Sea Scouts who fainted under the malevolent sun which beat upon Wembley Stadium with padded brutality.

King George VI, perspiring royally in his gold-braided sailor suit, and his missus, Queen Elizabeth, in some yards of pale blue fluff with a large, floppy hat to match, got in on passes (no tax or service charge). About eighty-two thousand cash customers paid up to two guineas apiece ($8.40) to watch the stately and magnificent rinky-dink that set off the games of the fourteenth Olympiad.

The King earned his free ticket, though. The gentry and the costers who bought theirs had only to sit and swelter in the great, steaming, concrete cauldron. His Majesty had to stand at rigid, humid attention for fifty minutes, which is the equivalent of clutching a strap on the East Side subway from Parkchester to Fourteenth Street; he had to salute the flags of fifty-nine nations carried past the royal box. He had to make a sixteen-word speech. Never were the hardships of the monarch business more amply demonstrated although, admittedly, the hours and salary are usually very good.

Besides sitting and sweltering, the cash trade beat sweaty palms red, yowled and chanted and waved flags as the musclemen of their countries marched by. For let there be no mistake about it, these

Olympics are the amateur sporting world's clearest expression of nationalism.

It was the desire of the games' founder, it says here in the program, that "the spirit of international comity be advanced by the celebration of chivalrous and peaceful contests," and Lord Burghley, the reformed Olympic hurdler who is chairman of the Organizing Committee which runs these games, spoke of "kindling a torch of that ageless and heartfelt prayer of mankind for peace and good will among men." But when their teams marched in, partisans hollered just as fight fans do for Rocky Graziano, who is no career torch-kindler.

They made clear the sound and healthy point that in the carnival of international competition which the ensuing fortnight will see, the idea is going to be, as it should be, to knock the spots off the other guy.

Wembley Stadium at two o'clock was a cooked gaboon of concrete, its gray slopes packed, its currycombed infield a vivid green encircled by a track of bright red clay. In one section of seats, the massed bands of His Majesty's Brigade of Guards blared and oompahed. Across the arena, about two-fifteen, a great covey of Olympic brass lined up in the sweaty elegance of silk hats and frock coats.

At two-forty-five exactly (in the king-and-emperor business, punctuality is of the essence) His Majesty came hiking out of a tunnel under the stands, shook hands with Burghley and the president of the International Olympic Committee, a silk-hatted Swede named J. Sigfrid Edström. With these two trailing him, the King then strolled the length of the waxworks, pumping hands with each exhibit. Amid a moderate patter of handclapping, he walked up to the royal box and sat at his spouse's left, directly under the tote board for Wembley's dog races.

Out of a runway at the east end of the oval came a Boy Scout with bare knees and a sign reading "Greece." Being the original Olympic nation, Greece's team led the march. The Greeks in the front ranks were all bald, obviously committeemen, caterers, and coaches. Their big silken flag, a white cross on a blue field, dipped as it passed the royal box. The King, standing, snapped to salute.

Thereafter, he remained standing as the flags passed in alphabetical order, never once shifting to relieve the heat on his royal bunions, saluting even those flags which were not dipped. About a half-dozen standards were not lowered, either because of national rules, or because their bearers hadn't been sufficiently rehearsed, or as a form of political criticism. Ireland's flag was half-dipped; grudgingly might be an accurate adverb. Colombia's didn't go down, but its bearer snapped into a majestic goose-step as he passed. By and large, the teams marched better than baseball squads do at the flag-raising on opening day.

The first wholehearted burst of applause came for Australia, first of the United Kingdom affiliates to show. However, the loudest enthusiasm manifested between A and E was inspired by the Danish team, whose claque set off a volley of yells and upped with a regular flurry of red Danish flags with their white crosses. Subsequently, this section boisterously hailed all Scandinavians—the Finns, Norwegians, Swedes, and even Iceland's team. As each such group appeared, the rooters gave off a chant that sounded, from this seat, like "Yale, Yale, Yale."

There were big teams and little. Panama was represented by one guy in a Panama hat, not Lloyd LaBeach, the sprinter. India's team wore baby-blue burnooses. New Zealand's had what looked like smoking jackets. The Swiss wore caps like lady softball players. The United States got a restrained hand; the last man in our ranks halted to snap the King's picture.

Well, the King finally got to sit down. He looked on while trumpeters trumpeted, speakers spoke, and attendants released a great mess of caged pigeons, which zoomed and swooped over eighty-two thousand unprotected skulls. The billing promised seven thousand pigeons, or one for every twelfth head, but it looked like maybe two thousand. Chances are the brass didn't dare turn loose that many squab in this hungry nation. Almost immediately twenty-one guns boomed. Sounded like first day of the duck season off Little Tail Point in Green Bay, Wisconsin.

Now a tall young blond in his underwear burst through the entrance and circled the track, bearing aloft the Olympic torch, a blinding magnesium sparkler which hurt the eyes. Theoretically, the torch had been lighted on Mt. Olympus and delivered by Western Union boys running in relays across Europe, with a Ford truck following with a spare torch in case the real McCoy went out. Actually, the torch that appeared here was a ringer, a special oversize job carried on the last relay from a suburb like Bay Ridge.

The torch-bearer dashed up into the stands, brandished his torch on high and dropped it into a tall concrete bird bath—from which red flame arose. That flame will burn throughout these games.

The crowd made with the tonsils. It was hokum. It was pure Hollywood. But it was good. You had to like it.

★ FISHING FOR TROUT ★

Opening Day

A Foursome Tackles the Banks of the Beaverkill

Roscoe, N.Y., *April 16, 1951*

At six a.m. the climate of the Catskills was dropping as the gentle rain from heaven upon the place beneath. In this instance the place beneath was a swatch of muddy turf outside a window of the Reed Cottage in Roscoe, New York.

As anybody knows, if he can read either English or the rod-and-gun columns, the stroke of six a.m. is to the angler as the clang of a bell to an old fire horse. In this case it was like the clang of a bell to an English heavyweight. There were snuffling sounds, such as a man makes breathing resin, and the creak of bedsprings as a body rolled over and snuggled deeper.

Two hours later the voice of Sparse Grey Hackle, angler, filled the house. The rain had abated, but this was a trick. It was lying in wait. It lay in wait through the hurried two-hour breakfast and the drive to the "Big River." Then it pounced, in hissing, gleeful torrents, mixed with one pounding rush of hail.

Harry Darbee, angler and fly-tier, had joined the party and suggested starting on the "Big River"—the Beaverkill below the Junction Pool, which is formed by the confluence of the Willowemoc and the upper Beaverkill, or "Little River." The theory was that with the water high and roily, the "Big River" would be less crowded than the smaller streams.

It wasn't exactly deserted, except by trout, but there was less congestion downstream than, for example, at the Junction Pool, where worm fishermen lined the banks. The Junction Pool is always patronized enthusiastically in the hope of landing a beamoc. The beamoc is a brown trout with two heads, one of which gazes longingly down the Beaverkill, while the other hankers for the Willowemoc. Unable to make up its minds, the beamoc lives its life out in the Junction Pool. Harry Darbee wears a portrait of one on the shoulder patch on his fishing jacket.

Mr. Darbee lives in Roscoe, and these waters speak to him with a thousand tongues. On opening day he listened to all the tongues, and what they said brought him no joy. Neither did Mr. Hackle's thermometer, which said the water temperature was 42 degrees. Harry said this meant the trout, if any, would be logy and disinclined to battle the savage current in midstream.

He advised working the slack water along the shore, where the malingerers would be loafing. The advice proved sound. In less than two hours, during which a tempting variety of bucktails, wet flies, and nymphs was offered on four rods, there came a strike. Meade Schaeffer, angler and artist, got the strike but not the fish.

Now and then a pale, domestic brand of sunshine was produced. If a guy happened to be out of the water detaching his fly from a willow branch, a semblance of circulation was restored at these moments. During one such interval it was decided to try the "Little River."

There the traffic was heavier and the fishing better, loosely speaking. That is, Meade Schaeffer caught a number of small trout on a spruce fly, and Harry Darbee had one strike that felt good, he said. Mr. Schaeffer said his were all gray trout, hatchery fish, and he released them. The other members of the party said nothing of interest.

Later in the afternoon a worm fisherman walked up and splotched his rig in where a fly-fisherman was working a streamer. The fly-fisherman reeled up, backed off, and asked: "Any action?"

"I got eight," the worm fisherman said bitterly. "No size. I'm fishing a pool, feller comes along, throws his bait right where I got my line. So I got to leave. So he catches a twenty-inch brown and an eighteen-inch brookie. Right in my pool!"

"Some people," the fly-fisherman said, "have no manners."

"You said it," the worm fisherman said.

He splotched his bait in again and caught a large sucker.

"Do you want it?" he asked politely.

"No, thank you." It was time to quit, anyhow, and go see what the boys were having in the Antrim Lodge. They were having plenty. This may account for the fact that traffic was lighter on the "Little River" the next day.

That second day was raw and splattery with a yammering wind that snatched flies out of the air and flung them into treetops. If there were trout in the treetops, they didn't seem to be feeding. The day's bag totaled one fish, caught, naturally, by Meade Schaeffer.

It was suggested that May would tell a different story after the water warmed and the hatches began.

"Yes," Harry Darbee said, "sometimes you can hook into a nice one. I tied into a pretty fair one last summer. He straightened out a bend in the river and took out two covered bridges before I landed him. And then I had to turn him loose."

"Why?"

"The water level," Mr. Darbee said, "dropped when I took him out. Would've ruined the fishing."

The Rills of Home

A Lovely Spring Morning in That Stream Just Out Back

STAMFORD, CONN., *May 11, 1952*

SINCE THE opening of the trout season there had been only one opportunity to join the booted host clamoring through the pools and stumbling over boulders in the home stream, which passes no more than a stone's throw—if you use a catapult—from the edge of the mortgage. One hurried hour at evening had been rewarded by one vicious strike, which was, naturally, missed.

Now it was midmorning, soft and bright, and the working stiffs who clutter the stream on weekends and in the evenings were off about their dreary affairs. The only other loafer in sight was casting a dry fly from the bank of a pool formed by a little dam just above a bridge. There were no rises.

Since the other vagrant was working upstream, etiquette suggested starting below him and going down. A brown streamer fly was dropped at the foot of the dam. It was this lure that had brought the strike several evenings earlier. Strictly speaking, a streamer isn't a fly at all, because it simulates no insect. Authorities who have consulted intelligent trout on the matter report that it looks, to the fishy eye, like a mentally retarded minnow.

Perhaps twenty feet below the dam, the brook funnels noisily under the bridge. There is an old saying that it's a poor bridge that doesn't have a fish under it. On a cast across the brook, the fly was swept close to the concrete abutment. In the clear, swift water there was a flash of pursuit, but the attacker merely pawed with a light jab, then turned and fled like Jersey Joe Walcott. Neither insult nor bribe could tempt him back to fight like a man.

Once through the narrow waist of the bridge, the stream relaxes with a soft sigh, like a lady who has removed her girdle. There is a deep, fast pool where the river takes a long breath before rushing at the boulders below. A search was undertaken for some morsel more tasty than a streamer.

Some anglers tie their own flies, some buy them. This one just has his. The tackle box is a sort of slum-clearance project, a dumping-place for reels without handles, rotting lines, bits of broken leader, and mangy, unkempt tufts of silk and feather, all preserved in a blend of fly dressing, mosquito dope, and machine oil.

Out of the debris came a thing that had started existence as a Coach-man, not recently. This was tied onto the leader, flicked out toward the head of the pool, and allowed to take over from there. The line swung downstream and tightened. Something yellow showed beneath the surface. A good fish cut across the pool, ran downstream, turned, and came back, silent and sullen.

Brought close to the net, he made one more short run, then shrugged his shoulders. He returned to the net, not willingly but resigned. He was no showpiece for mounting on a board over the mantel, no elder statesman of his tribe. Still, he was a respectable member of the younger set, probably a second vice president of the Junior Chamber of Commerce. A dressy number, with bright orange spots.

More than a year had passed since an adult member of his family had been led into this landing net. All of a sudden the woods were blithe with birdsong. Dogwood was the purest possible white in the new green foliage. The brook chuckled. It was a lovely day.

A little farther down, the stream plunges between big rocks and flattens out into a brief, rapid run. Trees crowd the banks, reaching out to catch backcasts. The only way to get a fly into the run is from below.

Fishing a wet fly upstream isn't the simplest trick in the world. A floating lure can be watched and the slack of the line retrieved as the fly rides down. A sunken fly disappears in fast water; keeping control of the slackening line is a matter of guesswork.

The trout lurking in this run, however, was young and inexperienced and had no way of knowing how unskillful an opponent he was matched with. Midway of the run, he hit that seedy old pensioner of a Coachman from below, making a small swirl on the broken surface. Fright, rather than skill, lifted the rod tip, and the barb went in.

The little fellow came out of the water, bounded down into swifter rapids, where the current lent him more weight than he owned. He was willing but overmatched, and the net got him, too.

Two trout inside the first hour. This strained plausibility. Might be a course record was in the making, if the old Coachman could hold out.

The old Coachman couldn't. A cleverly aimed cast caught a rock, and the hook broke off. Not that it mattered, probably, but there wasn't another fly of the same pattern at hand. Almost certainly it didn't matter, because the next couple of hours were devoted mostly to arboreal life, recovering backcasts from the treetops. Up among the birds' nests one pattern is about as good as another.

The place where a good strike had been felt on the earlier visit is a run below overhanging branches at the foot of rapids. On this return trip, the spot was worked from both sides, from above and below with wet flies, streamers, and dry flies.

No response. The ugly suspicion occurred that perhaps somebody else had come along between visits and removed the trout. That's the trouble with this modern forty-hour work week. It gives trout-rustlers leisure time to come stealing a man's fish when they ought to be selling insurance.

Young Man
with Fly Rod

A High-Summer Saturday with Mr. S.G.H. and Son

V<small>ACATION WAS</small> almost over when Mr. Sparse Grey Hackle called
and said how about a weekend of matching wits with the trout that
live in the Neversink River. Frankly, it looked like an overmatch from
the beginning, but it had been the sort of vacation that cried aloud for
relief.

N<small>EAR</small> C<small>LARYVILLE</small>, N.Y., *August 4, 1951*

A task force of three was made up swiftly. It included a young man
of twelve, going on thirteen, who had never before attempted to mislead a trout with a tuft of feather and barb of steel. He had, however,
shown an encouraging spirit several summers earlier when he was
eight or nine and used to accompany his parent on forays against the
smallmouth bass of Wisconsin. The pair would angle lazily through the
mornings from a rowboat until the noonday sun drove them ashore.
Then they'd seek out the nearest crossroads tavern, where each would
satisfy his appetite according to his needs.

On one such day the young man stuffed his face with a ham sand-
wich, slaked down the mess with a Coke, and observed: "Gee, Dad, this
is the life, ain't it? Fishing and eating in saloons."

There was to be no eating in saloons on the Neversink expedition.
Mr. Hackle had arranged for accommodations with Mrs. George Stail-
ing, a patient and gracious lady whose farmhouse near Claryville offers
immaculate lodging and prodigious fodder and commands a tempting stretch of river. Adroitly dodging thunderbolts that came crashing

down out of the Catskills, the car crept through the rainy darkness and made bivouac there.

At least one member of the party had a sleepless night and admitted it next morning, shamefaced, because it does seem childish to get so keyed up on the eve of a day in a trout stream. Always happens, though.

The young man and Mr. Hackle had slept soundly and they set a punishing pace on the mile-and-a-half hike into the water formerly held by Mr. Ed Hewitt. This is open water now, soon to be converted from river to lake when a dam, in construction, creates a new reservoir so that New Yorkers may have water to emasculate their scotch. It is beautiful water that comes boiling down out of the great, greenish Camp Pool through a long, rocky run; it was still perfectly clear after a night of rain and, said Mr. Hackle, who knows the river, it was low.

Mr. Hackle set one of his company to floating a dry fly into the broken water at the head of the run. The fly was a big White Wulff, and as it rode the wavelets tiny brook trout slapped at it impudently. They came to no harm. Perhaps they only flicked it with their tails, not actually trying to bite the fly. Or maybe they took sample nibbles, said "Pfui," and spat at leisure, properly confident that the dope holding the rod couldn't get his reflexes working in time to sink the barb into their sassy faces.

Meanwhile Sparse had tied a wet fly to the young man's leader and led him to the middle of the run and watched as the first cast was made. The first cast took a fish. Details can be distasteful. If it was a very young and very small and very inexperienced fish, there is no point in mentioning that. The young man was young and inexperienced, too.

The point is, the young man made one cast and got a rise and set the hook and got the trout home and then sent him about his business with a sore lip and, presumably, greater wisdom than he had possessed before.

Mr. Hackle, who realizes that the great teacher is the one who knows when to let well enough alone, retired to the tail of the run, where he caught and released a couple of juveniles. His pair and the young man's singleton were the only fish hooked that day. That didn't matter; there'd be another chance the next day.

"It's sure got it over bass-fishing," the young man said. When he was reminded that he had drawn blood on the first cast of his life, he had the grace to smile in deprecation of the size of his catch. He did not remark that there was, really, nothing difficult about this game.

When it was mentioned that he was the only member of his family to catch a trout in 1951, he laughed with pleasure and made no comment. No intelligible comment, anyway. He was down on all fours in a bramble patch at the moment and his mouth was full of wild raspberries.

Somewhat Like
Poetry

The Lessons of a Sunday on the Neversink River

O<small>N THE</small> first day of the great offensive against the trout of the Neversink River in the Catskills, the young man of the party had cast a fly into the rapids for the first time in his twelve years, had hooked and landed a speckled trout on that cast, and had released his prize undamaged. He had met successfully the first test prescribed by Mr. Walton, who observed some three hundred years ago that:

N<small>EAR</small> C<small>LARYVILLE</small>, N.Y., *August 5, 1951*

"Angling is somewhat like poetry, men are to be born so: I mean, with inclinations to it. . . ."

Now, on the second day, he was to meet a sterner test. He was to study patience and to learn that when the occasional angler goes fishing, conditions are invariably vile. There had been much rain in the preceding thirty-six hours and it rained again on the eve of the second day. The river remained tractable, however, and Mr. Sparse Grey Hackle, who was first on the stream that morning, had an encouraging report to make when his two pupils joined him.

Fishing the great pool just below the Stailings' farm Mr. Hackle had tied into a live one. The fish had taken the fly so lightly that Mr. Hackle thought he was another of the silly, suicidal little brookies that had been impaling themselves on the barb up to then. Had there been time for a second thought, no effort would have been made to set the hook in another of the tiny rascals. But when the strike came, reflex action lifted the rod tip, and the barb went home.

Reflex action guided the trout, too. He stripped line off the reel with a heavy rush. Now he was across the stream, sulking in a crevice of the rock ledge that rose on the far side. Mr. Hackle tried gingerly to coax him away, but as he tightened his line it came in slack. Against the rock, the leader had parted where it joined the fly.

All this was immensely promising. So was the look of the river. At the Stailings', the Neversink comes down out of a stretch of broad, flat water, dances across a rocky shoal, flattens out again, then pitches swiftly between boulders into a swirling run that fades into a tremendous pool several hundred yards long. For a distance you can see a stony rib in midstream, then the current swings deeply to the far bank, where a rock wall begins to take shape against the hillside. It was there, against the wall, that Mr. Hackle's trout had escaped.

Starting tardily, Mr. Hackle's pupils scarcely had time to survey the water before they had to reel up and report for midday dinner. Afterward a leaden lethargy lay on the senior members. They stretched out on beds and snored noisily while the young man pored through comic books, waiting out another rainstorm that blew in from the hills.

Later the task force deployed, Mr. Hackle working down into the huge pool, the young man taking the upper rapids, with their companion fishing a Light Cahill, wet, in the run at the head of the deep. Twice little geysers spurted up from the fast water alongside the Light Cahill as it swung down between boulders. Twice the angler responded too slowly to make connections.

It was getting more than slightly ridiculous. For the better part of two days now, small trout had been toying with both wet and dry flies, and this rod had flubbed every opportunity. The young man came through his run upstream and walked down to report that he had got one good rise and missed.

As he stood there, small rises dimpled the water in the head of the pool where it deepened and slowed against the far bank. Out in midstream, a trout took the Light Cahill and was coaxed to the net with a shout of incredulous triumph. At long last it became possible to boast that no member of the party had been skunked. After a conference it was decided to have a modest plaque struck off to mark the site of the triumph.

"I hope he isn't hurt," the young man said as the trout was netted. "He doesn't look as if he could stand much punishment."

"Just a cracked lip," he was told as the prize was released. "It's no worse than a bad cold."

Evening was coming on and there was every reason to expect lively action at last. But within a few minutes the young man said: "It seems to me this river's getting awful dirty." The water had clouded suddenly and now trash was floating, twigs and leaves and bits of forest debris. Just when activity should have increased, even the smallest rises ceased. Almost as swiftly as it can be told, the river rose, an ugly saffron.

"We've had it," the young man was told. "This, you must learn, is how it is when you go fishing. It rains or it freezes or it comes up drought or you break your last rod tip in a screen door. All this rain we've been having left the river clear, but now there's been either a flash flood or a landslide somewhere above us, and now we're through."

"Look," the young man said, "the river has cut through behind us and now we're on an island. How can it come up so fast?"

There was, he was told, no mystery about that. Mr. Walton wrote of a river in Judea "that runs swiftly all the six days of the week, and stands still and rests all the Sabbath." The Neversink was merely reversing the order, this being a Sunday.

No Orchestral Din

Fifty Strikes a Day

PARC DE LAURENTIDES, QUEBEC, *June 16, 1947*

An OPEN threat to the trout population of the Laurentian Mountains was issued in this space Saturday. Well, it turned out that this was kiddies' day among the fish of these parts and so the day was devoted to putting the hooks to the piscatorial knothole gang, Northern woods division, the idea being to take the little fellows on in a series of tune-up bouts preparatory to meeting more broad-shouldered adversaries later.

If a man came back from a day on a trout stream in New York or Pennsylvania or New England and said, yeah, he'd had medium luck, with maybe fifty strikes, you might be reluctant to cash his checks. Up here you take a faintly resentful attitude toward fifty strikes if the strikers are small. You find yourself deliberately jerking the fly away from the trout to teach them the vanity of greed. Using two flies on the leader, you sometimes have to jerk them simultaneously away from two or more trout as they elbow and jostle and shoulder one another like crowds at a mutuel window.

The morning was cold and cloudy with a toothy wind. We drove to the Piker River and started upstream on an overgrown trail. Vic led the way. Vic is a young gentleman with very little English, who used to be a prospector in the Hudson Bay territory. Now he works as a guide, which is the local term for a moving van. He walked ahead carrying a pack scarcely bigger than a grand piano.

Now and then Vic paused, pointed out a section of the boiling stream and said, "Here. Sometimes is good." We tried and got only moist. We'd wade ashore and go plodding on through the deep muskeg, which is a tweedy and outdoorsy name for mud. The trail was lavishly supplied with signs of moose, their cloven hoofprints deep in the muskeg. No moose made personal appearances, however, which suggested the possibility that the signs were left by a stock moose which the Laurentides management leads on leash up and down the trails to impress visitors.

A mile and a half of floundering brought us to a rotting dam. There, in the boiling water below the old sluice, the first good trout of the day made a pig of himself over a Parmachene Belle. He rushed around frantically, tried to run downstream, had to be checked and came lashing up through the current; he was still swearing a blue streak when the net went under him.

The commotion drew a crowd. In streams near home a single small splash frightens the trout for miles around. Up here you use flies the size of prunes and splotch them into the water with a noise like a troop of Boy Scouts swimming. This titillates the brutes.

We took enough fair-sized fish for lunch and returned a lot of smaller ones. We also missed strikes in outrageous numbers. Vic was courteous enough to suggest that this was the fault of the fish, which were young and inexperienced. The spring has been cold—snow still lies in the brush and the birches are not yet in leaf—and Vic says the big, big trout that know how to abuse a fly are waiting for summer in the Piker River.

We lunched on fish and bacon and cheese and ham and pork sandwiches and tea and cake and strawberry preserves, while a partridge in the brush near by whistled for love's sweet sake. The sound was the same that gallants in the front of the poolroom make when a babe walks by. Vic picked up a stick cut cleanly by a beaver and pointed to the neat toothmarks. He showed us the stump of a sizable tree, severed a foot from the ground in the same manner.

So we caught a few more small ones and worked downstream to the car. Back at camp we dined at a window overlooking Clarence Gagnon Lake. The sky had cleared and the water was the preposterous blue of a picture postcard, with evergreens rising steeply on the far side. There is no formal floor show at Le Gite, no orchestral din. You watch the tiny wind squalls racing across the lake and then you glance through the windows across the room and here comes a black bear waddling down a steep trail out of the woods. The first was a big guy who messed around behind a woodpile until some disturbance sent him lumbering back up the trail, running like Steve Owen.

"Was one," said Yvon Cote, son of the camp manager, "breaking into the icebox. We had to shot him. There." He pointed to a large fur rug, complete with teeth, on the floor.

Pretty soon a smaller bear arrived, accompanied by a tiny cub. The cub got scared right off. He made the furlong into the woods in eleven seconds flat. Mom watched him go and then sat down on her hunkers like a setter dog and looked at the people. The people looked back at her.

So then we went out to fish the evening rise on the lake. It turned out to be the evening settle, but we did get enough for breakfast. The best was about thirteen inches and stockily built, but he fought like Lee Oma.

Rainbow in the Dust

Catch and Release in a Desert Swimming Pool

PHOENIX, ARIZ., *March 17, 1952*

I T WAS late afternoon, the sun reddened the hump of Camelback Mountain, and horseplayers were streaming out of Arizona Downs, across the highway, when Old Scratch hit the fly. He was played with delicate skill, was led to the edge of the pool and lifted from the water.

Old Scratch wasn't the most muscular rainbow trout ever hooked, being a slender and spiritless seven inches. Still, he commanded a certain respect; he was the first trout ever snatched by this angler out of a concrete swimming pool in a desert. He was returned reverently to the water.

What must be the most densely populated trout pool in America lies ten minutes from downtown Phoenix in a broad and arid plain. A sign at the highway reads: "Trout Fishing." The motorist parks beside a shack tended by Mr. Pat Brazell, a thin, leathery party out of Rhinelander, Wisconsin, which is famous fishing country. Another sign announces: "You must keep all fish."

"I'll pay," Mr. Brazell was told, "but I don't want to take any fish. How do you charge?"

"According to size," he said. He had a board marked off in pencil, showing the scale of prices—thirty-five cents for the smallest, up to two dollars and a half for an eighteen-inch lunker. "Had a feller here from Boston," Mr. Brazell said. "He was a real sport. He'd ketch one, hold it up, and holler: 'How much for this one?' ''Bout fifty cents,' I'd say. "Right,' he'd say, and put the fish back and ketch another. Cost him plenty. You want a fly?"

He handed over a seven-and-a-half-foot rod, rigid as an icepick. On the reel was a light braided line meant for plug casting, not fly-fishing. A deer-hair fly with black body, white wings, and red tail was tied to the line without a leader. A sign read: "Poles, fifty cents; eggs, twenty-five cents."

"Who eats the eggs?" Mr. Brazell was asked. "The fish or the fisherman?"

"Salmon eggs," he said, displaying some red droplets of jelly about the size of small peas. "Good bait. They ketch 'em on everything here—eggs, meat, flies, flatfish, spinners."

About a dozen sportsmen fished from three sides of the rectangular pool. Concrete bleachers occupied the fourth side. Small boys were in the majority. They were all bait fishermen using stubby steel rods, and most of the boys fished with red bobbers. They splashed and yelled a good deal.

Every fifty seconds or so somebody wrenched a fish into the summery sunlight, but for a time only one trout took notice of the fly. That one approached just as the lure was being retrieved after the first cast, and he was an instant too late.

Strictly speaking, it was impossible to cast. Instead of running through the guides, the light line wrapped itself around the rod tip. The fly floated lifelessly on the still, murky surface. The inaction became slightly humiliating, for behind every other sportsman rainbows flopped on the ground, covering themselves with dust and dried grass.

Experiments showed that the trout could be interested by moving the fly, twitching it under water. That's how Old Scratch was mastered. Old Scratch fought with the game fury of a dead twig.

Catches ran generally small, but every now and then there was a cry: "Looka that big one!" A man with considerable stomach pulled in one of eleven or twelve inches and boasted: "They like this bread." Later, as the sun neared the mountain rim and the cocktail hour approached, he baited his hook with shrimp instead of bread, and caught a slightly bigger fish. His unbending rod could have lifted a shark, but he chose to play his prize long and proudly.

A tiny girl of perhaps four shared a rod with her father. When a fish took her shrimp, she would set her small, solemn face grimly and back away, dragging her catch up over the concrete curb. Then her sire would land one and roar with triumph: "Ho ho, Susy, look, look!" Little Susy jumped up and down. "My turn!" she squealed, "my turn!"

Trout were rising everywhere now, hitting the fly both on the surface and beneath. Wherever it moved, the flash of bellies showed just beneath and the surface bulged. The fly, however, had doubled back on itself so the hook caught the line. This made it difficult for the fish to hook themselves. One would take the fly, hold it an instant, reject it, and it would be grabbed by another and then another.

"It's, er, curious sport," it was observed.

"The kids," a man answered defensively. "I don't have the time to take 'em farther out to fish."

Mr. Brazell said he and his son hatched the trout in the mountains near Flagstaff and brought them here in a refrigerated tank truck. They opened the pool three weeks ago, he said, stocking it with four thousand rainbows—it's a swimming pool of ordinary dimensions—and about nineteen hundred had been taken out. This day, be said, there'd been about three hundred visitors, counting spectators, and 235 fish had been caught.

"One lady," he said, "took away twenty-nine dollars' worth of fish. Nice mess of trout."

The Brakes
Got Drunk

A Truckload of Happiness Up in the Andes

LAGUNA DEL MAULE, CHILE, *January 20, 1953*

THIS TYPEWRITER is being beaten with fingers whose knuckles are bleeding and nails broken after hand-to-fin struggles with trout exactly the size, shape, and disposition of Tony Galento. Up here in the Andes fishing is a more perilous game than Russian roulette. If you survive the mountain road, there are rainbow in Lake Maule ready and willing to eat you for bait. Nothing is impossible to fish that live a mile and a half up in the sky.

Lake Maule perches on the Chilean-Argentine border about twenty kilometers and two thousand feet above the sparse grove of maytenus trees at timberline where camp had been pitched the evening before. The last drop of fluid had drained out of the brakes of the old Chevrolet truck during the journey to campsite, and there are no filling stations along the narrow, twisting shelf that serves, more or less, as a road.

Herman, the driver, halted trucks that passed camp occasionally with construction crews working on a dam at the lake. They told him oil would ruin the brakes, but said wine could serve as an emergency fluid.

"Because it contains alcohol, eh?" said Captain Warren Smith, of Panagra. "We can do better than that. Where's the Vat 69?"

The Chevrolet scrambled up to the lake with a boiling radiator and a full brake cylinder, not the best truck in Chile, but by all odds the happiest.

Maule straddles a pass in mountains entirely devoid of vegetation. They are bare peaks of volcanic rock crumbling into gray dust under the wind that blows eternally up this gorge from the west, making even these midsummer days uncomfortably cold. A little way out from the shore there is a belt of seaweed just under the surface where the trout lie and feed on a small pink crawfish called *pancora*. This shellfish diet gives the rainbows their majestic size, but it is the barren landscape that gives them their evil temperament. In all this desolation they brood.

Captain Smith and his North American burden rode by outboard to the east end of the lake, where snow touched the Chilean mountains rising from the water's edge and Argentine mountains showed just beyond. They started casting over the weed beds, using a smallish bronze-finish spoon of scarlet and orange. Almost immediately there was a grunt from the captain and a wild splash. Something dark and shiny and altogether implausible came out of the water and returned. It looked like a trout, but not like the sort of trout people ordinarily see when their eyes are open.

"You go on fishing," Captain Smith said. "I'll be awhile with this fellow."

His rod was a bow and his line hissed through the water. The fish was in and out of the lake, in and out, and then it was in the boat flopping on a gaff, a pink-striped brute of black and silver. "He'll hit about nine pounds," the captain said calmly.

Thereafter the captain caught fish and his companion caught backlashes and weeds. So intense, however, is the dislike these trout have for people that even the least proficient angler is bound to be under attack.

Between backlashes, a distant relative of Primo Carnera sprang up for a look at the latest New York styles in outdoor apparel, made a face of hideous disapproval, and spat out the spoon.

Another grabbed the same spoon and went into a terrifying rage. Four times in quick succession he stood up on his tail, snarling and shaking his head and cursing horribly. On the fourth jump he snapped the leader.

Then Captain Smith had one that broke the leader and departed. Then it happened again to the amateur, but not before the whirling reel handle had smashed fingernails and stripped skin off awkward knuckles.

By now half the population of the lake had taken a passion for collecting hardware. Six leaders were snapped and six spoons confiscated by force before it was decided that the fifteen-pound-test nylon was faulty. There's an awful lot of trout in Maule going around with their faces full of painted metal with nylon streamers. Maybe the style will catch on, like nose rings in the cannibal islands.

With the spoon tied directly to the casting line, anybody could catch fish. Practically anybody did. The outboard would take the boat upwind to the lee of a point or island; then the wind would drift it swiftly over the weed beds. Duck and geese and tern and grebe swam on the water. Except for one other fishing party, the place belonged to them and the fish.

"Let's take one more drift," the captain suggested, "and call it a day."

Half a moment later his companion screamed. The reel handle was snatched from his grasp and the drag sang. A trout leaped, fell back on his side. He looked six feet long. He dived, wrenching off line. The boat drifted on, but he wouldn't come along. Twice the captain ran the boat upwind, cautiously undoing knots the fish had tied around weeds. At length the sullen beast came aboard.

He was a good twelve pounds, broad-shouldered, magnificently colored, and splendidly deep, like Jane Russell.

Laughing River

The Beaverkill Chuckles at the Greenhorn with a Fly Rod

ROSCOE, N.Y., *June 15, 1958*

PROBABLY IF a fellow looked up Willowemoc in a good encyclopedia he'd find it was an Indian word meaning "Place of the Evil-smelling Fisherman" or something equally romantic. It is pleasanter to fancy that the name was created by some early angler trying to imitate by phonetic spelling the chuckling, gurgling, chortling, gasping sounds of repressed, derisive laughter which the river makes when some booted oaf with a fly rod wades into it.

Harry Darbee, the fly-tier, had recommended something small and dark to tempt the trout during the bright hours of early afternoon. The stream behind his cottage, which is in the stretch restricted to fly-fishing, was laughing fit to split at the city guy offering a tiny black gnat. To the city guy, sensitive about his fly-casting technique, it was no laughing matter.

There were a dozen, perhaps two dozen casts in a stony run above the bridge. Then a little tongue of water spurted up near the fly. It was a slap rather than a strike, just a nose-thumbing token to indicate that fish were present and waiting for the angler who could prove himself.

This angler couldn't, though in the next several hours he did get the hook into one pretty little brown trout, too young and inexperienced to watch his diet. He was shaken off lightly, and as he splashed back to safety there was a fair rise at the head of a tan submerged rock a little upstream.

This fish kept right on working, but not on any of the patterns offered. One cast with a gray spider brought him out from under the rock but he didn't offer at the fly. For a moment or two he was silhouetted at full length against the tan background, then he moved back to his original position and went on feeding imperturbably on invisible tidbits.

Just above him, another trout lay almost perfectly still with his head between two small stones. Two others loafed in midstream, rolling occasionally with a silvery flash. One appeared to be a rainbow, for in the clear water a suggestion of color could be made out along his side. Now and then shadowy shapes moved by at a leisurely pace, cruising fish taking their ease on a summery afternoon.

Birdsong spiralled out of the mottled woods. Chances are it was only imagination which lent a jeering note to some of these calls.

"When you saw those trout," Harry Darbee said that night, "you should've gone down after them with nymphs or wet flies."

"We thought of that," he was told, "about the time it got pitch dark and we were quitting. How about tomorrow?"

"Sam," Harry said, "why don't you guide them tomorrow?"

Sam Hendrickson, of Homer, N.Y., had come in bubbling with pleasure over his day on the East Branch of the Delaware. In the morning he had worked a big pool that boiled with rises where the trout were taking everything offered. He said he must have released twenty fish between 9:30 and 10:30 A.M. Evening had brought a hatch of big red spinners that darkened the sky and there was more sport.

When Roy Steenrod invented the Hendrickson fly he named it for Sam's uncle. You don't often meet a man with the same name as a trout fly, except, of course, Mr. Sparse Grey Hackle. Sam didn't seem to mind that Harry Darbee was generous with his services. He said sure, he'd be at the Antrim Lodge at 3:15 A.M., and he was.

It was a gray day with fog wreathing the mountains. It rained, sometimes lightly, sometimes teeming, always cold. Waders that leak above the knee add little to sport. The icy water trickles down and is held in the boot, preserving the foot. Fish rose constantly in the big pool Sam had worked the day before but now they were shy of leaders. Sam's skill brought in three modest trout. John I. Day took one. Harry joined the group later to hook and release four small trout, three large chubs.

For the other member it was a day of nature study. Twenty feet overhead, a merganser flew upstream, honking brassily. Where the road skirts an eminence over the river, two big beaver were seen swimming in tandem formation through the pool below, one of them carrying about a peck of spinachy green vegetation. During the drive back to Roscoe, a doe strolled across the highway and stood posing for a calendar. She had an oddly mottled coat of beige and white, a piebald deer, a pinto.

In the cold evening there had been no hatches on the East Branch. Coming back beside the Beaverkill with some daylight remaining, the cars were halted by a traffic tie-up caused by a crash. That's how Sam happened to see the spinners overhead. Soon as he got clear of the traffic he parked and went fishing. Took three trout fast.

The man with the name of a trout fly is a fine fisherman. He is also a hero. Not once in that long, cold, almost fruitless day on the East Branch did he say, "You shoulda been here yesterday."

★ SPORTS IN THE FIFTIES ★

Grimacing
Greyhound

Five Thousand Meters of Agony with Emil Zátopek

HELSINKI, FINLAND, *July 24, 1952*
I N T H E morning there was a headline in a paper from Paris reading: "*La Finale du 5000 Metres? Ce Sera la Bombe Atomique des Jeux!* (This will be the atomic bomb of the games!)" In the afternoon there was thin sunshine, turned on specially for the occasion by the Finns, to whom nothing is impossible when it involves entertaining the thieves of time and destroyers of distance in congress here from all the nations of the world.

The steep slopes of the stadium were peopled with the greatest crowd yet drawn for Olympic competition here. Thousands of athletes not engaged on the day's card sat among the cash customers, taking time off from their rehearsals to see the *bombe atomique* go off.

Even on the field there was uncommon congestion. Judges scurried in flight as whirling hammer-throwers flung hardware about the huge playpen. Guy Butler, an old English Olympian now turned journalist-photographer, was stooping to dig into his equipment case when something hissed through the air and landed—kerchok!—just short of his unprotected flank. He whirled and saw, quivering in the real estate, the javelin of a Russian broad (the term is purely descriptive, not ungallant).

On the fifth day of boisterous combat, this conclave of gristle had achieved a climax with the second bid for a gold medal by the comical contortionist Emil Zátopek. Four years ago, this gaunt and grimacing

Czech with the running form of a zombie had made himself the pin-up boy of the London games. Witnesses who have long since forgotten the other events still wake up screaming in the dark when Emil the Terrible goes writhing through their dreams, gasping, groaning, clawing at his abdomen in horrible extremities of pain. In the most frightful horror spectacle since *Frankenstein*, Zátopek set an Olympic record for ten thousand meters in London and barely failed to win the five thousand from Belgium's Gaston Reiff. This year he broke his own records for both speed and human suffering at ten thousand, and two days ago he created a minor sensation in his five-thousand-meter heat. Leading on the last lap, he made the only political gesture yet seen on this playground, slowing up and beckoning to his Communist cousin, Russia's Aleksandr Anoufriev, to come on and win the heat.

Now he was back in the five-thousand final, trying for a distance double that had defied every mortal save Finland's Hannes Kolehmainen, who won these two tests in 1912. To the Finns, these are the races that count; anything shorter is for children.

For example, an old gaffer around here overheard mention of Andy Stanfield, the Jersey City sprinter, and asked: "Stanfield? Who is he?"

"The American champion," he was told. He blinked.

"How can he be champion to run two hundred meters?" the old guy said. "He should run anyway five kilometers."

That's what Zátopek was doing, along with Reiff; Alain Mimoun, the French Algerian schoolmaster; Herbert Schade, the German favorite; and Chris Chataway, the Oxford blue. These five were the leaders from the start, and they made up a sort of gentlemen's club on the front end, some distance removed from the ten other starters. Then Reiff quit the lodge, giving up on the eleventh turn around the track, with a lap and a half to go.

All through the race, Zátopek had commanded the rapt attention of spectators, and with every agonized step he had rewarded them. Bobbing, weaving, staggering, gyrating, clutching his torso, flinging supplicating glances toward the heavens, he ran like a man with a noose about his neck. With half a mile to go, Schade and Chataway passed him. He seemed on the verge of strangulation; his hatchet face was crimson, his tongue lolled out. A quarter mile left, and he went threshing to the front again, but as they turned into the backstretch for the last time, he was passed by Schade, then Chataway, then Mimoun.

Now he was surely finished, a tortured wreck three yards back of the three leaders, who ran in a tight little cluster into the last turn.

Suddenly, midway of the turn, there was a flash of red on the outside. Four times in front and four times overtaken, that madman was rushing into the lead with his fifth and final spurt. He went barreling past the rest in an unbelievable charge. There was a jam on the inside, and Chataway sprawled over the curb into the infield.

Mimoun took out after Zátopek. The little Algerian made a fine run, as fruitless as it was game. He tailed Zátopek home as he had at ten thousand meters. Even Schade, in third place, broke Reiff's Olympic record, and Chataway, who got up to finish fifth alongside his countryman Gordon Pine, was only four-tenths of a second off the London time.

A little later in the day, Mrs. Zátopek won the javelin throw in the dolls' department. Czech and double Czech.

Airborne Parson

The Rev. Bob Richards Vaults for Heaven

NEW YORK, N.Y., *February 6, 1956*

I N ANCIENT times—meaning prior to the last five years or so—
obese and over-age exhibits in the track-and-field waxworks would
creep courageously up stepladders and teeter in peril to adjust and
measure the crossbar for the pole vault. This is the age of technology,
however, and at the Millrose Games the dinner-jacketed subalterns
rode the elevator of one of those mechanical hoists which had been
wheeled into Madison Square Garden.

It was a little past ten o'clock and the Wanamaker Mile was just concluded when the Rev. Bob Richards cleared the bar at 14 feet 10 inches
for his tenth Millrose victory. In forty-eight previous meets, no man
had won an event ten times, not even demigods like Joie Ray or Paavo
Nurmi or Mal Whitfield, though the incomparable hurdler, Harrison
Dillard, was a nine-time winner. Dillard had scratched from this show.

The crowd paid little attention when Richards won, but now the bar
was raised to 15 feet 4 inches, and all of a sudden there were thousands
of eyes on the springing parson from California. He's probably the
most muscular minister in short pants, a great blond brute with scarlet
trim on his satin drawers and the tri-color sash of America's Olympic
team across his mighty chest.

A year earlier, Richards had established the Millrose record of 15-2.
Now he was going for a new mark, trying for his eighty-eighth time
over fifteen feet.

He tried, and missed. He missed again. As he balanced the pole for
the third and last attempt, Jack Lavelle's toy pistol sent runners away in

a club and college handicap relay. Their pounding feet made a thunder around Richards and the distracting voice of the public-address system was bellowing the names of the leaders, but vaulters must live in a world of their own, oblivious to all save the runway, the take-off mark and that slender bar overhead.

Through the clamor, Richards sprinted down the straightaway, dragged himself aloft, twisted in midair and plunged into sawdust. The bar wobbled but did not fall. The parson clenched his fists, beat the heels of his hands together, exulting.

Up went the bar to five full inches to 15-9. The Reverend was hell-bent for heaven this time, aiming at Cornelius Warmerdam's thirteen-year-old world indoor record of 15-8½.

Back up the runway he plodded, walking heavily on his heels like a laborer at the day's end. The toes of his running shoes curled up like the prows of small canoes.

At the outer curve of the banked track, a woman and two small boys were watching. This was, presumably, the better three-fourths of the Richards household, but local authorities on the domestic status of pole vaulters were too busy at their typewriters to confirm identification. Richards laid down his pole, crossed the track, and mussed the kids' hairdos for luck.

On his first try he kicked the bar from underneath. On his second he appeared to get high enough but couldn't get across. Getting set for the last time, he turned and took a long look over his left shoulder at his fans across the track.

Then he made his run. "Come on!" the crowd was crying, "come on!" The take-off was poor, jerky. He didn't get close. He rolled to his feet in the pit, brushed shavings away and trotted off, giving spectators an uplifted hand and a big grin.

Ordinarily, pole vaulting inspires no divine passion here. As a spectacle, it compares favorably with a typewriting speed contest or women's basketball. It is good to watch the best in any field, however, and this was fine, a rousing feature in a show that is always memorable.

Golf Is a
Gentleman's Game

But Is Sam Snead a Gentleman?

★ ★ ★

NEW YORK, N.Y., *December 22, 1955*

GOLF IS a gentleman's game. This is stated without fear of contradiction, on the unimpeachable authority of the gentlemen themselves. They keep repeating it, to remind themselves. It's supposed to have the same effect as a schoolboy's assignment to write, "I must not bust teacher in the eye with a spitball," a hundred times.

In a sport whose practitioners are known to exude honor, breeding, manners, and taste from every pore, it caused some commotion when Gentleman Tommy Bolt, a professional true-penny, publicly implied that his esteemed colleague, Gentleman Sam Snead, had been the beneficiary of practices abhorrent to the code of the clan. It seemed an almost ungentlemanly remark.

Mr. Bolt was "reasonably sure," he told the press, that when Mr. Snead swung the short irons, his ever-loving gallery was not content to let the chips fall where they might. He couldn't mention any specific time or place where a spectator had moved Mr. Snead's ball to improve the lie, he couldn't quote any witness to such an act, but he had talked to "thousands of people" who said this had been done.

To suggest that this bordered on gossip-mongering would be an implication that Mr. Bolt lacked the dignified reticence of a perfect gent. To mention that he was a loser lately defeated by Mr. Snead in the Miami Open would lend little to his delineation of Chesterfieldian grace.

As a class, the golfer doth protest too much, anyhow. He's interminably and everlastingly yacking about the gentleman's game, as though a mucker were instantly ennobled by the act of pulling a No. 2 wood from his bag.

The fact is, there are golfers who are vile mathematicians and can't count for sour apples. There are shuffling, unwary walkers who wouldn't dream of kicking a ball out of the rough, except by accident. There are myopic players who can't see all the way down to a clubhead grounded in the sand. The divine right of any golfer to concede himself all putts under twelve feet is honorably established, and if a man happens to sneeze while announcing his handicap, so it sounds like thirteen instead of three, he can hardly be blamed for his head cold.

In short, some players cheat. Not many years ago, a PGA committee deemed it necessary to have a heart-to-heart chat with one of the members and point out that the rules didn't require his wife to precede him around the course. The committee delicately refrained from accusing her of booting her husband's ball from woods to fairway.

For many years, Sam Snead has had a passionately devoted following. In a big tournament, the gallery watching his match may line the fairway from tee to green, making it difficult for a shot to veer off course. In their enthusiasm, his idolators may trample the opponent to jelly, but if any of them ever deliberately improves Sam's position there is no ground for implying collusion on his part.

The most widely remembered hole Sam ever played was the seventy-second at Spring Mill, outside Philadelphia, in the National Open of 1939, where he took eight strokes and blew a championship that was in his lap. It was either that same day or the next that Craig Wood hooked a shot into the crowd on the same hole and his ball ricocheted off the skull of a relative of Gov. Alf Landon, caroming into a lie that kept Wood in the running for the title.

This was, of course, a "rub of the green," a lucky break for Craig Wood. Good golfers learn to accept this sort of thing as quietly as Byron Nelson took an evil turn of fortune the year the Open was played at Canterbury near Cleveland.

Nelson had pushed a shot into the rough and his caddy was preceding him through a pack of spectators whom the marshals had allowed to cluster too close to the ball. Ducking under the rope which held the gallery back, the caddy kicked Nelson's ball accidentally before he could get his head up.

Byron immediately called the penalty on himself. It cost him the championship. Snead would do the same thing in the same circumstances. It would be ungentlemanly to speculate about others.

Mr. Bolt, expatiating on what he conceived to be Mr. Snead's unaccountably good fortune in money matches, said that Sam's ball was found in a surprisingly favorable position after what looked like a wild tee shot in the Miami Open. He admitted, however, that he hadn't actually seen where the ball landed and had no evidence that it had been moved after coming to rest.

Mr. Snead said he found it in a stinking lie and was lucky to bring off a splendid recovery, slicing it toward the green around a copse of trees.

"If anybody kicked it," Sam said, entering what seems a valid complaint, "he should have kicked it a little farther."

If there's kicking to be done around here, Sam's golf ball isn't necessarily the only target available.

Basketball in a Cage

Doing Time for Dumping Games

New York, N.Y., *November 21, 1951*

IF A man has any decent instincts at all, he's got to feel regret—not sympathy, but a sort of pain—over the crooked basketball players who are going to jail. He's got to feel bad because they are young guys whose lives are ruined. But he's got to applaud the decision of Judge Saul S. Streit to put the crooks in a cage.

There must be some deterrent to the spread of dishonesty in sports. Chances are it never occurred to the fakers that they could be put in jail for throwing in with sure-thing punks and dumping games for pay. Even the most stupid ones, who were dragged into college by the heels when they should have been working as longshoremen or grease monkeys, must have known that what they were doing was a dirty thing. They must have known that if the word ever got out, they would be put away as crumbs by the undergraduates and the neighbors and all decent associates.

Yet it is unlikely they realized they could be caught and tossed into pokey. It is time that realization was brought home to everybody. There has been far too much breast-beating about unfortunate, immature lads who were led astray by hoodlums. Everybody has been too ready to forget that the most doltish of students in ballroom dancing and finger-painting knew enough to count the money at payoff time. It is high time for the courts to teach what the colleges have neglected— that when you get caught stealing, there's a penalty for it. Maybe if that knowledge got around, it would make easy money look a little harder in young eyes.

It is unfortunate, of course, that these young men have to be put away. It is even more unfortunate that when they go behind the wall they will not be accompanied by their accomplices—the college presidents, the coaches, the registrars, the alumni, who compounded the felony. Regrettably, there is no law that can reach the educators who shut their eyes to everything except the financial ledgers of the athletic department, the authorities who enroll unqualified students with faked credentials, the professors who foul their academic nests by easing athletes through their courses, the diploma-mill operators who set up classes for cretins in Rope-Skipping IV and History of Tattooing VII, the alumni who insist on winning teams and back their demands with cash, the coaches who'd put a uniform on Lucky Luciano if he could work the pivot play. They're the bums who ought to go to jail with the fixers whom they encouraged. But they won't, and apparently they regret nothing except the fact that some crooks have been caught.

The most shocking feature of this whole sordid business is the attitude expressed by mature men entrusted with the guidance of the young.

"It isn't any of the judge's business in the first place," says Matty Bell, athletic director of Southern Methodist, about Judge Streit's comments on recruiting and subsidization in the Southwest.

"The public doesn't understand," says Clair Bee, of Long Island University, "that the players were not throwing games. They were throwing points. They were not selling out to the extent that the public believed, and somehow the players did not feel that what they did was wrong."

Admittedly, the public's understanding of many things is faulty. Yet one can't help believing it surpasses the understanding of some men who are supposed to set an example for boys. Recently a successful football coach was complaining about the bad press that college sports have received this year. He thinks the newspapers play up scandals and ignore news that puts athletics in a favorable light. "The sporting press," he said, "has let football down badly this year."

Foolishly, an effort was made to explain that the press wasn't letting football down. It was argued that many observers of the sports scene with a genuine respect for the good things in sports have been genuinely concerned about abuses and excesses which, they fear, threaten the very existence of amateur sports. It was foolish to attempt this explanation because the coach, a thoroughly honest, straight guy, doesn't want to see any imperfections in the game that makes him a good living. He should have tuned in the radio last Friday night when two newspapermen, probably the best friends football ever had in their field, laid some truths on the line.

These two men, Grantland Rice and Stanley Woodward, said all the things Judge Streit said later when he sentenced the basketball bagmen. They talked about the trapping and care and feeding of athletes, about slipping them through phony courses so they could make headlines and profits for the college with no danger of intellectual pursuits distracting them from the main job. They said that unless the colleges scrubbed up fast, there was sure to be a scandal that would invite the reformers to abolish intercollegiate sports altogether.

They are dead right, because if a college kid can dump a basketball game he can also dump a football game. As a matter of fact, who honestly believes it hasn't happened already?

Biological Urge

The Need to Be In on the Action

New York, N.Y., *April 8, 1951*

For a while, Butch said, there was no action at all around the joints. Instead of betting, the mob just sat and watched the Kefauver committee on the television. It was discouraging, somehow, the things that came over the air and the things you read in the papers. It took a lot of the fun out of betting.

"The way it is now," Butch said, "they tell you if you're betting basketball you should take the points. You figure if the favorite is dumping—that's what you must think of now, if they're dumping— why, then if they win they'll win inside the points or else maybe they lose the game. Either way, you must win if you take the points.

"But who wants to figure if a team is dumping? College kids already. Besides, if you're betting you don't know if you'll get paid off, because the bookies in action now are fly guys. The good, dependable regulars, they don't want that aggravation from the cops.

"Not that you'll ever stop gambling. This is the closest they'll ever get, now when it's maybe 80 percent off. But all that means, there'll be more guys going to the races and more guys betting cards and more corner crap games. You won't ever stop it, because it's a biological urge.

"What I mean about a biological urge, take Old Man Mose. He's a young guy, we grew up together. Back in the Depression, him and I run a $3 bill up to $500. Betting baseball, two-team parlays, three-team parlays, everything. Well, $500 in the Depression when we're working on the job for $10 a week, maybe $12 a week.

"We go down on the avenue and we buy white shoes. Not one pair of white shoes—two pairs of white shoes. Look, it was a treacherous thing buying one pair of white shoes in the Depression, because how do you get the polish for 'em? We buy two pairs of white shoes. We buy five sports shirts. Five. We want to go six blocks to the Turk Joint, we take a taxi. What the hell, in the Depression we got $500.

"Look, there was a girl I liked. She wasn't interested in me. But she sees the white shoes, the pressed suit, she sees the taxi, and she must start thinking. I made some time. Well, that's the way it was with Mose and me.

"Now it's the war, and in the Salerno landing, Mose is a scout and he lays in a ditch twelve hours. They're pinned down with mortars and stuff like that. Finally Mose says: 'I can't lay here. I'm gonna go take a look.' So he and another guy crawl up and stick up their heads to look and, whoom, everything hits 'em.

"Mose is hit here near the heart, and this is what he tells me. When he's hit, it's like he sees a great big fountain of light. And in the fountain he sees me. I'm sitting in Ebbets Field with a hot dog and a Coke and I got a long face on me and he knows I'm losing a bet. He says: 'That's Butch. I got to go help him get a winner.' And he can't hardly move, but he crawls back to the American lines.

"The Germans came over and they killed the guy was with Mose. He was wounded, but they killed him. Now what I mean about the biological urge, it wasn't in Mose's mind about the Germans coming over and killing him. What he had in mind was he must get back and help me get a winner. A hundred to one he can't even crawl back to the lines, but he's a gambler. He pretty near lost an arm and a leg, but he got back home finally. That's what I mean," Butch said, "how it's a biological urge.

"About this dumping in basketball," Butch said. "I read a column in the paper where it said the gamblers are just as guilty as the bookies. Look, there are gamblers and bookies and crumbs. I got no sympathy for these crumbs that want something sure.

"I got no sympathy for this Sollazzo, because if he's got the game fixed, he hurts me just like he hurts the bookie. I like to bet the home team, and if he's got the home team dumping, I can't win. I like to bet a twenty or forty and what I want is a good contest, which there's thousands of guys like to do the same thing.

"Look, I took my kid brother to the races the first time he ever went, when he was about twenty-two years old. We bet a horse and the horse win by fourteen lengths. My kid brother didn't like it, it was too sure. 'Where's these neck-and-neck finishes,' he asked me, 'like in the movies?'

"You understand? We want to sit back with a hot dog and a Coke and a little something going for us and a chance to win and a chance to lose. If I'm betting against the Yankees and it's a good game and DiMaggio hits a home run to beat me, I don't hate DiMaggio. I lose, is all.

"Who wants something sure? There's this guy we call the Bedbug because he's always biting you. He was around cutting the dice games, moving in here, moving in there, so one time they picked up his dice and he was using squares. Now, these are all level working guys and they must gamble, because it's a biological urge. So when they catch him with a pair of squares they empty the Bedbug's pockets and he spends two weeks in the hospital.

"It is the unwritten law," Butch said, "that if a guy pulls a phony, he must spend his vacation in the hospital."

Pattern of Violence

Sugar Ray Robinson Survives Randy Turpin

NEW YORK, N.Y., *September 13, 1951*

IN THE third round Sugar Ray Robinson smashed a straight right stiff to the chin of Randy Turpin, knocking the Englishman halfway across the ring, but when Robinson came plunging after, to punish him on the ropes, he found a fighter there with both hands working.

That was when the pattern took shape in America's biggest fight of 1951. The former middleweight champion of the world, fighting to regain the title as Stanley Ketchel and Tony Zale did before him, would land the sharper, cleaner blows. He would go fishing for Turpin's elusive chin, angling and angling patiently, missing wildly many, many times, looking often inept and sometimes foolish against the champion's strange but efficient defense.

He would send Turpin to the floor, dropping him cleanly, while Ruby Goldstein, the referee, tolled the numbers off to nine. But whenever Robinson punched, Turpin would punch him back. When Turpin went down, he would get up. Under the severest punishment he would have his wits about him. He would be a fighting man, ready to take more and give it.

That was the pattern, but there was no guessing when it might change. Turpin is tremendously strong, and as the rounds rolled away, his youth and strength might overcome the edge the older man had in class. The longer it lasted, the more likely it seemed that Turpin might come on to win.

He was coming on. By this score he won the eighth and ninth

rounds. He broke Robinson's left eye open as the tenth started—and then it happened.

It could be that Turpin's biggest mistake was to open that gash over Robinson's eye. "When that happened," Sugar Ray was asked afterward, "did you figure that was the time to go get him?"

"I figured that was the time to try," Ray said.

That's how it seemed from ringside, down in the sweltering funnel of the Polo Grounds. It seemed that when Robinson saw blood and knew it was his own, he opened the throttle all the way, reasoning that if he didn't get his man now, his neat face might come all apart soon and he wouldn't have many more chances.

He tore after Turpin, scoring well, but still unable to hurt the champion. They were in mid-ring, closing for a rally, when Robinson's right caught Turpin's chin. It was a short punch, almost a hook, and it stopped Turpin dead. The Englishman was bent forward at the waist, feet wide, legs rigid, knees seeming locked together.

Half an instant later, Turpin was in motion again, and though Robinson went after him hungrily, it looked as though Ray might lose his victim. The victim was fighting back. But, fighting, he left another opening. Robinson filled it.

A straight right to the chin spun Turpin in the first movement of a pirouette. He pitched forward into Robinson's arms, and Ray had to step back to let him fall. Turpin dropped on his back, but at the count of two or three he rolled over, brought up his head. His eyes were clear, and you knew he was going to get up.

Robinson knew it, too, of course. And he knew what to do. He was in on his man swiftly, slugging the head with both hands, batting him around the ring. He caught him on the ropes, punching frantically at first, then suddenly changing his tactics.

It was just as you see it on the screen when the slow-motion camera comes on to show the knockout in detail. Robinson took his time, steadying Turpin's head, aiming, then letting go. Turpin was defenseless, but neither senseless nor altogether helpless. He couldn't get his hands up, but he did raise his eyes and you could see them following

Robinson's gloves as he rolled and ducked and bent away from the blows. He was weaving like a cobra dancing to a flute.

At ringside they were beginning to shout for Goldstein to protect him. Then Robinson brought up a left hook and a right, and as Turpin sagged toward the floor, the referee burst in and stopped it. Ruby was right, though Turpin complained of his action in the dressing room and there will be louder protests as time goes on.

As Robinson turned toward his own corner, Turpin straightened, refusing to fall, and lurched after him as though to resume the fight. His handlers leaped into the ring and tackled him, but he wasn't trying to hit Robinson; he only meant to congratulate him, and he towed his handlers into the corner for that purpose.

It was a genuine gesture of sportsmanship from a first-class fighting man. There haven't been many better fighters than Turpin seen around here in a long time. There never has been a pluckier loser.

In the first row of ringside behind the working press, a woman was standing on a chair, gasping as her companions chafed her hands and fanned her. She seemed near to fainting. This was Ray Robinson's mother.

A few seats removed, another woman wept. Her face was wet with tears and she was crying. "The title is his!" Over and over. This was Ray Robinson's wife.

Night for Joe Louis

Rocky Marciano Knocks the Old Man Out

New York, N.Y., *October 27, 1951*

Joe Louis lay on his stomach on a rubbing table with his right ear pillowed on a folded towel, his left hand in a bucket of ice on the floor. A handler massaged his left ear with ice. Joe still wore his old dressing-gown of blue and red—for the first time, one was aware of how the colors had faded—and a raincoat had been spread on top of that.

This was an hour before midnight of October 26, 1951. It was the evening of a day that dawned July 4, 1934, when Joe Louis became a professional fist fighter and knocked out Jack Kracken in Chicago for a fifty-dollar purse. The night was a long time on the way, but it had to come.

Ordinarily, small space is reserved here for sentimentality about professional fighters. For seventeen years, three months, and twenty-two days Louis fought for money. He collected millions. Now the punch that was launched seventeen years ago had landed. A young man, Rocky Marciano, had knocked the old man out. The story was ended. That was all except—

Well, except that this time he was lying down in his dressing-room in the catacombs of Madison Square Garden. Memory retains scores of pictures of Joe in his dressing room, always sitting up, relaxed, answering questions in his slow, thoughtful way. This time only, he was down.

His face was squashed against the padding of the rubbing table, mulling his words. Newspapermen had to kneel on the floor like supplicants in a tight little semicircle and bring their heads close to his lips to hear him. They heard him say that Marciano was a good puncher, that the best man had won, that he wouldn't know until Monday whether this had been his last fight.

He said he never lost consciousness when Marciano knocked him through the ropes and Ruby Goldstein, the referee, stopped the fight. He said that if he'd fallen in mid-ring he might have got up inside ten seconds, but he doubted that he could have got back through the ropes in time.

They asked whether Marciano punched harder than Max Schmeling did fifteen years ago, on the only other night when Louis was stopped.

"This kid," Joe said, "knocked me out with what? Two punches. Schmeling knocked me out with—musta been a hunderd punches. But," Joe said, "I was twenty-two years old. You can take more then than later on."

"Did age count tonight, Joe?"

Joe's eyes got sleepy. "Ugh," he said, and bobbed his head.

The fight mob was filling the room. "How did you feel tonight?" Ezzard Charles was asked. Joe Louis was the hero of Charles' boyhood. Ezzard never wanted to fight Joe, but finally he did and won. Then and thereafter Louis became just another opponent who sometimes disparaged Charles as a champion.

"Uh," Charles said, hesitating. "Good fight."

"You didn't feel sorry, Ezzard?"

"No," he said, with a kind of apologetic smile that explained this was just a prize fight in which one man knocked out an opponent.

"How did you feel?" Ray Arcel was asked. For years and years Arcel trained opponents for Joe and tried to help them whip him, and in a decade and a half he dug tons of inert meat out of the resin.

"I felt very bad," Ray said.

It wasn't necessary to ask how Marciano felt. He is young and strong and undefeated. He is rather clumsy and probably always will be, because he has had the finest of teachers, Charley Goldman, and Charley hasn't been able to teach him skill. But he can punch. He can take a punch. It is difficult to see how he can be stopped this side of the heavyweight championship.

It is easy to say, and it will be said, that it wouldn't have been like this with the Louis of ten years ago. It isn't a surpassingly bright thing to say, though, because this isn't ten years ago. The Joe Louis of October 26, 1951, couldn't whip Rocky Marciano, and that's the only Joe Louis there was in the Garden.

That one was going to lose on points in a dreary fight that would have left everything at loose ends. It would have been a clear victory for Marciano, but not conclusive. Joe might not have been convinced.

Then Rocky hit Joe a left hook and knocked him down. Then Rocky hit him another hook and knocked him out. A right to the neck followed that knocked him out of the ring. And out of the fight business. The last wasn't necessary, but it was neat. It wrapped the package, neat and tidy.

An old man's dream ended. A young man's vision of the future opened wide. Young men have visions, old men have dreams. But the place for old men to dream is beside the fire.

Still Life

"End of the Road, for J.J.W.," by R. F. Marciano

★ ★ ★

PHILADELPHIA, PA., *September 24, 1952*

THE NOISY crowd had gone from Municipal Stadium, and the press rows were empty of all save the slowest writers and their telegraphers. A fellow who had finished his work was sitting at ringside at the foot of the steps leading down from the corner where J. J. Walcott, the Jersey schoolboy, had sat slumped and bleeding on a stool after Rocky Marciano's right hand separated him from his intellect and the heavyweight championship of the world.

The fellow was musing, reviving in memory the high spots of the fight. His gaze was at his feet but his mind was elsewhere and it was a little while before he really saw the little litter of symbols lying on the patch of turf beside the steps.

When he did, he thought: "Here is all that is left of the old champion of the world." There on the beaten grass were a swab stick, the soiled core of a roll of gauze, and the top of a Vaseline jar. If it had been a still-life painting entitled *End of the Road*, it would have won first prize in any exhibit.

When old Joe was gone last night, nothing remained save remnants, these used tools of the seconds' trade, and the memory of one of the most gallant battles any champion ever made in futile defense of his title.

It was a grand fight, possibly the best for the heavyweight championship since Jack Dempsey's famous "long count" match with Gene Tunney a quarter century ago. It was a wonderful fight in its own right, close and bruising and bloody and exciting, but especially good because Walcott's performance was so unexpected.

It is wearing a threadbare line to tatters to say that nothing in Walcott's reign as champion became him so well as his leave-taking. It is also true. Here was a pacific old gentleman who was justly recognized as a prince of prudence, an antique tiger who had lost to assorted mediocrities, who had never beaten any fighter of real distinction, who had shown himself possessed of many small skills and great contempt for the calendar's spite, but had never exhibited a consuming urge for combat. Yet he stood his ground against a young, rough, resolute bruiser and fought such a battle as nobody believed he could make, and he was winning when the sands ran out. He came suddenly to the end of the string, got nailed, and went out as a champion should, on his shield.

For the record, a majority of ringside witnesses had Walcott ahead until he was stiffened. A few unofficial scorers gave Marciano the edge. On this card they were even in rounds, but Joe had a substantial lead in points, which don't count in Pennsylvania.

Briefly, the fight went like this: Walcott outclassed Marciano at the start; the younger man won the middle rounds; then the old guy came on again and took charge, and it looked as though he was going to get away free when Rocky caught him.

On the official scores, Marciano couldn't have won after the twelfth round except by a knockout. Off the action in the first round, it didn't look as though he could win with hand grenades.

A magnificent fighter came out of Walcott's corner at the opening bell. He was feinting, punching, showing up his challenger as a gawky novice. He seemed a trifle tense, and in the corner his trainer, Dan Florio, kept screaming: "Relax, Joe!" but he was using his weapons superbly. He couldn't miss with his left hook.

As he slugged Marciano to the floor, it seemed impossible that Rocky could last five rounds. One had the shocked impression that here was a nice young fellow who'd been brutally betrayed. But Rocky had what everybody thought he'd had—courage, great recuperative power, and the strength to throw a killing punch after punishment that would have finished most men.

Cheap at
Half the Price

A Retirement Package for Jersey Joe Walcott

J. J. WALCOTT, the odd old gentleman from Jersey who has mocked $\qquad$ CHICAGO, ILL., *May 15, 1953*
the calendar for something like forty years, made a mockery of the
heavyweight championship of the world tonight in two minutes
twenty-five seconds. He also made a hooting, disgusted, short-changed
gathering in Chicago Stadium understand why there has been so much
confusion about his real age. He can't count his years; he can't even
count to ten.

Rocky Marciano, making his first defense of the title he won from
Walcott last September, threw one respectable punch. It was a right
uppercut to the expression, and it knocked Walcott to the floor. There
old Joe sat like a darkly brooding Buddha, thinking slow and beautiful thoughts while ten seconds drained away and he made no effort
whatever to get up.

That's all there was. Last autumn's wildly wonderful battle, one of
the finest, closest, and most exciting of all heavyweight title fights, was
replayed as one of the most sordid of all time.

Walcott was guaranteed a quarter of a million dollars for this night's
work. If its finish guarantees his departure from boxing, the price was
not too great.

After twenty-three recorded years as a professional fist fighter, the
former champion went out in a total disgrace that no excuses can
relieve. If he was truly knocked out by the only real punch of the bout,

then he didn't belong in the ring. If he was not knocked senseless and did hear the count of the referee, Frank Sikora, then it was a disgrace, because it was evident through the last several seconds that he was not going to get up, or even try. If he did not hear the count, then he was befuddled by Marciano's blow or else his hearing is no better than might be expected at his age, for the toll of seconds was clearly audible in the press rows half the width of the ring away.

In any case, there could be no justification for the complaints which he and his proprietor, Felix Bocchicchio, made to the referee, or the subsequent shouting in their dressing room, where Walcott's lawyer, Angelo Malandra, declared he would protest to the Illinois State Athletic Commission.

It was unmistakably a count of ten, and Walcott remained unmistakably on his hunkers throughout, and the Marquess of Queensberry rules unmistakably define this as a knockout.

Walcott compounded his own disgrace by putting up no part of a fight during the brief seconds preceding his sit-down strike. From the opening bell he backed away and grabbed as the champion moved in on him. Once, coming out of a clinch, he brought his right up to Marciano's face; once he dropped a looping punch that landed on the back of Rocky's head, and two or three times he pawed at the champion's celebrated nose with a long, timid jab.

He backed to a point near Rocky's corner, where the ropes were on his right and Marciano's left. Rocky threw a left hook, which some observers thought was blocked, though Walcott said later that it landed. The uppercut followed and Walcott sprawled on his back, rocked to a sitting position, and remained there.

Unfortunately for the reputation of a fine young puncher, Marciano will receive little credit for his successful defense. He was willing and even eager to fight, but it takes two even to tango.

While the customers jeered and cops and ushers cleared the ring of a half-dozen strangers who piled in, presumably confident that here was one former heavyweight champion whom they could whip, Walcott departed with only one possession intact. He still had his record of never getting off the floor in eight championship fights.

It had not looked like a killing punch and Walcott did not seem badly hurt. He sat in a kind of round-shouldered hunch, heels wide apart on the canvas, knees bent—the posture of a child playing jacks. By the time the count reached eight, it was clear he would not get up before the toll was completed. He didn't stir until the referee had cried "Nine," and he was not off the floor until well after "Ten."

"I was robbed in New York the first time we boxed Joe Louis," Mr. Bocchicchio announced with simple dignity in the dressing room, "but I never saw no robbery like this."

He could, just possibly, have been thinking of that quarter of a million cold quid.

The Fight Club
Upstairs

Beecher's Gym in Brownsville Is Boxing's Spawning Place

BROOKLYN, N.Y., *January 27, 1954*

L IVONIA AVE., in the Brownsville section of Brooklyn, isn't the pushcart street it used to be, but it is still a noisy tunnel under the I.R.T. tracks, and the pickle shops are still there, and the old ice plant and the stores with fiddle music on the windows. Now that there are no horses running in New York to distract the proprietor, Mike's Barber Shop is open, its windows bright in the early winter darkness. This is a gathering place for the sports crowd, a masculine clubhouse with triumphantly feminine art on the walls.

A short block along the street, steep, worn stairs lead from a dark doorway to a poolroom on the second floor, and across the poolroom a door opens into a fight club. This is Beecher's Gym, spawning place of Brownsville fighters.

Beecher's was home to Al Davis, the rough kid who died by a stick-up gun. Little Charley Goldman, trainer of Rocky Marciano, boxed there. Bernie Friedkin came out of Beecher's, and Herbie Katz and Morris Reif and Harold Green and Lew Feldman and the Silvers boys and scores of others. Years ago they would pack the place for smokers, and name fighters would drop in to referee a bout or just make a personal appearance, big shots like K. O. Christner or Jackie Kid Berg or Len Harvey.

Some of the kids who hung around, adoring the fighters, are doctors and lawyers and business tycoons today. Some of the others grew up to win their distinction with Murder, Inc.

Now it was early evening. The after-supper crowd was just beginning to arrive in the poolroom. Lights were on in the gym, where five or six fighters were working. The gym is square and neat, with tall windows on two sides, clear linoleum on the floor. The room contains one ring, a rubbing table and two heavy bags, one bearing the life-sized outline of a fighter's head and torso, with a wide black band at the belt labelled "FOUL." There is a small locker room and one shower.

Two stumpy, stocky guys were going at it in the ring with big gloves. One was young and wore a headgear. The other was a man in his middle forties, at least, with a pencil-line mustache.

"The old guy works in a tavern," said Patsy Fazio. "Used to box in the amateurs and he's just crazy about it. Always bringing kids up here, trying to get them started boxing, and he'll spar thirty, forty rounds with them in a day."

A fellow skipping rope looked familiar. This was Doug Ratford, who whipped Kid Gavilan twice back in 1947 and 1948 but retired three or four years ago. He's training for a comeback. "Wife and kids," he explained.

A boy was shadow-boxing before a mirror leaning against the rear wall. Another, a rather skinny kid with a mop of dark hair flopping over his eyes, was hooking the big bag. In a corner Vic Zimet watched a big fellow in baggy sweat clothes who was shadow-boxing without gloves. Zimet talked to him quietly, watching his shifting feet, trying to teach him to keep his weight evenly distributed so he could always punch with either hand.

Vic and Patsy run the gym now. For a while it was out of business, like most small clubs and neighborhood gyms these days. Vic was a kid around there in the boom days, worshipping an idol named Red Miller.

"Fighters were more colorful then," Vic said. "They had caps and sweaters and they wore patches over their eyes like a badge. When he was sixteen, Red Miller was a brilliantly promising lightweight. He boxed in the gym with Benny Leonard on Leonard's comeback. He boxed with Ray Miller, who would sink a left hook into your body and give you curvature of the spine. Red was a sweetheart at sixteen, and at seventeen and a half he was washed up."

Before he was twenty-one, Red Miller had tried two comebacks as a welterweight. Training down for a six rounder in Ebbets Field, he weakened himself so that he nearly fainted in the dressing room. He was alone. "This is nonsense," he thought, and got back into his street clothes and started home. "Hey, Red," a gate tender said, "ain't you fighting tonight?" "Well," Miller decided, "I'm not going to run out. I'll go back and take my lumps." He got 'em. It was the kid's last fight.

At thirteen Vic Zimet was sparring in Beecher's and he managed and trained fighters while still in knee pants. He had a string of boxers while he was going to college. Now he's in the steel business, doubling in leather in the evenings.

"That's a great-looking kid working on the bag," he said. "He has natural class and he learns fast. He's only seventeen. Now here's a prospect for you. Marvin Morris." He introduced a heavy-lidded young man wearing a windbreaker and peaked cap, sitting on the rubbing table.

"Marvin was captain of the Brooklyn College football team. Graduated in physical education. He played in all sports and he likes to keep in shape so he's started boxing. For five months we worked with him here before we let him put on a pair of gloves. Now he's in the Golden Gloves and he has won three bouts, two by knockouts."

Morris grinned sleepily. In the ring, the old guy and the kid finished another round. It was a normal, quiet evening in Beecher's.

Relentless Defender

Archie Is One Tough Turtle But Rocky Cracks His Shell

BRONX, N.Y., *September 22, 1955*

THE OLD man sat in his corner, but there was no stool there. His arms were wide, groping for support where there was no help at all. The mittened hands clutched the ring ropes, but the outspread hands were like a gesture of supplication. Head sagging but eyes turned upward with an expression unutterably forlorn, he gazed from under swollen brows at Harry Kessler, the referee, tolling the racing seconds.

At the count of eight, Archie Moore tried to pull himself erect. He got his feet under him, but his knees were wet spaghetti. At ten he flopped down again, and now Rocky Marciano came across, bleeding but solicitous for the man who had drawn the blood. Marciano was trying to help Moore up when Rocky's friend, Allie Colombo, came and pulled the heavyweight champion across to his own corner, victorious, invincible, indestructible as always.

Eight rounds, one minute and nineteen seconds had passed in Marciano's sixth defense of his world title. He had been on the floor, he had been outboxed, blood oozed from his nose and seeped almost imperceptibly from a nick in his left eyebrow.

Wounded but not hurt, sometimes bewildered and often frustrated, he had still got his man as almost everybody had believed he would. By plain strength and courage and resolution, he battered down an uncommonly skillful defense, smashed Moore to the floor four times, and scored the forty-third knockout of a career that has never included defeat.

The biggest fight in years was one of the best in years, twenty-five minutes of ripping excitement, uninterrupted and unrelieved.

It unwound very much as expected, though perhaps there weren't many who had foreseen what desperate courage Archie Moore would summon to fight back again and again from the ragged edge of extinction.

Most authorities, respecting Moore for the accomplished professional that he has been through a career of almost twenty years, believed his defensive excellence would make trouble for Marciano for eight or nine rounds. They recognized Archie as the more accurate puncher and deemed it likely that his left hooks and straight rights might cut the champion's face. Some suggested that he might punch sharply enough to put Rocky down, as only Joe Walcott had managed to do in Marciano's forty-eight earlier matches.

All this came to pass, and more. Archie furnished the additive with his wonderful, resolute hitting when it seemed to the great, howling crowd of 61,574 that he simply must go down and stay down. It wasn't just once that this happened; Archie did it in round after round when he seemed helpless against the ropes, a rolling, weaving turtle with his head retracted under a blizzard of blows.

He was still fighting like that when Rocky's left hand pulled the plug and the last drop of endurance drained away.

Probably there will be scornful things said and written about Marciano's punching power. Because he is known as the best one-punch hitter of them all, his antagonist is supposed to drop the first time Rocky swings a glove. No doubt it will be said and written that he hit Moore a thousand times before he could put the challenger away, so what kind of puncher is that?

It won't be the truth. The truth is that not more than one in a hundred of Rocky's blows found a spot where it would have serious effect, and whenever one did land solidly Moore's ears twanged like twin guitars. Archie didn't pass all that time on the floor just hunting sequins from his peachy black-and-gold dressing gown.

Time and again when it must have looked, to witnesses in the remote canyon of the Yankee Stadium stands, as though the champion was beating a defenseless victim eight to the bar, Moore was suffering no serious damage at all. In his extremities on the ropes he would turtle his head down into his chest, roll his shoulders up around his ears, and Rocky's thundering fists would slide off the shoulders or crash onto the very top of Moore's skull.

As seen from here, Marciano didn't land a really first-rate punch until the fourth round, though he won two of the first three heats. When he did connect cleanly it was a right that drove Moore backward toward Marciano's corner, followed by a left that made that challenger curtsy like a convent girl. That was the first time Rocky chased his man to the ropes and met frustration there, unable to find a chink in the turtle shell.

Every time thereafter that Marciano connected cleanly, Moore was in trouble, needing only a second shove to go over the edge. Yet almost every time, Moore's defense was equal to his need.

In one sense, this may have been Marciano's greatest fight, for he kept a relentless pressure on the most accomplished boxer he has ever met, dug into and clawed at and hammered upon an almost impregnable defense, stood up under some marvelously sharp and beautifully timed counters without flinching, and kept everlastingly at the task until the job was done.

He wants to be heavyweight champion of the world forever. Don't bet against it.

Two Champs
on the Ropes

Ray Closes Basilio's Eye But Can't Close the Deal

CHICAGO, ILL., *March 26, 1958*

THE LOSER walked wearily into his hotel convoyed by two cops and a knot of handlers. A big white patch covered the left side of his gaunt, high-boned face. He dropped on to a settee in the lower lobby, let his head droop clear down between his knees, and sat there shaking the head slowly, over and over, in a transport of dejection.

When an elevator was ready his escorts sought to help him in. He didn't exactly brush them off. He stood up, squared his shoulders and walked unaided through the pack. The doors slid shut behind the former middleweight champion of the world.

At almost the same time, the winner was receiving the press in another hotel across the Loop. He lay in bed answering questions, too exhausted to be exultant, uninterested in the telephone messages pouring in.

The job of whipping one side of Carmen Basilio had drained away the last of Ray Robinson's strength. In the last round his punches had nearly stunned his half-blind adversary, had doubled him up and made his knees sag. Basilio wobbled but didn't go down, and as they swayed into the ropes Robinson held and leaned heavily on the smaller man.

In the closing seconds you couldn't have scraped the winner off the loser with a putty knife. It was that sort of a fight.

Basilio won everything but the fight.

Robinson won the middleweight title, for the fifth time in an implausibly brilliant career. Let there be no niggling reluctance to pay him the full measure of credit that he has earned, to salute him as the incomparable craftsman that he has been. There has not been another like him in his time—and his time is running out as it must for the greatest and the least of warriors.

It is the conviction here that Ray could not have won without the little bit of luck that closed Basilio's left eye like a purple clam. To be sure, it was Robinson's punch that closed the eye, but a man might land a thousand such blows without accomplishing the same effect.

Until the eye swelled shut in the sixth round, Basilio had—it seemed here—a slight lead. He had been fighting from a sidewise stance, fairly well protected behind his left shoulder, offering a target that Ray was seldom hitting solidly. With his sight impaired, Carmen had to square around in order to find his opponent with his good eye, and from then on he presented a target that should have made Robinson's job easier.

Nothing is easy for Ray these days. Nothing ever will be again.

With his vision dimmed, his defense opened up and his timing off, Basilio chased the greatest fighter of his time all over the ring, and kept on chasing him. Ray jabbed and retreated, waiting for opportunities to take potshots. When he landed them he landed one at a time, almost never putting blows together, in combinations. There were rounds when he seemed lethargic and spiritless as well as physically exhausted.

Robinson did a curious thing, difficult to understand from the strategic view. After shutting Basilio's eye, he circled incessantly to his own left, moving into Carmen's line of vision rather than away from it. Maybe, like an aging shortstop, he can no longer go to his right.

Afterward, Robinson said he had hurt his right hand. If Basilio didn't hurt all over, then he is even tougher than he looked in the ring, and that is beyond conceiving.

There was, of course, immediate speculation regarding a rubber match between these two. Jim Norris mentioned June but in view of the fighters' conditions at the finish, three months seems hardly enough time for repairs and reconditioning. Anyhow, it always takes time to get Robinson's name on a contract, even when his hand is fit to hold a ballpoint pen.

Pride, and nobody has more than Robinson, no doubt will tempt the champion to retire on his matchless record. On the other hand, pride may impel him to try once more to prove himself Basilio's master in any circumstances.

Perhaps money will be the biggest consideration of all. Prize fighters fight for money. The doubts and arguments that were raised last night and the honor that Basilio won would combine to put an awful lot of money in a New York ballpark.

Patterson's Man

A Confused Cus D'Amato Puts Up His Dukes

NEW YORK, N.Y., *June 4, 1958*

O F ALL the stock characters in fiction, none is more fixed, frozen, unvarying, and trite than the fight manager. He is a gross and evil man, the embodiment of greed and cruelty, a fat and swaggering vulgarian with a fat cigar in his fat face and not an ethic on the premises. That's the popular-priced factory model. Contrasting with this version is the real thing.

He is a neat man of middle height, middle age, and almost ascetic tastes. He is physically presentable, well-scrubbed, well-dressed, with his gray crewcut impeccably barbered. He is a personable fellow, a trifle dull. He is a voluble man, rather prolix, with a tendency to misuse polysyllables. He is seldom, if ever, profane.

When others of his age were getting interested in girls, he was already wedded to the fight business. It consumed all his money, all his devotion. He is more than dedicated; he is obsessed.

All his life he has heard that when a man has the heavyweight champion of the world he has the fight business by the scruff of the neck. In his middle age, this manager got a boy who won the heavyweight championship but the fight business didn't sit up at his command and beg the way it was supposed to do. This bewilders him but he doesn't know he is bewildered. Convinced that he knows all the answers, he is suspicious of those who don't accept his answers on faith. He can only conclude that they're in league with the enemy.

This is a fair description of Cus D'Amato, manager of Floyd Patterson, a decent and confused fellow.

D'Amato is fighting a holy war against the International Boxing Club, which may or may not be the most sinister influence in sport this side of Frankie Carbo. It is difficult to establish exactly how and when and why this became a crusade.

When Patterson, the Olympic middleweight champion of 1952, was a rising young professional, the papers were full of complaints from D'Amato that mob guys kept trying to move in and the big promoters wouldn't give his tiger any work. In 1954 when the I.B.C. was matching Patterson in Madison Square Garden with Joe Gannon and Jimmy Slade, Cus denied that he had ever said any of those things that had been published.

At that time he was on cuddly terms with Jim Norris, the I.B.C. president who has lately retired to less hazardous pursuits like betting on his race horses. They were chummy enough for D'Amato to borrow $15,000 from Norris. Jim had a notion that it was an advance against Patterson's services but Cus said no, it was no more than any red-blooded American boy would do for a pal anytime.

Then Patterson won the title in a match promoted by the I.B.C. and Cus swore eternal vengeance against the firm that had given his tiger the big chance. Publicly he repeated all the charges of discrimination which he had denied making before.

Except for the principals in the quarrel, nobody cares a whoop about Cus' diplomatic relation with any promoter. The fight public is interested only in fights, and here the details are somewhat sordid. Having won the championship in November 1956, Patterson defended it in July 1957, against an unfortunate boy who was mistakenly designated as the leading challenger. It was a sorry thing, but it was a title fight nevertheless.

A month later Patterson took on an amateur for laughs. If the show had been telecast it might have put Sid Caesar, Phil Silvers, and Milton Berle out of business, but as a championship contest it fell short of the ideal. Nearly ten months have passed since that performance, eleven since the match with Hurricane Jackson.

There is a rule, observed mostly in the breach, that a champion must defend his title once every six months. At tardy last, the World Boxing Committee has declared that Patterson must take on a challenger by September 30 or forfeit his championship. That's giving him thirteen months since his last performance, fourteen since he boxed a professional.

Perhaps unreasonably, the World Boxing Committee insists on a qualified opponent. It has designated as eligible Eddie Machen, Zora Folley, Willie Pastrano, and Roy Harris. Cus says he won't have any part of them. He's making goo-goo eyes at Dan Hodge, an amateur wrestler; Pat McMurtry, who was whipped by Willi Besmanoff; and Allen Williams, a character from Australia.

It is inconceivable that official demands for a title fight could be satisfied by a match with any of these opponents. D'Amato says that if he is crowded by the men who are paid to supervise boxing he'll take 'em all into court—on what grounds? On the charge that they're doing their job?

Since he subscribes to other myths of the fight business, the chances are Cus believes the fiction that titles can be won and lost only in the ring. He doesn't realize that the only thing that establishes a champion is official recognition, that he and his tiger could be thrown away and forgotten unless he lets his guy fight.

Even at this late date, he's still saying that Patterson may defend his title three times this summer. This is June. Does Cus really think he's kidding anybody? He's such a nice guy, and so badly mixed up.

That Old Mary Ann

Max Baer, 1909–1959

NEW YORK, N.Y., *November 25, 1959*

THERE IS a handsome book almost thirty years old now called *The American Sporting Scene* with illustrations by Joseph W. Golinkin and text by John Kieran. One full-page drawing shows a grotesquely muscled gladiator, instantly recognizable as Primo Carnera, hung by the middle over the second strand of rope, his head and upper torso outside the ring.

Right behind him stands the man who has done this mischief. His feet are planted wide apart, his weight on the right leg. Both hands are low and the closed right glove is out here, wide of the hip and a trifle behind it, ready—if that sprawling galoot gets up—to whistle around in a sweeping arc with every ounce of its owner's weight and strength behind it. You can cover three-fourths of the picture, concealing everything but that right shoulder, arm, and glove, and there is no mistaking identities.

This has to be Max Baer winding up that old Mary Ann which no other fighter of any time could throw with quite the same gaudy and destructive and altogether unforgettable flourish.

When the news came that Max had died suddenly, the book was taken off its shelf and opened to this page. It was good to see Max Baer again at twenty-five, crackling with health, winding up to pitch the high hard one in from deep center field.

Max was on television refereeing a Zora Folley fight recently and he looked a little paunchy, though this may have been due to the cut of his working clothes or the tricks the camera sometimes plays. Certainly he looked great in San Francisco when Gene Fullmer fought Carmen Basilio there. Handsomely groomed as always, flat-waisted at fifty, straining the padded shoulders of his elegantly tailored jacket, he was full of bounce and full of a practiced patter about a heavyweight named "Johnson" who had recently won the championship from "Peterson" who had previously defended against an amateur named "Rutabaga."

When he died the papers told how he had won the world championship from Carnera June 14, 1934, clowned through exhibitions for a year and lost to Jim Braddock in his only title defense. Some papers described the wild and gory spectacle with Carnera, who was smashed down twelve times before Arthur Donovan stopped it in the eleventh round, and some told of his post-Braddock match with Joe Louis, when Max took the count on one knee in the fourth round.

He was savaged as a quitter after the Louis bout and he never denied that he could have gotten up, merely remarking that "if they want to see the execution of Max Baer it'll cost them more than twenty-five dollars a seat." To the best of my knowledge he never offered further explanation, but yesterday a man telephoned with a story which, if true, puts that incident in a new light.

The man had heard the tale years ago from Bayard Bookman, who was accountant for Max and his manager, Ancil Hoffman, and was in the dressing room on the night of the fight. It goes this way:

Max broke his right hand in training camp, but the injury was kept secret and the hand dosed with Novocain to protect the million-dollar gate. This is neither incredible nor unprecedented; other fighters have concealed injuries for far less money.

There was a threat of rain on the evening of September 24, 1935, and the fighters were sent to Yankee Stadium early to be ready in case the main event went on ahead of schedule, which sometimes happened in pretelevision days.

Actually, the bout didn't start until ten o'clock, but the fighters dressed and had their hands bandaged well ahead of time, too early to use Novocaine beforehand, for the effects would have worn off. During the bandaging, of course, there was a watcher from Louis' corner in

Max's room and he remained until fight time. As the hour neared, Max and the doctor slipped into the men's room where the doctor inserted the needle beneath the bandages.

Apparently the needle went in up near the wrist. At any rate, instead of merely numbing the hand, it deadened the whole right forearm. Within ten minutes Max was a frantic wreck, not far short of collapse. His friend Jack Dempsey almost literally had to drag him out for the fight.

"I knew Bayard Bookman well," said the man on the phone, "and there was no point in making up a story for me. If it was the truth, I can imagine what Max went through, and I saw the fight. Max had the intelligence and imagination to know what Louis could do to him, and here he was going in with his main weapon—the only weapon, actually—useless.

"Afterward they called him a coward, but I've always wondered."

Circus on Ice

Rangers, Canadiens Face Off at the Garden

NEW YORK, N.Y., *January 13, 1956*

IT STARTED sedately enough, if that adverb can ever rightly be applied to hockey, with the Rangers moving aggressively to the attack and keeping a steady pressure on the Montreal defense. At the beginning there was no reason to anticipate that the evening would produce some of the most rewarding fighting that has come off in Madison Square Garden since a Beau Jack or a Lew Jenkins used to drag in the crowds and keep them on their feet howling.

"Look at this," a girl said, caught in the crush of customers pushing in out of the rain just before the face-off. "You'd think the circus was in town."

In a sense, it was to be a small circus of the Roman type, starring Lou Fontinato, the Wild Man of Guelph, Ont., in gladiatorial combat with Maurice Richard, the Rocket of Mount Royal.

This was the big town's last sample of big league hockey before February. This season, for the first time in a decade, "big league hockey" has ceased to be a misnomer in the big town. For years the Rangers couldn't beat their mothers, with or without sticks, but this season they've been running second only to Les Canadiens, and even that redoubtable troupe had found the Garden no health resort. In four earlier visits, Les Habitants had gained three ties but won not at all.

Game and crowd and players seemed to warm up together. At first it was ebb and flow, swift skating, swooping forays, alert checking. Then oftener and oftener came the clash of sticks, the crash of big, padded bodies against the boards, the hunting cries of the fans sensing impending violence.

Halfway through the first period, with both teams at full force, Danny Lewicki scored for the Rangers. It was a double-barreled shot as Jacques Plante, the Montreal goalie, saved on Lewicki's first try and Lewicki, driving in close, caught the rebound and slammed into the net.

Skating back to battle stations, playmates pawed at Lewicki's haircut, warmly boxed his ears. Now all of a sudden the crowd was whooping and the rink was a battlefield. Little abortive clashes were breaking out all over the ice, mostly unseen or ignored by the officials.

Men slammed together against the boards, scuffed there briefly, straightened and glowered at each other, chest to chest like fighting cocks breasted in the pit. Here a man went halfway into a box. There a player scraped himself off the boards and took off after an opponent, bent on assault.

With the first period ending, the Rangers were holding their one-goal lead, partly, it seemed, because the Canadiens were getting more interested in physical combat than in hockey.

It wasn't clear exactly what happened in a skirmish near the boards on the Fiftieth Street side. Maurice Richard, skating to center ice, tossed his stick away but didn't seem to be aiming at anybody's head. He shoved with both hands against Fontinato's chest, like a small boy picking a fight on the playground.

The Rangers' dark defenseman is no admirer of the Marquess of Queensberry. Strictly a London Prize Ring man, he had his padded gloves off in the fragment of an instant. A lovely right caught Richard just outside the left eye. Skin burst and flesh cracked and blood ran in little parallel trickles down the Rocket's face, staining his white shirt.

Players and officials moved in and, to the crowd's astonishment, Richard drew back, showing no disposition for further action. Fontinato was raging, trying to shove past officials who held him off, starting little flank movements around the knot of men who fenced him off from Richard.

Pure joy swept the galleries. Crumpled papers and bits of waste were flung onto the rink. Photographers were out on the ice shooting eagerly. At length Fontinato was led to the penalty box for the second time in the evening, taking a comfortable lead over Detroit's Ted Lindsay as the league's most penalized badman.

The first period ended and the second started with Richard in the repair shop getting his wound closed with four stitches and a strip of tape. When he returned to a salute of boos, the Rangers had survived a perilous two minutes when, playing four men against Montreal's five, they controlled the puck chiefly on Andy Bathgate's elegant stickwork.

New York took control now, banging in three goals. The Rocket seemed chastened and his colleagues' tempers subsided, though at one point Boom Boom Geoffrion rose from the bench and shouted threateningly at an unperturbed Fontinato.

Less than three minutes of the game remained and New York had a fifth goal before Montreal scored. The Rangers got one more to restore their margin. When the teams skated off, you would have guessed wrong picking the league leaders.

Top Dogs

Best in Breeds and Breeders Strut
at Westminster Kennel Club

New York, N.Y., *February 9, 1954*

A N I D L E R dawdling in the crowd in Madison Square Garden yesterday was startled to feel a small, cold pressure on the back of his neck. It was made by a muzzle, but not the muzzle of a heater held by any of those sinister characters that Bob Christenberry is always throwing out of the fist fight business. This muzzle belonged to a Great Dane.

The old blood pit is currently occupied by pooches and people of assorted and sometimes mixed breeds, most of them growling and yapping at one another as they compete for scraps of silk in the seventy-eighth actual Westminster Kennel Club show.

For all the breeds and breeding on display at this most elegant of kyoodle carnivals, there is a wonderful sameness about people who go to the dogs. They sit for hours on little, hard chairs around the judging rings, gazing woodenly at the fauna on exhibition, or they go elbowing through the jammed aisles giving off little, excited yelps.

They wear something approximating a uniform. Males run heavily to hound's-tooth tweeds; the females favor pullover sweaters embroidered with animals of their fancy. In the great, rackety basement, for instance, a lady sat in a booth surrounded by several white poodles and the bosom of her blue sweater bore at least a dozen fuzzy replicas of the breed. She looked like a kennel all by herself.

Not far away, sleeping blissfully through the clamor, was a dog named Moe. Officially, he is Ch. Ernharkenburg's Stormson, one of the four hundred or so offspring of four-year-old Ch. Rancho Dobe's Storm, the Doberman pinscher that won best of show at Westminster last year, and the year before. Storm is retired now and two-year-old Stormson, called Moe when he's home in Willow Grove, Pa., carried on for the family yesterday by winning best of breed.

He snoozed under a blanket, only the tip of his black-and-tan nose showing, and in adjoining stalls his sons and daughters followed suit. Seems to be a tranquil family.

"He's a real showman," said Joe McGinnis, one of the dog men with the kennel of Mr. and Mrs. Fred T. Ueltzen, Moe's owners. "He didn't have a point last year when he came here and got winner's dog. Lately at a specialty show in Florida he got best of show, his son got winner's dog, one daughter got winner's bitch and the other was reserve bitch. Len Carey, who owns Storm, picked this one as choice of litter and sold him to the Ueltzens."

Incidentally, Storm and Mrs. Carey plan to watch tonight's finals on television.

Moe is handled by J. Nate Levine, who was a hockey player before he went to the dogs. Dog people, it seems, come from rather widely assorted fields. In addition to Levine, for instance, there's Tom Gately, a terrier-and-hound specialist. He used to be a prize fighter.

Then there's Mrs. Lina Basquette Gilmore, who works with Great Danes and German shepherds. She is a striking woman with glossy, dark hair and she wore a sweater of uncompromising red. She looks like a movie queen, and was. Lina Basquette was a siren in the silent films.

Between turns in the ring, the competitors live in the basement with accommodations varying according to their owners' taste. Here's one squatting elegantly on a leopard-skin pillow and there's a cocker spaniel wrapped in a bath towel swiped from a hotel.

Here's a row of stalls in which Irish wolfhounds sit alertly scanning the passing crowds, their eyes bright as though on the lookout for English wolves. There a man leads a miniature Boston terrier down an aisle, the tiny pooch flinching to right and left as chained Great Danes strain at him from one side and puffy white Great Pyrenees from the other.

Here among the poodles is a cinnamon job named Lu-Jim's Pixie Princess. She isn't a ch., yet she wears a crown on her brow, a tiara of silver that looks as though it started existence as a lady's bracelet.

There's one Bernese mountain dog in the show, and he came close to being the prime personal favorite here. A shaggy critter, he lay with his chin on the floor of his abode and gazed up through the most spectacularly bloodshot eyes this side of Skid Row.

An Irish setter was noted wearing a blood-stained bandage on a paw, but no mangled dog-lovers were in evidence. This was a surprise, for troops of small boys were sidling through the aisles reaching out to pat every beast en route. You'd think Eighth Ave. would swarm with fingerless children.

One Red Rose

The Green Kid on Middleground Plucks a Derby Trophy

LOUISVILLE, KY., *May 6, 1950*

THE BAWLING of the crowd still thundered up into the gray skies when the jockeys came striding through the alley from the track to the riders' quarters beside the Churchill Downs paddock. The seventy-sixth Kentucky Derby was over, and the losers walked swiftly, as though in a hurry.

Little Bill Boland, the eighteen-year-old apprentice who never won a stakes race before last Saturday, never visited Churchill Downs before this week, and never saw a Derby before this afternoon, wasn't with them. He was sitting on his horse, Middleground, in the big horseshoe of carnations growing in front of the tote board, fingering the blanket of roses they had hung over his lap while the King Ranch trainer, Max Hirsch, accepted congratulations, and the owner, Robert Kleberg, accepted $92,650 and a $5,000 gold cup.

In the second swiftest and perhaps the prettiest and most exciting of Derbies, Boland had brought Middleground around the rushing Mr. Trouble and the punctured California bubble, Your Host, to take command at the top of the stretch. He had run away from the powerful Hill Prince and swept under the wire the winner by a length and a quarter.

Now as the losers hustled away, Eddie Arcaro and Johnny Longden walked side by side. They'd been up on the two favorites—Longden on Your Host, which was 8 to 5, and Arcaro on Hill Prince, which was 5 to 2. Hill Prince had earned $10,000 in second money. Your Host had got there ninth, four lengths ahead of the bush-league rookie, Hallieboy, which made sordid company for a Hollywood immortal.

"I was lucky, too," Arcaro was telling Longden. "I got the breaks." He stepped along, lashing abstractedly at a boot with his whip.

"You never had any trouble anywhere?" Eddie was asked.

"Not anywhere," he said. "The only horses I had to come around were the leaders. I was lapped on the winner at the quarter-pole, but he opened up two lengths on me."

"You were coming hard in the last sixteenth."

"I didn't think I was catching him at the finish," he said. "Did it look like it? Well, maybe Hill Prince was picking him up a little, but I didn't think so."

Longden, an expressionless gnome, said he'd want Your Host to have another chance before he would be convinced the colt couldn't go a mile and a quarter. "I didn't worry when Mr. Trouble went past me the first time," he said. "I was pretty sure we could take him again. But I can't understand Your Host. He tossed it up corning into the stretch. Yeh, I'm a little disappointed. I thought he'd do better."

Newspapermen and photographers clamored through the jockeys' quarters, stumbling over benches, clambering onto one another. While they waited for Boland, Doug Dodson, who had ridden Mr. Trouble, explained that he was forced to make his move earlier than he'd wanted. Your Host's pursuers began to crowd him going to the far turn, he said, and he feared that if he waited he'd find himself with no place to go. So he took the lead from Your Host and finished him, but the battle finished Mr. Trouble.

Then Boland came in and there was a rush to his corner of the room. A jock who was nearly trampled looked up and muttered wryly: "Gosh, looks like somebody win something."

Boland is an immature kid with a lean, unsmiling face, ice-blue eyes, and wavy blond hair. The cameramen hollered to him and turned him this way and that and he complied reluctantly, never relaxing. They kept calling for a great big smile and he'd give them the faintest twisted grin, showing widely spaced teeth out of one corner of his mouth. He was in a hurry to get it over with. And you couldn't tell whether he was scared or bewildered or utterly indifferent.

His words were barely audible when he said he'd thought he was the winner in the upper stretch, but wasn't sure until he was home. He broke away from the shouting photographers, saying he wanted his shower.

He wore the same dead pan that had been on his face two days before when he sat in front of the King Ranch barn beyond the backstretch, staring straight ahead while a horseman came up and said to Max Hirsch: "Can I ride your boy on my filly in the stake tomorrow?"

"Is she a kind filly?" Max had asked. "Gentle?" Like a father solicitous of his small son.

"She's got very nice manners," the man had said. "She's very well behaved."

"All right," Max had said, and the man had gone away. He hadn't looked at Willie. Willie hadn't looked at him. But yesterday Willie won the Kentucky Oaks with the man's filly, Ari's Mona, earning $2,100 for himself. Last Saturday, getting his first stakes victory with Better Self in the Gallant Fox Handicap, he'd picked up something more than $4,000. And the jockey's 10 percent of today's purse was $9,265.

It's been a fair week for Willie.

A few minutes after the jockey room was cleared of its confusion, four people were seen walking down the track toward the backstretch stables. Hiking along just inside the clubhouse rail was a kid in a peaked cloth cap and leather windbreaker, with blue jeans clinging tightly to bowed legs. He carried one red rose from Middleground's blanket.

The thousand who saw him pass didn't recognize the kid who'd just won the Derby.

A Gold Cup

Bringing It Home from Louisville, Courtesy Count Turf

New York, N.Y., *May 8, 1951*

WHEN THE train from Louisville pulled into Penn Station, a great big man got off, watching his step as nervously as a man carrying a bowl of goldfish across Times Square. This man was carrying a polished mahogany case about two and a half feet tall. With him was a little, grinny guy almost exactly the size of the magnum of champagne which the porter held cradled in his arms. There was a rush of feet and a boy and girl plunged down the station stairs and hurled themselves on the big man.

"Look out!" Jack Amiel warned his son and daughter. "Don't scratch it."

"Is this it?" the kids asked. "Honest?" They stood off and regarded the gleaming box. Jack Amiel, who owns Count Turf, and Conn McCreary, who rode the colt in the seventy-seventh Kentucky Derby, stood off and regarded them. The case held the Derby Gold Cup, which the kids had ordered by telephone Friday night.

"We've got the place for it all picked out," they had told their father. Now their eyes were shining the way Amiel's and McCreary's had shone the night before.

The night before—Saturday evening—the only two men in the world who had truly believed in Count Turf had got aboard the train, got settled in a bedroom, and then removed the cup from its case and its swaddling of tissue and soft flannel. They had pulled a folding chair into the middle of the room and set the cup on its green marble base, both steadying it with anxious hands. Then they sat back and gazed with pious eyes.

A long while later they put the cup away, got out a deck of cards, and started to play gin rummy.

"What do you want to play for?" McCreary asked. "Tenth of a cent? Penny a point? Dollar?"

"Anything," Amiel said, "I'll play for anything."

Rakish mischief crept into the jockey's grin. "Let's play for the Gold Cup," he said softly.

His employer howled as though hit with a battery.

Whenever visitors came into the room, the cup was taken out again, set up, admired, and tenderly returned to its case. Once, gazing at it, McCreary said a curious thing.

"It seems to me," the little harp said, hesitantly as though the idea embarrassed him slightly, "that the Derby has come to be a kind of religious thing. Like for people that don't have any Confession."

There'll never be another night like that for Jack Amiel, the Broadway restaurateur—not if he wins a dozen Derbies. For this was his first. It was McCreary's second—he won on Pensive in 1944 and was eighth, fifth, third, and fifth in four others—but none was like this for him, either. This one was his answer to the guys who had said he was washed up, and to Amiel, who had vowed he wasn't.

"How did you happen to buy the horse?" Amiel was asked.

"I was crazy about Count Fleet," he said. "I used to see him race and I thought he was great. Well, I always buy a few yearlings at Saratoga, and when I saw this one in the ring, the muscling of his chest and shoulders impressed me. I thought he looked just like his sire, and later John Hertz, who owns Count Fleet, told me this was the first Count Fleet he ever saw that looked like the sire. I figured the yearling would bring $14,000 to $16,000 and he'd be worth it. But I got him for $4,500. Anyhow," he said, "his breeder, Dr. Porter Miller, called me before the race to wish us luck. I thought it was the nicest thing. I told him: 'You let this horse go so cheap, I hope you get the $2,500 award for breeding the winner.'"

McCreary told how he had sat in the jockeys' room plotting silently while other riders talked. "I know my orders will be to lay back and wait," one kid said, and then another and another said the same thing and Conn thought: Well, if all but three or four would be waiting with their horses, he'd be better off close behind the leaders, ahead of the heavy traffic.

So as soon as he could he tucked in behind the three pacemakers, "letting them run interference." When a horse started to move outside of him, he moved to avoid being shut off, passing everything but Repetoire.

"Repetoire bumped me," he said, "and I yelled: 'Hey, none of that!' and bumped him back. Then I was in front. I knew I had it."

The chart had Count Turf eighteenth at the start, eleventh at the half mile, sixth at three quarters, and fourth at the mile. "Actually," Conn said, "Count Turf got his nose in front at the three-eighths pole. That's seven-eighths of a mile from the start. I could have gone to the front any time after a half."

Another visitor had arrived and the cup came out again. McCreary eyed it. "I wish they'd give a little one for the jockey," he said. "I'd rather have it than the money."

He meant it. His 10 percent of the purse is $9,800 and, as a gift from the owner, there'll be a $1,000 bond for each of McCreary's four kids. But Conn meant what he said. When he said it, anyway.

The Swiftest Halfwit

Whirlaway and His World

B<small>EN</small> J<small>ONES</small> had been practically glowing with confidence when he

N<small>EW</small> Y<small>ORK</small>, N.Y., *April 8, 1953*

saddled Whirlaway in the Kentucky Derby and Eddie Arcaro had been dubious because this was Eddie's first ride on the colt and in his short racing life Whirlaway had committed some deadly sins, like finishing behind things named Agricole and Cadmium and Little Beans and Pony in Florida and running wide into the Keeneland homestretch to kiss off the Blue Grass Stakes by six lengths.

Now, on May 10, 1941, at Pimlico, it was Ben who was stall-walking fretfully before the Preakness, and Arcaro was laughing at his fears. Having won galloping by eight lengths in the fastest Derby up to that time, Arcaro was positive nothing in this field could be close at the wire.

He was so blandly sure of his horse, in fact, that when the others came out of the gate, Eddie and Whirlaway didn't. Not right away. King Cole, Ocean Blue, Dispose, Curious Coin, Our Boots, Porter's Cap, and Kansas, they came piling down past the stands with the jocks whipping and yelling and driving for position on the first turn. And away back, five lengths behind the field, Whirlaway came loping along counting the house with Arcaro sitting still as a blue point on the half-shell.

Eddie sat still down the backstretch as Whirlaway picked up horses in his own good time. Then with three still in front of him, Arcaro took the colt to the outside and clucked softly.

There was a curious sound from the crowd, a sort of deep bass "whuumph!" of exhaled breath—not a drawn-out "ooooohhh!" because the horse race didn't last that long.

"He moved around his field with a bold burst of speed," the chart reported afterward. Bold burst of speed? What he did to those horses was hard to believe even while you were seeing it. He cooked 'em, fried 'em. You could almost hear them sizzle, see them curl like froglegs in the pan.

The story was told later that Johnny Gilbert, setting the pace with King Cole, heard a rush of wind and glanced to his right, and Arcaro shouted, "So long, Johnny!" "So long, Eddie!" Gilbert shouted at the diminishing copper blur ahead of him.

That was all. Arcaro took hold of his horse and eased him in—five lengths behind the field going away, five lengths in front coming home. "Johnny," Arcaro said to Gilbert as they dismounted, "wipe the jam off my mouth, will you? I been on a picnic."

That was Whirlaway, whose death was reported yesterday from France, where he had been in stud on lease to the French breeder Marcel Boussac. The beautiful chestnut son of Blenheim had passed his fifteenth birthday last week.

He wasn't the greatest horse that ever lived, but he was just about the most exciting. Every time he stepped on a track you knew that some time during the race you were going to see that breathless, blinding, tremendous burst which was as stirring a spectacle as any field of sports could produce.

He was Babe Ruth, Jack Dempsey, Bill Tilden, Bobby Jones—not just a champion but a champion who was also the most colorful figure in his game. Today the memory of him is so vivid it is difficult to believe that a dozen years have passed since his three-year-old season. So many pictures come back to mind.

Arcaro in the Lord Baltimore Hotel after that Preakness and a guy asking him what happened at the start and Eddie saying, "I got left."

"No, Eddie, not really left."

"Well," Arcaro said, "he dwelled. But when you cluck to this horse, he gets to other horses faster than any horse I ever rode. When you move on this horse, it's like moving in a Cadillac."

Whirlaway in the Narragansett Special, beaten by War Relic in a finish so unexpected that the management had prepared the winner's blanket of flowers in the colors of Calumet Farm, Whirlaway's home. And had Whirlaway's name engraved on the cup too, if memory serves.

He was favorite that day, of course. He ran sixty times and was favorite forty-nine times. In his last forty-five starts the only time he wasn't bet down to favoritism was the Pimlico Special of 1942, when he walked over by himself and there wasn't any betting.

This was the horse that had seemed such an unpredictable rockhead as a two-year-old that Grantland Rice said to Ben Jones, "I hear your colt is a halfwit."

And Ben said, "I don't know, Granny, but he's making a halfwit out of me."

Great, Glittering, Gilded Fleshpot

Cutting the Ribbon at the New Aqueduct

P QUEENS, N.Y., *September 15, 1959*
REDICTABLY AT 11:45 A.M. yesterday George F. Seuffert upped with his baton, and the strains of the National Anthem spilled over the sunny landscape of Queens County, officially designating America's newest, biggest, and gaudiest gambling hell as the land of the free and the home of the brave. For the remainder of a golden autumn day, horseplayers prowled the premises of New Aqueduct in a brave quest for something free. They found it—misinformation.

The "change" board at Aqueduct is an electrified gizmo on top of the tote board which flashes messages in golden lights reading: "Scratch 1A," "No. 7 five pounds over," "Please bet early." Showing admirable restraint, management refrained from adding "and often."

As a matter of fact, the exhortation wasn't necessary. Unfamiliar though they were with the geography of the sprawling plant, distracted as right-thinking people must be when surrounded by sixteen bars and forty-six oases offering other refreshments, opening-day crowds relied on the animal instinct of the horseplayer and found their unerring way to the mutuel windows. There they yielded up their worldly goods as though it were their valorous aim to restore in a single afternoon the $33,000,000 spent to construct this great, glittering, gilded fleshpot. Home of the brave, indeed.

At 12:01 P.M. Gov. Nelson Rockefeller, Mayor Robert Wagner, and five assistant pants-cutters assumed a Matt Dillon stance at the finish line, drew seven pairs of gold-plated scissors, and snipped a red-white-and-blue ribbon stretched across the track. Having thus cleared the way for the horses, they repaired to the Man o' War Room, the club-house restaurant, to break zweiback with a thousand or so other V.I.P.s of assorted sexes.

Most of the guests wore lapel pins on which appeared a large block "A," similar to that worn by Hester Prynne.

Pains were taken to make sure that none of the 42,473 voters present would be deprived of an opportunity to view the distinguished father-in-law of Anne Marie Rasmussen in the flesh, or rather, in double-breasted worsted. The Governor broke away from the festive board in time to present a piece of hardware to the winning owner in the first race, then clasped hands over his head and strode about the paddock in front of the stands gesticulating like a victorious pug in Sunnyside Gardens. Some spectators were so unfeeling as to boo.

"They did?" said Eddie Arcaro incredulously when this was reported to him. Mr. Arcaro feels that his copyright is infringed when New York race crowds boo anybody else, but he was already under the stands, groping through the catacombs to the jockeys' quarters, when the Governor was saluted. His horse had finished out of the money in the first race.

"I got off to a great start," Eddie said wryly. "Dropped my stick leaving the gate."

"I," said Hank Moreno, "am the first jockey shut off at New Aqueduct." He, too, was out of the money, while Willie Shoemaker drove a chestnut gelding named Four Lane down the long brown stretch to win by half a length.

The first winner was an even-money favorite but Shoemaker's mount in the second race, Ira Eaker, was $9.10 and when Willie got him home in front, too, he wrapped up a $22 daily double.

Before the afternoon was done, however, Shoemaker was in a hospital with bruises, lacerations, contusions, and perhaps a cracked rib. Riding Amber Morn over the turf course in the fifth race, he was thrown when his horse stumbled midway of the backstretch.

Willie's remaining assignments were canceled, of course. Two other jockeys, Dave Erb and Bobby Ussery, gave up mounts during the afternoon, not because they were hurt but because they couldn't make the weight. They said the new steam room wasn't hot enough.

"It's a 1959 racetrack," one rider said mildly, "and the jocks are out doing road work like in 1900."

There were a dozen horses in the Aqueduct Handicap, the featured seventh, and Hillsdale, biggest money-winner of the year, knocked off the winner's share of $37,880 about as expected. Carrying a tall jockey named Thomas Barrow and enough lead to make top weight of 132 pounds, the handicap star held the rail fairly close to the pace to the top of the stretch, got out of a tight fit there to come outside and win by three-quarters of a length from Bald Eagle.

This time George D. Widener made the presentation, without audible objection. A lot of customers were still preoccupied trying to find their way around. Ordinarily the remarks most frequently heard at the grandstand rail are "I shoulda had 'im," and "Whaddaya know?" But not yesterday.

At Aqueduct the password was: "I been right here alla time. Where was you?"

Sportsmen of
the Fifties

Singular Acts of Greatness Redeem a Tainted Decade

NEW YORK, N.Y., *December 17, 1959*

O NE YEAR in sports is much like any other but decades are different. A decade can be viewed in perspective, and each has a character of its own. "The Era of Wonderful Nonsense," Westbrook Pegler called the Twenties, turning a wryly mellow gaze back on the days of his youth, which were also the days of Babe Ruth and Bill Tilden and Bobby Jones and Jack Dempsey and Gene Tunney and Red Grange and Earl Sande and the young Eddie Shore.

No Pegler applied so apt a term to the dizzy, depression-ridden Thirties. It was a time of dance marathons and endurance flights and flagpole sitters and walkathons, when crowds flocked to Yankee Stadium to see Jim Londos pin Ray Steele with his "unconscious hold." It was Dizzy Dean's decade and Carl Hubbell's, the age of Primo Carnera and Tony Galento and Pepper Martin and Gene Sarazen and Jesse Owens and Don Budge, of a young fighter named Joe Louis and a shy, inarticulate rookie from California named Joe DiMaggio.

Ted Williams batted .406 as the Forties unrolled, and before the era ended it produced Doc Blanchard and Glenn Davis, Stan Musial and the incomparable Chicago Bears and the matchless Eddie Arcaro. Mostly, though, it was a time of war, when a one-armed outfielder starred for the American League champions.

Now the Fifties wind to a close, and United Press International submits a list of the decade's top sports stories. It cannot escape attention that two of the ten are designated as outright "scandals," one is at least partly phony, and two others leave an unpleasant taste in memory. It was a decade of disillusion.

Prominent on the list are the college basketball sellouts of 1951–'52 and the so-called "cribbing scandal" that wrecked West Point's football team.

Ranked fifth in significance is the statement that "Russia outscored the United States in the 1956 Olympics," which isn't true because there is no national scoring in the Olympics and no team ever wins these games, but a guy gets mighty tired of pointing this out, especially when the adjacent column carries a meaningless tabulation captioned "Unofficial Score."

Third most important story in U.P.I.'s judgment was major league baseball's move to the Pacific Coast, and seventh was Ingemar Johansson's victory over Floyd Patterson.

The former was a development long overdue and greatly to be desired, but effected in an atmosphere of deceitful contriving which left the game wearing the dollar sign like a brand. The latter was a bona-fide upset that should have been a tonic for boxing, except for its shabby aftermath.

There is no quarrel about the other top stories—Roger Bannister's conquest of the four-minute mile, Don Larsen's perfect World Series game, Bobby Thomson's theatrical home run ending the 1951 baseball season, Ben Hogan's almost miraculous comeback in golf after his dreadful automobile accident, and the unrivaled record of Rocky Marciano, retired undefeated heavyweight champion of the world after forty-nine consecutive victories.

Bannister's achievement won top ranking and deserved it, for his was much more than a superior physical performance, more than a victory over the stopwatch. It was primarily a triumph of the spirit. When the blond Oxonian broke the time barrier he removed forever the psychological obstacles which had fenced runners off from this goal since man learned to walk on his hind legs.

Young Dr. Bannister went a mile in 3:59.4 on May 6, 1954. When he broke the tape, the impossible ceased to exist. He had hardly wiped the perspiration away when his record was broken, and in the five years since then runners have been beating four minutes in herds. For a little while, though, this man stood where none had stood before, in all the centuries in all the world.

Perhaps there will be another champion in the Sixties with a record to match Marciano's. Maybe some pitcher in the Continental League will deliver a perfect World Series game. Certainly many men will run faster than Bannister, some will shoot lower scores than Ben Hogan, and possibly there'll be another like Eddie Arcaro.

In their time, however, these stood alone. As long as the Fifties are remembered, they will be recognized as men of the decade. Remembering them, it may be possible to forget the cheaters, the bribers, the point-shavers, the quick-money operators.

★ BASEBALL 1952–1961 ★

The Mother Tongue

A Wannabe Sportswriter Makes His Pitch

NEW YORK, N.Y., *April 15, 1952*

THE MAJOR LEAGUE baseball season—which means, translated, the annual struggle for the gonfalon in both the senior circuit and the Harridge loop—opens today. It is an occasion which affects various individuals in various ways. It has impelled two normally law-abiding citizens to trespass upon a field legally posted by Mr. Frank Sullivan, the Sage of Saratoga, curator of clichés, platitudes, and bromides for the American Museum of Iniquitous Antiquities.

Somewhat surprisingly, the poachers are not baseball writers, or even baseball broadcasters. They are horse-race reporters fetlock-deep in turf lore, and each is better than a green hand with an inept aphorism himself.

They have submitted the following record of an interview, presumably overheard, between an applicant for a job as baseball writer and a sports editor who wonders whether the candidate can make the grade, fill the breach, and carry the ball:

Question (by sports editor): What is baseball?
Answer: The national pastime.
Q.: Good, very good. Now, what is the game played with?
A.: The horsehide and ash.
Q.: Excellent. And what else?
A.: The sphere, hassocks. . . .
Q.: Yes, yes, I see you have the idea. And what is the game played on?
A.: It is played on the velvety sward.

Q.: Identify the home team.

A.: Our heroes.

Q.: And they oppose?

A.: The hated visitors.

Q.: Now, where do both teams go in the spring?

A.: They head for sunny climes.

Q.: Where do they go on road trips?

A.: To the hinterlands.

Q.: Fine, fine. What is another name for umpires?

A.: The arbiters, the men in blue, or, collectively, the Three Blind Mice.

Q.: What is a rookie?

A.: A rookie is the New Dazzy Vance, the New Babe Ruth, the New Ty Cobb. In special circumstances, the Left-Handed Dizzy Dean.

Q.: What does the rookie who is the New Ty Cobb run like?

A.: A deer.

Q.: What has he for an arm?

A.: A rifle.

Q.: On days when he doesn't run like a deer, what does he run like?

A.: The wind.

Q.: Anything else?

A.: A gazelle.

Q.: Corking, corking! What is the manager?

A.: The Gallant Skipper, the Silent Strategist, the Tall Tactician, the Brain.

Q.: Fine, that's enough. What is the president of the club?

A.: The prexy.

Q.: And prexies as a group?

A.: Magnates.

Q.: What is a pitching arm?

A.: The old soupbone.

Q.: What sometimes happens to old soupbones?

A.: They get chips.

Q.: Where do the chips go?

A.: To Johns Hopkins.

Q.: What happens after they are removed?

A.: GIANT HOPES SOAR AS JANSEN PREDICTS 20 WINS.

Q.: What is the name of that type of headline?

A.: Set and hold for spring.

Q.: Describe a man who has played baseball for five years.

A.: An old pro with know-how.

Q.: With anything else?

A.: A take-charge guy.

Q.: Can you elaborate?

A.: He is a sparkplug.

Q.: What does the sparkplug do?

A.: He keeps the pennant machine rolling along.

Q.: What is it when a man hits the ball out of the park?

A.: A four-master, a round-tripper, a circuit clout. . . .

Q.: Good, good, you're doing splendidly. Now, let me ask you this: what do you call it when two men are retired on one play?

A.: A double play.

Q.: A double play! A double play! Anything else?

A.: Well, a—er, rippling double play?

Q.: Think, boy, think! Isn't there—uh—say, a twin answer to the question?

A.: A twin answer?

Q.: Yes, twin, twin, t-w-i-n.

A.: I'm sorry, sir, it's just a double play to me. I can't think of anything else to call it.

Q.: Well, son, maybe I'm being a bit hasty about this. Maybe I don't need a new baseball writer. Tell you what I'll do; I'm going to put your name on the list. Leave your address here and I'll drop you a line if anything turns up.

A Chapter Closes

But Willie Mays' Story Is Just Begun

I

I T WASN'T the end of the story, but a chapter was coming to a close. It began—well, of course it really began three or four years ago when Willie Mays was a high-school kid playing at nights and on weekends with the Birmingham Black Barons when the club was at home, but hardly anybody got to read any of it until a little more than a year ago.

Then Willie, who had moved swiftly up in the Giants' chain through Trenton, N.J., to Minneapolis, started hitting about .250 for the Millers. As Tom Sheehan, the Giants' chief scout, recalls it: "We pick up the papers one week and say, 'Hey, Willie's hitting .300.' Next week we look and it's .350. Another week and it's .400. Finally, holy mackerel, Willie's up to .477, which has to mean he's going at something like a .600 clip, after that slow start. So he's got to come to New York.

"When the Giants called him up, Tommy Heath, the manager out in Minneapolis, told me over the phone, 'Tom, you'll think I'm crazy but this is the only guy I ever saw can bat .500.'"

It was just one year ago yesterday when Willie Mays went to bat for the first time in the Polo Grounds. He had joined the Giants on the road and had gone up twelve times without a hit but now, in his first appearance in the park that was to become his home, he got hold of a pitch by Boston's Warren Spahn.

It cleared the fence in left. It cleared the seats in the lower deck. It cleared the tall upper deck. It cleared the roof above that, and disappeared.

"That," said Spahn after the game, "was one of the best curves I ever threw in my life. It must've broke a foot."

So now, a year later, Willie was in Ebbets Field wearing the gray flannels of the Giants for the last time in—a year? Two years? Eternity? Nobody knows.

This morning Willie reports to the Army Induction Center in Whitehall St. and when they fit him with a soldier suit his future becomes something nobody in the world can predict. The story may not be done but the chapter is ended. New York had whipped the Dodgers twice and taken first place away from them, and on any other occasion the Giants would have been replaying those victories before this game and chattering jubilantly about Sal Maglie's four-hit shutout of Tuesday night. Instead, they were talking about Willie.

Leo Durocher, who has become a genius among defensive managers—with Willie playing practically his whole outfield—was saying how he wished the Army would take him and leave Willie. Maybe he wouldn't hit with Willie in camp games, the manager was saying, but he could rack up pool balls in the PX and do K.P. and pick up waste paper in the area and handle other such soldierly chores in Willie's stead.

Up in the stands, a Brooklyn fan was saying, "He plays the outfield like he's there all alone. A ball is hit and he flaps his arms like a bird."

In the press box a man said, "Leo's instructions to Willie are to catch anything he can reach, in left or center or right. He has top priority on all fly balls and it's up to the other outfielders to get out of his way."

Another man said, "Somebody down on the field was saying that if the Giants think Don Mueller and Henry Thompson are slow, wait till they see that outfield without Willie and they'll learn what the word 'slow' really means."

When the batting orders were announced, there was a fine, loud cheer for Willie. This was in Brooklyn, mind you, where "Giant" is the dirtiest word in the language. And the Giant they were talking about and cheering is a baby, only one year old in the major leagues, a child who is only learning to play baseball.

As it turned out, the Giants made it three straight for the Brooklyn series, stretching their lead to two and a half games, with only a modicum of help from Willie. They didn't need his aid because Jim Hearn pitched a four-hitter, digging his own way out of difficulties created by some shoddy fielding, and young Dave Williams hit two doubles and a home run.

Willie took a third strike, flied out, grounded out, and lined out on his four turns at bat, and his only play in the field was on a line drive by Carl Furillo, which Willie charged so hard the collision would have been fatal if he'd missed the catch.

The score was 6 to 1 and Brooklyn fans had given up when Willie came to bat for the last time. Suddenly the playground bubbled with noise, everybody in the place howling, clapping, yelling for a farewell hit.

Willie took a mighty swing, topped the ball so that it cracked down on his left foot, sprawled across the plate, and the cheers went on unabated. He took another fierce riffle, and missed. Then he lined low and hard and straight to Pee Wee Reese at shortstop. Cheers followed him to the dugout steps, where he tipped his cap hurriedly.

He was standing with arms folded in center field when the game ended. As he jogged toward the dugout, all four umpires purposely cut across the diamond to wave good-bye. He caught up with the victorious Hearn, offered a hand, and hesitated at the dugout, where three or four kids were pushing scorecards and autograph books toward him.

Then he disappeared in the tunnel to the clubhouse, where his playmates gave him a portable radio and he got a tie clasp, suitable for dress uniforms, from Leo and Laraine Durocher.

On the organ, Gladys Goodding played "I'll See You in My Dreams."

Dept. of
Emotional Reactions

Dodgers' Carl Erskine Wrests Game 5 from Yanks

BRONX, N.Y., *October 8, 1952*

Wrest Carl Erskine was a kid pitcher in Montreal he was personally scouted by Branch Rickey, then the principal indoor genius of the Dodgers. Watching with broody gaze from under the dark tangle of his brows, Rickey saw the young man win a two-hit shutout, tossed away the cold carcass of his cigar, and took himself back to Brooklyn alone.

Rickey journeyed north again for the same purpose and Erskine responded by winning another, 2 to 1. The great man pulled his circuit rider's black slouch hat lower over his eyes and returned to his lair in Montague St., alone.

It happened again and again. Rickey made four, maybe five trips to Montreal just to look at Erskine, and not once did the International League hitters get more than one run off the kid.

"What in the holy name of A. Doubleday," Erskine was asking himself, "does the man expect me to do? Have I got the wrong idea about this game?"

There came at length a night when Rickey sat in the stands as Erskine struggled and scrambled through a game to win, 6 to 5. That's when Rickey took him for Brooklyn. He didn't bother to clear up the young man's bewilderment until much later. Then he told him:

"Carl, I was waiting to observe your emotional reaction in a game when you didn't have your best stuff."

Students of emotional reactions had 70,536 of them to ponder yesterday in Yankee Stadium while Erskine labored all through the sunny
afternoon and into the sultry dusk to win the fifth game of the World
Series for the Dodgers, 6 to 5, in eleven tremendous innings.

Customers expressed their emotions by wild animal cries, by boos
and cheers for a California politician named Richard Nixon—first
Republican to be jeered by a World Series crowd since Herbert Hoover
got it in 1931—and, in one instance, by slugging an usher earnestly
upon the mandible.

But if young Mr. Erskine felt any emotion himself he didn't show
it until he had thrown a third strike past Yogi Berra for the game's
last putout. Then, grinning like a billiken, he suffered himself to be
thumped and hugged and patted and mauled by all such Dodgers as
were able to lay a paw upon him.

Those who couldn't get through the pack around Erskine ran out to
intercept Duke Snider and beat upon him. Snider had won the game
once with a two-run homer which put the Dodgers in front, 4 to 0,
then tied it with a one-run single after John Robert Mize had sent
the Yankees ahead, then won it again with a one-run double in the
eleventh.

Erskine is an agreeable young man with good habits and an equally
good overhand curve. He does not drink, does not smoke, and does
not choke in the clutch. On out-of-town business trips, while his playmates sit in the hotel lobby waiting for somebody to discard a newspaper, he visits art museums.

He was a no-hit pitcher against the Chicago Cubs on June 19 and
no pitcher at all against the Yankees last Thursday, when New York
batted him out of the second game and beat him, 7 to 1. That day his
father may have wondered whatever gave him the idea of traveling
from Anderson, Ind., to Brooklyn to see his son pitch. Yesterday Erskine *père*'s doubts were dispelled.

Until the fifth inning, the only hit against Carl was a bunt by Mickey
Mantle. There were four hits in the fifth, including a home run by
Mize. Erskine must have been fairly beside himself after that destruc-

tive blow. At least, he was beside the Yankees, with both hands at their throats.

He retired the next nineteen batsmen who faced him. No others came up.

Unlike some men who forget their wedding anniversaries, Erskine is a dutiful husband. He was married five years ago yesterday.

Erskine, Snider, Mize, and Nixon—these were the featured actors of the most lurid entertainment yet offered in baseball's big show. Arriving late, waving and bowing, exchanging salutations with the Dodgers' Jackie Robinson, signing autographs, posing for pictures eating hot dogs, posing drinking pop, the Senator proved himself the most gifted grandstand performer since Happy Chandler.

Not even Republicans, however, hailed him as boisterously as they did Mize. When John Robert socked that three-run wallop for his third World Series homer in three successive days, the whole joint trembled. When he reappeared from the dugout to play first base, a noisier tumult saluted him; when it was announced over the public-address system that the hit was his two thousandth against big league pitching, eardrums split. The announcement was witless, for the figure includes hits made in World Series and All-Star games. No such figure will appear in the record books until Mize makes fifteen more hits in regular league games.

However, he deserved the applause. After all, he's older than Nixon, been around longer.

A Bus Named
Adolphus

The Cards' New Prexie Travels in Style

A ST. PETERSBURG, FLA., *March 14, 1953*
UGUST ADOLPHUS BUSCH, JR., the new president of the Cardinals, is a chubby gentleman called Gussie, about the size of a St. Louis brewer. He has horn-rimmed glasses, a zillion dollars, and an air of pleased bewilderment. He rides to the hounds and travels by bus.

The bus is named Adolphus, after Gussie's grandfather. It is a plush job that looks like a Greyhound wearing white tie and tails. It has a paneled interior, sleeping accommodations for eight, and several footmen out on the front porch.

If Adolphus carries Gussie through towns in the Cardinals' minor league chain this summer, chances are his well-shaped ears will be assaulted by hoarse, gasping cries of thirsty citizens. When the clubs were taken over by Anheuser-Busch, a firm that has specialized for generations in moistening the palates of this nation, the immediate result was to remove beer from the minor league parks.

The laws of many states forbid breweries to own or operate saloons, even indirectly. It doesn't apply to Sportsman's Park in St. Louis, where beers are sold, including Griesedieck, whose manufacturer spends $600,000 a year on the Cardinals' radio broadcasts to advertise his product in competition with Busch's Budweiser. However, because the Houston, Rochester, and Columbus clubs now are in the same stable as the brewer's big horses, beer of any brand will be illegal in those parks.

Comes the hot summer and fainting fans will be heaped in windrows in the grandstands clawing at their neckties and crying piteously for sustenance—"Buns! Hot dogs! Beer! For the love of heaven!"

The arrival of Gussie and Adolphus here this week was reminiscent of a story told about a similar occasion when Powel Crosley, having just bought the Cincinnati Reds, made his first visit to their training camp. Crosley was due to arrive for the opening of the exhibition schedule, and nervous lackeys attached to the club stalled around scanning the skies until his red plane hove into view.

The new owner was gathered up tenderly, convoyed to the ballpark by a fleet of scurrying junior executives, and eased into a box seat. One vice president slid a cushion under the presidential stern, another placed a scorecard in his lap, a third thrust a bottle of pop into one nerveless hand, a fourth produced a sack of peanuts.

"Now, Mr. Crosley," they told him, "our boys are the big fellows wearing red stockings. That's first base over there, second there, third, and that white thing is home plate. It's quite simple: The man with the stick, called a bat—"

The first hitter for the visiting team slashed a shrieking drive that lifted the Reds' third baseman bodily into the air, performed an appendectomy on him, and bounced crookedly into left field.

There was a strained silence in the presidential box, or so the story goes. More in sorrow than in anger, the new owner shook his head.

"Tch-tch-tch," he said. "Errors, so early in the season."

A similar air of taut expectancy was discernible here when Gussie, preceded into town by a public-relations expert, rolled up in Adolphus accompanied by assorted executives. Scarcely anybody connected with the Cardinals knew the new boss, for the sale of the club had been a hurried deal.

When it became necessary for Fred Saigh to dispose of his stock, Busch remarked idly to a vice president that it would be a shame if the Cardinals were to leave St. Louis. The vice president construed this as an order: Inquiries were made, and Saigh said he was about to accept an offer of $4,100,000 from a Milwaukee group.

In rapid negotiations, brokers' commissions were waived and cut off the purchase price; other details were arranged, such as having Saigh put $1,000,000 in escrow to discharge any tax obligations the club might have; and Anheuser-Busch bought for $3,750,000, subject to approval of the brewery stockholders. Holders of 1 percent of the stock voted no.

Aware of the boss's interest in the Bridlespur Hunt Club of St. Louis, the Cardinals half expected him to arrive on horseback wearing a pink coat and blowing on a horn. Instead, he showed up wearing a woolen shirt of burgundy hue and the bemused expression of a fox hunter whose horse had dumped him into a thicket of newspapermen, photographers, television cables, and newsreel cameras.

"How many ballgames have you seen?" he was asked.

"Not a hell of a lot," he said.

He said his elderly associate Mr. Anheuser was overjoyed in the new role as club owner, because he'd been a kid third baseman sixty years ago.

From the field, the players stared with faint apprehension, hoping the front-office enthusiasm for bus riding wasn't catching.

A Real Rough, Lovely Guy

The Late Bill Cissell and His Bad-Boy Ways

NEW YORK, N.Y., *May 7, 1953*

BILL CISSELL was a rough, tough, go-to-hell guy out of the cavalry who served a ten-year stretch in American League infields with a couple of years off for bad behavior. The White Sox paid a good chunk of gold for him as a rookie in 1928 and he should have been a great star, but he drank.

He drank with the White Sox and the Indians and the Red Sox and he never made any secret about it because he was a dead honest guy. In the autumn of 1936 Connie Mack drafted him from Baltimore and Al Horwits, who was a Philadelphia baseball writer then, said: "He is a good ballplayer and he has had a couple of years down in the minors and the chances are he has learned his lesson."

"Yes," Connie said, "I understand he is not drinking in the daytime now."

This story isn't primarily about Bill Cissell, but in order to make a point it is necessary to explain what sort of guy he was. It has been ten, maybe eleven years since Ciss was last encountered and that was out in California and he had a number of teeth missing. Not from age; probably from knuckles. He was a real rough, honest, lovely sort of guy.

Once he told a story about the first time he ever saw Ty Cobb. It was his rookie year with the White Sox and Cobb was an elderly gentleman playing out the string with the Athletics. Cobb went into third base,

Ciss related, and Willie Kamm was in the way so Cobb upped with his spikes and cut Kamm out of the way.

All the White Sox were enraged because they were fond of Kamm, the quietest, most inoffensive guy on the ball club. None was more furious than Cissell, the rookie at second base.

Next time Cobb reached first base and started for second, Cissell got the ball and, holding it in his bare fist, tagged Cobb squarely between the eyes. Then he invited Cobb to make something of it if he chose.

The ensuing dialogue, as Bill repeated it, eludes memory but the substance was this: Cobb, getting to his feet and dusting himself off, expressed willingness to meet Cissell under the stands after the game if Ciss insisted. But he managed to make it clear that he did not resent Cissell's energetic tactic and that he had used his spikes on Kamm without malice. Cobb had sought to reach third base and Kamm had endeavored to prevent it, and somebody had to lose.

Next day Cobb was out early giving Cissell a few pointers about playing ball.

There is another story which Grantland Rice tells about an evening in a hotel room with two retired ballplayers, Ty Cobb and Nig Clarke, the old Cleveland catcher.

Clarke was describing a technique he had perfected for retiring runners at the plate when there were two out. He'd catch the ball, make a sweeping gesture at the runner sliding home, roll the ball out toward the mound, and walk to the dugout. Half the time, he said, he'd never tag the runner but it enabled him to dodge spikes and the umpire seldom knew the difference.

"I probably got you out ten or fifteen times," he told Cobb, "without ever laying the ball on you."

Cobb came out of his chair and across the room and he had Clarke by the throat when Granny pulled them apart.

"I'll kill him!" Cobb was screaming. "He cost me ten or fifteen runs off my record!"

This, mind you, was years after Cobb and Clarke had retired.

The point is, that's the way guys used to play ball. Today they make a federal case of it when a guy named Martin belts a guy named Court-ney and a ruckus ensues on the field.

Maybe the old guys were wrong and the young guys are right. Per-haps the Browns' Clint Courtney shouldn't provoke the Yankees' Billy Martin by sliding into Phil Rizzuto with his spikes showing.

Maybe Sal Maglie shouldn't pitch high and tight to Carl Furillo, and Furillo shouldn't retaliate by throwing his bat at Maglie. If that's the case, the Dodgers' president, Walter O'Malley, certainly should not reward Furillo with a $50 bonus.

It is difficult to say which attitude is the wiser. Today a fellow runs considerable risk if he gets his features mussed up trying to win a ball-game. It may cost him a remunerative post-game appearance on televi-sion. Meanwhile, attendance at the games declines.

Like Rooting
for U.S. Steel

Martin's Hit in 9th Wins Yanks 5th Series in a Row

BRONX, N.Y., *October 6, 1953*
THE MORGUE doors yawned yesterday, snapped shut, then swung open again, and as they carted the remains away a man in the press box gazed thoughtfully at the knot of Yankee baseball players at first base tossing Billy Martin aloft like a beanbag. "You wouldn't think," said Mike Lee, the man in the press box, "that they could get so mercenary over a lousy $2,000."

The fiftieth World Series was over and this time the Dodgers really and truly were dead, beaten 4 to 3, in the sixth and final game after Carl Furillo had snatched them to temporary safety when they were only four strikes away from destruction.

In a florid finish that stretched dramatic license to the breaking point, Furillo saved the Dodgers from routine defeat by tying the score in the ninth inning with a two-run homer with one out and a count of three balls, two strikes on the scoreboard. Then Martin lowered the boom.

The gray and chilly day, suitable for funerals, had thickened into grayer, chillier twilight and some of the Yankee Stadium crowd of 62,370 had departed when Martin walked to the plate in the rusty glow of the floodlights. Hank Bauer was on second base, Mickey Mantle on first, and Yogi Berra had been retired. Clem Labine, Brooklyn's best pitcher, threw once for a called strike.

He threw another and Martin slapped a ground single over second base into center field. Duke Snider fielded the ball but didn't trouble to throw as Bauer went ripping home with the winning run.

The Dodgers trudged to their dugout behind third base, looking over their shoulders toward first, where the Yankees were spanking Martin. It was a sight worth at least a backward glance. Never again, perhaps, will it be possible to look on a baseball team that has just won the championship of the world for a fifth consecutive year. It never was possible before, never in any age.

Martin's single was a mercenary stroke, worth something like $2,000 to each Yankee, this being the approximate difference between winner's and loser's shares. On the holy pages of the record books— and these are sacred writings to a ballplayer—it represents a good deal more, for the blow broke a noteworthy World Series record.

It was Martin's twelfth hit of the six games. Nobody ever made more, even in an eight-game series, and nobody ever made so many in six. Twelve hits had stood as a record since Washington's Sam Rice made that total in seven games in 1925, and the Cardinals' Pepper Martin did the same in 1931.

Those Martin guys. Pepper personally took the Athletics apart in 1931. Billy was a rookie star against the Dodgers last year and this time the brash, combative, fist-slinging little hellion tortured them as a child might pluck the wings from a fly. His namesake needn't be ashamed of yielding his share of the record to a ballplayer like this.

It is an extraordinary achievement which the Yankees have brought off and the manner of its completion was so outrageously melodramatic that witnesses were shrieking senselessly at the end. Even so, it was a Dodger crowd. Even in the Yankee fortress, the alien cries for Furillo were wilder than the cheers for Martin.

"How can you root for the Yankees?" an actor named Jimmy Little had asked a friend earlier in the series. "It's like rooting for United States Steel."

"Do not forsake us," the page-one bannerline of the *Brooklyn Eagle* had implored yesterday following the Dodgers' third defeat. They weren't forsaken in enemy territory. They were only defeated in splendid competition.

For a show with such a taut ending, the last act began limply. The Dodgers made three errors in the first three innings, and the Yankees three runs in the first two. Even the incomparable Billy Cox booted one, and he's the man who, Casey Stengel says, should be required in fairness to the opposition to play third base in chains.

Whitey Ford, who is really pinker than he is white, allowed the Dodgers only one run in seven innings, confirming Stengel's conviction that there's a future in this Ford. Carl Erskine, making his third start for Brooklyn, went out for a pinch batter after four innings and might have departed earlier except for Ford's overdeveloped sense of sportsmanship.

In what should have been a big second inning, Ford was on third with the bases filled and one out when Berra hit a long fly to Snider. Ford tagged up, started home an instant before the catch. Twenty feet down the line his conscience overtook him. He started back, saw Joe Collins arriving from second base, turned toward the plate again, and was an easy half of a double play ending the inning.

This was light comedy. They came on with the corn in the eighth. First Allie Reynolds appeared unexpectedly, tramping in from the bullpen with purposeful stride, like a players' delegate come to make demands on the owners. He made demands, but chiefly on the Brooklyn hitters. Striking out Roy Campanella to close that inning, the Indian was really pouring that Kickapoo Joy Juice.

With two out and two on in the Yankee eighth, the crowd put in a pinch batter. Joe Collins was up for his turn, but from everywhere came cries of "Mize! Mize!" Yielding to popular demand, Stengel sent John Mize up to howling applause for what John and the fans agreed would be his last time. He grounded out.

Silence fell, but not for long. It has only returned just now, as these last lines are written. Down in the clubhouse, Ford has had the last word.

"I felt bad when Casey took me out," he said. "Then I thought, 'Well, he hasn't been wrong in five years.'"

"And Take
d'Batboy Witcha!"

Statistics Prove Baseball a Scandalous Dawdle

NEW YORK, N.Y., *April 27, 1954*

I N A delectable denunciation of the "figure-drunk, record-crazy micromaniacs" who describe baseball for radio and television, Mr. Richard Maney offered a striking statistic yesterday.

Mr. Maney, an authority on the home life of the Cree Indian, a Shakespearean scholar, and a St. Louis Cardinal fan who publicizes Broadway plays in his spare time, was writing a "guest column" for John Crosby, the vacationing radio-television critic. Wielding his truncheon against the quidnuncs who deafen their audience with twaddle about the ancestry, collar size, and political complexion of each batsman, he cudgeled them cruelly and defiantly tossed in some arithmetical data on his own.

The difference between Mr. Maney's statistic and those which pullulate in the ether is that his was both enlightening and germane to the subject. In a three-hour ballgame, he declared, "the ball is actually in play about twelve minutes."

Though this seems incredible, anybody who has ever engaged Mr. Maney in debate over a dish of sauce in the Artist and Writers (formerly Club) Restaurant knows better than to dispute the gentleman on a point of information. "Any stopwatch will prove it," he testified.

Assuming that Mr. Maney has personally clocked games and established the accuracy of his statement, we are shown what a scandalous dawdle the sport has become in recent years. It is bad enough that an operation which could be completed in fifty-one minutes (the record for a nine-inning game) now consumes more time than a Senatorial filibuster. It is worse when you realize that the filibuster offers more sustained action.

When there is published criticism of modern baseball's tortoise pace, Mr. Warren Giles, president of the National League, is wont to put the complaint away as the snivel of a sportswriter weary of his job. Nobody hollers about long games, he says, except newspapermen.

Mr. Maney's stopwatch furnishes an effective rebuttal. The time the ball is actually in play includes, of course, the time consumed by intentional bases on balls and the leisurely pick-off throws that pitcher and catcher make for their own amusement when there is no possible chance of trapping the runner.

A twelve-minute period constitutes one-fifteenth of a three-hour span. If that's all the entertainment the fans are going to get for their money, then the clubs should refund fourteen-fifteenths of the admission price, or $2.80 on a $3 ticket.

Barring Mrs. J. DiMaggio in a sarong, there is no more captivating spectacle in the entertainment field than the action of a ballgame. No mountain brook is lovelier than St. Louis' Stan Musial in his knee-sprung crouch at the plate glowering around the corner at the pitcher, or Cincinnati's Roy McMillan gathering in a ground ball and firing it to first in one fluid movement.

The show sorely needs competent direction, though. The pace is such that if the entertainment were presented in a theater the reviewers would horse-whip it clear into Cain's Warehouse.

Now and then authorities make a token gesture toward "speeding up the game." They'll limit the number of delegates to a conference on the mound, or demand that the pitcher kneel in the "on deck" circle while awaiting his turn at bat. This is bootless nonsense, for Leo Durocher can talk as long in a phone booth as in an auditorium and any man can shuck his windbreaker, select a bat, and lounge up to the plate while the pitcher is still performing his mumbo-jumbo with the resin bag.

What delays the game are those frequent and interminable powwows on the field, that eternal haranguing of the umpires. Managers feel they are unfaithful to their television public if they don't make a dozen appearances a day, and they won't tolerate umpires walking on their lines.

This year's rule forbidding fielders to leave their gloves strewn about the field has been attacked as a time-waster, though it has not been demonstrated that the additional weight retards the fielder's progress from his position to the bench. It never was brilliantly consistent to interrupt play while the public-address announcer implores a customer in center field to remove his hat from the wall, and at the same time permit the playing field to be littered like a schoolgirl's boudoir.

Trifles like these do not speed or delay the game materially. What baseball needs is a staff of tyrants like the noble old umpire Bill Guthrie, who could chase Babe Ruth from the premises with one imperious gesture and, seeing little Miller Huggins advancing from the dugout, could add: "And take d'batboy witcha!"

The Color of Money

Will Yankees' Elston Howard
Make Lineup in Birmingham?

NEW YORK, N.Y., *December 16, 1954*

BEFORE THERE were Negroes in organized baseball, Jim Crow's affairs were none of baseball's business. When the teams went South in the spring it was for physical, not social, training. If the players noticed that Negroes sat only in one section of the bleachers, or if they read the signs on the railroad stations, "Waiting Room, White," why, they accepted it as local custom that had nothing to do with them.

The visitor who mentioned the position of the Negro in the South heard a stock answer: "We know how to treat them down here and they keep their place. They're happier here than in your big cities up north with their slums and race riots."

Then Branch Rickey and Jackie Robinson broke baseball's color line. Baseball became an important area of influence in the nation's uncertain groping toward real democracy. It is no longer possible for baseball men to regard Jim Crow regulations in sports as something as remote from their affairs as voodoo drums in Haiti. Whether they like it or not, baseball men now must set an example in interracial relations.

That is why the Yankees should not knuckle down to Birmingham's Jim Crow baseball ordinance and play an exhibition game in the Alabama city next spring. Because of their preeminence in the game, the Yankees should be the last to conform to any local segregation policy.

Up to last year, Birmingham forbade "mixed" sports events involving Negro and white participants. Then the ordinance was repealed, and both the Dodgers and Giants played exhibitions there last spring. The Dodgers' weekend game drew well, the Giants and Indians only moderately in mid-week, Negroes making up a large majority of the crowds.

Since then, through a referendum in which balloting was very light, Birmingham restored the ban on mixed sports. The Dodgers are bypassing the town on their spring tour. So are the Giants, at a substantial financial sacrifice, for this is Willie Mays' home and Willie, playing with the world champions, could fill the park.

Chances are the crowd that would pay to see Willie and the other Giants would be mostly Negro, too, but the pigmentation of a fan's skin doesn't affect the color of his money. The Dodgers or the Giants and their Cleveland traveling companions couldn't give a bona fide exhibition without using their Negro players. The Yankees can, and have scheduled a game there.

Elston Howard, a catcher-outfielder, is the only Negro expected to report to the Yankee training camp. He has not yet made the team and perhaps he may not make it, though his chances are highly regarded in the Yankee office. Whether he makes it or not, he won't be used in Birmingham.

Jackie Robinson, barnstorming with a Negro team that included several white players, ran afoul of the Birmingham ordinance a couple of years ago. In this instance, "no mixed sports" meant "no whites allowed," and although at first blush it might seem ludicrous to consider this racial discrimination, it wasn't ludicrous at all because it was merely a reverse application of the same abhorrent principle.

A Negro newspaper in Birmingham called upon Robinson to resist. Editorially, it urged him to defy the ordinance and thus test its validity, or else cancel the game. Instead he knuckled down as the Yankees mean to knuckle down.

Robinson explained that he hadn't booked the tour but was merely lending his name and services to the organization, playing wherever the booking office scheduled a game. It was a mistake on his part.

Robinson is keenly and properly conscious of his importance in the Negro's struggle for recognition. Here was an opportunity to dramatize the cause in far more sympathetic circumstances than Jackie has encountered on other occasions. He blew the chance.

Even if he wins a job as a regular, there will be times in the spring when Elston Howard won't play, in order that he may have a day off or so Casey Stengel can try out another candidate. There is no reason why he shouldn't get his day off in St. Petersburg or Miami or Birmingham—except that in Birmingham it's a matter of yielding to pressure.

The Yankees could play Howard and make a test case of the ordinance's dubious legal standing. That would be an uncharacteristic bit of crusading, though. The Yankees have the Southern Association farm in Birmingham. They have no special wish to alienate any of the population through a political-social dispute.

They don't have to carry a torch, but they do their credit no good by giving aid and comfort to the voodoo worshippers. They could stay out of Birmingham—except that a crowd of fifteen thousand there would represent a nice financial touch for their local affiliate. Curious how often that consideration bobs up.

Knothole of Memory

My Old Home Team, the Green Bay Bays

NEW YORK, N.Y., *January 19, 1955*

NOSTALGIA IS thicker than sour cream around here today, all on account of a clipping from the Green Bay, Wis., *Press-Gazette*. The clipping turned up in the mail and all of a sudden winter melted away and it was 1912 again and under the grandstand in Hagemeister Park a small boy shivered with ecstasy at the unimagined, unforgettable privilege of shaking hands with Bobby Lynch, third baseman and manager of the Green Bay team in the Wisconsin-Illinois League.

There's a high school now on the ground where Bobby Lynch played, and the wooden stands and board fence with its strategically placed knotholes are long gone. A kid of the right height could see part of the field through a knothole, but for a fan with initiative there were better accommodations.

In right and left field were small gates to enable members of the ground crew to recover balls hit over the wall. If a kid got there by 9 A.M., say, he didn't have to be a skilled cracksman to unlatch a gate or, failing that, scoop away the soft earth and squirm under the fence. (Going over was a more ticklish business because of the barbed-wire along the top.)

Once inside, you could hide under the bleachers, and within four or five hours the crowd would start arriving and then you were safe, though a little hungry, having blown the noonday dinner.

The W.-I. League must have folded about 1915 but it had its share of pretty good ballplayers. There was Red Ormsby, a spitball pitcher for Green Bay who was an American League umpire for nineteen years, and Fred Mollwitz, the first baseman who went on to the Cubs, Reds, Pirates, and Cardinals. Freddie Thomas and Adam Debus, who were shortstops, and a pitcher named Frank Scanlan had brief hitches in the majors.

Heinie Groh was a shortstop with Oshkosh; La Crosse had Fred Luderus and Ed Konetchy, and one season a hawk-faced outfielder named Charles Dillon Stengel tore up the league for Aurora, Ill., batting .352.

Remembered best of all, perhaps, is Chief Williams, an outfielder off the Oneida Indian Reservation near Green Bay. The chief lives in Lac du Flambeau, Wis., now and recently he met up with Bobby Lynch, who has been a State Assemblyman for years. That's what this story in the *Press-Gazette* was about, the two of them together for the first time in twenty-five years, cutting up old touches.

They recalled the league's two twenty-three-inning games, one of which Bobby still regards with the pleasure a jeweler might take in a flawless gem. Oshkosh played Fond du Lac. There wasn't an error or a base on balls, a stolen base or a passed ball or a wild pitch, and both starting pitchers finished. The Fond du Lac second baseman had fourteen putouts and eighteen assists.

They talked about the time Green Bay scored nine runs with two out in the ninth to beat Sheboygan, 10 to 9, and chuckled over the job they did on Oshkosh in 1914 after Oshkosh had won twenty-six straight. It was a home-and-home series of six games and Green Bay won 'em all.

Seems that in the first game in Oshkosh, Williams spotted a spy stealing the Green Bay catcher's signs through a peephole in the Bull Durham sign on the center-field wall (you got a free suit of clothes if you hit the bull on the fly). The chief tipped off the manager and they switched their signs but continued to flash the old ones as a decoy.

When they moved to Green Bay, Bobby planted a fellow named Al Van Dyke in a tree beyond the fence to pick up the Oshkosh signs through binoculars. Van Dyke had a stick suspended on strings. He swung the stick horizontally for a curve, hung it straight up against the sky for a fastball.

"Remember Joe Benz?" Bobby asked the chief. "He should have made the majors. In fact, I sold him to Pittsburgh for $5,000, but the deal fell through." The clipping doesn't say so, but the chances are Bobby allowed himself a grin at this point.

"Benz was a good pitcher," Bobby said. "Chick Fraser scouted him for Fred Clarke, who was managing the Pirates. Chick liked the kid but he wanted to know about his habits, because Clarke wouldn't touch a fellow who took a drink. I told him Benz behaved himself.

"Benz pitched a fine game in Racine and Fraser said he'd give me $5,000 for him—after he checked further on his habits. Then he invited Benz and some others out for the evening. Late that night Fraser came to my room.

"'You're drunk,'" I told him.

"'I know it,' he said, 'and guess who got me stiff. For five cases of beer, I saved the Pittsburgh club $5,000.'"

Straws in the Pasture

Is the Pastime Passé?

MIAMI, FLA., *February 24, 1955*
THIS COULD be nothing but coincidence, the merely happen-so, but this is how it is. On the drive south this year, not a single game of baseball or softball or one o'cat was seen anywhere along the fifteen-hundred-mile route from New York to Miami. Never before, over a period of years that has got much longer than a fellow would care to mention, had this happened.

Often enough in the past, there'd be snow on the ground when you left New York, as there was this time. Generally you get out of the snow on the first day's drive, but for a while there may be rain and mud and fog. Then you get down into the Carolinas and then Georgia, and always in past years there were kids playing ball on the school yards and in pasture lots.

It was always good to see. It was the surest harbinger of spring, and it took a fellow back to his own boyhood and the lazy, happy summer days on cow-pasture diamonds which, it has always seemed here, were the real source of the love so many of us feel for the game of baseball.

Perhaps a one-paragraph digression may be taken to labor this point.

The only reason baseball is our national sport, instead of cricket or soccer, is that practically all American males play baseball or its equivalent—stickball on the city streets, softball on the school yards—when they are young. When they grow up they go watch the games, not so much to enjoy the thrill of appreciation that anybody must feel seeing a Phil Rizzuto scoop up a grounder and get rid of the ball in one fluid motion, but more because the spectacle restores their youth, warms them with nostalgic memories of the fun they had as kids.

It follows that if the kids aren't playing ball now, they're not likely to flock to the big league parks in great numbers tomorrow. Maybe they are playing, but they weren't on the route down here. Kids were shooting baskets on the playgrounds and in one lot there was a football game going on, but not a baseball was seen.

There was another discovery to be made on arrival here. It seems that in 1955, for the first time since World War II, there will be no organized baseball in Miami. There will be no professional baseball at all in southern Florida, and it may be that this situation hasn't existed since Ponce de León came barnstorming through these regions.

Perhaps that doesn't seem important up North, but it is important. For many years, Florida has been a breeding ground for ballplayers and baseball fans. Big league clubs have been training here for half a century; the state has been the hub of preseason operations for more than thirty years. If there is any place where the game ought to be booming, it is here.

Already there are guys playing pitch-catch all around here. It's entirely unofficial, because there is a rule against teams starting training before March 1. All the clubs do is lend uniforms, bats, and balls to fellows like Roy Campanella and Don Newcombe, who wish to entertain themselves on their own time. Their employers realize that they simply can't keep boys from playing baseball in a free country.

Next week Florida will be flooded with big league players, and for the next month there'll be games everywhere. Then the teams will start north, and that will be the end of it. Summer will come on, without baseball.

There's something wrong about this. In recent years, Miami—just to mention one town—has had some pretty exciting times, even if the baseball was minor league stuff. The incomparable Pepper Martin was operating here as a manager, and livening things up by trying to choke an umpire.

("When you had your hands on that man's throat," Pepper was asked by Happy Chandler, who was baseball commissioner then, "what were you thinking?"

"I was thinking I'd kill the ——!" Pepper said, being a dead honest guy.)

That's the way it was around here only a few years ago, and now it has ceased to be that way. Miami is a big city. If towns like Richmond, Va., Havana, and Charleston, W. Va., can support teams in Class AAA ball, so can Miami. There's a splendid ballpark here, and plenty of money.

However, the Florida International League collapsed last year. A town that ought to be able to support Triple-A ball isn't going to have any ball at all.

George Trautman, boss of the minors, was around the other day saying the minors were in pretty good shape. He said it was unfortunate that there would be no baseball in southern Florida this year, but he said maybe this would make the consumers hungry for the stuff and encourage them to bring it back in 1956.

You can't even excuse this by calling it wishful thinking. Absence doesn't make the heart grow fonder of baseball. The only thing that can stimulate baseball interest in any area is baseball itself. When the men who make a living from the game let it die in any part of the country—as it has died in the whole of New England—they are simply banging themselves on the sconce, and not with a hammer. They are using an ax.

All Guys
Finish at Last

Leo Durocher Leaves the Polo Grounds

NEW YORK, N.Y., *September 26, 1955*

THE BRIDGE at 155th St. still spanned the Harlem yesterday. No part of Coogan's Bluff had crumbled. The seismograph was quiet at Fordham, and along Eighth Ave. not one numbers bank collapsed. The departure of Leo Durocher was a sensation, but the earth didn't tremble.

Speaking of sensations, they varied. In some quarters there was regret, in others relief, here a sigh for the past, there a hope for the future. In no case where the name of the Giants means anything was there indifference.

It wasn't a shattering surprise when the Little Shepherd of Coogan's Bluff hung up his crook. Since June it had been evident that this must he a year of decision for the Giants. The defending champions of the world were not only third in their league, but also third in their town, which is far more important from a business point of view.

There is a hard core of Giant fans, mostly members of the Old Guard, who never were reconciled to the presence of Durocher in the seat formerly occupied by John McGraw, Bill Terry, and Mel Ott. The team's dramatic success in 1951, last year's front-running race and four-game conquest of Cleveland, won new followers and brought in fresh business to counteract earlier losses. This year those Johnny-come-latelies deserted to the Yankees and Dodgers, and the old dissenters still held out.

The problem had to be faced, and everybody knew it. Nearly everybody assumed it would be tackled as Horace Stoneham has attacked it—by reshuffling the deck for a new deal.

If nice guys finish last, what sort of guys finish third?

Well, in this case, it is a controversial guy, and that may be the understatement of the decade. It has never been easy to characterize Durocher either as a man or as a manager, not because he is an especially complex personality, but because so much depends on where you stand when you view him.

Regarding him as an athlete and competitor, there is no room for disagreement. He was a first-rate ballplayer and he is an altogether intractable antagonist, obsessed with winning, a stranger to physical fear. He will fight anybody anytime for anything.

Combative, quick-witted, and knowledgeable, he was truly the practically peerless leader on the field, a superior gambler with a nice balance of calculation and recklessness. Like any good gambler—horseplayer, card expert, or pool shark—he has the gift of absolute concentration. Half an hour after a long doubleheader he can recite every detail of the eighteen innings, play by play. An hour or so later he has forgotten it all.

As a director of tactical operations, then, he was as good as a manager can be. As a leader of men—that's something else again.

He is ambitious, brassily assertive, and impatient. Though he can be gracious when he chooses, instinctive regard for others is not ingrained in him. Some players responded to his goading, played better for him than they would for another man. Others found him impossible to live with, and these weren't necessarily congenital sulkers.

Durocher did play favorites, he did indulge in personal dislikes, he was swayed by enthusiasm and prejudice, he could be outrageously unreasonable. Some of the Giants will rejoice in his departure and perhaps flourish under more temperate leadership. Some will miss him.

In his first couple of seasons as manager in New York, the personnel of the Giants changed rapidly. Leo wanted, he said, "my kind of ball club." What that appeared to mean was that he wanted the team staffed with men just like himself. Chances are there aren't nine major league ballplayers just like Durocher, let alone twenty-five. This is not an unmixed evil.

However, he did get enough of "his kind" to win two pennants and a World Series.

That's got to be a major item in any accounting of his stewardship. Some felt from the beginning that it was a mistake to bring him across the river from Brooklyn. From July 1902 to July 1948, none but a Giant had ever managed the Giants. Now Stoneham brought in an alien, and one of the most devoutly detested enemy aliens ever to invade the Polo Grounds.

Those who insisted the fans never would stand for Durocher were partly correct. Some never did. Yet the Giants, who had not won a pennant in eleven years, won two in the next six. It's in the records.

Long before the decision was officially made, Durocher's successor had been selected and was waiting in the wings. It has been taken for granted everywhere that when a change was made, Bill Rigney would become the Giant manager. He's a Giant, personally popular, and he has been successful on the Minneapolis farm. He's going to take over a team that isn't good enough. No miracles need be expected.

Curtain Call

Branch Rickey Was a Baseball Man, and More

BROOKLYN, N.Y., *October 28, 1955*

CONSIDERING THE nature of the team's performance over the last decade, it might be said that the Pittsburgh Pirates have hired the wrong Joe Brown. When Branch Rickey, the greatest of all double-talk monologists, withdrew to the wings, the role as his successor cried aloud for Joe E. Brown rather than the comedian's serious-minded son. Who'll do the entertaining now, unless Bing Crosby sings for his fellow-directors?

Since Rickey relinquished the general manager's swivel chair to young Joe L. Brown and backed off into a never-never land identified as "an advisory capacity," practically everybody has been trying to call the score on his fifty-eight years in baseball. It can't be done. The man confounds arithmetic as easily as he confuses an audience.

This inept mathematician undertakes the task knowing in advance that it's impossible. Add Rickey up? How? As a player, manager, executive, lawyer, preacher, horse-trader, spellbinder, innovator, husband and father and grandfather, farmer, politician, logician, obscurantist, reformer, financier, sociologist, crusader, sharper, father-confessor, checker shark, friend, or fighter?

As Rickey said, wilted by a salary debate with a rookie named Dizzy Dean, "If there were one more like him in baseball, I'd quit the game." If there were one more like Branch—well, Judas priest!

Rickey is inimitable, but that doesn't mean he hasn't had plenty of imitators in addition to Arthur Mann, whose parodied impersonation of the master has convulsed audiences for many years at the annual baseball writers' show in New York. Junior executives learning the baseball business under the great man have tried to adopt his methods, not always with unmixed success.

When Al Gionfriddo was chattel of the Dodgers, he made a winter visit to the Brooklyn office to plead his financial case. He was intercepted in an outer office by a subaltern who undertook to soften him up for the Old Man.

Gionfriddo brought forth all his carefully rehearsed arguments for a wage commensurate with his ability. The subordinate replied as he fondly imagined the Maestro would have done.

"You don't know anything about baseball," he told the player. "You're a rotten base runner, haven't the first idea how to steal a base. Look, this is the way to steal."

He sprang from his chair, hurled himself across the room, and slid into a wastebasket.

Gionfriddo walked over and stood gazing moodily down upon the apprentice magnate, prostrate on the rug.

"What base were you stealing?" he asked softly.

"Second!"

"You're out. Hooked the wrong way into the bag. Lemme see the boss."

Most players dreaded to approach Rickey at contract time, fearing that after ten minutes under the spell of his persuasive eloquence they would emerge minus salary increase and underwear. If Gionfriddo had been as good at belting baseballs as at bearding lions, he wouldn't be a star outfielder today for Visalia in the Class C California League.

Yet there are players and managers and scouts and pensioners, men in baseball and out of it, who have worked for Rickey and will say of him sincerely, "All that I am and hope to be, etc." in terms that make Mother Machree a fishwife by comparison.

There is no doubt here that Rickey brought into baseball the finest, liveliest, most inventive and resourceful mind the game has attracted. To hear him speak, in public or private, is to be allowed a glimpse of that mind's operation. When the topic is one he wishes to consider, he goes directly to the heart of the matter, sorting out, analyzing, and cataloguing each point in beautiful order. When he chooses to avoid a direct statement, he numbs his listeners with rhetoric and leaves them bound hand-and-foot in circumlocution.

He has built many monuments in baseball. The farm system that he devised brought about the greatest single change of this century in the business structure of the game. By breaking the color line, he revolutionized the social structure of baseball and, in a lesser degree, the nation.

It is the notion here, however, that when he looks back on what he has accomplished, he does not consider first the social progress made. More important than that, to a baseball man, was tapping a great pool of talent that had been dammed up and ignored. He is a baseball man first, and that was his proudest achievement.

Connie, As Ever Was

Cornelius McGillicuddy, Sr., 1862–1956

NEW YORK, N.Y., *February 10, 1956*

IT IS not for mortals anywhere to suggest that another has lived too long, yet for those who knew and, necessarily, loved him it is difficult to regard Connie Mack's last years as part and parcel of a life that was a beacon in our time. Toward the end he was old and sick and saddened, a figure of forlorn dignity bewildered by the bickering around him as the baseball monument that he had built crumbled away.

That wasn't Connie Mack. Neither was the bloodless saint so often painted, a sanctimonious old Puritan patting babies on the skull and mumbling minced oaths and platitudes. As long as he was Connie Mack he was tough and human and clever. He was tough and warm and wonderful, kind and stubborn and courtly and unreasonable and generous and calculating and naïve and gentle and proud and humorous and demanding and unpredictable.

Many people loved him and some feared him, everybody respected him, and, as far as I know, nobody ever disliked him in the ninety-three years of his life. There may never have been a more truly successful man, for nobody ever won warmer or wider esteem and nobody ever relished it more.

Only the most fortunate men can appreciate their own success and enjoy it fully. Connie entered professional baseball when it was a game for roughnecks. He saw it become respectable, he lived to be the symbol of its integrity, and he enjoyed every minute of it.

He had an innocent vanity that could delight those who knew him. He liked going places and, of course, he was recognized everywhere.

To see him introduced, say, at a fight in the Hollywood Legion Stadium was something to remember: He would spring through the ropes as nimbly as a preliminary boy and draw himself erect, hands clasped overhead, acknowledging the spontaneous cheers.

There were unexpected demonstrations of the affection felt for him in far places. It could be in Dallas or Houston or Fort Worth just before an exhibition game in the spring. All of a sudden, in the lull between infield practice and the first pitch, applause would go rippling through the stands, swelling to a roar, and the customers would be on their feet and here Connie would come hiking from dugout to dugout with his bouncy, long-legged stride, his scorecard waving high. For a moment, swallowing would be difficult.

He could laugh at himself. One winter he obtained title to the renowned orator and pitcher Bobo Newsom, and brought Bobo up to Philadelphia for a formal signing. When the press was admitted to the tower office in Shibe Park, Connie was on his feet and Bobo relaxed in the swivel chair behind the desk, a big cigar in his face. A little later Newsom stepped outside to take a phone call and Connie dropped absentmindedly into the boss's seat.

As the door opened for his employee's return, Connie sprang up in mock alarm, reinstalling the great man with wonderfully exaggerated humility. Bobo was quite nice about it.

It is the little things one remembers most happily, the small foibles of his great humanity, like his sudden flash of real anger one day in San Francisco. It was a nippy morning and one of Connie's companions suggested closing the windows of a car that was taking them to San Quentin for an exhibition. He was astonished when his solicitude infuriated Connie.

"Dammittohell!" the old man exploded. "Don't worry about me! Dammit, everybody's always worrying. Mrs. Mack says, 'Con, wear your overcoat; Con, don't forget your rubbers!' So I put on my dam' coat and my dam' rubbers and go out to the drugstore to get medicine for her!

"And that Blackburne!" Lena Blackburne, coach with the Athletics, had a leg infection that had kept him in bed in Anaheim, California, when the team broke camp there. "That Blackburne!" Connie said. "It's 'Boss, are you comfortable? Boss, are you warm enough? Sit still, boss, and I'll get it for you.' And where's Blackburne? Down on his tail in Anaheim, dammit!"

So many little things. He could fight a player for the last dime at contract time and win. Yet he confessed that after fifty years two jobs still made him miserable—haggling with a player and telling a kid from the minors that he had to go back.

Little things. His unfailing gift for getting names wrong, from the day of the pitcher Addie "Josh" to the time of the young Cleveland manager "Mr. Bordiere." "It is a great pleasure," he told fans in Long Beach, California, before an exhibition game with Gabby Hartnett's Cubs, "to be here in Long Branch playing my old friend, Pat Hartnett."

His Athletics are gone. Memories are his monument, and small things like the elevator built for him in Shibe Park before the place was renamed Connie Mack Stadium. The elevator was tailored to measure, eight feet tall and narrow as a phone booth, and there was an old press-box attendant named Smitty assigned to take the lift to the ground floor each day in the eighth inning and hold it so Connie could ride up to his office directly after the game.

One day in 1945, the score was tied 1–all when Smitty went down in the eighth. It was still tied when the game was called after the twenty-fourth. Smitty stood with his foot in the door for sixteen innings.

The Name Is Averill

Earl Sr. Was Bad for Pitchers

NEW YORK, N.Y., *April 5, 1954*

O DD WHAT memory can do to a guy. There was this line in a story about an exhibition game between the Giants and Indians. "Cleveland," it read, "tied the score on Earl Averill's three-run homer off Hoyt Wilhelm in the eighth." That was the name—Earl Averill. The calendar did a backflip.

It was a warm and sunny July afternoon in Griffith Stadium in Washington, for this was a way back in 1937 when baseball was played by daylight even in the nation's capital. President Franklin D. Roosevelt was there along with Cabinet officers and Supreme Court justices and senators and congressmen, watching the fifth annual All-Star Game between the American and National leagues.

The center fielder for the Americans was a Cleveland player, name of Earl Averill. He batted fifth in a lineup that included Red Rolfe, Charlie Gehringer, Joe DiMaggio, Lou Gehrig, Joe Cronin, Bill Dickey, Sam West, Lefty Gomez, Tommy Bridges, Mel Harder, and Jimmie Foxx, a pinch hitter. Where are they now?

With two out in the third inning, Gehrig hit a home run with DiMaggio on base, and the Americans led 2 to 0. Then Averill hit a ball that ended both the inning and, though nobody suspected it then, the great days of a pitcher named Jerome Herman Jay Hanna Dizzy Dean. It was a low liner that caromed off Dean's shoe to Billy Herman, who threw Averill out, but the smash had broken Dean's big toe. Trying to pitch for the Cardinals a fortnight later before the toe was repaired, Dizzy was off-balance throwing his hard one and something came loose in his shoulder. After that he never got anything for the Cardinals except $185,000 and three players in a deal with the Cubs.

That Earl Averill, he was bad for pitchers. "The Rock," they called him, because he'd play in 155 games in a season for the Indians and bat .333, and to stand in front of one of his line drives was untidy suicide.

There was one summer when Clark Griffith, believing the Senators had a chance for the pennant, swung a deal for Bobo Newsom to make assurance doubly sure. Over the years, that was always Griff's solution of any problem. Get Newsom.

Newsom slipped surreptitiously into Washington at the head of a sixty-piece brass band roaring, "Have no fear, Bobo's here." It is not recalled that Congress adjourned to see him make his first start for the Senators, but the event stirred at least as much excitement as the fire that burned Dolley Madison out of the White House during one of Bobo's earlier administrations in the capital.

Early in the game, like the second inning, he pitched to Averill. The Rock rifled one back that caught Newsom on the knee. Bobo fell, and away up at Fordham the seismograph reared like a startled colt.

Bellowing with pain, Bobo crawled after the ball on all fours, recovered it, and tossed Averill out at first. He remained in the game, grimacing horribly, trumpeting like a wounded elephant with every pitch. Between turns on the mound he would sit swaying in the dugout, massaging the knee and groaning.

"The damn thing's broke," he kept moaning, and his playmates hooted.

"A big slob like you couldn't even stand on a broken leg. Keep pitching."

He went the whole distance and, if memory serves, lost by a score of 2 to 1. Incidentally, the Senators didn't win the pennant, which astonished nobody, but there was rioting in all the theaters when Bobo was not awarded the Pulitzer Prize.

Anyhow, the evening after that game he was encountered hobbling with a cane through the lobby of the Wardman Park Hotel, where he had living quarters commensurate with his splendor.

"I'm going over to have this damn thing X-rayed," he said. "I still think it's broke."

It was. Averill had shattered the knee.

There was another line in that story about the Giants' exhibition with the Indians. It said that in the fifth inning Grissom went in to pitch for New York. Grissom? That name appears, too, in the nineteen-year-old box score of that All-Star Game where Dean got his from Averill.

Bill Terry, manager of the Nationals, sent Lee Grissom in to pitch in the fifth inning. Successive doubles by Cronin and Dickey scored a run against him, but before that he had made Gehrig and Averill throw their bats away. You never saw great hitters look so pitiful striking out.

This is all just pretending, of course. Everybody knows it isn't Lee Grissom, lean and left-handed and balefully fast, who works for the Giants these days. It's his brother Marvin, no mewling infant himself but born eleven years after Lee. And, of course, the fellow who hit that three-run homer for Cleveland, that was Earl Averill, Jr.

That's the trouble with memory. It starts a guy adding up the years.

Connoisseur of Bottles

The Giants' Whitey Lockman Dodges Glassware in Philly

PHILADELPHIA, PA., *April 25, 1956*

I T WAS Kitty Foyle or one of her friends who commented on the unbending punctilio of Philadelphia where public functions have, as a rule, the proud and puffy stiffness of a swollen thumb. Philadelphians, Kitty said, felt that they had been unpardonably rude to British visitors in 1777 and had been doing a sort of social penance ever since.

Well, 179 years have gone by since manners on the Main Line caused Sir William Howe to raise his eyebrows, and a certain gaucherie seems to be creeping back into the deportment of the natives. At least, the Giants' Whitey Lockman thought he detected something less than Chesterfieldian grace among the clients in Connie Mack Stadium who wiled away a recent afternoon bouncing bottles off his skull.

"I wouldn't mind getting hit by a regular bottle," Mr. Lockman said plaintively, "but when they break the necks off then throw 'em at you, that's going too far."

A sampling of opinion has been taken among the social arbiters in Stillman's Gym, and they are unanimous in the view that Mr. Lockman has a legitimate beef. Moreover, it is felt that Mr. Lockman's comments reflect a capacity for discrimination that is surprising in him, for he is by no means the most noted connoisseur of bottles among the New York outfielders.

A rather ugly sullenness on the part of Philadelphia baseball fans is, perhaps, not to be wondered at. They're still rankling under the municipal insult delivered a year or so ago when it was decided that their city wasn't fit for the Athletics, which is like saying a man isn't good enough for a broken hip. Also, they have dangerous drinking habits. Any visitor who has drawn a glass of city water from a tap, blown the dust off the top, and chewed the residue must realize that habitually swilling this heady stuff is bound to rouse the passions and bring out the beast in any man.

Neither Whitey Lockman nor the other Giants should be blamed for this, of course, but after watching two or three double-play grounders sift through a porous infield, a fan is likely to strike out blindly. It was the Giants' tough luck that they were in town when the customers started heaving glassware and obsolete vegetation into left field and strafing the visitors' bullpen with empty hot-chocolate tins.

Players leaving the park were besieged for autographs, as they are in every town. Some who paused in the crush to scrawl their names discovered hero-worshippers attempting to pick their pockets. The Giants resented this, but on sober consideration it seems inaccurate to describe it as unsportsmanlike conduct.

This was an example of international enterprise inspired by the profit motive. According to what one reads in the political speeches, that's the very foundation stone of our national economy.

A question has been asked: Where were the cops? It seems they were across the street in a parking lot guarding automobiles owned by players and officials of the Phillies. This is an important civic duty, not to be taken lightly.

Guarding automobiles has been an honored Philadelphia custom since the invention of the horseless carriage. The motorist fortunate enough to find a parking space on the street seven or eight blocks, say, from the ballpark, is set upon by a horde of juvenile delinquents as he backs into the curb.

"Wotcher car, bud?" they offer shrilly. In Philadelphia, all news boys and other urchins address all male adults as "bud"—"paper, bud?" "shine, bud?"—and if the man has been brought up properly he will reply, "If you please, mister." This is standard cultural practice, like saying the nearest trolley line is three squares to the left, instead of blocks, and employing the plural nickname "Reds" for any redhead.

Anyhow, the motorist parking for a ballgame is invited to have his car watched, and is allowed a choice between two alternatives. He can accept the offer and disgorge suitable tribute in cash, or he can decline politely. The latter choice is favored by those who believe that ice picks improve the appearance of their tires.

Not all these little points of etiquette are unique to Philadelphia, though it does seem that some of the more ingenious practices, and the marksmanship of fans, have been brought to their highest state of refinement there. They are all aspects of a situation which represents a continuing problem in baseball.

The research firm which Ford Frick employed to do a survey of baseball last year encountered again and again the same complaints—deterioration of the neighborhoods in which some parks are located, unsatisfactory transportation, inadequate parking facilities, and assorted discomforts. Many persons cited these as reasons why they seldom attended games. There'll be fewer and fewer at the games unless steps are taken.

Now there is legislation pending in Pennsylvania to permit sale of beer in ballparks. In some cities like Chicago where brew is served in the stands, agitation has been growing for some kind of control, because some customers do get loaded and become pretty objectionable. With regard to Philadelphia it is difficult to take sides.

It is a hard fate to be a Phillies' fan and have to drink hot chocolate, too.

Ted Williams Spits

The Kid Doesn't Suffer Fools Cheaply

BOSTON, MASS., *August 10, 1956*

B Y N O W some modern Dickens, probably in Boston, must surely have brought out a best seller entitled *Great Expectorations*. It was a $4,998 mistake when Ted Williams chose puritanical and antiseptic New England for his celebrated exhibition of spitting for height and distance. In easygoing New York's insanitary subway the price is only $2.

It was bush, of course. There is no other way to characterize Williams' moist expression of contempt for fans and press, even though one may strive earnestly to understand and be patient with this painfully introverted, oddly immature thirty-eight-year-old veteran of two wars.

In his gay moods, Williams has the most winning disposition and manner imaginable. He can be charming, accommodating, and generous. If Johnny Orlando, the Red Sox maître de clubhouse and Ted's great friend, wished to violate a confidence he could cite a hundred instances of charities that the fellow has done, always in deep secrecy.

This impulsive generosity is a key. Ted is ruled by impulse and emotions. When he is pleased, he laughs; in a tantrum, he spits. In Joe Cronin's book, this falls $5,000 short of conduct becoming a gentleman, officer, and left fielder.

The price the Boston general manager set upon a minute quantity of genuine Williams saliva, making it the most expensive spittle in Massachusetts, suggests that the stuff is rarer than rubies. However, this is one case where the law of supply and demand does not apply. Actually the $5,000 figure is a measure of Cronin's disapproval of his employee's behavior and an indication of Ted's economic condition. Rather than let the punishment fit the crime, Cronin tailored it to the outfielder's $100,000 salary. As it is, considering Williams' tax bracket, chances are the federal government will pay about $3,500 of the fine, though it may cause some commotion around the Internal Revenue Bureau when a return comes in with a $5,000 deduction for spit.

Baseball has indeed put on company manners since the days when pitchers like Burleigh Grimes, Clarence Mitchell, and Spittin' Bill Doak employed saliva as a tool of the trade and applied it to the ball with the ceremonious formality of a minuet.

Incidentally, the penalty was applied after Williams drew a base on balls which forced home the winning run for Boston against the Yankees. He must have realized that a few more victories at those prices would leave him broke, yet the next night he won another game with a home run. With Ted, money is no object.

Nobody has ever been able to lay down a rule determining how much abuse a paid performer must take from the public without reciprocation. It was either Duffy or Sweeney, of the great old vaudeville team, who addressed an audience that had sat in cold silence through the act:

"Ladies and gentlemen, I want to thank you for giving us such a warm and encouraging reception. And now, if you will kindly remain seated, my partner will pass among you with a baseball bat and beat the bejabbers out of you."

Baseball fans consider that the price they pay for admission entitles them to spit invective at a player, harass him at his work, and even bounce a beer bottle off his skull. It is not recalled that Williams' hair was ever parted by flying glassware, but verbal barbs from Fenway Park's left-field seats have been perforating his sensitive psyche for years.

There are those of a sympathetic turn who feel it was high time Williams be permitted to spit back. Miss Gussie Moran, trained in the gentle game of tennis, remarked on the radio that she approved, "as long as he didn't spray anybody." As in tennis, Gussie believes, marksmanship and trajectory count.

All the same it is a mark of class in a performer to accept cheers and jeers in stride. One of the soldier citizens of the Boston press—it could have been Johnny Drohan—pointed this out to Williams years ago. Ted was a kid then, a buff for Western movies.

Hoots and jeers were a part of the game, the man said, and everybody in the public eye had to learn to accept them.

"Take actors, for instance, Ted. You see one in a good show and you applaud and go around talking about how great he is. Then you see him in a bad vehicle and you say, 'He stinks. Whatever gave me the idea he could act?'"

"Oh, no, Johnny," Ted protested, "not that Hoot Gibson. He's *always* great!"

Perfection

Larsen's Feat a First in Any Series

BROOKLYN, N.Y., *October 9, 1956*

THE FIFTH game of the World Series had been finished for forty-five minutes but the crowds didn't want to go. They moved slowly through the stands like files of army ants. In front of the visitors' bench a throng swelled steadily, packing more and more tightly around a man who stood pinned against the dugout corner, signing programs with stiffening fingers.

Dear diary! It was exciting! They were getting Ed Sullivan's autograph.

Upstairs a stray thrust a scorecard into the press box, interrupted a newspaperman at work, and asked for *his* signature. The interruption didn't matter, for there was no story to write. The Dodgers hadn't got any hits.

Down in the catacombs where the Yankees bathe and dress, a big man sat and sweated. His name is Don Larsen. He is a pitcher, the first who ever lived to pitch a no-hit game in the World Series, the first in thirty-four years to pitch a perfect game anywhere in the major leagues.

Nobody asked him to sign anything. From San Diego to Baltimore, bourbon drinkers arose and lifted glasses in a solemn, silent toast.

Let's make it simple, this: Behind Larsen's strong pitching, the Yankees defeated the Dodgers, 2 to 0, yesterday for their third victory and now require only one more for their seventeenth world championship. They made five hits off schoolboy Sal Maglie, including a home run by Mickey Mantle.

Now, then. When Don Larsen was born in Michigan City, Ind., Aug. 7, 1929, seven years had passed since the last big league team played nine innings without getting a man to first base. Charlie Robertson, of the White Sox, pitched that perfect game.

Larsen grew up big, six-feet-four and 225 pounds. He came to the American League with the Browns, where his pitching equipment and his power at bat set the more excitable scholars babbling about a second Babe Ruth. Then the Browns became Orioles, and although Baltimore isn't exactly a nine o'clock town, it couldn't hold Donald. One of the first orders Paul Richards received as manager was to get rid of Larsen.

Dealt off to the Yankees, Larsen was sent down to Denver for a while, came back and helped pitch New York to the 1955 pennant. This year he did nothing spectacular until September, when he won four games and discarded his windup.

During his next-to-last game this season, in Boston, he experienced blinding intellectual flashes. If hitting was all a matter of timing, he reasoned, why couldn't a pitcher unsettle the batters' rhythm by leaving out the big motion they were accustomed to seeing? Since then he has just bowed from the waist, straightened up and thrown.

"I still say," a Brooklyn fan insisted yesterday when the deed had been done, "that the big stiff throws like a girl."

From the beginning, this was the best game in a struggle that has been getting better and better. It was just five years to the day since Maglie, as a Giant, had lost a World Series game to the Yankees, yielding a home run to Mantle's predecessor in center field, one Joe DiMaggio. It was thirteen days since Sal himself had pitched a no-hitter against Philadelphia. It was five days since he had beaten the Yankees in the opening game of the World Series.

He had better control in this second start, this swarthy and poisonous descendant of the Borgias, but he had Larsen against him and Larsen had Yankees behind him. When Don didn't take care of the hitters, his playmates did. A savage line drive by Jackie Robinson, a bitter ground ball hit by Junior Gilliam, a long fly by Gil Hodges, all became putouts.

From the seventh inning on, 64,519 witnesses screamed with every pitch. As Larsen completed each hitless, runless inning, they howled hoarsely. When he walked to the plate to lead off the Yankees' last turn at bat, they rose in salute, beating their palms and emitting wild animal cries. Then in the ninth—

Well, Carl Furillo fouled off two pitches, took a ball, fouled twice more, and flied out. Roy Campanella fouled once and grounded out. Dale Mitchell, batting for Maglie, took a ball, a called strike, swung and missed, took another ball, hit another foul. The last pitch came in. Mitchell leaned forward, twitched, and took the final strike.

Yogi Berra plunged out to intercept Larsen, wrapped arms about his head, put a leg-scissors on his middle, and swung ponderously off the ground. He might have pulled even that tower of gristle to earth, but now the other Yankees closed about the pair. Larsen vanished in the middle.

In the confusion, Benny Weinrig won $9. Benny is press-box steward in Ebbets Field. Whenever the Dodgers or their opponents are hitless for three innings, somebody starts a pool on the first hit. If nobody wins, Benny gets the swag.

Benny loves the Dodgers. To him, this was blood money.

Wake for a Ball Club

The Late, Great New York Giants

NEW YORK, N.Y., *September 30, 1957*

I N THE sixth inning the Pirates scored their seventh run and Bill Rigney walked out to call for a new pitcher. The crowd booed the Giants' manager, and this was the first time its voice was loud, though there had been decent applause before the game for Mrs. John McGraw and some of the old players.

Probably it is fanciful and sentimental to suggest that the quiet was that of a wake. Of course it was a wake. There were 11,600 customers for a game between the Giants, moored in sixth place, and the Pirates, tied for seventh. If it hadn't been the very last game that New York's oldest team would play in the hallowed Polo Grounds, the count might have been closer to Saturday's 2,768.

When they were simply the New York Club in 1883, they played down at 110th Street. It was there they received their name from their first manager, James Mutrie, who wore a top hat and frock coat and carried a gold-headed cane. "My big fellows!" he cried exuberantly. "My Giants!" It was 1891 when they took over Brotherhood Field and renamed it the Polo Grounds.

Here Amos Rusie fired the fastball that inspired a line which batters still use, probably believing they are coining it: "You can't hit it if you don't see it." Here a kid out of Brooklyn, Willie Keeler by name, broke in as a third baseman, not very good. Buck Ewing was good, though. Saloons all over town displayed a garish lithograph of "Ewing's famous slide."

There was a pretty fair cheer for Bobby Thomson when he went to bat the first time. He got a single but was trapped off base and was doubled on a fly ball. He was playing third base.

That's where Thomson was playing that unforgettable day in 1951, and he was having a time of it then, too. He messed up a promising inning by stealing second with a playmate already there, and when the Dodgers scored the runs that seemed to sew up the pennant playoff, it was through Thomson's position that their big hits whistled.

Then Bobby swung his bat, and the Giants were champions of the National League. Maybe they'll win other championships, some day, for San Francisco. Surely there'll be other home runs hit at timely moments, but will there ever be another scene like that? The season was over but the fans wouldn't leave. Thousands stood cheering beneath the clubhouse windows in center field, singing, sobbing, calling again and again for the heroes to show themselves. Twilight deepened, and still the clubhouse windows blazed with the flashes of photographers' lamps.

Yesterday's customers were equally reluctant to leave. Most of them sat it out as the Giants dragged wearily to defeat. Pigeons kept circling overhead, as though impatient to move in, and one could fancy Robert Moses, blueprints of a housing project in hand, waiting to pounce.

These Giants played as though they couldn't wait to get to San Francisco. They couldn't hit the ball or catch it, pick it up, or hold it, and Rigney kept calling the bullpen for another bull.

One day John McGraw handed Bugs Raymond a new ball and sent him out to warm up for relief. When Bugs got into the game he was loaded. Leaving the bench, he had hiked right past the bullpen to a gin mill across the street.

Pitchers with the old Giants got knocked out, too. After Rube Marquard arrived here as the "$11,000 beauty," it wasn't long before they were calling him the "$11,000 lemon." Rube Schauer had to relieve Ferdie Schupp so often that Sid Mercer wrote in the *New York Globe*, "It never Schupps but it Schauers." And there was even a Giant manager who tried Christy Mathewson at first base and shortstop and in the outfield because he said Matty couldn't pitch. Horace Fogel was the name of that genius.

In the ninth inning a Pirate named John Powers hit the last home run that will be struck in the Giants' New York home. It went clear over the roof and stirred scarcely a murmur.

The crowd shouted for Willie Mays on his next-to-last time at bat, when he beat out an infield single, and fans stood up to cheer him on his last, when he grounded out. A thunder of boos responded when it was announced that "after the game, patrons will not be permitted on the field until the players have reached the clubhouse."

The instant Dusty Rhodes hit a grounder for the last putout— remember the World Series of 1954 when he did everything but walk on water?—hundreds of kids rushed onto the field and Giants ran for their lives, fending off souvenir hunters who snatched for caps and gloves. Adults followed the boys.

Kids tore up the bases, clawed at the mound for the pitchers' rubber and dug for home plate. Boys scooped earth from the mound into paper bags and pulled outfield grass which they stuffed into pants' pockets. They ripped the green canvas from the screen behind home plate, gouged sponge rubber from the outfield walls, tore the roof off the bullpen bench in right field.

A man took a photograph of the plate. Another pried the number tag from the railing of a box. A woman walked off carrying a big cake of sod from beneath the plate. Below the clubhouse windows, a forlorn throng lingered. Somebody out there held up a sign. It read: "Stay, team, stay."

East Goes West and
League Goes South

N.L. President Makes Disastrous Call

NEW YORK, N.Y., *October 15, 1957*

WHEN THE gallant skipper, Walter O'Malley, gave orders to abandon ship in Brooklyn, there issued from the office of Warren Giles, president of the National League, a paragraph or so of singularly rancid prose which received less attention than it merited chiefly because ears were deafened at the time by applause for Lew Burdette.

"The National League," its chief executive crowed, "has again demonstrated that it is a progressive organization—," at which time this reader asked permission to leave the room. Thus did the guiding genius of the senior major league gloss over the despoliation of two of baseball's most valuable franchises, the abject surrender of the world's greatest market, the boldest step backward since the league was born in 1876.

Warren Giles is an old friend and a nice guy. Unless they can make some vestige of sense, nice guys should finish speaking, but immediately.

The departure of the Giants and Dodgers from New York is an unrelieved calamity, a grievous loss to the city and to baseball, a shattering blow to the prestige of the National League, an indictment of the men operating the clubs and the men governing the city.

It is difficult to apportion the blame because so many must share it. Horace Stoneham sat still for twenty years watching the deterioration of the wonderful organization he had inherited. When at long last

the noose had tightened around his neck, he cried, "All is lost!" and
scuttled for San Francisco.

O'Malley, operating like a dealer of three-card monte, made threats
and half-promises, blew up smoke screens, played one city against
another, took millions of dollars out of Brooklyn, and then took Brooklyn's ball club in order to latch onto a big chunk of property near the
heart of Los Angeles.

Los Angeles and San Francisco are major league towns where major
league ball probably will enjoy great success, for a while at least. Yet
suppose you manufactured ladies' garters and your sales manager said:
"I can't do business here among fifteen million consumers. Let me go
sell to San Francisco's one million or Los Angeles' two million and I'll
show you some real business." You'd fire him, wouldn't you?

Outside of New York there are six owners of National League
teams who sat on their hunkers last summer and voted permission for
O'Malley and Stoneham to abdicate the New York territory. Some of
them regret it now. Even while his team was winning the championship of the world Milwaukee's Lou Perini was telling everybody he
encountered: "We must have a team in New York, even if it means a
nine-club league."

Where was he three months ago when the deed was done? If a single
dissenting voice was raised in that meeting in Chicago, the fact was not
reported to the newspapers.

As to those dim bulbs in the city administration maybe the Greeks
have the word for them. This edition has to go through the mails.

If they don't know what major league baseball means to a town,
financially and in prestige, then they're alone in their ignorance
among all the municipal authorities of the nation.

If they weren't aware of what was going to happen unless they took
steps to avert it, then they are blind or illiterate, for the warnings were
published in the papers no fewer than a hundred times.

An inescapable comparison forces itself into attention. Last spring
a party of political space cadets headed by Los Angeles' Mayor Poulson
flew into the Dodgers' training camp in Vero Beach, Fla., to bid for the

Brooklyn franchise. The mayor mouthed a lot of Hollywood malarkey about "thinking big," but he also said, in practically these words: "It is our duty to go all out to get a major league team for the entertainment and pleasure of our citizens."

New York's Mayor Wagner has said a number of things, too. After the city had lost both the Giants and Dodgers, he said that "in a few days" he would appoint a committee of businessmen to inquire into the possibility of getting a nonexistent National League team to come and play in a park that's never been built and probably won't be.

So go ahead, put the blame where you feel it belongs. An incredibly stupid thing has been done. Some of the men responsible are stupid and some are not. All must share the discredit.

A hundred years ago, give or take, a man named Browning wrote a toast that seems to fit the occasion still. All together now:

> *Just for a handful of silver he left us,*
> *Just for a riband to stick in his coat.*

Man You Listen To

Phil Rizzuto Speaks from Experience

NEW YORK, N.Y., *May 14, 1958*

A RUNNER on first base broke for second and was thrown out by Lawrence Peter Berra. "I wonder," Red Barber said on the air, musing, "if that was an all-out attempt to steal. Looked as if somebody might've missed a sign." He put it up to Phil Rizzuto, who concurred; yes, it was altogether possible somebody had goofed.

"On a play like that," Barber asked, "what would you say the percentage would be—that is, who'd be more likely to have missed the sign? The runner or the batter?"

Rizzuto reckoned it would be the batter.

"You mean that's what the percentage would be," Red said hastily. "You're not saying that it was the batter."

"That's right," Phil said, and there must have been at least several members of the great unseen audience who fell to wondering how fearlessly forthright a television commentary could be, how bluntly candid and four-square. If the hit-and-run is on, and the runner goes down but the batter doesn't offer at the pitch, can the matter of responsibility be a secret?

When a player did miss a sign, Red asked, was his misfeasance mentioned in the dugout? Or did the bench preserve a discreet silence so that gentle reproof might be administered privately by the lovable old manager with heart of gold?

"No sir!" Phil said emphatically. "He hears about it, and right away."

After a moment Barber returned to the subject. It was true, then, that in big league baseball signals were missed from time to time? Oh yes, Phil said. Teams usually changed their signs for each series with a different opponent and consequently the codes could get a mite confusing.

"But how can that happen?" Barber asked. "I thought the player was supposed to flash a return sign to indicate that he got the message."

"Not necessarily," Rizzuto said. "Some teams don't ask you to return the sign. Now, the Yankees, for instance—well, maybe I'd better not say that either. Let's just say some teams don't use the return sign."

So he didn't say that the Yankees' codebook omitted responses. The inning ended about this time and, obedient to the commercial, a trip was made to the refrigerator. In the interval Red must have asked a direct question, for the next voice heard was Rizzuto's.

No, Phil was saying thoughtfully, he couldn't remember an instance when he had missed a sign while he was with the Yankees. He hastened to add that he wasn't putting himself away as infallible.

"The fact is," he said, "I had to be alert. I had to be awake and watch everything. With the sort of power I had, I wasn't going to be around very long if I took to missing signs."

This, of course, is why Rizzuto was the best shortstop the Yankees ever had. He brought the physique of a boy to a man's game but he came to play, and because he couldn't hit like a DiMaggio or Keller or Henrich, he had to make up for it by employing all the gifts he did have—his speed and agility and resolution and attention and industry and intelligence.

He learned to bunt and to drag a bunt, to dart in on the slow, high bounders past the mound and race back for those pop flies that clear the infield but are too short for the outfielders to handle. He knew where to be for a relay from the outfield and where to throw the ball when he got it.

He learned all the plays and could execute them so well that even in Phil's last days as a player Casey Stengel still pointed to him as an example for rookies who thought they were ready for the major league.

"We had to wait eight years for Rizzuto to give up," Casey said this spring, explaining why he had employed Gil McDougald so long at third base and second before assigning him to shortstop.

The fact that Rizzuto is rich in knowledge and can share it with the fans is his greatest asset on the air. Barber draws him out skillfully when they work together and their little chats are agreeably instructive, filling in gaps in the action, heightening the entertainment.

A commentator who paraded his knowledge, struck a pose as an expert, lectured his audience, or second-guessed the actors—a fellow like that could be pretty obnoxious on the air. Phil just tosses in pleasant little bits. For example, the pitcher asks the umpire for a new ball and Phil remarks that pitchers have educated fingers which can discern small differences between baseballs, discovering whether the seams are perfectly even, the cover as snug as it should be, and so on.

It does not follow that a man must have excelled in sports in order to excel as a sportscaster or sportswriter, nor that anybody who was good at a game can describe the game well. It does seem here, however, that Rizzuto offers an outstanding example of the simple truth that, when other things are equal, the man you listen to is the man who knows what he's talking about.

Hutch and The Man

Musial Won't Save Record-Book Hit for Hometown Crowd

NEW YORK, N.Y., *May 21, 1958*

FRANCE AND Algeria heaved in ferment, South Americans chucked rocks at the goodwill ambassador from the United States, Sputnik III thrust its nose into the pathless realms of space—and the attention of some millions of baseball fans was concentrated on a grown man in flannel rompers swinging a stick on a Chicago playground called Wrigley Field.

Warren Giles, president of the National League, had come down from Milwaukee to sit in the stands and watch Stan Musial make his three thousandth hit against major league pitching. When the event came to pass, the game would be halted. Giles would walk out on the field to congratulate Musial with full benefit of Kodak and formally present to him the ball he had struck—if it could be found. Then the Cubs and Cardinals would return to their play.

On his first time at bat, Musial made his 2,999th hit. He got no more that day. There were still only seven men in history who had made three thousand. To be sure, there were only eight who had made 2,999, but nobody thought of that. Giles left town.

"I'll do it tomorrow," Stan said, but just before dinner the Cardinals' manager, Fred Hutchinson, phoned Jim Toomey, the club publicity man, and asked him to notify the press that Musial wouldn't start the next day's game. Unless he were needed as a pinch batter, Hutch would let him wait until the following evening to try for the big one before a home crowd in St. Louis.

At dinner, Toomey and the newspapermen and the club secretary,

Leo Ward, talked about it. Musial hadn't asked to be held out the next day. Nobody in the St. Louis office had suggested it. It was Hutchinson's own idea, prompted by his respect and affection for Musial and his realization that Stan would derive a special satisfaction out of attaining his goal in the park where he had grown to greatness.

"Maybe I'm speaking out of turn," said Bill Heinz, who was there on a magazine assignment, "but it seems to me Hutch is sticking his neck out. His team got off to a horrible start and now it's on a winning streak and he's got a championship game to play tomorrow, without his best man because of personal considerations.

"Not that the guy hasn't earned special consideration, but from a competitive point of view I think it's wrong. If the Cardinals lose tomorrow, Hutch will be blasted. He'll be accused of giving less than his best to win and it will be said the club rigged this deliberately for the box office, gambling a game away to build up a big home crowd."

"You're absolutely right," another said. "I've been thinking the same thing and I'm glad somebody agrees."

They talked it over but didn't mention it to Hutchinson. He's the manager. He must have known what he was doing.

Now it was the next day and Musial was sunning himself in the bullpen and the Cubs were leading, 3 to 1. Gene Green, a rookie outfielder, was on second base. It was a spot for a pinch batter. Hutch beckoned.

Musial hit the sixth pitch to left field for two bases, scoring Green. The game stopped, Hutchinson walked out to second and shook hands. Frank Dascoli, umpiring at third base, got the ball when it was returned from the outfield and gave it to Musial. Eight cameras fired away.

You don't see that often. They don't stop games in the major leagues and let photographers invade the playing field to celebrate individual accomplishment. Baseball is as ceremonious as a Graustarkian court, but they butter the Golden Bantam before the game, not during play. Maybe this sort of thing has been done before, but not in thirty years of firsthand observation.

When the last picture was taken, Hutchinson called for a runner and Musial left the game. The manager was sticking his neck out again.

The score was still 3 to 2 against the Cardinals and Musial's bat might still be needed to win, but Hutchinson took him out. It could be that Hutch lost sight of the score in the theatrics of the moment. It is no discredit to him if, just for that little while, the personal triumph of one great man meant more to the manager than team success.

As it turned out, the Cardinals kept the rally going and won the game. The next night Musial got his twenty-one guns from the fans in St. Louis, and on his first time at bat acknowledged the salute by flogging one over the pavilion in right.

So everything worked out happily. The way it happened was theatrical but it wasn't staged. There was nothing planned, nothing tawdry, no prearranged billing to disfigure the simple reality. Stan got his hit in honest competition, and it helped his team win.

Like anybody else, Musial relishes personal success and takes pleasure in the honors he wears so gracefully. Above all, though, he's a ballplayer in a team game, and the object is to win. Circumstances saved his greatest moment from the carnival vulgarity that would have debased it. That was good for baseball, good for the Cardinals, good for Hutchinson, and good for The Man.

Pity the Poor Umpire

The Major Leagues vs. the Bean Ball

G
NEW YORK, N.Y., *June 10, 1958*

OLD, SILVER, and bronze foundries of the land operated double shifts over the weekend striking off suitable medals for the first umpires to display the red, raw courage to enforce the major leagues' new beanball rule. Up to now no blue-jacketed paunch has been decorated for valor, but we can look forward to some stirring scenes as soon as the strike zone Hawkshaws have had time to brush up on their mind-reading.

Apparently baseball was left, like Alexander, with no new worlds to conquer after Walter O'Malley met and defeated the forces of darkness on a hilly goat pasture called Chavez Ravine. Pining to open up frontiers of their own, Will Harridge and Warren Giles, presidents of the American and National leagues, turned their attentions forthwith to the deplorable practice of skipping fastballs off the skulls of batsmen.

Hereafter, they decreed, any pitcher who throws at a batter on purpose automatically becomes liable to a $50 fine. If he persists in his unneighborly attitude, a severer penalty will be imposed.

The task of divining the pitcher's intentions is assigned to the umpire, who has trouble enough deciding where the pitch goes, let alone why. This may be a mistake. Perhaps the job should have been turned over to Dr. J. B. Rhine, the authority on extra-sensory perception who occupies the Chair of Mind-reading at Duke University.

Announcement of the new regulations appeared in the morning papers last Saturday and perhaps escaped the umpires' attention if they happened to be concentrating that day on the past performances of Tim Tam and Cavan. This may account for the fact that although there must have been some wild pitches delivered over the weekend, none was priced at $50.

Surely it cannot be that baseball's house dicks are unsure of their ability to plumb the depths of any pitcher's soul, to see and interpret the innermost workings of his psyche. Directing the umpires to distinguish between the accidental wild pitch and the intentional duster, the Messrs. Harridge and Giles are crediting them with omniscience worthy of a Broadway gossip columnist, a lofty compliment.

Not exactly going out of their way to make the job easier, the league presidents have instructed the umpires to consider the degree of wildness and the wisdom of the pitching tactics as well as the matter of intent. That is, Giles and Harridge emphasized that it was not their purpose to deny a pitcher the right to brush the batter back and loosen him up.

"Our regulations," they wrote, "are not intended to interfere with accepted pitching practices which are now and have been accepted for many years, but the intentional throwing at batters must stop."

The term "accepted pitching practices" means the brush-back pitch. You get two strikes on the hitter, then you nudge him back a trifle with an inside pitch, then come through with the curve or fog the hard one across the outside corner. This is the classic pattern, as rigidly formalized as the minuet.

Under the new edict, umpires are not to obstruct this strategy. The batter may suspect the waste pitch is coming, may even invite it by crowding the plate, and may seek to dramatize it by flinging himself backward in exaggerated terror. The umpire is not to be deceived. "Get up, you bum," he says, "wanta live forever?"

Suppose, however, that the pitch is a half inch farther inside. Is this due to faulty control or misanthropy? "Ball one," says the believer in man's essential humanity. "Fifty bucks," says the skeptic. These are the questions that try men's souls.

Rewriting the beanball regulations, Giles and Harridge erect no sign posts to guide their deputies on the field. On the contrary, they warned them that the evidence of their eyes can be misleading.

"We recognize fully," the law givers concede, "that many incidents which may appear to be the result of intent are definitely unintentional. Many of these entirely unintentional incidents have been dramatized out of all proportion."

They're correct in that last statement, anyhow. Today's crop of baseball players, fans, and writers seem to get much more hotly exercised about knockdown pitches than their elders did. Maybe this is the erroneous memory of an old curmudgeon, but it is the impression here that a good hitter of twenty-five years ago went to the plate expecting to hit the dirt—and he wore no protective helmet.

He got annoyed, of course, and sometimes he resorted to reprisals. But it was not then a tacit rule that a pitcher with shaky control must always be wild low and outside, never high and inside.

There is a line so fine as to be almost indistinguishable between the viciously callous and the coldly competent. When Luke Easter played in the American League, he confessed that the pitcher who gave him more trouble than any other was that estimable aborigine, Mr. Allie Reynolds, of the Yankees. Asked why, he replied in a tone more respectful than resentful.

"He throws too hard," Luke said, "and too close."

A Demigod of
Picturesque Grace

Napoleon Lajoie, 1874–1959

NEW YORK, N.Y., *February 9, 1959*
IT COULDN'T possibly happen today. Baseball has no backwoods today, no frontiers, no dark continents. Stop in at 745 Fifth Avenue in New York and ask George Weiss who's the best ballplayer in Australia; he'll tell you all about a cricketer named O'Neill.

Olanta, South Carolina, is a nodule on Highway 301 six miles north of Turbeville and about equidistant from Florence and Sumter. On the day Don Buddin finished high school, representatives of fifteen major league clubs waited at his home in Olanta. For *Lebensraum,* he took them to the funeral parlor next door and interviewed them one by one before selecting the bonus offered by the Red Sox. That's how baseball's intelligence service works today.

In August of 1896 Bill Nash, a scout for the Philadelphia Nationals, went up to Fall River, Massachusetts, to look over an outfielder named Phil Geier. He saw a strapping twenty-year-old playing second base, and forgot all about Geier. The kid was leading the New England League with a batting average of .429 but scouts had not heard about him yet. Charley Marston, the Fall River manager who had signed the rookie on the back of an envelope, sold him to Nash.

That is how Napoleon Lajoie reached the big leagues en route to the Hall of Fame. In those days, it could happen.

Nap Lajoie had been a hack driver in Woonsocket, Rhode Island, playing ball between fares, when Marston picked him up. In his first season as a professional, after only eighty games with Fall River, he got to Philadelphia in time to play thirty-nine games and bat .328. That fall he went back to Woonsocket and his job as a hack driver.

The next year he hit .363, went back home and climbed into the hack again. The following season his average dropped back to .328 but he led the league in doubles and topped all second basemen in putouts. He was in the hack again as soon as he got home. Wasn't sure he could stick in the big leagues.

As it turned out, the baseball job wasn't permanent. It lasted only twenty-three years. When he was forty-two and finished in the majors, he went up to Toronto, where he played 151 games and batted .380. The Enos Slaughter of his day, they call him.

That wasn't bad for a washed-up antique, but the chances are Lajoie didn't regard it as a noteworthy season. He would compare it with 1901, when he batted .405 and led the American League with 220 hits, 145 runs, 48 doubles, 13 home runs, and 403 putouts. When they built the Hall of Fame in Cooperstown, he came with the deed.

Considering the excitement that was stirred when Stan Musial became the eighth player in history to make three thousand hits, it would be interesting to know whether anybody even noticed it when Lajoie attained that figure. That was in 1914, his last season in Cleveland. Two years later, when he left the majors after his second tour of duty with the Athletics, he had 3,251 hits, fifth in the all-time list.

These days when a club gets a hitter like Lajoie the club keeps him, as the Yankees kept Joe DiMaggio, the Red Sox Ted Williams, the Cardinals Musial. Lajoie moved from the Phillies to the Athletics to Cleveland to the Athletics, but there were special circumstances.

When the American League moved into Philadelphia, Lajoie jumped to the Athletics for $2,400, which was double his National League salary. His ingratitude infuriated the Phillies, for whom he had averaged only .349 over four seasons, and they sued. The courts were making curious decisions even then. Lajoie was enjoined from playing in Pennsylvania but he wasn't restored to the Phillies. Cleveland got him instead, letting him sit on the bench when the club played in Philadelphia.

He managed Cleveland from 1905 until midseason of 1909. The team was called the Napoleons in those days, and Lajoie's roommate on the road was a young sportswriter covering the club, name of Grantland Rice. It is indicative of Lajoie's disposition that when Jim McGuire succeeded him as manager it wasn't deemed necessary to trade him away. In 1910 he played 159 games, led the league with 227 hits and 51 doubles, and batted .384. Must've been sulking.

After his death in Daytona Beach, the obituaries mentioned the minor scandal of 1910, when the St. Louis Browns, playing Cleveland a doubleheader on the last day of the season, tried to hand Lajoie the batting championship because they did not love his rival, Ty Cobb.

In spite of their efforts, Cobb won. Chances are Ty regarded Lajoie with something less than cuddly warmth thereafter. At any rate, he dissented from the popular estimate of Lajoie as a demigod of picturesque grace.

Choosing Lajoie on his All-Star team in 1908, the Reverend Billy Sunday wrote, "He works as noiselessly as a Corliss engine, makes hard plays easy, is great in a pinch, and never gets cold feet."

In a letter to E. J. Lanigan, Hall of Fame historian, in 1945, Cobb put Eddie Collins at second base. "Lajoie," he wrote, "could not go out, nor come in, and did not cover too much ground to his right or left."

His Last Bow?

Casey Stengel at 70

WHEN HAL SMITH hit the ball Jim Coates turned to watch its flight over left field, and as it vanished beyond the ivied wall of brick the pitcher flung his glove high, as though renouncing forever the loathsome tools of his trade. Before the runners had circled the bases, C. D. Stengel was out of the dugout, his knee-sprung gait taking him rapidly toward the forlorn young man on the mound.

Five times earlier this sultry, sunny, hazy, implausible day, the greatest man in baseball had shaped up front and center, asking questions, making decisions, issuing orders, while the Yankees and Pirates threshed and clawed through the sudden-death seventh struggle for the championship of their species.

Now Casey spoke briefly to Coates, who turned and shuffled to the dugout on dragging feet, his head low. The manager waited until Ralph Terry arrived from the bullpen, then walked warily back to his seat.

It may have been his last exit from the stage he has occupied through most of his seventy years. Maybe it wasn't, and next year they may have to write pieces captioned "The Return of Casey Stengel." But if this was his final bow, then it was made in circumstances more gaudily theatrical than the wildest mummery this old trouper could have dreamed up for himself.

Perhaps there have been other World Series games as extravagantly melodramatic as this, which the Yankees seemed to have won with a come-from-behind rush in the middle innings; which flipped over to dizzy abruptness when Smith's home run with two on base topped off a five-run burst for Pittsburgh in the eighth; which slipped out of Pirate paws when the Yankees tied the score with two runs in the ninth, then blew up with the shattering crash of Bill Mazeroski's bat against Terry's last pitch.

The home run went where Smith's had gone, giving Pittsburgh the game, 10 to 9, and the set, 4 to 3. Terry watched the ball disappear, brandished his glove hand high overhead, shook himself like a wet spaniel, and started fighting through the mobs that came boiling from the stands to use Mazeroski like a trampoline.

Maybe there've been other finishes like this, but this is Pittsburgh's first world championship in thirty-five years. As this is written, the pitching mound heaves and squirms with kids whose parents may not have been born when the Pirates last won a pennant. From somewhere under the stands comes burst after burst of cheering for every blessed little Buccaneer down to Joe Christopher, a pinch runner from the Virgin Islands. Over and over, screeching trebles sing a tinny horror entitled "The Bucs Are Going All the Way." On the field a meaty introvert in a brown suit poses for snapshots with a spade over one shoulder and, on the other, the Forbes Field home plate which he dug up as cops looked on.

In his own good time, Casey Stengel will reveal whether he means to manage again or retire with his matchless seasons. His Yankee teams won seven world championships and it was obvious from the outset that he wanted this eighth title so much he could taste it.

He sent his non-alcoholic, de-nicotinized, clean-living, right-thinking, brave, pure and reverent right-hander, Bob Turley, out to pitch against the equally unblemished Latter Day Saint, Vernon Law, but the lofty moral tone of the duel didn't stay his hand. When Rocky Nelson hit a two-run homer in the first inning and Smoky Burgess led off the second with a single, out came Turley like a loose tooth, and when Pittsburgh added a third and fourth run off Bill Stafford, that young man vanished also.

For five innings, Bobby Shantz stopped the Pirates cold with one single while the Yankees got hunk with Law and the accomplice who had helped him win two games, Roy Face. Bill Skowron got a home run against Law and a six-inning rumpus brought in Face, in time for a three-run shot that Yogi Berra smashed high and far to the right-field gallery.

The four runs scored in the sixth put the Yankees ahead 5 to 4, and there was lovely poetic justice in this. If this was Casey's last game, how sweet that it should be a gift from Yogi, the only Yankee who was a Yankee when Casey arrived in New York, the only one who has shared his triumph and disaster since 1949.

Somebody up there hates sentiment. Somebody up there waited until the Yankees padded their lead by two more runs, then slipped a pebble in front of a double-play grounder hit by Bill Virdon. The double play would have averted trouble in the eighth inning, but the ball leaped and struck at Tony Kubek like an angry cobra, sending him to hospital with a smashed larynx. Moments later, Shantz was out of there and Hal Smith was capping that five-run binge.

With the score 9 to 7 against them, fortune turned a false smile on the Yankees. Singles by Bobby Richardson, Dale Long, and Mickey Mantle got one run home, put men on first and third with one out. Berra grounded out to Nelson, who stepped on first base for what he may have believed the final putout, then gazed incuriously at Mantle, sprawled face down a few feet from the bag. Mickey wriggled like a snake back to safety as Nelson made a belated stab and the tying run scampered home.

Casey's old heart sang. A swan song? A brief song, and how. Maze-roski was first up for Pittsburgh.

59 Homers
and Counting

Maris Chases Babe Ruth's Ghost

BALTIMORE, MD., *September 21, 1961*
THE YANKEES won it early, and it didn't matter, somehow. Everybody knew they were going to win the pennant. What everybody wanted to know was, how about Roger Maris and the great ghost-hunt?

"If Maris has any class," a guy said, joking, after Maris went hitless in the first game of Tuesday's twi-night doubleheader, "he'll go empty tonight and then rap three tomorrow."

At this point Maris had fifty-eight home runs. He did go empty in Tuesday's second game, so that he went to work last night needing two home runs to tie Babe Ruth's record sixty, three to break it within the 154-game limit imposed by Ford Frick, the tradition-loving baseball commissioner.

"I'll tell you how he'll do it," a romantic said before the game began. "First time up, he'll hit one. Next time he'll strike out. They'll walk him on his third trip but he'll smack No. 60 on his fourth. This'll be one of those games where he comes up five times. So on the last shot, he'll make it sixty-one—and win the pennant in the bargain."

In Hollywood they would have done it that way, but this is Baltimore—Babe Ruth's home town. Maris got No. 59 and he's the first since Ruth or before him to reach that figure. But the Yankees could have and would have won without his hit.

It's hard to describe how this was, the last crazy rush in pursuit of Babe Ruth's ghost. Maris himself had been saying right along that he took no stock in the commissioner's view that Ruth's record couldn't be broken unless it was done in a season of 154 games, such as Ruth used to play. Nobody doubts that the fellow will hit sixty-one or more before the expanded season of 162 games ends.

Just the same, Maris was keenly aware of the deadline. So were the 21,032 witnesses who saw him come up against Milt Pappas in the first inning. Pappas is big and tough and able, but at least he's right-handed and he pitches like people.

That is, he pitches fastballs and curves. He must have looked good to Maris, a left-handed hitter. In the first game Tuesday evening, Maris had to swing against Steve Barber, the youngest and meanest left-handed pitcher in the American League.

In Tuesday's second game they hit him in the face with two knuckle-ball throwers, and hardly anybody hits the knuckler far.

Last night the wind that had been blowing in from right field moderated, but on his first time up Maris got only a piece of the ball and pulled a line drive to Earl Robinson in right.

The crowd relaxed for a while, making no great disturbance when Bill Skowron's triple and Cletis Boyer's single put the Yankees in front, 1–0, in the second inning.

It was still 1–0 and Pappas was still pitching when Maris came up in the third inning with one out and nobody on base. In fact, the Yankees' Ralph Terry was pitching a perfect game up to this point, and he was destined to wind up with a four-hitter.

Maris took the first pitch for a ball. He swung at the second and missed. The third was low for a second ball.

The fourth—well, there never was a moment's question about the fourth. Maris nailed it with that lovely, level swing of his and it looked so remarkably easy. Even as it left the bat, customers in the sparsely settled seats in right were on their feet getting ready to scrap for it.

Yogi Berra followed with a home run and the Yankees scored again before the inning ended, on a single by John Blanchard and a double by Elston Howard.

Nobody cared much, though. Everybody knew the Yankees were going to win the pennant: It was only the ghost-hunt that counted.

By the time Maris came up again, a tall kid named Dick Hall was pitching. Hall is a sterling young man out of nearby Towson, Md., whom Branch Rickey snagged off the Swarthmore campus a few years back when Rickey was running a day nursery in Pittsburgh.

Hall knocked around a few years before anybody discovered what he was good at. He is good at throwing strikes, on the very edge of the plate.

Hall fired one over the outside corner and Maris took the strike. Hall brushed the inside edge, and Maris took his second strike. He swung at the third, which was also inside, and pulled a screaming foul to right. He just plain missed the next.

There was one out again when Maris came up in the seventh. The first time they had faced each other, Hall had thrown nothing but strikes. This was the second time, and again they were all strikes. Maris took one, fouled one, and flied out to right on the third.

Roger was the Yankees' last hitter, with two out and none on in the ninth. Now Hoyt Wilhelm was throwing that nauseous knuckler. Maris took a half-swing on the first pitch and fouled it back. He took a half-swing at the second and dribbled down the first-base line where Wilhelm fielded the ball and tagged him out. The crowd had been giving off animal noises, but suddenly there was an odd silence. The great chase was ended.

There is, however, one bit of good news. Seems there's a new strip-tease artist playing the joints, a smasher, they say. Her name is Mickey Maris.

★ SPORTS IN THE SIXTIES ★

Bike Ride

The Mad Pursuit of the Maillot Jaune

GAP, FRANCE, *July 11, 1960*

FROM THE summit of the mountain called Col de Perty, misty Alpine peaks stretched away in wave after gray-blue wave, as far as the eye could reach. The morning had been hot in Avignon in the soft valley of the Rhône, but up here, four thousand feet in the sky, a fresh wind was blowing, stiff and chilling. Col de Perty is a barren knob not close to anything or anybody, yet it looked like the bleachers in Yankee Stadium on a good day with the White Sox.

From somewhere, by some means, they had come by the hundreds— wide-eyed kids and old-pappy guys and wizened peasant women and young guys and exuberant girls waved at the press cars whirring by. A smiling doll had a counter of plain boards set up, where she sold razor-thin salami in yesterday's bread, and nearby was another hutch offering soft drinks and beer.

They had been waiting for two or three hours, perched on rocks or camp chairs or just meandering about. Now a sense of expectancy came over them all as a squadron of cops on motor bikes came around the shoulder of the mountain. Then from the crowd on the highest slope came a buzz that grew into a hum and finally a babble.

Bicyclists in bright jerseys emerged from behind a rocky promontory. They came straining bitterly, leaning on the pedals, teeth clenched, shaved limbs glistening with sweat—a little group of leaders in single file, then a gap, then a long cluster, then the laggards.

This was the Tour de France topping the first challenging peak of the Alpine section of the course. There would be more and tougher heights to scale later, but this was enough to split out the men from the boys.

The Tour de France, now being contested for the forty-seventh time since 1903, is an annual bike race of 2,600 miles around the perimeter of France, over the Pyrenees and over the Alps. Some of the roads are terrifying in a car, but these characters go pumping a hundred-odd miles a day at something like twenty-five miles an hour.

There is nothing in America even remotely comparable with it. We think the World Series claims the undivided attention of the United States, but there is a saying here that an Army from Mars could invade France, the government could fall, and even the recipe for sauce béarnaise be lost, but if it happened during the Tour de France nobody would notice.

Today's leg was the fifteenth of the course that began June 26 at Lille in the North, took the riders up into Belgium through Brussels and down the west coast, then east to this corner near Italy and Switzerland. Of the 120 starters, eighty-eight had made it into Avignon last night, hoping to reach Paris on July 17.

In that ancient walled city which once was the seat of popes, there was festival last night but there was also mourning for the loss of a favorite, Roger Rivière from the French team. On yesterday's run he had plunged off the road, hurtled through a gap in the retaining wall, and plummeted seventy-five feet, winding up in the hospital with a broken vertebra and a highly intelligent statement: "You shall see me no more on a bicycle."

In the over-all time reckoning, he had been second, only one minute thirty-six seconds behind Italy's Gastone Nencini, who set off again this morning in the yellow jersey of the leader, probably the most coveted, and sweatiest, piece of apparel in Europe.

This is the order of march in this implausible parade: An hour before the cyclists start the "publicity caravan" departs, a great parade of sound trucks and shills advertising commercial products. Then a platoon of motorcyclists clears the road for the racers, who are followed by a control car and then a double file of press, radio, television, and team cars carrying the team managers and spare parts for broken bikes.

Out of Avignon it was fairly level going for a while, with the whole field pumping along in one great clot. In every village, streets were jammed. All along the country roads there were family groups waving and cheering.

For the first fifty miles of this 110-mile leg, the road climbed gently toward the foothills of the Alps. Then the high hills began, capped here and there by fortifications left over since the Roman Empire. Past a village named Pierrelongue, Albertus Geldermans of Holland went into a ditch, crawled out with blood streaming down his left leg, swiftly replaced a bent wheel, remounted, and pumped hard to catch up with the pack. (There is short-wave radio control that brings up a team car or the race's attending doctor on quick notice.)

As the narrow road wound through a gorge, a Belgian named Louis Proost crashed against the retaining wall. He remounted but he was badly knocked about, and in a mile or so he had to give up. He wobbled over against the wall and sagged there, crying like a child.

They went sweating up Col de Perty, went ripping down the far side at a bloodcurdling fifty miles an hour, and now the field had stretched out, with five riders in a cluster about a mile ahead of the main pack. Behind the latter were the stragglers, followed closely by a car that is called the *camion balai*, the "broom truck," which gathers up the debris.

Then it was up again around devastating hairpin turns to Col de la Sentinelle and finally down to this village, with a wild sprint down a tree-lined street with Belgium's Michel Van Aerde beating a Dutchman named Van den Borgh by inches for the day's lap prize. The villagers milled and swooped and cheered and a dozen radio announcers babbled and a truck rolled by advertising bananas, "the fruit in the yellow jersey."

Who Broke the Tape?

A Relay as Tangled as a Plate of Spaghetti

ROME, ITALY, *September 8, 1960*

I T TOOK 'em two perishing weeks and it cost an almighty lot of sweat, but they finally brought off a barmy beauty today—a disqualification in a relay race that left a whole blooming stadium bewildered, bemused, and full of wild wonder as to who got there first.

The disqualification was entirely proper in the opinion of press-box witnesses who saw—or thought they saw—America's Frank Budd bootleg the baton to Ray Norton outside the legal zone at the end of the first of four one-hundred-meter legs.

Then everybody saw Dave Sime, of Duke, run a desperate anchor leg nose-and-nose with West Germany's Martin Lauer. They're still wondering whose manly bosom broke the tape—and as far as the brass in this carnival is concerned, everybody can go right on wondering, period. This is Italian snafu at its finest.

Most watchers in the press box thought Sime finished first. So, apparently, did some vice president in charge of confusing issues, for the teletype flash sent out of the stadium to the information-processing center read: STAFFETA 4X100M. (four-thousand-meter relay): USA NUOVO CAMPIONE OLIMPIONICO (new Olympic champion).

There has not yet been, however, any official announcement of the order of finish but only the final decision: Germany first, Russia second, Great Britain third, and the United States nowhere.

Chances are that by tomorrow there may be further details cached in the time capsule out on the edge of town that is called a press center. Meanwhile, here's how it looked:

It was the final day of track and field in Stadio Olimpico and about eighty thousand customers showed up, in spite of cloudy skies and a fair warning from the weather bureau. Romans have been observing Roman weather for better than two thousand years, which puts them ahead of woolly bears as seasoned forecasters. On the basis of their experience, they announced before the games began that there'd be two rainy days. Sure enough, this was the second.

The rain wasn't heavy, though, and it let up before the start of the 400 relay. Twilight was settling when the runners left their starting blocks on the clubhouse turn. Around the bend where the track straightens out down the backstretch, Norton was waiting to get the stick from Budd.

Inexperienced watchers could see only a tangle of runners at the exchange point. Keener observers said Norton started running too soon and had crossed the boundary of the legal zone before Budd got the baton to him. Norton handed over to Stone Johnson at the end of his hundred meters, Johnson passed to Sime, and Sime flashed down the stretch abreast of Lauer.

Lauer made like a winner. He and a colleague pranced on around the turn, waving to wildly cheering customers in the cheap seats, which aren't seats at all but only standing room in the end zone. On the infield turf, red-coated jurymen drew into a tight little covey like quail seeking cover from a hawk.

They huddled there while the runners cooled out and got into sweat suits. Then an amplified voice announced Germany as the winner. From one end of the stadium, two Germans came running. From the other end, their two playmates dashed toward them. The four met at midfield, flung arms about necks, danced, swirled in a jubilant knot.

There will be no protest as there was twelve years ago in London, when exactly the same ruling was made in the very same event. On that occasion a patrol judge watching the first exchange thought he saw America's Lorenzo Wright slip the stick to Barney Ewell beyond the legal zone.

The United States finished first, by a comfortable margin that time, but Great Britain got the gold medals—on lend-lease. It was England's one short-lived moment to howl during that track meet, and a mighty roar shook Wembley Stadium.

"We did that on cold mutton," a British journalist said. Wartime rationing was still in effect, for this was 1948 and England still subsisted on Brussels sprouts.

Actually, they had done it on one judge's myopia, as films of the race were to demonstrate. Medals were exchanged, but that won't happen this time.

For all practical purposes today's snafu wrapped up the Seventeenth Olympiad. Champions still have to be decided in basketball, cycling, fencing, gymnastics, and such nonsense, but Stadio Olimpico has had it. Saturday evening they'll clean it all up with the marathon over Rome's ancient pavements and along the Appian Way.

Considering that this is Italy, it's kind of nice to finish this way, all tangled up like spaghetti.

Subway Alumni

The Secret Notre Damers of New York

NEW YORK, N.Y., *November 28, 1963*

Once they were known from coast to coast as the Subway Alumni and there seemed to be millions of 'em, though you hardly ever met one in person. Whether they were college football fans in the strict meaning of the term it is hard to say, for New York never has been a college football town in the sense that Philadelphia used to be and Boston and Chicago still are.

They were faceless customers buying entertainment when they helped fill the parks for Fordham–New York U. or Fordham–St. Mary's, or when Army came down to play Michigan or Illinois or Navy, or when Columbia had a Cliff Montgomery or Paul Governali or Sid Luckman in the showcase.

The Subway Alumni weren't Irish, they weren't Catholic, they weren't anything, but once a year they became an entity, and only once a year. When Notre Dame came to town to play Army, they took on identity, they found their voice—and they were all Notre Damers, even though a lot of them regarded Hoboken as the western frontier.

Notre Dame–Army day was the World Series, it was a heavyweight championship fight . . . but with a difference. You could hear the difference on the streets and in the saloons; you could see it among the crowds on Long Island and New Haven station platforms, carrying their thermos jugs and binoculars and plaid blankets; you could smell it in the used air of the subways.

Notre Dame hasn't played Army in New York since 1946. Fourteen years have passed since a Notre Dame football team came in to play anybody. In fourteen years a lot of classes are graduated, even in the subway, and a lot of alumni grow old.

They grow old and a new generation grows up, but in New York they grow up as fans of professional football. Today the town is populated by kids who think the game was invented by Y. A. Tittle.

Ask these kids if they ever heard of Johnny Lujack and they'd say sure, the sportscaster, usen't he to play with the Bears or somebody? He was the Notre Dame quarterback in the last Yankee Stadium meeting with Army.

But try to tell them about Frank Spaniel's 78-yard touchdown run against North Carolina when Notre Dame last hit town in 1949, and they'd look at you like you were some kind of nut or something. Spaniel? Football? Not the Westminster Kennel Club?

Still, when Notre Dame plays Syracuse today there will be a crowd in Yankee Stadium, the first real college football crowd in New York in too many seasons. And that is a remarkable thing, for the Notre Dame football "image" is not the one the Subway Alumni used to know.

The 1949 team they saw beat Carolina, 42–6, was undefeated in thirty-five games and stayed that way the rest of that season and into the next. To be sure, there was a bit of Irish luck involved, for when Notre Dame beat Washington early that year, the Cougars' Hugh McElhenny was on the sidelines; in the North Carolina game, Charlie Justice appeared only to hold the ball for an unsuccessful conversion kick; in the closing game Southern Methodist had to get by without Doak Walker—and mighty near did get by on account of a boy named Kyle Rote.

Lucky or not to escape the ministrations of the country's three best backs, the Irish won ten for ten and took the national championship in 1949. That was the last Notre Dame team New York saw, and the last to go through unbeaten and untied.

This year Notre Dame has won two and lost six. The record could be better. The defeats by Wisconsin and Purdue were close things. Stanford, Pittsburgh, and Staubach Academy won decisively, but on the last Saturday that football seemed worth watching, Michigan State tried valorously to thrust a victory upon Notre Dame.

Only by the sternest exercise of will, the most ascetic self-denial, did the boys from South Bend decline the proffered gift.

Nobody need be reminded, of course, that this is the playoff (two years delayed) of the 1961 Syracuse game, which Notre Dame won, 17–15, in a welter of controversy. Both sides have rejected the suggestion of Newark's Jerry Izenberg that they play this one double-or-nothing.

Chances are Syracuse is the stronger side this time. This, at least, is the apprehensive judgment of Bill Earley, a specialist in an age of specialization. Earley, a Notre Dame back of the Frank Leahy era now in the paper business in South Bend, was drafted to scout Syracuse this year because he is an expert deeply versed in Schwartzwalder lore.

When Bill was a clear-eyed youth in high school in Parkersburg, W. Va., Ben Schwartzwalder, now the Syracuse coach, took over the chair at Parkersburg and started winning state championships. For two seasons before the Black Forester's arrival, football had been fun to Earley.

"And then," Bill says, "we went to war."

The Hessians

Buck Shaw's Eagles Eye Third NFL Championship

PHILADELPHIA, PA., *November 27, 1960*
B ETWEEN HALVES of the Giants-Eagles football game today, a drill team stomped bravely through complicated maneuvers with live bayonets affixed to rifles. This enchanted the customers jammed into Franklin Field, who realized that if somebody should goof they'd see a head cut off. Nothing else could tickle the professional football fan's fancy so much.

Unhappily, nobody was decapitated and none of the padded gladiators got killed, not even Chuck Bednarik, the Philadelphia bogeyman who rendered New York's beauteous Frank Gifford null and void a week ago. Just about everything else happened, though, this warm and sunny Sabbath as the leaders of the National League's Eastern Division had at each other in the money game the Giants had to win—and didn't.

On their first two plays from scrimmage, the Giants gained 105 yards. Inside the first thirteen minutes, they romped away to a lead of 17 to 0. Fourteen minutes later the score was 17 to 17, a scandalous lot of sweat and blood had been wasted, and a new ballgame was starting. The Eagles won that one, 14 to 6, for a net profit of 31 to 23 on the day.

This just about consummated the unfrocking of New York and investiture of Philadelphia as champion of the East. The Giants now have won five games, lost three, and tied one; the Eagles, with eight victories and one defeat, can play the Western Division winner here December 26 for gold and immortality, pro tem, if they win just one in the next three weeks.

In reports on professional football, an inflexible convention demands that every game must be described in purple and amethyst superlatives—the greatest game ever played, the greatest team that ever played, the most heroic defense ever mounted, the most God-awful literature ever committed.

This one could be put away as one of the goofiest, wherein the opposing quarterbacks, George Shaw and Norm Van Brocklin, threw passes with high technical skill and unfailing impartiality, utterly indifferent to the color of the receiver's jersey. There were six interceptions in the first half and one in the second, New York's Shaw scoring four bull's-eyes on the green bosoms of Eagles and Philadelphia's Van Brocklin hitting the white Giant haberdashery three times.

By this means, and with the aid of a few timely fumbles, the teams managed to exchange both possession and the lead whenever success became a burden. Breaking the game down into quarters, it can be said that New York won the first period by seventeen points, lost the second by fourteen, won the third by three, and lost the fourth by fourteen.

After taking their first-quarter lead of 17 to 0, the Giants were tied at 17–all in the second period, inched ahead for an advantage of 20 to 17 before the half ended, extended their margin to 23 to 17, then fell on their shapely heads.

Philadelphia, in a state of municipal rapture over prospects of its first divisional title in eleven years, snatched up all 60,547 accommodations in Penn's double-decked playground, and such was the excitement stirred by this event that university authorities reversed a policy of long standing. There were cops patrolling the grounds for the first time in a dozen or so years; ever since Philadelphia's gallant horse brigade rode with drawn night sticks across this hallowed turf, cracking the skulls of undergraduates scuffling under the goal posts after a Penn-Princeton game, the law had been barred.

Packed in solid ranks from the cinder track to Thrombosis Terrace on the upper deck's rim, the witnesses rose for the National Anthem—sung by a character wearing smoked glasses and a green sweater with a big white "E"—sat down, and then stiffened with astonishment. They were looking, with justifiable incredulity, at an opening attack such as few had ever seen the Giants put on.

In all their most successful years under the direction of Steve Owen and then Jim Lee Howell, the Giants have been distinguished primarily for defense. Such offense as they have shown in recent seasons depended largely on the passing of Charley Conerly and the running of Frank Gifford, both ailing and unavailable today.

Yet on their first play they went seventy-one yards for a touchdown and their second gained 34 yards toward another score.

The first was a long, lovely pass from Shaw to Kyle Rote, who had sneaked past Don Burroughs in the Philadelphia secondary. Rote caught the ball on the Eagles' 34-yard line and was gone.

The second New York play from scrimmage sent Ed Sutton through the line for thirty-four yards, then Joe Morrison peeled off gains of seventeen and eighteen yards, the first on a pass from Shaw, to set up another touchdown pass to Rote.

It was beginning to look downright ridiculous, but after making three more points on a field goal by Pat Summerall, the Giants put on the drunken sailor act.

So freely did they squander their wealth that Philadelphia, making four touchdowns and a field goal, had to travel more than thirty yards for a score only once. On that occasion the Giants waited until they were almost at midfield before handing over the ball, and the Eagles went forty-nine yards in one piece on a pass from Van Brocklin to Ted Dean.

Though harsh language had been employed last week after a tackle by Bednarik put Gifford in the hospital, no knives, blackjacks, or knuckle-dusters were in evidence today.

Late in the game the Giants' Jim Leo took a swing at Philadelphia's Jerry Reichow. The officials, probably fight fans, disdained to score it as a real punch.

Skinning the
Sacred Bear

Packers Roll in the Snow and the Dough

GREEN BAY, WIS., *December 28, 1961*

O UT OF the Stone Age comes the memory of an afternoon in Joannes Park when a rare old Wisconsin blizzard was shaking tons of snow out of a sky that seemed about nine feet high. Through swirling clouds of white, monstrous shapes threshed and floundered, emitting low animal growls. The Packers, champions of the West, were heating up for their 1938 match with the Giants for the championship of the National Football League.

Over the swacking sounds of combat, the voice of Buckets Goldenberg, guard, could be heard: "C'mon, guys! Whoosh! This is for dough! Whuh! Big dough! Whup!"

Greed was the spur that drove them through the blizzard. Greed and pride took them to the Polo Grounds in New York where they lost the playoff, 23–17, on a forward pass from Ed Danowski to Hank Soar. The big dough Goldenberg spoke of came to $135.61, the difference between each Packer's $368.84 from the players' pool and the winners' $504.45.

That championship game drew 48,120 customers on Dec. 11, approximately ten thousand more than Green Bay's City Stadium normally accommodates. Yet when the same clubs contend for the same title here on the last day of this year, there will be a million dollars in the house, counting television swag, and the loot for each Hessian will top $5,000 on the winning side with about $3,500 for the losers.

By the standards of polar bears, penguins, and professional head-breakers, this is good pay for a roll in the snow.

By the 1919 standards of guys named Tubby Bero, Fritz Gavin, Natie Abrams, Gus Rosenow, and Riggie Dwyer, today's rewards represent wealth beyond the dreams of avarice. They were among the home-town mob that Curly Lambeau recruited for the Packers' first season—Rosenow, the coach at West High, was a one-handed end and a remark-able pass receiver—and they played on an unfenced lot in Hagemeis-ter (later Joannes) Park, which is clear across town from the present stadium.

George Whitney Calhoun, sports editor of the local paper, passed the hat among the straggle of spectators standing on the sidelines, for there were no seats. The Packers whipped ten other town teams in a row, scoring 565 points against six, lost their eleventh and last game to the agreeably named Beloit Fairies, 6–0, then assembled to cut the melon. There were twenty-one shares of $16.75 each.

By 1929, though, the gold was really rolling in. That year the Packers won the first of three straight National League championships and the citizenry tossed a banquet where each man received a watch and $200 raised by public subscription.

There was only one division in the league then, with no intersec-tional playoff to create a special players' pool. For winning again in 1930 and 1931, the players got their regular salaries, about $100 a game. They also got drunk on Brown County moon. Heading home after their last 1930 game, Johnny Blood fetched Lavvie Dilweg a swat with a wet towel, fled the length of the train with an angry Dilweg in pursuit, swung aloft like Tarzan from the rear platform, and scampered for-ward over the roofs of cars to swing into the cab with the engineer.

Remembered also is an evening in 1936 after the Packers had beaten the Boston Redskins in their first East-West playoff. Because of poor attendance in Boston, George Preston Marshall moved the title game to New York, as he would later move his franchise to Washington. The game drew only 29,545 customers and the Packers' winning shares were $224.

In their hotel that night, they used language about Lambeau, the leader whose genius had brought them this wealth. It could have been then that Cal Hubbard, the tackle, summed up team sentiment toward the coach: "They'll have trouble finding six men to bury the ————."

The Packers' story is the story of pro football's soaring progress from the sandlots to the Chase Manhattan. Twenty years after Lambeau's pioneers sold out their amateur standing for $16.75, Green Bay and New York were playoff rivals for the second time in the only title game scheduled for this town before this year. Lambeau, however, moved that one to Milwaukee and upped ticket prices to an unprecedented $4.40. When the Packers won, their shares were $703, the Giants' $455.

That was 1939. In 1960 the Packers played off with the Eagles in Philadelphia, with $747,876 in the house. The winning Eagles got $5,116.55 apiece, the Packers $3,105.14. Franklin Field seats sold for $8 and $10. The price here is a flat sawbuck.

There was no new snow yesterday on the fourteen-inch base which makes a frosting over City Stadium's cover of canvas and straw. Skies were brilliant. The temperature was a kindly 3 degrees.

Excitement was building in town, where nothing as exciting as this has happened since the night they cracked the crib in the Farmers' Exchange Bank.

This is a week of carnival in Titletown, U.S.A. "The eyes of the world," one of the city fathers has told the electorate in an inspired address, "are on Green Bay, and we're putting on a promotion which will justify our position as the biggest little city in America."

Three centuries ago, according to Father André, a Jesuit historian, the Indians who lived here acted the same way exactly. They would skin the sacred bear, set up the hide with its nose painted green, and dance around the effigy, "yelling all night like one in despair."

One Drunk, Unarmed

A Nation in Mourning and a Game for Children

NEW YORK, N.Y., *November 24, 1963*

BETWEEN HALVES of the Army-Navy football game last year, cadets and midshipmen formed a double row across the field and John F. Kennedy walked between the ranks from a flag-draped box in the west stands to another in the east.

Hatless and without an overcoat in the November cold, he went jauntily—one football fan among one hundred thousand. He was a Navy veteran but he was also Commander in Chief of the Army. In the first half he had seen Navy take a lead of 15–6.

Halfway across, a drunk broke through the line and was almost within arm's reach of the President when Secret Service men grabbed him. Laughter started in the crowd but choked off.

Suppose the drunk hadn't been drunk? Suppose he had a gun? It could have happened there in Philadelphia, before one hundred thousand witnesses.

No doubt the sixty-fourth Army-Navy game will come off as scheduled next Saturday, if anybody cares. It is difficult to conceive of anybody caring but life has to go on, and work, and probably play, too.

John Kennedy enjoyed games as a participant and spectator, and sports had his hearty official support as President.

There is no disposition here to condemn the few college authorities who did not call off their games yesterday or the men in the National Football League who decided to go through with today's schedule. A while back some promotion man on the *Herald Tribune* lumped the paper's book reviewers and drama and television critics and a few others into a group he called the Tastemakers but this peanut stand wasn't included.

What seems bad taste to one man is plain common sense to another. What one considers decent respect is mawkish in other eyes.

Maybe it's important to determine whether the St. Louis Cardinals can upset the Giants in Yankee Stadium today, whether the Bears can push on against the Steelers in Pittsburgh. There's a race to be finished and there's money invested. Money.

Maybe a lot of people will feel it perfectly proper to attend. Like it or not, we newspaper stiffs will have to be there because that's our job as much as it's Y. A. Tittle's job.

If Yale and Harvard had played yesterday, we'd have had to be there, too. Thank heaven they didn't. Work must go on, but there'll be other days to shiver in that crepe-gray heap called Yale Bowl being light-hearted about a game for children.

Fight Night New York

Fridays at the Garden in the '40s and '50s

NEW YORK, N.Y., *October 21, 1966*

"THIS WAS New York in the elegant eighties," Frank Graham wrote, "and these were the Giants, fashioned in elegance, playing on the Polo Grounds, then at 110th Street and Fifth Avenue. It was the New York of the brownstone house and the gaslit streets, of the top hat and the hansom cab, of oysters and champagne and perfecto cigars, of Ada Rehan and Oscar Wilde and the young John L. Sullivan. It also was the New York of the Tenderloin and the Bowery, of the slums and the sweatshops, of goats grazing among the shanties perched on the rocky terrain of Harlem. . . ."

Some day before the memory grows too dim, somebody with Frank's gift for words—if such there be—ought to write, "this was Friday night in New York in the 1940s and '50s," and try to make readers understand what fight night at the Garden used to be like.

The early dinner crowds and the talk in Shor's and Gallagher's and Al Schacht's and 21 . . . The feeling after dinner that all the traffic in Manhattan was moving toward Eighth Ave. and 50th, sluggish and noisily impatient . . . The swirling throngs under the marquee that reads "Madison Square Garden" and the cops not bothering to try to keep the sidewalk open . . . The sharp, cheap mob in the lobby, and at ringside the Broadway guys with their varnished blondes (until television came in with the cameras looking down from the 50th St. balcony, whereupon the guys with the dolls swapped their seats on the 49th side for locations out of range of a picture going into the home).

The buffs from the Bronx and Brooklyn and Harlem in the galleries

. . . The thunder they made, and the tobacco smoke in clouds under the ring lights . . . Afterward, in Leone's or back at Shor's the arguments, the laughter, the crackling electricity in the air.

The big guys like Joe Louis and Rocky Marciano packed them in, of course, as the big guys always do. There was a time when lightweights like Beau Jack and Bob Montgomery wouldn't take their pants off with less than $100,000 in the house. But best of all were the middleweights.

Big enough to take a guy out with one punch, light enough to move with the animal grace of a Ray Robinson, they made the evenings that are still unforgettable. Mickey Walker and Billy Conn. Robinson and Jake LaMotta and Marcel Cerdan and—to be remembered to the grave—Rocky Marciano's three wars with Tony Zale.

Nights like these come around ever so seldom now. Now basketball players do the fighting in the old Eighth Ave. house.

Once in a long while, though, the old excitement comes back. It could happen on Nov. 10, even though that's a Thursday night. That night Emile Griffith fights Joey Archer. They are middleweights and the world championship is on the block.

In the best and busiest of the divisions, Griffith is the busiest of champions. No man has ever had three middleweight title bouts in six months, but it was only last April 25 when Emile won the championship from Dick Tiger, and on July 13 he defended it against Archer.

This malingerer was in Ireland in July, standing by a Connemara pool cursing foully at a salmon that wouldn't stand and fight, and isn't qualified to testify on the first Griffith-Archer match.

Opinion varied as to the winner, among the officials and among the citizens. Today most qualified observers seem to agree that Griffith ran the game, ducking Archer's jab and working Joey over inside, seldom letting the Bronx boy fight his fight. They feel Artie Aidala had it about right giving Griffith nine rounds to five with one even, though the other judge, Al Berl, made it only 8–7 for the champion and Johnny LoBianco, the referee, made it a draw at 7–7–1.

That's why they're at it again, of course. For all his slave bracelets

and foppish threads and his enthusiasm for the Frug and the Booga-
loo, the Monkey and the Watusi, Emile Griffith is a fighter who ducks
no arguments. Last March when Archer's interests were screaming
that Joey, not Griffith, should have the shot at Tiger's title, Emile told
Teddy Brenner, "Make me with Archer first. If he wins I'll tear up this
contract and he can have Tiger."

Now if you ask Griffith why he's taking Archer right back when he
could collect on the title with far less risk, he says simply: "A lot of
Joey's friends thought he beat me, especially when he caught me with
that right in the fourteenth. I have to fight him again."

Most Alone

Patterson's Year in the Wilderness

★ ★ ★

NEWTOWN, CONN., *June 14, 1960*

I F HENRIK IBSEN was right that "the strongest man on earth is he who stands alone," then Floyd Patterson ought to bat Ingemar Johansson bubble-eyed in the Polo Grounds next Monday night. For here is a deeply lonely man.

For ten months Patterson has lived and worked and had his being up here in the woods. Dan Florio, the trainer, has been with him, and most of the time he has had sparring partners to work with him. They seem to get along well enough, but they seem also to have nothing in common. It is noticeable that outside working hours they leave Floyd to himself unless he seeks company.

The others are here to do a job and make a buck. For Patterson, alone, this is a crusade, a ten-month capsule containing his whole purpose in life. He is dedicated to the single goal of winning back the heavyweight championship of the world, and in that dedication he lives within himself, withdrawn from those around him. Nobody shares his thoughts, his hopes, his dreams, his doubts.

From small things observed, one judges that he and his wife have a close understanding, that she shared his confidence before his knockout last June and his despondency afterward. But for ten months Floyd has been cut off from his family except for occasional visits.

Sportswriters and photographers come with questions and cameras. They do not reach him. He is polite without warmth. He answers questions thoughtfully, with careful reserve, volunteers little.

Tourists and fans and acquaintances come visiting. Patterson is polite with them, too, poses patiently for snapshots, signs autographs, makes small talk, and watches them drive away with no sign of regret.

He runs on the road, boxes and exercises, sleeps, eats, watches television. He rarely goes to a movie, thinking that when he gets home his wife may want him to take her to a picture and perhaps it would be one he has seen. He can't abide sitting through a show twice. He gets a lot of mail, especially from abroad and particularly from Sweden, which he reads and sends to an office in New York where it is answered for him. Otherwise, he reads very little. He regards excessive reading as a disease and can't understand an omnivorous reader like Ed Bunyan, formerly a sparring partner and now the camp chauffeur.

"That Bunyan!" Floyd said one day. "If there wasn't nothing to read but"—his glance fell on the parquet floor of that abandoned roadhouse, where visitors had stubbed out cigarettes—"but one of those butts, he'd read that."

A visitor stooped for a butt. "Not much plot," he said, "it just says 'Camel.'"

This is wilder, prettier country than the hillside near Summit, New Jersey, where he trained for Johansson the first time. No naturalist, Floyd gives no indication that he notices. His surroundings, indoors and out, apparently mean nothing to him.

There were more people around the Summit camp, other fighters coming and going, and Cus D'Amato, an enemy of silence, was there, not having been unfrocked as Patterson's manager then. Even there, the fighter lived like a monk.

Visitors were struck by the contrast between Floyd's celibate existence and Johansson's life of coeducational cheer in the teeming Catskills. Between workouts at Grossinger's, Ingemar and his retinue relaxed on a broad estate nearby, with wide lawns, terraces, swimming pool, and other trappings of gracious living.

There were trips to New York for television appearances, and when you have to go to New York you might as well hit a night club or so for a spot of dancing. Wherever Ingo went, the tinkle of girlish laughter followed. This year the party occupies less pretentious quarters up the road, but it is still a gay bit of Sweden in those jumping hills.

Before the first fight, scholars fancied they could read a sturdy moral in the contrast between the champion's Spartan existence and the challenger's Lucullan revels. Then Ingemar lowered the boom. It played hell with the copybook maxims, but it was the greatest ad for womankind since Ziegfeld was around glorifying the American girl.

Ibsen was a Scandinavian and ought to understand about these things, but maybe he overlooked one point. It may not have occurred to him that when the house lights go down and the ring lights go up and two men face each other across a white square of canvas, each stands utterly alone. Between them, these two haven't got one manager to say, "He can't hurt us," and count the house.

The Road Back
to Göteborg:

The Floyd-Ingo Street Fight, Resumed

NEW YORK, N.Y., *June 21, 1960*

TEN MINUTES after the fight they scraped Ingemar Johansson off
the floor, propped him on a stool, bundled him in white like a sore
thumb, and nudged him gingerly into his first step on the long road
back to Göteborg. Reaching center field in the Polo Grounds, they
supported him up the stairs to the old baseball clubhouse, then had to
grab him as he stumbled and almost fell down the short flight to the
locker rooms.

His womenfolk came in—his mother, his sister, his Birgit Lund-
gren, and Miss Elizabeth Taylor, an added starter. The ladies talked
together for a while on the landing where the ballplayers used to lose
their pay to Leo Durocher at gin rummy. Liz waited while the others
visited the sickroom. An hour after Floyd Patterson's fist had reached
his dimpled chin, Ingo's eyes were glazed.

Six days less than a year from the night Johansson had dismantled
Patterson and become heavyweight champion of the world, that chin
had become a landmark, a tourist attraction, a unique curio in boxing's museum. It was the target for the only blow that ever restored a
deposed heavyweight to his throne.

Let this be said of the winner, who lived in aggrieved obscurity the
three years he held the title, ignored by the public and derided by
many: On this one night he earned his place in pugilistic history. If

· 358 ·

his unlicensed, unsilenced manager will allow, he can bask now in the fame that has been denied him.

It was a fascinating fight, full of seeming contradictions. From the first minute when Floyd charged in with two hard hooks that drove Johansson back into the ropes, witnesses were on notice that this was not the same overcautious Patterson whom Johansson had plugged like a sitting hen last June. This wasn't the lackluster winner over incompetents like Pete Rademacher, Roy Harris, and Brian London. This was, instead, the street fighter from the Bedford-Stuyvesant district of Brooklyn, a fair match for a street fighter from Göteborg.

Taking the initiative had seemed to many the only way Patterson could possibly beat the Swede, yet taking the initiative also means taking chances. And all the while, there was Johansson's right hand cocked, the right that had smashed Floyd down seven times in their first fight. Every instant until the fifth-round knockout, the menace of that right was present, imminent, and suspenseful.

Only once in the second round did the right land cleanly. This time Floyd saw it coming and was ready, took it high and stayed on his feet. He said later that when he didn't go down he saw astonishment and dismay in the Swede's blue eyes, and felt assured then that he would win.

Johansson kept trying with the right, but Patterson had a plan, and it worked. Last year Ingemar had set him up with a lazy hook. Floyd had stopped moving just long enough to block the hook, and in that instant the right shot through. This time when Johansson fished with the left, Floyd ducked, going under the left and the following right.

Patterson began and ended the fight with his left hand, hooks in the first round, swings in the fifth. It is dangerous to throw a round left at a man who can shoot a straight right inside it, but Patterson prepared for this risk with jabs. Ingemar brought his right glove across his face to brush the jabs aside, immobilizing the hand as an offensive weapon.

These were planned tactics, but there was too much street fighter in Floyd this night for him to operate always on plan. Sometimes he leaped and lunged, throwing punches, as he did in his amateur days. Through the first two rounds he had the oddest way of attacking—just sticking the left out like a pole and rushing in behind it as Johansson backed away.

Sometimes he was able to connect with rights by this means, because Johansson has little lateral movement in the ring. The Swede moves straight back and forth on a trolley.

Forget tactics, though. The essential thing was that here was a fighting man, brave and able, displaying qualities he had never shown before as a heavyweight, except perhaps in his first title fight with a listless Archie Moore.

He had left much to be desired against the likes of Rademacher, Harris, Tommy Jackson, and London. Hacking away at these defense-less stooges, he had made an interminable task of putting them away. Where was that take-out punch then, a punch so effective that even a long left swing could leave a man for dead?

"I had so little respect for those other fellows," D'Amato said, "that Floyd had no incentive. This time he was emotionally ready."

Death of a
Welterweight

Benny Paret and the Case Against Boxing

NEW YORK, N.Y., *April 3, 1962*

T HE PITIFUL case of Benny Paret moves each according to his nature. The habitually hysterical raise the scream of "legalized murder," and their number includes some who are equally quick to revile any fighter who, unlike Paret, quits under punishment. The politicians fulminate as politicians must, like that cluck in the South Carolina legislature who wants a law requiring circular or ten-sided rings so a fighter can't be trapped in a corner.

Prodded perhaps by fear or maybe by conscience, Manny Alfaro, Paret's manager, gave a disgraceful performance trying to pin the blame on Ruby Goldstein, the referee. Nobody involved has any right to blame anybody else for a tragic accident, least of all a manager who gets his boy cruelly beaten by Gene Fullmer, then sends him back against a man who has already knocked him out.

To me boxing is a rough, dangerous, and thrilling sport, the most basic and natural and uncomplicated of athletic competitions, and—at its best—one of the purest of art forms. Yet there is no quarrel here with those who sincerely regard it as a vicious business that should have no place in a civilized society.

They are wrong, of course, those who think boxing can be legislated out of existence. It has been tried a hundred times, but there were always men ready to fight for prizes on a barge or in a pasture lot or the back room of a saloon. It is hard to believe that a nation bereft of such men would be the stronger or better for it.

Still, if a man honestly feels that boxing should be abolished, he has every right to cite the Paret case in support of his position. The quarrel here is with the part-time bleeding hearts, the professional sob sisters of press and politics and radio who seize these opportunities to parade their own nobility, demonstrate their eloquence, and incidentally stir the emotions of a few readers, voters, or listeners.

Some of the fakers now sobbing publicly over Paret have waxed ecstatic over a Ray Robinson or Joe Louis. It must be comforting to have it both ways.

Sometimes it seems there are more frauds outside boxing than in it. At least, the professionals are realists who recognize the game for the rough business it is, and accept the stern code which demands that a beaten man go on fighting as long as he is able to stay on his feet.

This doesn't mean that all card-carrying members of the fight mob are cut to the Hollywood-and-pulp-fiction pattern—scheming, selfish, dishonest mercenaries devoid of all decent feeling. A gentleman like Ray Arcel, the great trainer, can spend a lifetime in the dodge without dishonor, but he must subscribe to the code.

One night Ray was in the corner of a boy pacifist whose innate repugnance of violence was aggravated by the shots his adversary kept bouncing off his chin. Between rounds the boy expressed a devout wish to be elsewhere.

"Hang in there," Ray said. "He's as tired as you are."

Reluctantly the young man returned to the conflict. With a most unneighborly scowl his opponent advanced and the boy backed off warily, into his own corner.

"Ray," he said from behind a half-clenched glove, "throw in the towel, will ya?"

"Just keep punching," Ray said. "You're all right."

The tiger fled backward, buffeted and breathless. His knees were wobbly but he managed to stay up for a full circuit of the ring.

"Please, Ray," he gasped, passing his corner, "throw in the towel now."

"Box him," Ray called after him. "Stick him and move."

The pursuit race continued for another dizzying lap.

"Ray," the hero begged, "please throw in the towel. I won't be around again."

It should not be inferred that Arcel is impervious to punishment or in any degree lacking in compassion. Among the hundreds of fighters he has handled, a special favorite was the gallant Jackie Kid Berg, whom he called by a pet name, Yitzel.

Crouching in Berg's corner one night, Ray winced and shuddered in vicarious pain as a ferocious body-puncher poured lefts and rights into Jackie's middle. Sometimes the whistling gloves seemed to disappear altogether, bringing a gasp from Berg and a groan from his handler. Still up and fighting back when the round ended, Jackie did an about-face at the bell and marched back to his corner.

"Yitzel!" Ray said shakily. "How do you feel?"

"Fine, thank you," the Kid said. "And you?"

"I'm the Greatest"

Cassius Clay Wins Bragging Rights from Sonny Liston

MIAMI, FLA., *February 25, 1964*
Cassius Marcellus Clay fought his way out of the horde that swarmed and leaped and shouted in the ring, climbed like a squirrel onto the red velvet ropes and brandished his still-gloved hand aloft.

"Eat your words," he howled to the working press rows. "Eat your words."

Nobody ever had a better right. In a mouth still dry from the excitement of the most astounding upset in many roaring years, the words don't taste good, but they taste better than they read. The words, written here and practically everywhere else until the impossible became unbelievable truth, said Sonny Liston would squash Cassius Clay like a bug when the boy braggart challenged for the heavyweight championship of the world.

The boy braggart is the new champion, and not only because Liston quit in his corner after the sixth round. This incredible kid of twenty-two, only nineteen fights away from the amateurs and altogether untested on boxing's topmost level, was winning going away when Liston gave up with what appeared to be a dislocated shoulder.

He might have been nailed if the bout had continued, but on the evidence of eighteen frenzied minutes, Cassius was entitled to crow, as he did at the top of his voice before Liston retired: "I'm the greatest. I'm gonna upset the world."

"That's right," his camp followers howled. "That's what you're doin'." And he was.

On this score, Clay won four of the six rounds, and in one of the two he lost he was blinded. Apart from the unforeseen ending, that was perhaps the most extraordinary part of the whole wild evening. It started between the fourth and fifth rounds. "Floating like a butterfly and stinging like a bee" as he and his stooges had predicted, Cassius had made Liston look like a bull moose plodding through a swamp.

Dancing, running, jabbing, ducking, stopping now and then to pepper the champion's head with potshots in swift combinations, he had won the first, third, and fourth rounds and opened an angry cut under Liston's left eye.

Handlers were swabbing his face in the corner when suddenly he broke into an excited jabber, pushed the sponge away, and pawed at his eyes. As the bell rang he sprang up waving a glove aloft as though forgetting that a man can't call a time-out in a prize fight. In the corner, frantic seconds sniffed the sponge suspiciously.

Cassius couldn't fight at all in the fifth, but he could and did show a quality he had never before been asked for. He showed he could take the sternest hooks and heaviest rights Liston could throw—or at least this Liston, whose corner said later that the shoulder had slipped in the first round.

Just pawing feebly at the oncoming champion, Clay rocked under smacking hooks, ducked, rolled, grabbed, and caught one brutal right in the throat. He rode it out, though, and at the end of the round he had ceased to blink.

"You eyes okay, champ," they were screaming from his corner as the round drew to a close. "Everything okay."

He didn't confirm that until the bell rang for the sixth. Then, getting up from his stool, he looked across the ring, nodded with assurance, and went out to enjoy one of his best rounds, pumping both hands to the head, circling, dancing.

"Get mad, baby," his corner pleaded. "He's retreatin', champ."

It was at the end of this heat that he came back crowing about upsetting the world. Yet he couldn't have known how quickly his words would be confirmed.

Just before the bell for the seventh, Cassius sprang up and waved both hands overhead in a showoff salute to the crowd. He took a step or so forward, as the gong clanged, then leaped high in a war dance of unconfined glee. He had seen what scarcely anybody else in Convention Hall had noticed.

Liston wasn't getting up. Willie Reddish, Sonny's trainer, had his hands spread palms up in a gesture of helplessness. Jack Nilon, the manager, swung his arm in a horizontal sweep, palm down. The fight was over, the championship gone.

Dr. Robert C. Bennett of Detroit, who has treated Liston in the past, hastened into the ring and taped Liston's shoulder. The former champion told him he had felt the shoulder go midway in the first round and the left hand had grown progressively number from then on.

They'll fight again to answer the prodding question of what might have been, and it will be a big one. Although return-bout clauses are frowned upon these days, Bob and Jimmy Nilon, Jack's brothers, have an independent contract with Clay entitling them to name the time, place, and opponent for his first defense.

As Bob Nilon explained this, Clay rode the ropes. "Eat your words," he bawled.

Greaseniks

The Grand Prix of Endurance Racing

Sebring, Fla., *March 27, 1960*

I N T H E dew-drenched grayness of 6 A.M. the doodlebugs screeched down Highway 27, howling like the damned. Roaring and coughing, they made their way through this normally tranquil village and out across the flatlands to the abandoned bomber base that is now a shrine of the sports-car faith, a booming religion whose ritual includes human sacrifice.

For ten years now, each March has brought from thirty thousand to fifty thousand greaseniks of the sports-car persuasion here for the twelve-hour orgy of noise and grime called the Sebring International Grand Prix of Endurance. They come in their MG's and Porsches and Anglias and Triumphs and in tribal attire—checkered caps or berets with bright pompoms, full beards, stained windbreakers bearing the emblem of their sect or club. Their consorts wear Bermuda straw hats lashed on with scarves under the chin, striped sweaters, skin-tight slacks.

By 7:30 A.M. they were driving six abreast through the main gate. Infidels caught in the procession in conventional sedans looked and felt as square as dice.

To the right of the entrance was a squalid straggle of tents and trailers on a barren within chummy earshot of the bawling motors. For ten gritty days this canvas slum had been growing; there wasn't, it was said, a vacant motel room within sixty miles.

The morning sun took on a hot, metallic brilliance, but a light breeze persisted, strong enough to pick up and distribute equitably grimy dust and an oil-blackened chaff of dried grasses. This stuff sifted everywhere, working itself down to the roots of the hair, under finger-nails, inside collars and ears.

Over the ear-shattering roar of warming motors, Alec Ulmann, the promoter, presented the Reverend Gordon Strickland, of Sebring's First Methodist Church. Three or four pits away from the microphone—the pits are diagonal parking spaces along the rail—a bearded Swede named Joakim Bonnier raced the motor of his Porsche, so the invocation sounded like this:

"As we—*rraaughww*—at these machines which are a work of art—*yooowaowowowow*—all of us may run life's race—*rowoowauawff*—be acceptable in Thy sight—*howlloowlah!*"

Similarly accompanied by Bonnier, a high-school band played the National Anthem. Soon a horn sounded the five-minute warning, and drivers lined up across the track from their cars. On a count-down at ten o'clock they would rush across the track, slide behind the wheel, hit the starter button, and go burping away in smelly clouds of glory.

Several started running a count or two ahead of the starting signal, beating the gun to save one second in twelve hours. They pulled out of the pits in a wild tangle and swayed thunderously down the two-lane strip of concrete, sixty-odd spitting monsters funneling under a pedes-trian overpass to disappear around a bend to the left. It would take the fastest about three and a half minutes to negotiate 5.2 miles of twisting concrete and blacktop and return to the starting line.

From now on there would be no rest, no quiet, no relief until 10 P.M. It was all heat and grime and clutter and clatter and the incessant *brrruppp, brrruppp, brrruppp* as the iron beasts blasted past. On the straightaways they hammered along at speeds up to 180 miles an hour. On the sharp turns they braked down as low as 15 mph. On bends like the snaky strip of blacktop called "the esses," the cars swayed through the curves with all four wheels skidding as the drivers steered by the gas pedal.

After two laps, a stocky, mustached little man pulled into the pit and waved to his partner to take over. This was Vic Lukens, of the steel family, driving his first big race with an untested machine called the Bandini, a hand-tooled job that the veteran Red Vogt had literally strung together in the last ten days with parts flown in from New York, Miami, and Italy. Lukens' accelerator had stuck immediately after the start, he had plowed across a field at the very first bend and got so rattled he took himself out to simmer down.

He had just finished telling of his ordeal when word came that Jim Hughes, of Napa, California, twenty-nine-year-old father of three, had missed the hairpin turn, struck and killed George Thompson, twenty-three-year-old photographer for the *Tampa Tribune*, and died a few minutes later.

Guys said "Gee, what a shame," but fatalities had to be expected in a field full of inexperienced drivers. Sebring has been proud of its record of only two deaths in nine years. Now it's four in ten, including a young working guy just doing his assignment. They kill spectators at Le Mans, they kill little girls at Watkins Glen. A remark made by Ernest Hemingway rang in memory, one made two winters ago after a car plowed murderously through the crowd in Havana.

"A bullfighter," Hemingway said, "can take as much risk or as little as he chooses. These slobs always take somebody with them."

The Patrioteers

Nobody's a Winner in Fight over Draft Status

NEW YORK, N.Y., *February 23, 1966*

G OVERNOR OTTO KERNER of Illinois finds Cassius Clay's shrill complaints about his new draft status "unpatriotic and disgusting." So do millions of other Americans. Equally objectionable to many are posturing patrioteers in political office who miss no chance to take bows wrapped in righteousness and the American flag.

As published, Clay's remarks on being reclassified 1-A have been stupidly odious. He says there are a lot of Muslims in the world and "maybe they'll be angry about this." He says Selective Service is picking on him because of his religion. He says he has "no personal quarrel with those Viet Congs" and wants no part of a war with them.

None of which justifies Kerner's request to his Illinois boxing commissioners that they reconsider their approval of Clay's match with Ernie Terrell in Chicago, March 29. Clay's loud and tasteless quarrel with his Louisville draft board has nothing whatever to do with his defense of the heavyweight championship.

Squealing over the possibility that the military may call him up, Cassius makes himself as sorry a spectacle as those unwashed punks who picket and demonstrate against the war. Yet in this country they are free to speak their alleged minds, and so is he. If he burned his draft, library, Diners Club, and American Express cards together, this would not excuse a politician for singling him out in denying him the right to work at his trade as long as the Army leaves him free to work.

When Rocky Graziano won the middleweight championship, patrioteers around the country discovered he had been AWOL during

World War II and publicly persecuted him for it. Joe Triner, chairman of the Illinois commission, held the same office then. His was among the groups that ostracized Graziano for a bad war record—which he had paid for with a hitch in Leavenworth.

To their credit, Triner and his present colleagues, Lou Radzienda and Joe Robichaux, have not yet acquiesced to their boss's demand for reprisals against Clay. They did call a special meeting, heard apologies from Clay by telephone, and agreed to have him up in person for a hearing on Friday before making a decision.

Cassius, who can be an extremely attractive young man when he chooses, will be winning and contrite. He has already conceded that he did pop-off out of turn. He says he is not "going to let newspapermen maneuver and trick" him into any more foolish statements on "politics or Viet Nam."

It is not difficult to believe that something along this line actually happened. Probably nobody was deliberately trying to trick him, but he talks so incessantly and thinks so little that an occasional leading question is almost sure to elicit provocative replies.

Clay needs no help from headlines to look bad. He will find that out if he takes an appeal on his reclassification. If he thinks he has encountered adverse criticism in the past, let him go to the draft board as heavyweight champion of the world, twenty-four years old, unmarried, rich, and superbly healthy, and beg to be let out of his duties while other kids are dying.

As far as the Terrell fight is concerned, he doesn't have to appeal now, for the Louisville draft board has filled its March quota without his name coming up. One reason for the planned appeal, no longer material, was to stall the Army off until after March 29.

Now that there is no immediate need for legal delays, perhaps his lawyers will advise him against appealing. They can't believe he would win. On the other hand, it is evident that Cassius does what the Muslim leadership tells him to do, and there is a discernible difference between tithes from a GI and tithes from the heavyweight champion of the world.

Of course, Joe Triner's commission may still tug the forelock and withdraw its sanction of the fight. Reserving decision, the boys did not promise they would tell Kerner to go tend his pork barrels in Springfield, though they should.

Meanwhile, Irving Schoenwald and Ben Bentley, the Chicago promoters, and the Muslims' closed-circuit firm, Main Bout, Inc., are sweating it out. This match is running true to the off-again-on-again pattern of all Clay's fights on the championship level.

His first bout with Sonny Liston laid a large egg at the box office and Bill Macdonald, who had bought the live promotion for $625,000, went to court to avoid paying off.

The Liston rematch came down with a hernia the first time it was made. When it was rescheduled for Boston, the district attorney chased it clear up to the Maine woods, where a phantom punch put Liston down for a count which he heard and the referee didn't.

Finally Clay went to Las Vegas to box Floyd Patterson, and a sort of hernia developed there, too—a herniated spinal disc that made Patterson a cripple going into the ring. Cassius is young and inexperienced. He must think this sort of thing is normal in heavyweight championships.

A Yank at Ascot

The King George VI and Queen Elizabeth Stakes

ASCOT, ENGLAND, *July 16, 1960*

INSIDE THE brick wall surrounding Ascot Heath stands a sentry box with a sign promising that a ring official will visit this point after each race to assist with regard to any dispute which may arise between bookmakers and backers. The first race was just over but there was no official on the spot, nor any bookmakers, backers, or signs of dispute. Half the Royal Family was on the premises, and horseplayers were being so polite their teeth hurt.

In the royal box at the front of the members' stand were Queen Elizabeth in pink and the Queen Mother. Meandering about on the clipped green turf near the walking ring were Princess Margaret in blue and her squire, Antony Armstrong-Jones, sans camera. There was no sign of the Queen's consort, Prince Philip, who leaves the family gambling to his womenfolk.

A slightly bewildered Yank plodded among innumerable brick structures asking gate guards in iron hats hard questions like how to get to the press room. "Afraid I don't quite know, sir," was the standard reply. "Suppose you try that chap over there."

Memory recaptured a day at Belmont when Alfred Vanderbilt was encountered frowning over the page in the program giving location of change and information windows. There was a list of windows providing both change and information, then at the bottom: "For change only, window 22, ground floor, clubhouse." "What do you make of this guy in Twenty-two?" Alfred asked. "Do you suppose he is just an ignorant slob?"

Ultimately the Yank found himself at the rail in front of the members' stand, where he didn't belong. To his right were the shouting bookmakers in front of crowded stands extending down to the "silver ring," where the costers get in for $1.40 instead of $5.60, the grandstand price. To the left and behind were the paddock and level green walking ring with mutuel windows taking bets of fifty-six cents.

The main event, third in a program of six races, was the King George VI and Queen Elizabeth Stakes, for entire horses and mares of three and older at a mile and a half, worth $65,366 to the winner. This is one of England's great races, which frequently produces a candidate for the Washington, D.C. International at Laurel. Everybody knew it would go to Petite Etoile, the young Aga Khan's four-year-old, who has been regarded as the finest of her sex in this land since Pretty Polly, winner of the Oaks in 1904.

"It must be Petite Etoile," read the headline in one morning newspaper. "Petite Etoile can set seal on great career," declared the conservative *Daily Telegraph*. "Big Ascot prize should go to Petite Etoile," announced the *Times*. Forty of forty-two handicappers published in the *Sporting Chronicle* picked Petite Etoile. She had won nine races in a row, including the 1,000 Guineas, the Oaks, the Champion Stakes, and the Coronation Cup, and today's prize would give her a bankroll of $230,642, a record for the English turf.

Petite Etoile is a handsome Amazon with the iron-gray coat of Native Dancer, a silver face, and silvery tail. Sir Harold Wernher's Aggressor was in a nervous lather. He is a big bay five-year-old that trounced Parthia, last year's Epsom Derby winner, in the Hardwicke Stakes here last month, but he carried only 130 pounds then against Parthia's 136. Today both would have 133 like the other males of four or older. Petite Etoile had a three-pound sex allowance, and the three-year-olds Flores III, His Story, and Kythnos had 119.

The field started in front of a background of trees and ran clockwise, the wrong way for American tracks. De Voos, a speed horse from France, rushed away in front as expected, with Flores III second and Parthia next. Petite Etoile and Kythnos brought up the rear.

They flashed into view on the backstretch, disappeared, and the public-address caller said De Voos led for a mile, then was caught by Flores III. Parthia was still third, Petite Etoile and Kythnos still seventh and eighth.

Coming down the green homestretch, Jimmy Lindley moved Aggressor to the front, but with two hundred yards to go Lester Piggott had Petite Etoile coming hard at him on the outside. The filly didn't get there. "That's the boy, Jimmy," a man at the rail said, and his voice sounded loud in the hushed English crowd as Aggressor flashed in with Petite Etoile second and Kythnos third.

Lindley rode back to unsaddle, slapping his mount affectionately on the stern, grinning back at the polite applause. Piggott was solemnly expressionless on the beaten favorite.

Some horseplayers started home, down a roofed walk to the railway station. Somebody had been ahead of them with a piece of chalk. Scrawled on the wall of the tunnel was a name: ELVIS PRESLEY.

Dead Sea Downs

A Racetrack Where It All Began

JERICHO, OCCUPIED JORDAN, *November 11, 1967*
THE LOWEST gambling hell in the world lies hard by the shore of the Dead Sea, 1,291 feet below sea level. Nowhere on the face of the earth can you get lower, not at Charles Town or Suffolk Downs, not even at Aqueduct on a Tuesday in November.

The gambling hell has no official name. Call it Dead Sea Downs or Qumran Park. It is a little Shoeless Joe of a racetrack on the desert, at present a casualty of last June's Six-Day War but in its time a center of cheerful debauchery in a region where sin isn't exactly an innovation. (After all, when Joshua brought the walls of Jericho tumbling down, the only house in town left standing was that of Rahab, the harlot.)

Dead Sea Downs sits beside the highway leading south from Jericho. A faded wooden sign over the gate shows a running horse with a jockey in silks, and squiggly Arabic lettering identifies it as the "course for horses Arabian."

The track is a one-mile oval of sand crusted with little white drifts of salt, overgrown now with clumps of thorny burnet called netish, meaning "scratcher." Except for a panel or two of fence at the finish line, the inside rail consists of rusty oil drums set on end, and a low ridge of sand substitutes for an outside rail.

What's left of the grandstand looks out across the saltiest puddle in creation, steely under the fierce sun, to the Moab Mountains on the east shore. Behind the stand a rude fence encloses the paddock walking ring, and behind that rise stark cliffs pitted with caves where the Dead Sea Scrolls lay hidden for two thousand years.

Today the grandstand is just a grand place to stand, a roofed platform like the New Haven station platform at Rye or Greenwich. Before the war it had chairs for the beauty and chivalry of Jordan, who gathered each winter Sunday to play the ponies and the camel race that concluded each program. Everybody says the Bedouin jockeys pulled their camels.

In the spring, racing moved across the Jordan River to Amman, the capital, so Dead Sea Downs was idle when the war came. Now that Israel occupies this West Bank territory, neither the horses nor the horseplayers are welcome back.

At its peak, Dead Sea Downs must have been something, but not much, like Saratoga when the games were running at Canfield's or Riley's or Piping Rock. A player who tapped out at the track could repair to the Dead Sea Hotel on the lake shore where Sharif Ben Nasser provided an opportunity to recoup at baccarat or roulette.

Ben Nasser, uncle of King Hussein and formerly Jordan's prime minister, is an Arabic version of James Cox Brady, president of the New York Racing Association, and Ogden Phipps, chairman of the Jockey Club. His huge racing string is the Middle Eastern equivalent of the Phipps family's Wheatley Stable, and last month, when the Shah of Iran threw a coronation for himself, Sharif sent his gaudiest steeds to dress up the show.

Ben Nasser is a tycoon of many parts, though some of his most profitable enterprises might not appeal to the Messrs. Cox and Phipps. His Dead Sea Hotel was an embarrassment to the king because things went on there which might be all right in other seashore resorts like Sodom or Atlantic City but, in the opinion of local Bedouins, tended to give this neighborhood a bad name.

Twenty-one centuries ago this land was occupied by the Essene sect, an extraordinarily strict religious body, some of whose puritanism seems to have survived. At any rate, Uncle Ben's casino finally was shut down, ostensibly because of illegal gambling, which was the least of its pleasures.

In a way it's too bad that there is no racing here now, for this is where it all started. There is a legend that when Mohammed was wheeling and dealing, he turned loose a herd of horses on the desert within sight of water. As they raced to drink, a trumpeter sounded recall. Most of the steeds ran on but those that wheeled back in obedience became the foundation for Mohammed's breeding operation.

That's how the expression "improvement of the breed" began, but of course horses had been used for cavalry earlier. In the Maccabean war about 170 B.C., Lydias led a force of one hundred thousand foot-soldiers, twenty thousand horses, and thirty-two elephants to subdue the Jews. The campaign was bad for Eleazar, brother of Lydias. He got hit on the head with a falling elephant and snuffed it.

As history goes in these parts, all this is modern. Archaeologists have established there were people here in the Mesolithic era, at least ten thousand years ago, and everybody knows that where you have people you have horseplayers, except maybe in Appleton, Wisconsin. Not even Max Hirsch goes back that far.

A Not-So-Typical
Day at the Races

A Horse, a Jockey, Hurdles, Death

W<small>HEN THE</small> field broke in the fifth race, a dark gelding named
SARATOGA SPRINGS, N.Y., *August 17, 1962*

Exhibit A dashed off in front as though he could read the tote board, where he was a smashing favorite at 1 to 3. Just off the pace was Otsego, a three-year-old owned by Mrs. Stephen C. Clark, Jr., of Cooperstown, which had raced five times and broken his maiden the last time out. He was 15 to 1 on the board.

This was a race called the Promise, a mile-and-five-eighths over hurdles, with $12,500 added. The rider on Otsego was Jimmy Murphy, a small man in his upper thirties who has been riding jumpers trained by Sidney Watters, Jr., about as long as anybody can remember.

Jimmy Murphy hasn't been the luckiest man on the racetrack. They say he has brittle bones, which isn't ideal equipment for a rider of jump races. He's had his collarbone broken something like seventeen times. In the first week at Saratoga last August he went down with a smash that meant a longish stretch in hospital with a broken leg.

He keeps getting up and riding, though. If they grow 'em brittle in Ligonier, Pa., they don't short-change 'em on courage. He has kept busy this year, and stands second to Pat Smithwick in the national rankings, with twelve winners, twelve seconds, and eight thirds in fifty-five races.

Up front on Exhibit A, Willard Thompson had two fistfuls of running horse. The favorite drew off easily with his rider sitting still—two lengths, three, five. Murphy had Otsego third behind Kantikoy, then second, then third again.

From the stands, 13,363 watched with pleasure. It was one of the finest days of the meeting, bright and mild, and the green turf was firm. Horse fans like hurdle races, where the jumps aren't frightening like the steeplechase fences but just high enough to add a fillip of excitement to the pretty spectacle.

Eight of the nine jumps went off smoothly. Coming around the last turn, Thompson let his mount out a notch and Exhibit A went to the last barrier leading his field by six big lengths. He was over and reaching out for the last stretch of flat when Murphy sent his tiring mount into the fence.

When a horse is tired, young riders are told, don't let him loaf into a jump unless you enjoy being hurt. Send him at it as hard as he'll go. Murphy did. For an instant horse and rider seemed to hang in midair. Then both came down head first.

The horse came down on his head, somersaulted, gave two or three convulsive kicks, and lay still. Murphy, thrown just ahead, was a limp little figure in white as the field jumped clear. From the grandstand area a girl started running, his wife.

Ambulance, outriders, Dr. John A. Esposito, Pinkertons, and assistant starters were moving before the favorite reached the wire, twelve lengths ahead of the 35-to-1 Scuderia, who came on from far back under a drive by Tommy Burns, a fugitive from the flats.

Murphy was lifted on a stretcher and the ambulance cut across the infield bound directly for the hospital. The doctor rode with him. Steve Clark, who had joined the group, bent over his horse. Otsego was dead, his neck was broken. A wooden screen was set up, and behind it the horse was dragged into a van.

"The result of the fifth is official," Fred Capossela said over the public-address system. "The winner, Exhibit A——" The tote flashed the shortest price of the meeting, $2.70, but there were cries for the return on Scuderia, $14.30 for place.

A horse was dead, a rider unconscious. The horseplayers scanned their form sheets on the sixth race. In the press box, a phone wire was opened to the hospital.

Murphy, the first report said, had regained consciousness and his only visible injury was a laceration on the forehead. A little later, lacerations of face, arms, and hands were reported. Finally came word of a mild concussion. The patient would remain overnight for observation. For jumping horse riders, that's the name of the game.

"We are happy to report," Capossela told the crowd, "that jockey James Murphy is not seriously injured." There was quite a polite little patter of applause.

The Daddy of 'Em All

Pros Pay Their Own Way at Frontier Days Rodeo

CHEYENNE, WYO., *August 1, 1967*

CLYDE VAMVORAS was sitting first in bareback riding when he came out of the gate aboard an unguided missile named Pee Wee. Spurring high, he stuck to the leaping, whirling beast the required eight seconds, and when he tried to bail out after the gun, his right hand hung up in the rigging.

For what seemed an interminable time he was a rag doll flopping helplessly in midair as the horse, terrified by the lifeless thing tied to his withers, went frantic. At last the hand came free and the cowboy limped back to the chutes, the mauled paw cradled under his arm.

The judges held up their slates and Chuck Parkinson announced the score—a good mark of 70, giving Vamvoras a total of 203 for the three head he rode in Cheyenne's Frontier Days Rodeo, "the daddy of 'em all," according to some Chamber of Commerce poet.

It wasn't good enough. Jim Mihalek, of Broomfield, Colorado, had gone into the third go-round with a marking of 125 for his first two head against Clyde's 133. Mastering a wild sorrel named Red Rebel, he scored 79 for a total of 204, giving him $1,018 for his six rowdy, dusty days in the showcase of the world's most violent sport. It made a juicy July for this twenty-eight-year-old, for earlier this month he walked off with $3,281 from the Calgary Stampede. His Cheyenne loot brought his 1967 earnings to $12,551.

Vamvoras, holding a wide lead in the scramble for the 1967 world bareback championship, had reached the last go-round with $15,889 in his poke and a lovely lavender paint job decorating his left eye. Beating by one point for top money, he came out with a limber wing and $1,400 for his pains, having picked up more than Nihalek in day money.

Clyde's fortunes were typical of the short, happy life of a rodeo cowboy. So was the experience of Marty Wood, three-time world champion saddle bronc rider who collected a record $179,250 in the ten years through 1966. Now the defending champion, Marty came to Cheyenne sitting second on the year with $12,310 and after two go-rounds had 127 points, only one point behind the leader, Bill Smith.

He was delighted to draw a critter named Joker for the finals. He knew that this new one in Harry Knight's string was really rank, though he had never seen the horse. (No matter how well a cowboy rides, he can't score well unless his mount bucks.)

In the finals a kid named Mel Hyland flung a fierce challenge into Marty's teeth. With a superlative ride on a celebrated outlaw named Reckless Red, this eighteen-year-old got the highest marking of the whole show, a rare 86 (out of a theoretical but impossible 100). This gave him 206, meaning that Wood had to score 80 to top him.

Joker was a firecracker. He bucks, cuts back on his rider, spins, and reverses direction. Marty handled him beautifully, but the horse, still boiling with malice at the gun, flung himself headlong to the earth with the rider underneath. Marty was pressed like a flower.

Three or four cowboys peeled him off the ground. He got up clutching his right thigh—and heard the announcer invite him to do it again. Because Joker had fouled him against the gate leaving the box, the judges ruled he hadn't received a fair chance to score high and was entitled to a reride.

Less than ten minutes later he was up again on a steed named Gambler. Neither a Reckless Red nor a Joker, Gambler got him only 66 points for fifth place.

"A lovely afternoon, Marty," a guy said. "How is it?"

"It's gonna be all right," Marty said, his face twisted.

No doubt it will, but each man must be his own judge as to what constitutes all right. Athletes in team sports work for a salary. In boxing even a loser is guaranteed a payday. In only two games do the pros pay their own way, get up entry fees, and depend for a living on what they can win—rodeo and professional golf.

The difference is that Arnold Palmer has never in his life been hooked by a bull, kicked by a steer, or pitched against the fence by a horse. Rodeo is a living, but so is opening oysters.

Biting the Hand
of the Masters

Straight-Hitting, Straight-Talking Lee Trevino

BECAUSE HE said out loud that he'd never again play in the Masters golf tournament, some of the pros are staring at Lee Trevino, the United States Open champion, as though the sleeves of his underwear were showing beneath his cuffs. And small wonder.

AUGUSTA, GA., *April 21, 1968*

This is clearly a case for the House Un-American Activities Committee. A man can burn his Diners Club card in public and fly the Viet Cong flag from the antenna of his Bentley, and in this permissive society nobody will lift an eyebrow. He can put the knock on motherhood and apple pie, and they still won't refuse to serve him in Nedick's.

But to say a word against the Masters, against the Augusta National Golf Club, against Bobby Jones, who runs it—why, the fellow's got to be some kind of Commie or something.

If Trevino really means to stay away from Augusta in the future, then good riddance. The folks down there would as lief welcome Charlie Sifford to the clubhouse as give locker space to a Bolshevik who isn't reduced to jelly by the beauty of the azaleas flanking the sixteenth hole.

Most God-fearing pros would concur with Bob Charles, the left-hander from New Zealand, who says in a scandalized stage whisper: "I never heard of anyone disliking the Masters. It's the most wonderful tournament in the world."

Actually, Trevino never said that it wasn't, and he didn't say the

National wasn't a good golf course. All he said was that he couldn't play it because it demanded lofted shots which he didn't have in his bag.

In short, he was knocking his own game, not the course. His real sin was making his remarks within earshot of an Associated Press reporter who put them in the paper. If he had used the language other players have employed about the course, the words wouldn't have got through the mail.

For thirty-five years now it has been possible to sit in the grill room and hear the National described as a "dishonest" course because it overemphasizes putting or because of the sneaky way it has been lengthened over the years or because of the new fairway traps rung in a couple of years ago. It doesn't always turn out that the speaker has that day put two balls in the water at No. 12, but sometimes it does.

Trevino was strictly in character when he stated his position. The reason he is the most refreshing character to burst on the sports scene in years is that he is an original who has not, thus far, yielded to pressure to conform.

There is no sham or pretense about him. When he showed up two years ago as a straight-hitting, uninhibited stranger, he made no effort to conceal his background as an eighth-grade dropout who had given up a career as a bootblack to become a $30-a-week assistant pro at a freewheeling club outside El Paso.

He talked freely and happily of the days when he hustled customers at a par-three course into betting him that he couldn't break 60 hitting every shot with a family-sized Dr. Pepper bottle.

He told how his young wife Claudia ran the family, handling their meager funds and doling out allowances for his entry fees and walking-around money. He was gay and natural and articulate, and what he said he meant.

Happily he has not changed. Winning the Open fattened his purse but not his head. He has enjoyed his success without being especially impressed by it or by his own grandeur.

"But Lee," Gary Player said when Trevino declared he was through with hilly Augusta, "don't you think that if you're a champion, you'll have to play every kind of course? Over the last few years I've got the second best record there behind Arnie Palmer, and I don't hit the ball that high."

"Yeah," said the honest Texan, "but you've got to remember one thing, Gary. You're a lot better player than I am."

The Black Berets

Raised Fists on the Victory Stand

MEXICO CITY, MEXICO, *October 19, 1968*
THE FOUR-HUNDRED-METER race was over and in the catacombs of Estádio Olímpico Doug Roby, president of the United States Olympic Committee, was telling newspapermen that he had warned America's runners against making any demonstration if they should get to the victory stand. A fanfare of trumpets interrupted him.

In stiff single file, the three black Americans marched across the track. All of them—Lee Evans, the winner; Larry James, second, and Ron Freeman, third—had broken the recognized world record. Rain had fallen after the finish and, although it was abating now, the runners wore the official sweatsuits of the United States team, plus unofficial black berets which may or may not have been symbolic.

Each stopped to enable John J. Garland, an American member of the International Olympic Committee, to hang the medal about his neck. Then each straightened and waved a clenched fist aloft. It wasn't quite the same gesture meaning "We shall overcome" that Tommie Smith and John Carlos had employed on the same stand after the two-hundred-meter final.

Lord David Burghley, the Marquess of Exeter who is president of the International Amateur Athletic Federation, shook hands with each, and they removed the berets, standing at attention facing the flagpole as the colors ascended and the band played the Star-Spangled Banner. Smith and Carlos had refused to look at the flag, standing with heads bowed and black-gloved fists upraised.

Evans, James, and Freeman stepped down, and out from under

every stuffed shirt in the Olympic organization whistled a mighty sigh of relief. The waxworks had been spared from compounding the boobery which had created the biggest, most avoidable flap in these quadrennial muscle dances since Eleanor Holm was flung off the 1936 swimming team for guzzling champagne aboard ship.

The four-hundred-meter race was run Friday, about forty-eight hours after Smith and Carlos put on their act and twelve hours after the United States officials lent significance to their performance by firing them from the team. The simple little demonstration by Smith and Carlos had been a protest of the sort every black man in the United States had a right to make. It was intended to call attention to the inequities the Negro suffers, and without the aid of the Olympic brass might have done this in a small way.

By throwing a fit over the incident, suspending the young men and ordering them out of Mexico, the badgers multiplied the impact of the protest a hundredfold. They added dignity to the protestants and made boobies of themselves.

"One of the basic principles of the Olympic games," read the first flatulent communiqué from on high, "is that politics play no part whatsoever in them. . . . Yesterday United States athletes in a victory ceremony deliberately violated this universally accepted principle by using the occasion to advertise their domestic political views."

Not content with this confession that they can't distinguish between human rights and politics, the playground directors put their pointed heads together and came up with this gem:

"The discourtesy displayed violated the standards of sportsmanship and good manners. . . . We feel it was an isolated incident, but any further repetition of such incidents would be a willful disregard of Olympic principles and would be met with severest penalties."

The action, Roby said, was demanded by the International Olympic Committee, including Avery Brundage, president, and by the Mexican Organizing Committee. They are, as Mark Antony observed on another occasion, all honorable men who consider children's games more sacred than human decency.

Soon after the committee acted, a bedsheet was hung from a sixth-floor window of the apartment house in Olympic Village where Carlos has been living. On it were the letters: "Down with Brundage."

There were, of course, mixed feelings on the United States team. Lee Evans was especially upset, but when asked whether he intended to run as scheduled, he would only reply, "Wait and see."

"I had no intention of running this race," he said over the air after taking the four-hundred, "but this morning Carlos asked me to run and win."

Said Carlos: "The next man that puts a camera in my face, I'll stomp him."

★ FISHING FOR BASS ★

On Kangaroo Lake

The Elusive Smallmouth of Comely Door County

K ANGAROO LAKE is a comely tract of pale green water about three
STURGEON BAY, WIS., *August 1, 1955*
miles long near the Lake Michigan shore of Wisconsin's Door County.
It takes its name not from any great concentration of marsupials in the
vicinity, but rather from its shape which, seen on a map, looks a little
like the silhouette of a kangaroo and a lot like that of a sea horse. Its
soft bottom supports a luxuriant crop of weeds which, in turn, furnish
cover for a dense population of fish.

There are perch and bluegills, northern pike and walleye, but the
aristocrat of the marine colony is the smallmouth black bass, so called
because he is not black and has a mouth suitable for storing oranges.
Apparently he has taken a protective coloring from the weeds and
water; he is a striking blond with a vague greenish cast instead of the
dark bronze back typical of his breed.

He is pale but not wan. Ordinarily the smallmouth is a cold-water
fish and there is a theory that his vile disposition is traceable to the
chill in which he lives. The water of Kangaroo Lake is as warm and
relaxing as Milady's bath, but this has not softened the temper of the
tenants. In all this wonderful smallmouth country, there are no uglier,
angrier, meaner fish than these pallid brutes, none more eminently
fitted by temperament for burning down orphan asylums.

There were four men in the car that arrived at Fischer's Happy
Landing at one end of the causeway that carries a county highway
across the kangaroo's neck. This day there was only one boat available

on the main body of the lake, but there was another across the highway in the shallow, overgrown head.

In a small boat or on a park bench, three's a crowd. Four constitutes a DeMille mob scene if they are all waving fly rods to any useful purpose, but this day there was no commotion and no especial congestion. The bass weren't feeding, not even in the dependable spot at the south end of the lake where twin weed patches darken the surface like brown birth marks.

Unable to arouse interest in their live bait, the anglers docked for lunch and one announced he would try the other side of the causeway alone. Walter Fischer had said this reedy lagoon often produced largemouth bass and northerns, especially in the morning and at evening.

"It's pretty bright today," he said dubiously, frowning at the blue sky. "Wonder if it's too clear for my pet fish."

He scooped several dead minnows from a live-box, tossed them off the end of the dock and fluttered a hand in the water to cause a commotion. Half a dozen perch heeded this mess call, swam lazily up, and gulped the hand-out.

The bait-soakers went about their business and the lone oarsman started working the brushy shore of the north end. The water was extremely shallow, the sun bright until a sudden, drenching shower blew in. Within five minutes the sun was out again, drawing steam from sodden clothing. The work went on under difficulties, bugs and poppers and flies hooking up among the thick rushes on every other cast.

There is a point of land where the kangaroo's neck meets the chin. The tall, shattered stump of a birch tree split by lightning stands there in a clump of cedars. A pair of kingfishers was doing glides and barrel-rolls, filling the air with rattling cries. In desperation, a flatfish was tied on to the leader, though this is no proper fly-rod lure. It is too heavy to cast satisfactorily and its vicious little triple-gang hooks catch up on everything.

Just off the point, a bass assaulted this wiggling, foamy minnow. He came up out of the dark roots of some rushes, clearly visible all the way.

All strut and swagger and confidence, he snatched the lure, wheeled, and started for home. A tight line brought him up short. He cursed, dived, threshed about, was mastered. He was a smallmouth.

Another cast dropped into a school of minnows, whose leisurely demeanor suggested that there couldn't be a bass within miles. There was, though. Picking the flatfish out of the crowd, he took a swipe at it; caught by surprise, the angler failed to set the hook.

Alongside a small garden of lily pads, another fish struck, was on briefly, escaped. Just a few feet away came a heavy hit. This one, hooked soundly, tore through the lily pads, ripped out of the flora and headed for a tangle of brush near the shore, was checked, turned, raced right and left. He looked long and angry and as he dashed about another fish of exactly the same length raced beside him, either running interference or cheering. "Yah, yah, you and your big mouth!" He was right, for the one that came into the net was a largemouth.

That was it for the day—five bass seen, two rendered obsolete as a junior senator. Back at the landing, a small boy saw the victims and his eyes popped. "Gee, I'd like some fish like that!"

"Would you like these?"

"Boy, would I!"

"Take 'em, then." Now he protested politely, but his heart wasn't in it. As he carried the fish up the causeway bank an auto halted and a man asked what kind of fish those were. Black bass, the young man said indulgently.

"Gosh, do you catch 'em like that here all the time?"

"Not always," the young man said truthfully.

The Mysteries
of Europe

Local Shows Stranger "Peace That Passeth Understanding"

L ARRY SERVAIS came up from Green Bay with his plywood canoe
STURGEON BAY, WIS., *July 31, 1957*
on the station wagon, making it feasible to undertake research in the
quantity, size, disposition, and appetites of the bass in Europe Lake.
Of all the famous smallmouth waters on and around the Door County
peninsula, Europe Lake gets the least fishing, partly because it is away
up near Gills Rock where this craggy sliver of limestone tapers off into
the strait called Death's Door, and partly because there are no boats
for hire on the lake.

Now and again over a dozen Julys there had been undocumented
reports of great fish taken from Europe's pale green water. Once two
bass were exhibited in a hardware store window, each weighing more
than eight pounds, and they were supposed to have come from there,
though there are always cynics around to imply that a guy who could
net, dynamite, or pitchfork fish like these wouldn't necessarily be scru-
pulous about revealing the place and method.

From the highway, a narrow country road bores through birch
forests and peters out on the shore of the lake. The canoe had been
launched and fly rods were being set up when a motorist arrived with
a boat and outboard on a trailer.

"Do you know this lake?" he was asked.

"Sure do."

"Any advice for well-intentioned strangers?"

"Yep. Take down your rods and go home."

Europe Lake, the man said, had fewer fish than any other water in the whole county—"a few scrawny perch, a very few bass, lots of big suckers." In half-hearted protest, mention was made of the occasional tales about big bass here.

"Tales," he said, dripping scorn. "They're started by a fellow who gets his fish in North Bay."

"Oh, one of those men who won't tell where he takes the big ones?"

"Not exactly. He's got property for sale on this lake."

The man had backed his trailer into the water and launched the boat and now he went puttering off toward the wooded shore opposite.

"He'll be back," Larry said. "Did you see his shoulder patch? He's a state game warden. Didn't ask to see our licenses here because he means to nail us fishing." Not many licenses are sold in Door County because they are required only for the few lakes and streams; 90 percent of the fishing is done offshore in the coves of Lake Michigan and Green Bay.

At the road's end, the lake has the sort of cobbled bottom where bass love to lurk. The canoe was drifted through sparse bullrushes. On the fifth or sixth cast, a bucktail streamer was dropped over a big rock and a bass took it hard. He felt good, but the hook didn't go in and he escaped unseen.

"No fish here, eh?" Larry said. "Here comes that big chunk of law."

"Any luck?" the warden asked, coasting alongside. One missed strike, he was told. "Well," he said, elaborately casual, "might as well check the licenses now that we're here." Finding the papers in order, he turned on the friendly interest. He pointed upwind to the far end of the lake.

"About two hundred feet off that point," he said. "Man I know tells me he's caught a lot of bass there. Want a ride up?"

A line was tossed to him and he towed the canoe. "We put test nets in here," he said, "just to see what the lake had, and results were very poor. We wanted to check the population before stocking, so we'd do it right. Here's the place. You can drift down toward that red cottage."

The drift which he pointed out was straight down the middle over the deepest water. The bottom was sand, with no cover for fish except a few weeds. Here was the peace that passeth understanding, unbroken by swirl or splash of a single feeding bass.

Something like two hours was wasted working around the shoreline to the starting point. As soon as the canoe was back over the rocky bottom, another bass hit the bucktail. He was a long dark shadow in the clear water, sullenly swift, arching the rod with steady pressure. Then all of a sudden he was gone.

The third strike came almost immediately, but this bass, firmly hooked, was small and peevish. He went back with a split lip. Then Larry took one on a night crawler and released it. Two more darted for the fly, and were missed by overeagerness when the lure was snatched out of reach. Over some sunken timbers came two more rises, but both of these fish rejected the fly, turning aside at the last instant.

It was time to go fry a steak. In a total of perhaps thirty minutes, eight bass had been encountered among the cobblestones and bullrushes. An unworthy suspicion intruded.

"You don't suppose, Lawrence, that that devious dastard deliberately hauled us away from the best fishing?"

"Preposterous," Larry said. "He's a public servant."

Matted with Bass

The Largemouth Are Feeding on Verona Lake

AVON PARK, FLA., *February 27, 1948*

T HE STORY was that Arbuckle Creek was matted with bass. They were also getting 'em in Arbuckle Lake, the big, shoal pond out of which the creek flows through jungle, but the lake merely teemed with fish; the largemouth didn't have to queue up there to take turns hitting the lure. However, in spite of this it was decided to try the lake first, largely because a lake is easier to find than a creek.

It was a lovely summer day, sunny, with fluffy cumulus puffs and scarcely enough breeze to wrinkle the surface. As the outboard pushed the boat out from the shore, a mamma duck swam past with a brood of ducklings that couldn't have been out of the shell more than an hour. There must have been a dozen ducklings in the brood but they swam in such tight wing-to-wing formation they made a bright yellow cluster no bigger than a dinner plate. They went chunking along an inch or so behind mamma's tail and she kept looking back fretfully, worried stiff by the sputtering outboard.

A pair of loons perched on two stakes rising from the water near the shore. The birds waited while the boat bore down on them, twisting their heads nervously right and left on their long, skinny necks. But they weren't loony enough to sit and be run down, like pedestrians. They got up and flew when the boat was maybe forty feet away.

The boat worked along the shoreline, pausing at this likely spot and that one. With three men aboard, two fished and the third handled the boat, shutting off the motor and using a paddle to work along the edges of weed beds. The fishermen tried assorted lures on their fly rods—

a tiger-striped popper, a big bucktail, a wooden-bodied frog with tufts of bucktail behind to simulate legs.

There should have been a vast and congested bass population alongside the patches of water hyacinth in the rushes, just off the tough, elephant-eared weeds they call "bonnets," and around the roots and knees of the big cypress trees that stand out in the water like bathers. The lures plashed and popped and jiggled on the surface. Nothing else happened.

It was decided to try the creek after all. It was a gingery job getting into the stream, for the cypress trees on the bank thrust their knees far out under the water, and you can't see these obstructions until your propeller grabs onto one and wallops itself out of shape.

The creek flowed swiftly and quietly out of the lake. The left bank was all tangled undergrowth, but a sort of path ran along the right bank for perhaps a quarter mile, and all along here were grown-up pickaninnies fishing. They were all barefoot, all costumed like cotton pickers in a Shubert musical, all using long cane poles with cork bobbers.

All of a sudden around a bend, a deep hole was alive with fish. The surface dimpled and swirled and here and there came a man-sized splash as a fish rose clear out of the water. There was a moment of panicky haste, and a lure got itself hung high in a tree. (The creek isn't wide, and you must watch your backcast while fishing from midstream.) It was necessary to bring the boat right into the fishing hole to disentangle the hook. But that didn't bother the fish. They continued to make the water bubble and gurgle on all sides. Yet they would take no lures.

Maybe they weren't bass. They could have been bream, locally pronounced "brim." Maybe they were "specks"—speckled perch, which are like the crappies of the north—or war-mouth perch or stumpknockers or shellcrackers. Anyhow, they paid no attention to a meal that should have made any bass's mouth water.

A man came along the bank and explained that he'd set his pole down and a fish had pulled it across the stream and he couldn't recover it. The long cane pole was found snagged in some brush on the far bank. Lifted, it brought up a slate-blue channel cat, long and snaky and ugly, which had swallowed the hook.

The boat drifted swiftly downstream. Now it was in dense jungle. Spring was in the woods, green as green. The new leaves were out on the gum trees, pale and bright and shaped exactly like maple leaves. The creepers and climbing vines were a lush, rich green. White elder was blossoming thickly. There were trees garnished with orchids.

Every few seconds came the resounding splash of a feeding bass. At long last, one took a floating frog and was boated after an infinitesimal struggle. He was maybe two inches under the legal minimum of one foot. Back home he went with a sore mouth.

He was the only catch. Another bass struck twice and the hook missed him twice. By that time the current had carried the boat out of range. Bass still rose occasionally along the weedy, overgrown banks. But they paid no attention to the bugs cast their way.

The boat was turned around and headed back upstream. A snake went twisting across the creek, a water moccasin, which is poisonous if you challenge him but will run if he can. The boat ran him down and, just as its prow came on him, he whirled and struck at it. He went down under the boat and wasn't seen again.

That was all. The trip back to Avon Park was finished before evening. The sun went down during dinner. The house is on a hillside overlooking Verona Lake, which was a mirror red with evening. "Too bad about today," the man said. "You should have been around a few days ago. Did I tell you about the bass we caught down in the canal?"

He had. Out on Verona Lake, big rings kept spreading across the surface. The bass were feeding.

Island Derby

Casting for Prizes at Menemsha Bight

MARTHA'S VINEYARD, MASS., *October 13, 1950*
The rain, which had been falling in sudden sullen bursts all day,
backed off just before the arrival of Mr. Al Brickman, proprietor of
Vineyard Haven's popular stores Abercrombie & Brickman and
Bergdorf-Brickman. Mr. Brickman had contracted to show an igno-
ramus a thing or two about fishing in the annual Martha's Vineyard
striped-bass derby, a month-long competition in which anglers who
snatch the largest comestibles out of the ocean are rewarded with
automobiles, cruisers, fishing tackle, and the like.

Mr. Brickman was accompanied by Stan Bryden, an island man,
and General Charles W. Ryder, who switched his address this year
from one island, Japan, to another island, Martha's Vineyard. On the
drive down to Menemsha Bight, all three explained that experience of
surf-casting was not essential to a derby candidate.

"That boy Drake," said Stan Bryden, "whose forty-pounder is leading the field right now, never caught a bass before he hooked this one.
And George Marshall, who won the derby two years straight, had
never caught a striper before he got his first winner, and I don't think
he caught another one until he got his second winner. He won two
cruisers."

"One day," said Al Brickman, "there was an off-island kid over here
on his honeymoon, borrowed some tackle and made one cast and got
a backlash. While he was untangling the backlash, a bass took his plug.
He couldn't reel in, so he just backed up inland and dragged the bass

onto the beach. He lost the plug, and that night he came down to my store, bought another plug, went back, and caught another striper."

At Menemsha Bight the bass-slayers got into hip boots and rubberized overalls and waterproofed parkas and lugged their tackle down to the beach. The tide was rampaging out through a narrow cut and there were perhaps half a dozen fishermen casting into the current from the rocky jetty, with a dozen or so more strung out along the beach flinging their feathered jigs into the surf. The jigs, or plugs, or tin squids are cigar-sized gobbets of lead with feather tails, which, it is optimistically hoped, will look edible to large stupid fish.

Either there weren't any large fish or they weren't stupid enough. The anglers kept heaving their jigs out to sea and reeling them in and nothing else kept happening. Nobody worked too hard. A guy would make a few fruitless casts, then thrust the butt of his rod into the sand and go light up a cigarette and tell some lies.

"When I was a kid," Al Brickman was saying, "a buddy and I used to camp down here in two pup tents and go fishing, and the things we'd catch you wouldn't believe. Ever see a goosefish? They have two feet on 'em, webbed just like geese."

"See old Levi Jackson fishing down the beach there?" said Ted Henley, an island man. "Every time I see him I think of one time I saw him with a monkfish, which are as fat as this with a mouth that big. He'd stuffed this monkfish full of rocks and old scrap iron and all sort of heavy stuff and then I saw him sewing up the fish's big mouth. I watched, wondering what in the world he could be doing.

"Well, he finally got the fish sewed up and then he picked it up like this and threw it overboard. I heard him say: 'There, you slob. You've torn up my nets enough. You'll never do it to anybody else.'"

A gull flew in from sea, wobbling crookedly, with something dangling from its claws. The bird alighted on the jetty close enough so you could see it had a surf-casting plug looped to one foot. Apparently it had been stupid enough to think this gadget of lead and feather was a fish.

"I'm going to get that jig," Ted Henley said, and he picked up a stone and crept toward the bird. When he got close he threw the rock. It missed, but the gull took flight with a scream and the plug shook free and Ted recovered it.

The tide was changing and bluefish were breaking water in the rollers out beyond the reach of the beach casters. Now one of them hooked into a fish and a man beside him shouted, pointing, and all the yarn-spinners snatched up their rods and rushed to the water's edge and began casting relentlessly. Nobody got anything, except the one who had brought in a bluefish.

As evening came on, more cars rolled down to the beach and more fishermen went to work. When the setting sun broke through clouds on the horizon, there were about twenty-five anglers strung along the beach casting earnestly. Some of them would keep at it all night.

Al Brickman's party stowed tackle and started for home. General Ryder was telling about bass-fishing in the spring in Menemsha Pond during the spawning run of herring. The herring, he said, come through a cut from the ocean and go into the pond to spawn, and the stripers follow them in.

"You net some herring," he said, "and put one on your line for bait, hooking it through the fleshy part of the back. Then you toss him out and teach him to swim. A bass comes along and slaps the herring, stunning him. You wait, because the bass will then go around and try to eat him head-on. When the bass takes the herring in his mouth and starts swimming away, you tighten your reel and you have him.

"The gulls, though, they come in with the bass and they hang up there waiting. When a bass stuns a herring, the gull dives and grabs the stunned bait. Then you've got a gull in the air on the end of your line, and that's something."

"Did you see cormorant-fishing in the Orient?" the general was asked.

"You mean where they have a cormorant with a ring around his neck so he can't swallow the fish, and they send the bird out fishing and he grabs the fish and they take it away from him? Yes," the general said, "I saw it, and the cormorants love it. They get to eat the little fish, which slip down their throats.

"I have also," the general said, "netted ducks in the private preserves of the Emperor of Japan. You use a long-handled net and catch the ducks on the wing. That's quite a sport, too."

That's what a bass derby is like. No bass, but much education.

Right Little,
Tight Little Isle

The Treasures and Trash Fish of Lake Muckasie

CHAMBERS ISLAND, WIS., *August 1, 1950*

D UNCAN THORPE, a somewhat reformed newspaperman who now serves the Door County Chamber of Commerce as personal publicity man for every fish that lunches along this peninsula's shores—he thus has more clients than all other public-relations counselors put together—came around with a proposal.

"Why don't you leave off killing these smallmouth bass," he said, "and go pick on something your own size?"

His idea was to take on the largemouth and the northern pike and other critters that tenant Lake Muckasie, on Chambers Island. Chambers is a bright green-and-yellow swatch of sand and woods in the middle of Green Bay, about four miles long and nine miles by balky outboard from the mainland village of Fish Creek. On the island there is a lake, and in the lake there are two small islands, and when it rains, naturally, there are little lakes on these islands, and tiny islands in them, and so on and on.

Buried treasure, which is still there, brought Chambers Island its earliest distinction. A century or two ago, two mutineers snatched the payroll for Fort Howard, at the mouth of the Fox River in the tip of the bay, and fled by boat. When they were collared, and probably hanged, in Chicago, they said they had buried the swag on an island in Green Bay with a shoreline of tall sandbanks. There's only one sand island in this whole area.

Afterward Chambers supported a year-round colony of commercial fishermen until the lake trout and whitefish quit these waters. Sam Insull, the Midwestern utilities tycoon, built an airfield and golf course on the island and was developing it as a summer resort when the Depression came and he had to lam for Greece with the law at his heels.

Nature has scrubbed out all trace of his handiwork. There are now four cottages on the island, only one occupied this summer. There is a small Coast Guard station, there is a lighthouse, and what few campers and yachtsmen drop in are outnumbered by deer two hundred to one. Wherever you walk, you tread on deer tracks.

Mr. Thorpe furnished provisions, guide service, a large pack containing two eiderdown sleeping-bags, a boat, and an outboard motor. The boat had lain out in the rain all summer. At eleven the expedition was ready to start. By noon the boat was too, having been bailed. By one P.M. the motor responded, having been cranked scarcely more than five hundred times.

The bay sparkled like the eyes of a hungry blonde. The bluffs of the mainland towered cool and green. The Strawberry Islands were emeralds nestling in rumpled blue satin. The golden banks of Chambers shimmered on the horizon. It was beauty to be sipped and savored slowly. When the outboard quits every half mile and the passenger cranks, you travel slowly, you savor everything.

At length the boat limped into a cove, was made fast to a ruined dock, and the duffel was stored in an abandoned boathouse occupied by barn swallows, whose young yeeped bitterly at the intruders from their nests of mud and grass up in the rafters. The lake wasn't a quarter mile distant. Fishing started immediately.

Mr. Thorpe took the oars, and a trolling lure was put out. Lake Muckasie is richly undergrown with weeds. Something came up out of the vegetation, splashed once as it hit the lure, dived, and departed, leaving the hook loaded with greenery. Mr. Thorpe rowed close to one of the islands and anchored. Fishing started in earnest, the host using a casting rod, the supercargo working with flies.

Mr. Thorpe brought in a northern pike, just about the legal size of nineteen inches. The critter fought with frantic speed when hooked, then quit cold and came in like a dead stick. He was sent home with a wounded mouth.

The supercargo, preparing to cast upwind, let his fly sink while he reeled up slack line. When he tried to lift the fly, there was a legal largemouth bass attached to it. The bass had cooperated by hooking himself and now he cooperated by coming in without a kick or struggle. Largemouth fight as ferociously as ballplayers.

During the long afternoon two largemouth were boated along with one boisterous bluegill. Mr. Thorpe caught several northerns and released them with an expression of repugnance. Up here, northern pike that run smaller than cows are treated with inexpressible disdain. The Wisconsin attitude toward these varmints is expressed by a friend who was fishing in the north woods.

He came back to camp one evening with several walleyed pike and one large northern. He offered the northern to his Indian guide, who declined without thanks. Having no facilities for refrigeration, the angler cleaned his fish and hung them from a tree limb where he thought they'd be safe overnight.

He miscalculated. In the morning there was unmistakable evidence that a skunk had visited the premises. The walleyes were entirely consumed; the northern was untouched.

"Which proved to me," the man has said, "that neither a skunk nor an Indian will eat northern pike."

You Give Up

How Typical Can a Fishing Story Get?

A

CHAMBERS ISLAND, WIS., *August 2, 1950*

As reported yesterday, an afternoon of fishing on the lake on Chambers Island, which is a bosky sandbar in Green Bay, produced two dispirited largemouth bass, one bluegill, and several northern pike, which were released disdainfully by Duncan Thorpe, of the Door County Chamber of Commerce. The bass were invited to dinner, but after Mr. Thorpe had got a fire prepared for them they couldn't be found. They'd been left on a stringer tied to the boat, and now they were gone. Three small sea scouts from Menominee, Michigan, had a tent near by, but suspicious sniffs in that area could detect no bouquet of frying fish.

Bacon and eggs provided enough energy for night fishing on the lake, and a big yellow moon furnished light for the purpose. The evening was warm and beautiful and so quiet in the lee of one of the lake's small islands that the splashing of feeding fish seemed monstrously noisy.

Whatever the fish were feeding on, it wasn't artificial flies or bugs or poppers or plugs or spinners. In almost four hours just one bass rose for a fly, missed it, and went away to brood. There was no choice save unconditional surrender.

Duffel stashed on shore had included a jug of Old Forester, an ancient Indian remedy for infection caused by the teeth of angry pike. Now as midnight approached and fatigue arrived, medication seemed indicated. But the jug was missing. In their tent the sea scouts slept deeply, pure of heart and, perhaps, of breath.

Permission had been received to sleep in one of the island's three unoccupied cottages. By the light of candles it was discovered that the cottage had not been entirely unoccupied. Some zillions of bats had been using it for not altogether sanitary purposes of their own. Eiderdown sleeping-bags were spread on beds, however, and employed effectively until four A.M., when Mr. Thorpe made like an alarm clock.

In the brightening dawn, a big buck deer was browsing. He paid no attention to humans emerging from the house, and when Mr. Thorpe said "Whoosh!" loudly, the deer merely lifted his horny hatrack and stared. "Whoosh!" Mr. Thorpe said again, and the buck loped into the woods, breezing.

The lake was flat as a fried egg. In shallow water on the beach, where it had blown ashore during the night after working free from the boat, lay a stringer holding two bass and one bluegill. On one count, anyhow, the sea scouts were acquitted.

Six hours of relentless fishing ensued. The world holds no deeper peace than that which lay on Chambers Island that morning. The three bass and several northern pike which were caught were about as truculent as Whistler's Mother. Once a big northern surfaced near the boat, thrust his ugly undershot face out of the water, looked around sleepily, and submerged. A pair of loons flew overhead, taking their time. The only contentious note was struck by two kingbirds quarreling with some enemy on one of the islands.

The sun got high and hot. For the bass and pike it was siesta time, but bluegills were busy all along the shore. They developed a deep and lasting affection for a tiny yellow popper, swatting at it again and again with a small kissing sound. It would have been possible to land almost any number of bluegills, but the whole purpose of the two-day visit to Chambers was to wrench heavy largemouth out of the island's lake.

By ten o'clock every yard of the lake's surface had been lashed with flies and plugs. There were, at least, enough bass for breakfast, and obviously there would be no more. Back in the cove on the bay shore, where the outboard had been left after the trip from the mainland, Mr.

Thorpe built a fire and started coffee. His companion carried the fish down to the water to clean them.

There was a splash just off shore. Then another and another. The joint was loaded with smallmouth bass feeding on minnows. A fly dropped among them took two legal bass inside a minute before the flurry ceased.

After breakfast some hours were devoted to mechanical pursuits involving the outboard. Fouled sparkplugs were removed, cleaned, restored, removed again, recleaned, and finally replaced. Once the motor started perkily, but the boat didn't move. A shear pin had broken and the propeller wasn't turning. Among timbers from an old wreck some rusty nails were found. Cut to the proper size, one of them served as a new pin.

Every now and then the motor started, the boat made brief trial runs, and the motor sputtered out. On each such occasion a trolling lure was tossed over the stern. And on every little run there was at least one strike.

How typical can a fishing story get? You wrestle a motor across nine miles of water, moor your boat in an island cove, and go ashore to fish an inland lake all afternoon, all evening, and all morning. You flog that lake for something like thirteen hours, laboring vastly, and you get a practically irreducible minimum of spiritless fish.

You return at last to the spot you had abandoned in the first place. And the water is practically solid with bass trying to jump into the boat. You give up.

★ SPORTS IN THE SEVENTIES ★

Constant Reader

Charles L. Liston, 1932–1970

NEW YORK, N.Y., *January 8, 1971*

SONNY LISTON's death brings memories, some rather personal in character. One has to do with a breakfast among the slot machines and blackjack games in Las Vegas before Liston's second match with Floyd Patterson.

Not many heavyweight champions have been distinguished for their scholarly attainments, as Gene Tunney was, but Liston was the only real illiterate among them, unable to read or write. His wife Geraldine often read from the sports pages aloud and Sonny listened. He was generally uncommunicative, though, so it was difficult to guess how much he retained and whether he associated the writer's name with what was written.

The Las Vegas match was his first defense of the championship that he had won from Patterson with a first-round knockout in Chicago. When Patterson agreed to fight him, some of the Eagle Scouts in and around sports had been scandalized. They insisted that a labor goon and head-breaker who had done time for armed robbery should not have a chance to win the heavyweight championship of the world and so qualify as a model for hero-worshipping youth. Their attitude inspired a column in this space asking what was wrong with having jailbirds in boxing all of a sudden.

The breakfast engagement in Vegas was the idea of Benny Bentley, the publicity man in Liston's camp. Setting up the date, he started to brief the fighter about the party of the second part. "Now, Red Smith..." he began, but an uplifted palm silenced him.

"He's the one," Sonny said, "wrote there ain't hardly no archbishops win the heavyweight championship."

Even so, the big guy's mood wasn't exactly expansive when he showed up for breakfast. In the interview written immediately afterward, his boyish charm was mostly beneath the surface. Only in a few passages did his repartee sparkle. Once he said, "Uh." Later, expanding a trifle, he said, "No." And at last, taking off the conversational wraps, he said, "Unhuhn."

Colloquies like that spread an impression that he was scowling, sullen, suspicious, and unmannerly. He wasn't always. To be sure, the first time he met Jack Murphy, the San Diego sports editor, Jack was smoking a cigar. When they were introduced, Sonny didn't offer a hand or say he was charmed or even hello. He said, "The cigar mus' go."

On the other hand, there was one afternoon at Aurora Downs, the abandoned racetrack outside Chicago where he trained for the first Patterson bout.

"Sonny," a guy said, "you're such a giant in the gym. You look so huge, in the shoulders, the arms, the hands, the chest. And yet you're about two hundred and fifteen pounds. Compared to the guys who play in the line in pro football . . ."

"Oh," he said, and his tone was downright diffident, "I'm too puny for that game."

When he was training in Dedham, Massachusetts, for the second performance with Cassius Clay—the one that eventually came off in Lewistown, Maine—I sat chatting with his trainer, Willie Reddish, whom I had known when Willie was a Philadelphia heavyweight and I was a reporter on the old *Record*. We rapped along about old Philadelphia days and at one point I said, "Yes, I did ten years hard in Philadelphia."

A little removed, Liston was sitting with his back to us and he hadn't appeared to be listening, but now his head swiveled around.

"Hard," he said. "No good time?"

"Not a bloody hour, Sonny," I said.

After the workout when I entered the tiny cubicle that was his dressing room he snatched a stack of towels off a chair to make a seat for me. With every evidence of confidence and candor he answered all my questions. At length I rose to leave, wished him luck, and we shook hands.

"Any time," he said cordially. "Any time." Obviously, any old con from Philadelphia was a friend of Sonny's.

Nor could anybody have been more at ease, or enjoying himself more obviously, than Liston was receiving the press the morning after he won the championship in Chicago. He sat up front at a long table like the chairman of the board and handled a microphone as though he had invented it.

A visiting author came weaving into the room, took the floor, and held it, making an ass of himself. Working stiffs tried to shout him down, but the new champion lifted a restraining paw.

"Leave the bum speak," he commanded, benevolence itself.

The Big Fight

Joe Frazier Whips Muhammad Ali

NEW YORK, N.Y., *March 9, 1971*
EARLY IN the fifteenth round a left hook caught Muhammad Ali on the jaw and it was as though Joe Frazier had hit him with a baseball bat, Frank Howard model. Several times earlier Ali had sagged toward the floor. This time he slammed it like a plank. He went down at full length, flat on his back.

He rocked back on his shoulder blades, both feet in the air, rocked forward to a sitting position and pushed himself wearily, sadly, to his feet. He was up by the count of four but Arthur Mercante, the referee, counted on for the mandatory eight seconds. He stepped aside and Joe came on, bloody mouth open in a grimace of savage joy.

Another hook smashed home, and Ali's hands flew up to his face as if to stifle a scream. When they came down, he had an advanced case of mumps. The comely visage he describes with such affection—"I'm the prettiest; I'm the greatest"—was a gibbous balloon, puffy and mis-shapen.

"Broken jaw," somebody said at ringside, but the diagnosis was not confirmed. As the fifteenth round started, Angelo Dundee, Ali's han-dler, had said the jaw was broken. But X-rays taken later showed there was no fracture.

On one point there was no shadow of doubt. Joe Frazier, whom they had called a pretender, was heavyweight champion of the world—the only champion of the only world we know.

Though he was on his feet at the final bell, Ali took a licking in the ring and on all three official scorecards, his first defeat in thirty-two bouts going all the way back to the days when he answered to the name of Cassius Marcellus Clay.

Losing, he fought the bravest and best and most desperate battle he has ever been called upon to make. In all his gaudy, gabby years as a professional, he had always left one big question unanswered: Could he take it? If ever he was hit and hurt, how would he respond?

He not only took it, he kept it. Each fighter got $2.5 million for his night's work, and earned it. At least they did in the estimation of 20,455 witnesses, but those beautiful people have so little respect for money that they paid $1,352,961 at the gate.

This was not only the biggest "live" gate for any indoor fight; the loot was almost twice as great as the previous record, established in the same Madison Square Garden by a doubleheader featuring the same Joe Frazier (with Buster Mathis). Chances are it will be weeks before the swag from television is counted up, for the match was shown on closed-circuit all over the United States, Canada, and Great Britain and on network TV in thirty-two other countries.

It was the most hysterically ballyhooed promotion of all time, and not only because of the obscene financial figures. If these men had been fighting on a barge for $500 a side it would still have commanded extraordinary attention, for never before had a single ring held two undefeated heavyweights with valid claims to the world champion-ship—Ali unfrocked but still a champion because he had never been whipped for the title, Frazier his rightful successor because he had whipped everybody else—both at the peak of youth and strength.

So great was the interest that a bad fight would have left the Sweet Science sick unto death. A performance that left any shadow of suspi-cion behind might have destroyed boxing. This one destroyed nothing but Muhammad Ali.

It didn't do a thing for Frazier's health either. It did, though, prove Joe just about as close to indestructible as a fist fighter can be. He walked into hundreds of clean, hard shots, flashing combinations that drilled home with jolting force, and never for an instant did they halt his remorseless advance.

Outpointed as expected in the early rounds, he hurt his adversary
in the sixth, batted him soft in the eleventh, knocked him into a grotesque backward slide along the ropes in the twelfth, and wrecked
him in the fifteenth. Not many men could have survived the attack.
But then not many athletes have Ali's armor of arrogance. Even in his
deepest trouble, the loser pretended he wasn't losing, shaking his head
to deny that a punch had hurt him, beckoning Frazier in to slug him
again, trying by every trick of the theater to support the "secret" he had
confided just before the start to a closed-circuit microphone:

"I predict, first of all, that all the Frazier fans and boxing experts
will be shocked at how easy I will beat Joe Frazier, who will look like an
amateur boxer compared to Muhammad Ali, and they will admit that
I was the real champion all the time. Frazier falls in six."

Before these men ever saw Madison Square Garden, the English
music critic Ernest Newman wrote of something he called the magic
chemistry of genius:

"What is the artistic faculty? Is it just a knack, which some people
are born with and others are not, for moving the counters of art—
words, sounds, lines, colours—about in a particular way? We do not
expect of a great billiards player or boxer that he shall have read Kant
or Aeschylus, or understand the political problems of the Balkans. We
do not even expect Mr. Joseph Louis to have studied the rudiments
of that science of the impact of forces upon moving masses, upon the
correct application of which his success depends. Indeed, were he and
his like to try to get their results by reason, by 'culture,' they would find
themselves in the company of Mr. Belloc's nimble water-insect:

If he ever stopped to think
how he did it he would sink."

Joe Frazier has now fought twenty-seven boxing matches as a professional and won twenty-seven. The Olympic heavyweight champion
of 1964 has won the championship of the professional world three
times—by knocking out Buster Mathis when Cassius Muhammad Ali
Clay was ostracized as a draft-dodger, by knocking out Jimmy Ellis,

whom the World Boxing Association called champion, by knocking Muhammad Ali down but not out.

All his fights were cut to the same pattern, yet he could not tell you how he does it any more than Beethoven could.

Joe can talk a little about tactics, about "cutting the ring," which means advancing obliquely on a circling opponent to cut off the escape routes. As for his own bobbing, ducking attack: "I'll be smokin'," he says. "Right on." A witness within earshot of his corner Monday night could have heard his manager, Yank Durham, enlarge on this:

"Down, Joe, down . . . for the body, Joe, the body . . . bring the right over . . . don't wrestle him, Joe; let the referee do the work."

What Joe says and Yank says merely brushes the surface. These two don't begin to explain what makes Joe the best fist fighter in the world at this time. Neither truly understands it. Yet one thing they do know.

If they fought a dozen times, Joe Frazier would whip Muhammad Ali a dozen times. And it would get easier as they went along.

It Takes Two

Ali–Frazier: The Thrilla in Manila

MANILA, PHILIPPINES, *October 2, 1975*

A GAGGLE of pretty girls got aboard an elevator for the press center in the Bayview Plaza Hotel, where they had been working for the last ten days. "It's over," one of them said, "and we're glad." Were they satisfied with the way it had ended? "No," they said, "no," every one of them. "How about you?" a girl asked a man on the lift. "I'm neutral," he said, "but I'll say one thing: Joe Frazier makes a better fighter and a better man of Muhammad Ali than anybody else can do." "Right," the girls said, all together, "that's right."

A small, strange scene came back to mind. It was two days before the fight and Ali lay on a couch in his dressing room, talking. If this had been a psychiatrist's couch it would not have seemed strange, but he wasn't talking to a psychiatrist and he wasn't talking to the newspaper guys around him. He just lay there letting the words pour out in a stream of consciousness.

"Who'd he ever beat for the title?" he was saying of Joe Frazier. "Buster Mathis and Jimmy Ellis. He ain't no champion. All he's got is a left hook, got no right hand, no jab, no rhythm. I was the real champion all the time. He reigned because I escaped the draft and he luckily got by me, but he was only an imitation champion. He just luckily got through because his head could take a lot of punches. . . ."

Why, listeners asked themselves, why does he have to do this? Why this compulsion to downgrade the good man he is going to fight? It had to be defensive. He was talking to himself, talking down inner doubts that he would not acknowledge. He will never feel that need again, and he never should. If there is any decency in him he will not bad-mouth Joe Frazier again, for Frazier makes him a real champion. In the ring with Joe, he is a better and braver man than he is with anybody else.

Muhammad Ali loves to play a role. He is almost always on stage, strutting, preening, babbling nonsense. But Frazier drags the truth out of him. Frazier is the best fighter Ali has ever met, and he makes Ali fight better than he knows how.

They have fought three times. In the first, Ali fought better than ever before, and lost. In the third he fought better still. This one ranks up there with the most memorable heavyweight matches of our time— Dempsey-Firpo, Dempsey's two with Tunney, both Lewis-Schmeling bouts, and Marciano's first with Jersey Joe Walcott.

It was really three fights. Ali won the first. Through the early rounds he outboxed and outscored Frazier, doing no great damage but nailing him with clean, sharp shots as Joe bore in.

The second fight was all Frazier's. From the fifth round through the eleventh he just beat hell out of Ali. When the champion tried to cover up against the ropes, Frazier bludgeoned him remorselessly, pounding body and arms until the hands came down, hooking fiercely to the head as the protective shell chipped away. When Ali grabbed, an excellent referee slapped his gloves away.

Then it was the twelfth round and the start of the third fight, and Ali won going away. Where he got the strength no man can say, for his weariness was, as he said, "next to death." In the thirteenth a straight right to the chin sent Frazier reeling back on a stranger's legs. He was alone and unprotected in mid-ring, looking oddly diminished in size, and Ali was too tired to walk out there and hit him. Still, Ali won.

This evening Ali dined with President and Mrs. Ferdinand E. Marcos in the Antique House. Frazier was also invited but he begged off, sending his wife and two oldest children instead. Afterward the winner disappeared but the loser had several hundred guests at a "victory party" in the penthouse of his hotel. Like a proper host, he shaped up, trigged out in dinner clothes with dark glasses concealing bruises about the eyes.

"There was one more round to go, but I just couldn't make it through the day, I guess," he told the crowd. "Hey, fellas, I feel like doin' a number." That quickly, the prize fighter became the rock singer. "Lemme talk to this band a moment, because I sure don't want to get into another fight tonight." In a moment he had microphone in hand.

"I'm superstitious about you, baby," he sang. "Think I better knock-knock on wood." He did a chorus, he urged everybody to dance, and then a member of the Checkmates took over. The Checkmates are a trio and at the fight they had sung the Star-Spangled Banner in relay.

"We are all here tonight," the Checkmate said, "because we respect a certain man."

He got no argument from listeners. They all stood smiling, watching Joe Frazier dance at his own funeral.

Homecoming
in the Slammer

Don King Returns to School of Hard Knocks

MARION, OHIO, *March 6, 1977*

For TWO rounds a Brooklyn heavyweight named Kevin Isaac shuffled, shrugged, feinted, and circled warily while huge Stan Ward of Sacramento fixed him with a beady glare of waiting.

"Come on!" yelled a fan at ringside as the bell rang for the third round. "I've only got twenty years!"

Number 125734 was back in the slammer today, and he got a standing ovation. Up to September 29, 1971, No. 125734 was Don King, now perhaps the most widely known alumnus of the Marion Correctional Institution. Returning to alma mater, where he did four years for manslaughter, the least diffident promoter in boxing presented another round in his "United States Championship Tournament" for the edification of his former classmates and the entertainment of the American Broadcasting Company's viewing audience. "King's back," read one placard held high in the bleachers. "We told you so." Another struck a note of resignation: "Some dudes ya can't chase away with a club. Welcome back, Don King."

The former resident in Room 10, Cellblock 6, stepped into the ring wearing a gold-encrusted jacket and waistcoat, brown pants with a crease that could draw blood, a frilled white evening shirt and fan-wing bow tie. His Afro haircut quivered with pride.

"I look around and see many familiar faces," he told the crowd of 1,400. "I am one of you." They cheered. "It is with mixed emotions that I am coming back to what was a trauma in my life. I am happy and proud to be able to bring back some entertainment for you because you have been part of my life." They yelled. "Wherever I have gone outside, I have never tried to hide Marion C.I. I never forgot No. 125734." That was for openers. When he went on to tell them they must "deal with the pragmatic thing realistically," they howled.

He introduced the prison chaplain, Father Fred Furey, and got mostly cheers; Pete Perini, the superintendent, who was warmly booed; his own daughter and son, Debbie and Carl, who were politely received; Joe Louis, who brought down the house. There were boos for Walter Hampton, head of the parole board, but Don reminded them: "That's the dude that sprung me."

Gesturing toward a microphone at ringside, he presented "The Mouth of Boxing—Howard Cosell." Up went placards: "Finally, Howard is where he belongs" and "Howard got in—will he get out?"

It was a homecoming to warm every cockle this side of Sing Sing.

Photographers were waiting when the returning prodigal strode through the big gate at the end of Victory Road. "I used to mow that grass," he said, pointing. Sure of his way, he walked to Cellblock 6 with the superintendent. Pete Perini was a linebacker at Ohio State, played some pro football with the Cleveland Browns and Chicago Bears and came to this post in 1967, the year Don King matriculated, fresh from command of the numbers racket in Cleveland.

"And I have to believe Don has done better," said Irving Rudd of the promoter's staff, "because he's out and Pete is still inside."

Residents recognized King as he passed. They exchanged greetings. At the door of his old quarters he spoke to the present occupant: "You're making this room famous." As he entered with the warden, the occupant, Obie Brooks, stepped out. Brooks said he was doing ten to life for murder, too. He said he had five years in, with two to go before he could apply for parole. "Did it happen in a fight?" he was asked, for it was in a street fight that King killed a man.

"During an armed robbery," Obie said.

The warden and the graduate walked together down the quarter-mile corridor to the gym. "Don didn't serve time," Perini has said. "Time served him."

Cordiality has been rampant here for days. When King arrived, the Mayor of Marion gave him the key to the city. "Mr. Mayor," Don said, "when I was here before, nobody gave me a key to anything."

Members of the press were frisked courteously on arrival and given a mimeographed sheet of do's and don'ts. "Keep track of your valuable equipment," came ahead of "do leave all weapons (knives) and medication outside the main stockade." Inside they met an old friend, Peter Rademacher, the only man who ever fought for the heavyweight championship of the world as an amateur. That was twenty years ago and Floyd Patterson dropped him seven times. Rademacher, now an Akron businessman, refereed the Isaac-Ward bout. Some of the fights were good, some funny. Mike Dokes, who lost flashily to Cuba's Teófilo Stevenson when Dokes was a flashy amateur, was in with an oval personage named Charlie Jordan. Charlie is known as "Big Tuna" but he is built more like an angry blowfish. Ignoring his billowing belly, Dokes aimed for his bobbing head and opened a cut near an eye. The doctor seized the opportunity to stop it, but not before Vic Ziegel of the *New York Post* had spoken: "This fight belongs here."

"Nevertheless," said Ed Schuyler of the Associated Press, one who survived the street gangs and pickpockets at last fall's Muhammad Ali-Ken Norton affair. "Nevertheless, the security is better than in Yankee Stadium, and there's a better class of people."

Massacre in Munich

The Black September Killings

MUNICH, WEST GERMANY, *September 5, 1972*
Olympic Village was under siege. Two men lay murdered and eight others were held at gunpoint in imminent peril of their lives. Still the games went on. Canoeists paddled through their races. Fencers thrust and parried in make-believe duels. Boxers scuffled. Basketball players scampered across the floor like happy children. Walled off in their dream world, appallingly unaware of the realities of life and death, the aging playground directors who conduct this quadrennial muscle dance ruled that a little bloodshed must not be permitted to interrupt play.

It was 4:30 A.M. when Palestinian terrorists invaded the housing complex where athletes from twelve nations live, and shot their way into the Israeli quarters.

More than five hours later, word came down from Avery Brundage, retiring president of the International Olympic Committee, that sport would proceed as scheduled. Canoe racing had already begun. Wrestling started an hour later. Before long competition was being held in eleven of the twenty-two sports on the Olympic calendar.

Not until 4 P.M. did some belated sense of decency dictate suspension of the obscene activity, and even then exception was made for games already in progress. They went on and on while hasty plans were laid for a memorial service.

The men who run the Olympics are not evil men. Their shocking lack of awareness can't be due to callousness. It has to be stupidity.

Four years ago in Mexico City when American sprinters stood on the victory stand with fists uplifted in symbolic protest against injustice to blacks, the brass of the United States Olympic Committee couldn't distinguish between politics and human rights. Declaring that the athletes had violated the Olympic spirit by injecting "partisan politics" into the festival, the waxworks lifted the young men's credentials and ordered them out of Mexico, blowing up a simple, silent gesture into an international incident.

When African nations and other blacks threatened to boycott the current Games if the white supremacist government of Rhodesia were represented here, Brundage thundered that the action was politically motivated, although it was only through a transparent political expedient that Rhodesia had been invited in the first place. Rhodesia and Brundage were voted down not on moral grounds but to avoid having an all-white carnival.

On past performances, it must be assumed that in Avery's view Arab-Israeli warfare, hijacking, kidnapping, and killing all constitute partisan politics not to be tolerated in the Olympics.

"And anyway," went the bitter joke today, "these are professional killers; Avery doesn't recognize them."

The fact is, these global clambakes have come to have an irresistible attraction as forums for ideological, social, or racial expression. For this reason, they may have outgrown their britches. Perhaps in the future it will be advisable to substitute separate world championships in swimming, track and field, and so on, which could be conducted in a less hysterical climate.

In the past, athletes from totalitarian countries have seized upon the Olympics as an opportunity to defect. During the Pan-American Games last summer in Cali, Colombia, a number of Cubans defected and a trainer jumped, fell, or was pushed to his death from the roof of the Cuban team's dormitory.

Never, of course, has there been anything like today's terror. Once those gunmen climbed the wire fence around Olympic Village and shot Moshe Weinberg, the Israeli wrestling coach, all the fun and games lost meaning. Mark Spitz and his seven gold medals seemed curiously unimportant. The fact that the American heavyweight, Duane Bobick, got slugged stupid by Cuba's Teófilo Stevenson mattered to few besides Bobick.

Even the disqualification of sixteen-year-old Rick DeMont from the fifteen-hundred-meter free-style swimming, in which he has shattered the world record, slipped into the background. This may be unfortunate, for it appears that the boy was undone through the misfeasance of American team officials and if this is so the facts should be made public.

The United States party includes 168 coaches, trainers, and other functionaries, which seems like enough to take care of 447 athletes. It wasn't enough, however, to get two world-record sprinters to the starting blocks for the one-hundred-meter dash and it wasn't enough to reconcile young DeMont's asthma treatments with Olympic rules on drugs.

After the boy won the four-hundred-meter free-style, a urinalysis showed a trace of ephedrine, a medicine that helps clear nasal passages. A list of forbidden drugs, released before the Games, includes ephedrine. The fact that DeMont uses it for his asthma appears on his application sheet for the Games.

Why didn't the American medical staff pick this up and make sure there would be no violation? Efforts to get an answer today were unavailing. Dr. Winston P. Riehl, the chief physician, couldn't be reached. Dr. Harvey O'Phelan declined to talk.

The Round
Jack Nicklaus Forgot

World Cup '63 All Over Again

★　★　★

FT. LAUDERDALE, FLA., *March 3, 1978*
JACK NICKLAUS' golf is better than his memory. When he came charging home in the Inverrary Classic last weekend, picking up four strokes on Grier Jones, three on Jerry Pate and Andy Bean, and two on Hale Irwin, with five birdies on the last five holes, he was asked whether he had ever put on such a finish before. "I can't imagine any other time," he said. "It was the most remarkable thing I've ever seen in my life," said Lee Trevino, comparing it with Reggie Jackson's three home runs in the last World Series game and Leon Spinks' victory over Muhammad Ali. Well, it was remarkable but it wasn't unprecedented.

Fifteen years ago, Nicklaus and Arnold Palmer represented the United States in the World Cup competition at Saint-Nom-la-Bretèche near Versailles in France. If Jack has forgotten his performance there, perhaps he wanted to forget it. Maybe he deliberately put it out of his mind as too outrageously theatrical to bear remembering.

The things he did on the very first hole were downright scandalous. The hole was a legitimate par 5 for club members but a trifle short for a pro with Jack's power, measuring somewhere between four hundred fifty and five hundred yards. In his four rounds, Jack played it eagle, eagle, eagle, birdie, and that was just for openers.

Bretèche may have been a trifle shorter than Inverrary's 7,127 yards, but this was no exhibition on a pitch-and-putt course, and the opposition was at least as distinguished as the field Nicklaus encountered last week. The World Cup, now twenty-five years old, is a movable feast that leaps from continent to continent, usually playing national capitals, matching two-man teams from virtually every land where the game is known. Though it hasn't the prestige of the United States or British Open, it is probably the closest thing there is to a world championship.

In 1963, Saint-Nom-la-Bretèche was a comparatively new course built on land that had been the royal farm when Louis XIV was top banana. The clubhouse, once the royal cow barn, was a splendid building of ivy-covered stone set in a terraced stableyard ablaze with roses, snapdragon, chrysanthemum, and pansies.

The galleries had a touch of quality seldom associated with, say, Maple Moor in Westchester County. Among those who followed the play were two former kings and one former Vice President—Leopold of Belgium, the Duke of Windsor, and Richard M. Nixon.

Before play started, Prince Michel de Bourbon-Parme, the club president, dispatched ten dozen fresh eggs to a nearby convent. This, he explained, was an ancient custom in the Île de France. Anyone planning an outdoor binge like a wedding or garden party sent eggs to the poor and this assured him of good weather. The standard fee was one dozen eggs, but the Prince had laid it on to guarantee a week of sunshine.

Morning of the opening round found the Prince glowering through a clammy fog. "So," he said, "I am sending to the sisters to get back my eggs."

Soggy turf made the course play long for little guys, but not for Nicklaus. His second shot on the opening hole was twenty feet from the pin, and he ran down the putt for his first eagle 3. After that he had five birdies and three bogeys for a 67. Palmer's 69 gave the pair a tie for first place with Al Balding and Stan Leonard of Canada.

Prince Michel changed his mind about reclaiming the eggs, but the weather didn't relent. Day by day the fog thickened, until the green hills and yellow bunkers were all but blotted out. Realizing that if a hitter like Nicklaus tried to fire a tee shot into that soup the ball would never be seen again, officials postponed the final round for twenty-four hours.

It didn't help much. Next day a gray soufflé garnished the fairways. The climate dripped sullenly from the trees. Windsor and Leopold showed up as they had for each earlier round, but the weather reduced the gallery to a minimum. Reluctantly, the committee decided to cut the final round to nine holes. At this point Nicklaus and Palmer were tied with Spain's Ramón Sota and Sebastián Miguel for the team trophy, with Nicklaus and Gary Player all square in individual competition.

Automobiles were driven out past the first green, where they made a U-turn and parked with headlights on. From the tee, lights were blurred but visible, giving the players a target. For the first time in four rounds, Nicklaus needed four shots to get down. Then he got serious.

With that birdie for a start, he played the next five holes as follows: 3-3-3-3-3. When he walked toward the seventh tee, a spectator asked: "What are you going to do for an encore?"

"Try to finish," Jack said.

On the first six holes he had taken nineteen shots. On the last three he took thirteen for a 32. It won.

Pound for Pound, Our Greatest Living Athlete

Willie Shoemaker Is America's Jockey

IT WAS March of 1952 and a couple of guys in the walking ring at Santa Anita bumped into their equestrian friend, Eddie Arcaro, accompanied by a bat-eared wisp of a kid in silks.

"Meet the new champ," Eddie said, and William Lee Shoemaker acknowledged the introduction with a tiny, twisted grin.

In 1952 Arcaro had been riding races for more than twenty years. Only two men in the world—Sir Gordon Richards and Johnny Longden—had brought home more winners. In about six weeks he would ride his fifth Kentucky Derby winner. He was rich and famous and destined to go on as top man in his field for another decade, yet he was cheerfully abdicating his title to a twenty-year-old only recently sprung from apprentice ranks.

Gifted with the class of the true champion himself, Arcaro could recognize class in another. Before he was through, Eddie would ride winners of $30 million, but if somebody had asked him to name the jockey likeliest to break that and all other records for success on horseback, he would without hesitation have named the painfully bashful, almost wordless Shoe.

Last Monday Bill Shoemaker won the fourth race at Del Mar aboard a horse named Dares J. It was Shoe's 6,033rd visit to the winner's circle, an all-time record. Characteristically, he explained that he had profited from opportunities that weren't enjoyed by Johnny Longden, whose record he had broken.

"I had a lot more mounts early in my career than Longden did," he said. "He didn't ride many horses in his first ten years. When I came along there were more racetracks and more racing."

That is true, but it took Longden forty years and more than thirty-two thousand races to get 6,032 winners. Shoe did it with twenty-five thousand in twenty-two seasons.

Opportunity has no great value without the talent to capitalize on it. When Shoe was a sixteen-year-old working horses for a man in California, his boss told him he'd never make a race rider and turned him loose, keeping another exercise boy whom he deemed more promising. The other boy hasn't won a race yet, though once he came close. Put up on a horse that was pounds the best, he came into the home-stretch leading by six lengths, turned to look back, and fell off.

At seventeen Shoe was a winner. At eighteen he tied Joe Culmone for the national championship with 388 winning rides. At nineteen he led the country with purses of $1,329,890. At twenty-one he rode 485 winners for a world record.

His mounts have brought back $41 million. If he receives only the standard fee of 10 percent, he has earned more than $4 million in the saddle. No other performer in any sport ever collected that much directly out of competition.

And that isn't counting what the little bandit takes from large, muscular golfers who simply will not believe that this imperturbable scamp can go on scoring in the early 70's round after round and even outhit them from the tee when he's in the mood.

If Bill Shoemaker were six feet tall and weighed 200 pounds he could beat anybody in any sport. Standing less than five feet and weighing around 100, he beats everybody at what he does. Pound for pound, he's got to be the greatest living athlete.

He hadn't been around long before horsemen had to discard a belief that had been handed down for generations. It was an article of faith that "live" weight was easier on a horse than "dead" weight; a man whose horse had drawn a heavy load from the handicappers shopped around for a big jockey who needed no ballast.

Then along came Shoe weighing well under 100 pounds with all his tack. With enough lead in the saddle pockets to sink a battleship, he won every stake in sight, and that took care of that old husband's tale.

Not that Shoe was out to prove anything. That isn't his style. He goes along quietly doing his thing and if he kicks one for an error, as we all do, he cops no plea. It can't give him any pleasure to remember the 1957 Kentucky Derby that he lost with Gallant Man because he misjudged the finish line and eased his horse too soon. Yet because Ralph Lowe, who owned Gallant Man, took defeat like a gentleman, Shoe endowed a Ralph Lowe Trophy to be presented annually to a racing man distinguished for sportsmanship.

Instead of hiding out and hoping people would forget his mistake, Shoe puts up his own money to remind people of it every year. The word for that is class.

A Little Greedy, and Exactly Right

Secretariat Wins the Triple Crown

BELMONT, N.Y., *June 11, 1973*

T H E   T H I N G to remember is that the horse that finished last had broken the Kentucky Derby record. If there were no colt named Secretariat, then Sham would have gone into the Belmont Stakes Saturday honored as the finest three-year-old in America, an eight-length winner of the Kentucky Derby, where he went the mile and a quarter faster than any winner in ninety-eight years, and an eight-length winner of the Preakness. There is, however, a colt named Secretariat. In the Derby he overtook Sham and beat him by two and a half lengths. In the Preakness he held Sham off by two and a half lengths. This time he and Sham dueled for the lead, and he beat Sham by more than a sixteenth of a mile. There is no better way to measure the class of the gorgeous red colt that owns the Triple Crown. Turning into the homestretch at Belmont Park, Ron Turcotte glanced back under an arm to find his pursuit. He saw nothing, and while he peeked, his mount took off.

Secretariat had already run a mile in one minute, 34⅕ seconds. Up to three weeks ago, no horse in Belmont history had run a mile in less than 1:34²⁄₅. He had run a mile and a quarter in 1:59, two-fifths of a second faster than the Derby record he had set five weeks earlier. Now he went after the Belmont record of 2:26³⁄₅ for a mile and a half, which was also an American record when Gallant Man established it sixteen years ago. With no pursuit to urge him on, without a tap from

Turcotte's whip, he smashed the track record by two and three-fifth seconds, cracked the American record by two and a fifth, and if Turcotte had asked him he could have broken the world record. If he had been running against Gallant Man, the fastest Belmont winner in 104 years, he would have won by thirteen lengths. Unless the competition spurred him to greater speed.

"It seems a little greedy to win by thirty-one lengths," said Mrs. John Tweedy, the owner, and then repeated the rider's story of how he saw the fractional times blinking on the tote board, realized there was a record in the making, and went after it in the final sixteenth.

It is hard to imagine what a thirty-one-length margin looks like, because you never see one, but Secretariat lacked eight panels of fence—eighty feet—of beating Twice a Prince by a sixteenth of a mile. This was the classic case of "Eclipse first, the rest nowhere."

The colt was entitled to his margin and his record. At the Derby he drew a record crowd that broke all Churchill Downs' betting records and he set a track record. He set attendance and betting records at the Preakness and may have broken the stakes record, but if he did discrepancies in the clocking denied him that credit. Last Saturday belonged to him.

Indeed, Belmont was kinder to the Meadow Stable than Pimlico had been, in more ways than one. On Preakness day, while the Tweedy party lunched in the Pimlico Hotel near the track, a parking lot attendant smashed up their car. They walked to the clubhouse gate, found they hadn't brought credentials, and paid their way in. While the horses were being saddled in the infield, somebody in the crowd accidentally pressed a lighted cigarette against Mrs. Tweedy's arm. On his way back to his seat, John Tweedy had his pocket picked.

"Boy," he said after that race, "we needed to win this one today, just to get even."

At Belmont there were the few scattered boos that most odds-on favorites receive here, but the prevailing attitude was close to idolatry. Well, perhaps that isn't the best word because it suggests a cathedral restraint. Idols are remotely chilly. This congregation was warm. Horseplayers passing the Tweedy box raised friendly voices:

"Mrs. Tweedy, good luck."

"Thank you."

The voices followed her to the paddock where her colt was cheered all around the walking ring. They followed as she returned to the clubhouse.

"Mrs. Tweedy, good luck."

"Thank you."

Secretariat was cheered in the post parade, cheered as he entered the gate, and when he caught and passed Sham on the backstretch the exultant thunders raised gooseflesh. At the finish the crowd surged toward the winner's circle, fists brandished high. After twenty-five years, America's racing fans had a sovereign to wear the Triple Crown.

Parallels are striking between this one and his predecessor, Citation. Both colts raced nine times as two-year-olds and finished first eight times. At three, each lost once en route to the Derby, Preakness, and Belmont. Both made each event in the Triple Crown easier than the last. After the Belmont, Citation won his next ten starts for a streak of sixteen straight. Secretariat's stud duties won't permit that. Love will rear its pretty, tousled head.

The Frenchman's
Rare Day in June

A Slew of Happiness for Jean Cruguet

THREE OR four strides before he reached the finish line, Jean Cruguet stood up in his stirrups and flung his right fist aloft in triumph. It was a typically Gallic gesture, an emotional flourish such as had not been witnessed in 108 earlier Belmont Stakes, but this was the 109th and Cruguet was astride Seattle Slew, the only undefeated horse that ever won a Triple Crown. Cruguet had a right to his moment of melodrama, but that didn't silence the dramatic critics in the jockeys' quarters.

"You do that again," said Jacinto Vásquez, who had finished fourth aboard Mr. Red Wing, "and you'll fall on your butt."

Not yesterday. Jean Cruguet has been riding races for eighteen of his thirty-seven years, but he never knew a day like this. Fall off this colt, which he has ridden every step that Slew ever took in a race? Mess it up now when he and his horse had their ninth straight victory in hand with the Kentucky Derby and Preakness behind them and the Triple Crown only yards away?

This was a day when nothing was beyond him. Not only did he and Slew complete the most sensational winning streak ever compiled by an American horse at this stage of life, but the little Frenchman also polished off three other races, including the $85,800 Mother Goose Stakes. Jean took that one, the second event in the fillies' triple crown series, aboard Road Princess, who was trained for Elmendorf Farm by

Cruguet's severest critic, John Campo. It is a rare day in June when Jean can look good in John's eyes.

Indeed, he looked so good that when he got off Road Princess, the trainer kissed him. However, Cruguet reported later that Campo had not been all sweet surrender. Even as he smooched the rider he growled in his ear: "You're still a bum."

Why had the jockey saluted the crowd as he coasted down toward the wire? It was the second-largest crowd that ever saw the Belmont Stakes, by the way, 70,229 immortal souls who tore their pants shoving $6,498,117 through the mutuel wickets.

"Happiness," Cruguet said, "just happiness."

This is the rider whose chances in the Derby were assayed by Campo thus: "Two minutes is a long time for the Frenchman not to make a mistake." He has been on and off Seattle Slew since the colt got to the races last Sept. 20. That is almost nine months, and the Frenchman has yet to make his first mistake with him.

"What can I say?" Billy Turner said when the trainer was asked about Seattle Slew's Belmont. "He runs the same race every time."

He meant the colt wins every time, and that is all the trainer asks. Actually, every one of his races differs from the last. Where he has shown devastating speed in the past, he took his time with this job, obediently cooperating with the rider trying to conserve him for a mile and a half.

The result was a comparatively slow trip over a bridle path drenched by thirty-six hours of rain.

"We knew up front," Billy Turner said, "that this wasn't a track for record-breaking, and this isn't a record-breaking horse. He does what he has to do. If something presses him, it's like his first race this year when he destroyed the track records, but it's hard to find a horse to press him."

One of his old rivals and one who had never hooked him before tried pressing him in the Belmont. A newcomer named Spirit Level went after the favorite right after the start, ran with him to the far turn and chucked it, finishing sixth in the eight-horse field. Run Dusty Run ranged up alongside Spirit Level and Seattle Slew turning into the backstretch, but the winner went along on his untroubled way. Run Dusty Run is always close. He can't run with Slew, but he ran second.

As a rule, no horse that comes to the Belmont has ever tried the Belmont distance of a mile and a half and there are always doubts about a steed's ability to stay that far until he does it. Before this race, as a voice in the jock's room was saying, "It's another quarter mile. He has to go a quarter mile farther."

"Yes," said Joe Imperato, who had no Belmont mounts, "another quarter mile to look at his rear end."

"I'm Always Ready to Lose"

Buddy Delp's Spectacular Bid

BELMONT, N.Y., *June 10, 1979*

HUNG ON the rail around the Belmont Park walking ring was a hand-lettered salute to Spectacular Bid's jockey. "Ron Franklin," the sign read, "is spectacular." Horseplayers were jammed eight or ten rows deep around the paddock as the field for the Belmont Stakes paraded, but there must have been at least one fight fan among them. "Franklin will whip your tail," he cried as Angel Cordero, the jockey who moonlights as Franklin's sparring partner, was hoisted aboard General Assembly.

Nobody said anything just then to Ruben Hernandez on Coastal, but earlier in the week when the prospect arose that this colt might be made a supplementary entry, Buddy Delp, Spectacular Bid's trainer, said: "I beat this horse by seventeen lengths in Jersey. Why is he coming in here?"

Delp got the answer yesterday, and he accepted it like a champion. Along with 59,073 paying guests, he saw Coastal ramble home on top in the 111th and richest running of the gaudy old cavalry charge, he saw his tired gray colt beaten back to third by Golden Act, breaking a winning streak of twelve straight stakes, and he saw his dream of a Triple Crown shattered. Then he went back to Barn 14, opened a can of Heineken's, and said:

"He may not be a mile-and-a-half horse. The best horse won. I got beat, that's all. Tomorrow's another day."

He took a long swallow of beer. "I couldn't see any excuse for my horse at all. He was strong until he ran out of gas. I'm not shocked, I'm disappointed. I understand horse racing better than a lot of people do. I'm always ready to lose. I've lost a lot more than anybody."

Over on the front side of the track, the experts were already dissecting Ron Franklin's ride with the sure touch of sophomores in the biology lab dissecting a frog. "A turf expert," one definition goes, "is a baseball writer with borrowed binoculars."

"Around the racetrack," another says, "an expert is somebody who's been right once."

Now they were saying that Franklin pulled his mount's cork by sending him to the front early and going the first mile in 1:36. On the back side, Buddy Delp sipped his beer.

"The kid rode a fine race," he said again and again.

In a little while Franklin joined him. Trainer and jockey climbed into a car to ride back home to Laurel, Md. A woman handed Franklin a scrap of paper for an autograph. "Make it quick, Ronnie," Delp said. In the front seat, he reached across and scribbled his own signature below the jockey's. "There, lady," he said. "You've got the losers."

At just about that time, William Haggin Perry, who owns Coastal, and David Whiteley, who trains him, visited the press box. They had waited till the last moment to make their colt a starter, putting up $5,000 to enter him last Thursday but deciding only about 2 P.M. yesterday to pay the remaining $15,000 of the supplementary fee. That money was due because Coastal had not been nominated by Feb. 15, as the others were.

Coastal's training for the Belmont had been retarded. He had won two of five starts last year but finished fifth in the World Playground at Atlantic city in September, seventeen lengths behind the victorious Spectacular Bid. He suffered an eye injury in the fall when he was hit by a clod, and didn't start as a three-year-old until April 28. Running in blinkers, he won three times in a row, and the third was a smasher in the Peter Pan, which he polished off by thirteen lengths.

It was that race that got Coastal's people thinking about the Belmont. If they didn't remember, there were others who reminded them how Counterpoint, Gallant Man, High Gun, and Cavan had all used the Peter Pan as a prep for Belmont, had knocked off that race and gone on to take the big one. So they invested the $20,000—other starters paid only $3,100 to get the post—and they got back $161,400.

Spectators were astonished when Spectacular Bid took out after Gallant Best soon after the start and went to the front early in the backstretch, though in most of his successful races he had run fairly close to the pace. When David Whiteley was asked about this, a trace of a smile touched his lips. He recalled that at the press breakfast last Thursday, Harry Meyerhoff, the colt's owner, had teased Delp by asking whether he thought Spectacular Bid could spring a mile and a half.

"Maybe they were trying to prove something," Whiteley said, "because the boy was riding him on the back side." He looked around at the assembled press. "You all been comparing him to Secretariat," he said. "Maybe they were worried about thirty-one lengths." That was Secretariat's stunning margin in the Belmont of 1973.

Beaten in the third and last leg of the Triple Crown series, Spectacular Bid joins a distinguished company that tired and fell back in the past. Starting thirty-five years ago, eight horses before him won the Kentucky Derby and Preakness but failed in the Belmont. They were Pensive in 1944, Tim Tam in 1958, Carry Back in 1961, Northern Dancer in 1964, Kauai King in 1966, Forward Pass in 1968 (though he finished second in the Derby and was moved up later when Dancer's Image was disqualified), Majestic Prince in 1969, and Canonero II in 1971.

"So your horse won't be remembered with Secretariat," a man said to Buddy Delp.

"No," the trainer said. "He sure won't be, but I'll remember him pretty good."

Undefeatable

Giants Can't Stop Miami Dolphins

Bronx, N.Y., *December 11, 1972*

I N T H E sixtieth minute of the thirteenth football game of his eighteenth season as a professional, compassion softened the flinty old heart of Earl Morrall. The Miami Dolphins had the New York Giants whipped, 23–13, and were in possession two yards short of another touchdown with time for one last play.

Massed around the hog wallow that rains had left in Yankee Stadium, 62,728 witnesses looked on moodily, waiting for the final blow to fall. All through the raw and foggy afternoon they had seen the home forces attack and fall back, attack and fall back, attack and fall back again, frustrating their own admirable efforts by giving up the ball on fumbles and interceptions.

The Dolphins broke from their huddle and hunkered down in the mud. Morrall crouched behind center prepared to turn loose one of the rampaging bulls who have given Miami the most formidable running attack in football. Perhaps at that moment the quarterback remembered his three seasons as a member of the Giants and went dewy-eyed for auld lang syne. Maybe he was aware of the abuse and contumely heaped upon Coach George Allen of the Washington Redskins a few weeks ago when that villainous character stopped the clock in the last half-minute to give his men time to double a seven-point lead over the Giants.

Whatever it was, something stayed his hand. He just crouched there in silence and let the seconds tick away until Miami's thirteenth victory of the season and New York's sixth defeat became official.

On that clement note, the curtain came down on the season in the

Bronx, and the first performance ever given there by the Dolphins. They shouldn't have waited so long; guys like Jim Klick and Larry Csonka, Paul Warfield and Mercury Morris and Nick Buoniconti were born to play on Broadway.

Last winter when the Dolphins made it to the Super Bowl in New Orleans, they were pictured as faceless, nameless silhouettes. Today they are one game away from the National Football League's first perfect season in thirty years. Already champions of the Eastern Division in the American Conference, they can complete their regular schedule undefeated by beating Baltimore next Saturday.

In thirteen games, their runners have gained more than half a mile, and they need only 105 yards against the Colts to replace the Detroit Lions of 1936 as the top rushing team in history. The record is 2,885 yards. Against a recalcitrant defense they made 204 yards on foot yesterday, and the names of those who carried the goods are known to people who never heard of Henry Kissinger.

Biggest of the bulls is Csonka, six-foot-two, 237 heaving pounds, of whom Bob Griese, the disabled quarterback, says: "He attacks the earth." He had gains of 1,016 yards before this game, and added thirty yards on what amounted to a day off.

Morrall knew what most outsiders did not—that Csonka has done his running this year on feet swollen by gout. Possibly on this account, the quarterback called on him only nine times.

Chances are Miami could have got the job done without using Csonka at all, considering the way Klick and Morris were operating. The electrifying Morris, who moves so fast he seems to flicker, darted, whirled, and fled for ninety-eight yards to bring his season total to 905. If he can do as well against Baltimore, the Dolphins will be the first team ever with two one-thousand-yard runners.

Klick has been troubled this year because Don Shula, the coach, has used him and Morris alternately. There is no animosity between the players, but Jim never had to share his job with anybody during his undergraduate years at Wyoming or in his five previous seasons as a pro.

Yesterday some of his neighbors in Lincoln Park, N.J., came across the Hudson to see him perform. He gave them a show, making an average of eleven yards on every carry in the first half and winding up with sixty-nine yards on ten rushes for the day. On one play he ripped through the secondary for twenty-six yards, carrying the Giants' Pete Athas piggyback over the last ten.

Then there was Warfield, the little old pattern-maker whose name used to be a household word in the White House. Last season Richard M. Nixon, helping Shula lay out a game plan for the Super Bowl, recommended using Warfield as pass receiver on a down-and-in pattern. Miami got whomped, and this season Warfield has been hurting.

Yesterday he still had discomfort in the arch of one foot, but a damaged ankle had shown improvement. To celebrate, he caught four passes for 132 yards and one touchdown.

This was a game that meant nothing in the league standings, for the Giants were already consigned to third place in their division and the Dolphins' future was assured. Furthermore, the climate had the color and consistency of a blue point on the half-shell, providing a setting of unrelieved dreariness.

Yet the day furnished entertainment of the first order because both teams responded to the spur of pride. Victory over the only unbeaten team in the league would have made this a successful season for the Giants. Except for their errors, their performance was uniformly excellent. It would have been good enough to beat many teams, but not this one proudly resolved to win 'em all.

Ambush at
Fort Duquesne

It's Frenchy to Franco with Five Seconds to Spare

I N T H E raucous streets, Frenchy's Foreign Legion honked at Bradshaw's Brigade, Gerela's Guerrillas hailed Ham's Hussars, and foot soldiers in Franco's Italian Army waved red, white, and green flags. Back in the bowels of Three Rivers Stadium, Frenchy Fuqua's mutton-chop whiskers twitched rapturously. Art Rooney's cigar was limp. The first postseason football game in Pittsburgh history was over, and not since Braddock was ambushed at Fort Duquesne had the town known a day like this.

Forty years ago little Arthur Rooney, 135-pound playing coach of the Majestic Radios, the Hope Harveys, and the James P. Rooneys, paid $2,500 for a franchise in the National Football League. Never in all the cold autumns since then had the Steelers got the whiff of a championship of any kind, and now here they were: Half-champions of the American Conference with a date to play again next Sunday for the conference title and a chance to earn $25,000 a man in the Super Bowl. And of all the 478 games they had played before last Saturday, none was more gaudily theatrical than the 13–7 conquest of the Oakland Raiders that brought them to this plateau.

Five seconds this side of defeat, the victory was accomplished on a busted play in which the Oakland defense performed flawlessly.

With fourth down, ten yards to go, on the Pittsburgh 40-yard line, twenty-two seconds remaining on the clock, Oakland on top by 7–6, and a horde of predators clawing for Terry Bradshaw's eyeballs, the Steelers' scrambling quarterback threw a pass that Oakland's accomplished safety man, Jack Tatum, deflected out of Frenchy Fuqua's reach. The play was designed to gain about eighteen yards—enough to get the ball into field-goal range for Roy Gerela—and Fuqua became the target only because the defense wouldn't let the primary receiver, Barry Pearson, get downfield.

Blocked by Tatum around the Raiders' 35-yard line, the ball flew back about seven yards to Franco Harris. The rookie runner fielded it at his knees and crossed the goal line forty-two yards away with the clock showing five seconds to play.

"We'll take those little crumbs," said Chuck Noll, the Pittsburgh coach. His tone was devout.

The Steelers reached their dressing room in a daze. Fuqua, who had been knocked down in a collision with Tatum, had thought the pass was incomplete. "When I got up I saw Franco about the 5-yard line."

"I didn't see the ball bounce away," Bradshaw said. "I just saw Franco take off. I thought, 'Man! It musta hit him right on the numbers!' I've played football since the second grade and nothing like that ever happened. It'll never happen again. And to think it happened here in Pittsburgh in a playoff!"

"We're putting the play in tomorrow," Noll promised.

Before Fred Swearingen, the referee, ruled the touchdown official he checked with Art McNally, the NFL supervisor of officials, who had watched the televised replay in the press box and confirmed Swearingen's observation that a defensive player (Tatum) had indeed touched the ball and the pass had not gone illegally from Bradshaw to Fuqua to Harris.

Jim Kensil, the league's executive director, hastily denied that the decision had been made in the press box for fear such a precedent would be cited forevermore by coaches and players demanding that officials consult the instant replay before rendering judgments. However, Noll, who had huddled on the field with all the officials and John

Madden, the Raiders' protesting coach, already had reported that the referee had agreed "to check upstairs, I didn't know how."

Heightening the melodrama of the finish was the primeval stodginess of the defensive struggle that preceded it. For fifty-eight minutes the teams played antediluvian football. After a scoreless first half, witnesses were saying, "It took the Steelers forty years to get here, and they're setting the game back eighty." Somewhere in the gray nothingness overhead, Dr. Jock Sutherland must have been watching with a smile of benign approval. When that dour Scot, that rock of conservatism, coached the Steelers he considered the forward pass downright obscene.

Harking back to the days of the Minnesota shift and the flying wedge, the Steelers smothered Oakland's attack so effectively that a 6–0 lead on two field goals by Gerela seemed safe until, with a minute and thirteen seconds left, Ken Stabler slipped around end for a thirty-yard touchdown run and George Blanda's conversion put Oakland in front, 7–6.

Now Chuck Noll remembered that on fourth-and-two on Oakland's 31 in the first half he had ordered a line plunge that failed instead of a placekick by Gerela. The three points he might have got but didn't would have meant a 9–7 lead now. "If I'd had a third leg I would have kicked myself," he confessed.

With a kicker like Gerela around, that would have been another mistake.

Super-Sloppy Football

The Cowboys-Broncos Boo-Boo Bowl

NEW ORLEANS, LA., *January 15, 1978*

FOR ALMOST a dozen years, critics have scoffed at the frenzied bally-
hoo, the hype and the hokum surrounding the annual game for the
championship of the National Football League, contending that nothing this side of Armageddon could justify the buildup. What came to
pass tonight in the roofed showcase called the Louisiana Superdome
ought to shut them up.

Super Bowl XII, won by the Dallas Cowboys from the Denver Broncos, 27–10, was truly something special, an entertainment in a class by
itself: It may be possible to play sloppier football, but not at $30 a copy.
Perhaps the most interesting aspect of the entire production was that
although 76,400 customers paid $2,352,000 at the box office, nobody
is going to be arrested except for a few scalpers and pickpockets.

Seven and a half minutes into the first quarter, two pigeons buzzed
the field of phony grass but the symbolism wasn't clear to witnesses
that early. They needed a little longer to discover what tender pigeons
the Denver forces were, and what a turkey this performance would be
for Craig Morton, the retreaded quarterback who had led the Broncos
to the championship of the American Conference.

Cruelly harried by carnivores named Too Tall Jones, Harvey Martin,
and Randy White, Morton threw four interceptions for a Super Bowl
record, threw another pass that bounced off the lofty wishbone of the
same Mr. Jones and watched the last twenty minutes of play from the
sideline while his understudy, Norris Weese, directed the Broncos'
diaphanous attack.

Morton's misdirected passes established only one record for futile misfeasance.

Ten fumbles by the two teams put another standard in the book, and there were more mental, mechanical, and physical errors, more botched opportunities than some clients get to see in a whole season.

One witness watched serenely, a small, compassionate smile on his face. This was Tom McEwan of Tampa, who saw the Tampa Bay Buccaneers play like this twenty-six weekends before they won the last two games of the 1977 season.

"It is obvious to me," Tom said, "that Denver somehow got the Tampa playbook."

Since the National and American leagues mated and produced two conferences, many of the title matches have left something to be desired. It's not only that the advance billing promises more excitement than humans can produce; the overheated magnitude of the occasion frazzles the performers' nerves and induces errors.

In that respect, this production topped them all. Even the Cowboys, toughened by three previous appearances in the big one, were jittery at the beginning and sinned in uncharacteristic fashion.

On the very first punt of the game, Dallas' Tom Henderson knocked Denver's Rick Upchurch loose from his intellect just as Upchurch was about to catch the ball. The interference cost Dallas fifteen yards, giving Denver possession near midfield, and for the next seven or eight minutes all the action was in Cowboy territory.

Moments after Henderson's misdemeanor, Denver's Bucky Dilts hung a punt high above Tony Hill, who was waiting just a yard from the Dallas end zone. Tony is a rookie, and rookies dream of returning kicks ninety-nine yards for touchdowns. So instead of letting the punt bounce across the goal line for a touchback, Hill tried to catch it, felt it slither through his paws and was lucky to fall on the ball on the 1-yard line.

That helped pin the Cowboys down and create the illusion of a genuine contest.

By the middle of the first quarter, however, the Cowboys had settled down, more or less, and begun to play their game—such as it was.

Statistics for the first quarter underlined the illusory quality of Denver's participation. In that period the Cowboys gained fifty-six yards, thirty-six by rushing, twenty by passing, and scored ten points. The Broncos' eight-yard offense showed five yards gained by rushing, three by passing, and their figure on the scoreboard was 0.

However, once they gained the upper hand over Denver, compassion got the upper hand on the Cowboys. It was obvious that they had the guns to blow the Broncos out of the tub, but when they beat Minnesota for the National Conference title two weeks ago they practiced diligently at squandering chances to score. That experience yielded results tonight; in the first half alone they blew four or five chances.

Efren Herrera, the Mexican sidewinder who usually puts points on the board when he kicks a football from placement, took personal charge of this department.

In his first two appearances he kicked field goals of thirty-five yards and forty-three yards.

On the next three he missed from forty-three yards, thirty-two, and forty-four.

So it came about that the Broncos trailed by only 13–0 at halftime, but it was the most lopsided 13–0 within memory.

Early in the second half the margin became 13–3, then 20–3, and after that nothing mattered.

It is becoming more and more obvious that the Super Bowl needs a new name, a designation the players can live up to. Superficial, maybe? Superfluous?

★ BASEBALL 1962–1981 ★

A Character
and a Constant

Yogi Catches Game 2,000

W
NEW YORK, N.Y., *June 12, 1962*
HEN YOGI BERRA shuffled up to the plate, the game stopped. Jim Honochick, the umpire, called for the ball from Dick Hall, the Baltimore pitcher, handed it to Berra, and produced a new one. Yogi kept the first and lost the second in the right-field seats. In his two thousandth game with the Yankees, his home run was the winning blow.

Two thousand games earlier was the first half of a doubleheader on Sunday, Sept. 22, 1946. Berra caught nine innings against the Philadelphia Athletics and nobody stole on him. He whacked little Jesse Flores for a home run and a single and drove in two runs as the third-place Yankees won, 4–3, for Johnny Neun, the manager pro tem. This was the Yankee batting order that day:

George Stirnweiss, 2b; Tommy Henrich, 1b; Bobby Brown, ss; Joe DiMaggio, cf; Charlie Keller, lf; Bill Johnson, 3b; Johnny Lindell, rf; Berra, and Spud Chandler, p. "Of considerable interest," wrote Harold Rosenthal in the *Herald Tribune*, "was the appearance of several recent Yankee acquisitions. Bobby Brown, Newark's hard-hitting shortstop, made his debut as did Larry Berra, Newark catcher." The next day a "likely looking lad" named Vic Raschi pitched and won his first game for the Yankees.

No need to ask where they all are now. Where was Dick Hall, the Baltimore pitcher, in September 1946? He was approaching his sixteenth birthday in St. Louis. And Jim Honochick? He was a rookie umpire in the Eastern Shore League, having played until midsummer as an outfielder for Baltimore in the International League.

In terms of service to an organization, just what do two thousand games mean? Well, if Johnny Neun, Bucky Harris, Casey Stengel, and Ralph Houk had decided, in their infinite wisdom, to play Yogi at one position all the time, he would by last year have caught more games than any other man who ever wore the tools of ignorance. Because he was employed also as an outfielder, third baseman, and first baseman, he leaves the lifetime catching record to Al Lopez, with 1,918 games.

In the fifteen seasons completed since 1946, the Yankees have won twelve pennants and nine world championships, finished second once and third twice. They have had stars of the first magnitude through those years, DiMaggio and Keller and Henrich, Phil Rizzuto and Mickey Mantle and Roger Maris, Allie Reynolds and Ed Lopat and Whitey Ford.

One constant factor has remained while the others came and went. One was there before Stengel and is there now that Stengel is gone. Nobody can say the Yankees would not have won all those championships without Berra, but the simple fact is that he was there helping with every one, and playing a huge part in the winning.

It is not possible to exaggerate his importance. He has been the keystone, the binder, the adhesive element that has held this team together when everything else changed.

Early in 1947 a visitor was sitting on the Yankees' bench between Bucky Harris and Al Schacht. Berra slouched by on his way to the water cooler. Bucky nudged the visitor and, speaking behind a hand, muttered into his left ear, "A character." At the same moment there was a nudge from the right. "A character," Schacht murmured into that ear.

Actually, Yogi was not yet either a character or a catcher, officially. His name was Larry Berra, not Yogi. Harris was using him as an outfielder and his defensive talents reflected no high polish, either out there or behind the plate.

Later Bill Dickey was to take him in hand to smooth the rough spots from his technique. "Bill is learning me his experiences," Yogi said.

That helped make him a character, and Dickey helped make him a catcher.

To say merely that he became a great one is to underplay his value to the team. In spite of his curious construction, he moved with astonishing agility around the plate. He learned the hitters and he never forgot anything he learned. He could, and still can, con and cosset and calm a harried pitcher who would spit in the manager's eye if he were to walk out. His throwing and running were exceptional, and with a stick in his paws he is pure poetry.

"And," Casey used to say, "he knows what they're thinkin' in the front office."

At first he was so eager to hit that he swung at pitches Wilt Chamberlain couldn't reach. Somebody, memory suggests Birdie Tebbetts, remarked that it would be easy to run Yogi out of the league. "Walk him intentionally four times in a row," he said, "and he'd quit baseball." Today they say that when Yogi discards a bat which he has squeezed dry of hits, it is marked only in a single spot, the fat part which that lovely swing of his brings around to meet the ball again and again.

Over sixteen years Yogi accepted all the hazards and suffered all the catcher's occupational ills—the split fingers and cracked knuckles, the sprains and spavins and bruises. Yet summer after summer he hung in there doing the work of two, sometimes catching doubleheaders when he was hot with fever or aching with flu, catching even while he nursed, of all things, an allergy to the leather mitt.

The Yankees have had many great ones, but no other quite like this one. "Why," the late Rud Rennie protested the first time he saw this rookie up from Newark, "he doesn't even look like a Yankee." Perhaps he didn't then. Today if somebody were to ask what a Yankee looked like, whose image would come to mind?

Vexed Vigilantes

Terry Keeps Giants at Bay for Yankees' 20th Series Win

SAN FRANCISCO, CALIF., *October 18, 1962*

IN THE last World Series game, Mickey Mantle added thirty-four points to his batting average. One single in three chances brought him to .120. He also walked once, whereupon Jack Sanford picked him off first base with admirable celerity.

Nothing could illustrate better the quality of pitching which lent such rich, crunchy goodness to the rounders tournament. The curtain scene, gripping though it was, may have lacked a little of the wild and implausible melodrama that closed the 1960 Series in Pittsburgh, but this was finer baseball and cleaner theater throughout. Stretched out over seven games and thirteen days, it had everything but continuity.

Nevertheless, the Vigilantes were riding the unlittered streets yesterday, thirsting for Whitey Lockman's blood. It's hard to blame the natives. They never had a World Series before and hardly expected to see this one. Having come to believe in miracles, they would have been crushed if their demigods had got clobbered in the final match; to have the decision slip down the drain, 1–0, enraged them.

Even though allowances are made, however, the oral and printed abuse of Lockman is slightly outrageous. The second guess is almost always unfair because it is a judgment made at leisure and influenced by subsequent developments which could not be foreseen at the instant of the first guess. In this case it's doubly scandalous because Lockman was right and his critics are downright wrong-headed.

The issue, of course, was whether the Giants' coach at third base should have let Matty Alou try to score the tying run from first base on Willie Mays' double to right with two out in the ninth inning. The Yankees played the ball cleanly, and it says here the odds were 10 to 1 against Alou. However, even with a fifty-fifty chance, Lockman would have been foolish to send Alou in.

When your team is only one putout this side of extinction, you simply must not run any considerable risk of giving away that last out. If the score were tied and Alou represented the winning run, the gamble could be justified, for the Giants would still be entitled to another turn at bat. That was the situation in 1946 when Country Slaughter ran home from first to win the championship for the Cardinals.

In this case, Willie McCovey was coming to bat. He is a left-handed batter. On his last turn against the right-handed Ralph Terry, he had ripped a monstrous triple into center field for one of San Francisco's four hits.

When he tore into Terry's first pitch with Mays on second and Alou on third, Lockman's decision looked good. McCovey hit that pitch far over the fence, but the wind pushed it foul. He hit the next pitch even better. Luck alone steered it straight into Bobby Richardson's glove instead of a yard to right or left for the ballgame.

Had that drive gone safe, Lockman would be immortalized as the Sage of San Francisco and Ralph Houk would be getting chewed out for not ordering an intentional base on balls for McCovey. That would have been unfair, too, for it was Terry who made the decision to pitch to the big guy.

Before the commotion raised by Mays' hit had subsided, the Yankee manager was on the mound consulting his pitcher. First base was open, and putting a runner on would cost the Yankees nothing because the game and Series would end if Mays scored from second.

Orlando Cepeda, a right-handed hitter, would be up behind McCovey. Though Cepeda had been a terror in the sixth game when he got a double and two singles, they were his only hits of the Series and he had been in a wretched slump for weeks. Against Terry in this game, he had struck out twice and popped up.

"I'd rather pitch to McCovey," Terry said.

"You're pitching the game," Houk told him. "Go ahead."

As Yogi Berra would say in his Left Bank French, Terry had *raison*. With the bases filled, he would have to use extreme caution with Cepeda. If he got behind him in the count, he would have to come in with good pitches, suited to Orlando's educated taste.

So Terry aimed for McCovey's fists—"jamming him" is the trade term. McCovey hit where he was supposed to hit, and the Yankees had their twentieth championship in forty years. When you consider that over most of those years, there were fifteen other clubs after the same prize, then seventeen and now nineteen others, the record makes the Yankees look a mite hoggish. And slightly good.

Incidentally, there'll always be a Willie Mays. Almost invariably after a player had made a noteworthy home run, such as Chuck Hiller's blow with the bases filled in the fourth game, he says, "I was just trying to meet the pitch for a single."

After slicing his double, Willie was asked whether he'd been deliberately aiming for right field.

"No," he said, "I was only trying to hit it out of the park."

Gotham's Urchins

These Second-Season Mets Might Actually Be a Ball Club

NEW YORK, N.Y., *April 22, 1963*

BASES FILLED, two out, Mets leading 3 to 1, and Duke Snider at the plate—the Polo Grounds seemed to rock and shudder. Grown men bawled and beat their bosoms. Women screamed. The treble screech of small fry shivered among the rafters. Dear Diary, might this go on forever?

It couldn't, of course. One victory was glorious. Two straight were fantastic. Three in a row? Why, that would match the longest winning streak in the whole history of this matchless nine, and with the season a mere eleven games old.

The dream died hard. It was only the second inning when the Mets went ahead. They struggled on through the third. The fourth found them still clinging to that two-run lead. They made it through the fifth. Now it was the sixth and the Braves tied the score but with two out. Jay Hook might still escape his third defeat if—oops, wild pitch, two more runs in and Milwaukee on top, 5 to 3.

Rain started to fall. The Mets aren't giants, after all. They are honest, earnest, artless lads who wear knee britches—the short and simple flannels of the poor. May Providence postpone the evil day they rise to mediocrity.

Wait, though. Now it is the home half of the eighth and the rain has stopped. Ed Kranepool leads off, an eighteen-year-old just learning to play this game. He triples. Choo Choo Coleman up. He gets three balls from Ron Piche and Milwaukee's Bobby Bragan, thinking deeply, reluctantly signals the bullpen for Claude Raymond, who throws a fourth ball. Mets on first and third, nobody out.

Charlie Neal slices a double to right. Kranepool scores easily. Coleman is the tying run on third. If Neal can get around, the Mets will be ahead. Ted Schreiber bats for the young shortstop Al Moran and flies to short right. Coleman can run, but he dare not challenge Hank Aaron's arm. One out and the Braves still lead, 5 to 4.

Tim Harkness bats in the pitcher's place. He is a left-handed hitter and first base is open. The right-handed Raymond puts him on, filling the bases for Jim Hickman.

Hickman swings, and it is a high fly to left, curling toward the foul line, arching toward the stands, sailing, sinking—in for a grand slam.

Mets 8, Braves 5—and this is no ballpark. It is a garbage dump, a vast rubbish heap, and play is suspended while groundsmen gather up programs, torn newspapers, paper cups, obsolete fruit.

The Polo Grounds is an ancient ruin with a long and purple history. Excitement is no new commodity in the yard where Christy Mathewson pitched and Buck Ewing swung; where King Carl Hubbell in an All-Star game struck out Babe Ruth, Lou Gehrig, Jimmie Foxx, Al Simmons, and Joe Cronin in a row; where Fred Merkle did not step on second base.

It has known scenes like this before, but not since that October day in 1951 when Bobby Thomson swung for these same left-field seats.

Ron Hunt, whose bat started this whole implausible nonsense last Friday, follows Hickman in the batting order, is brushed by a pitch and goes to first base. Snider grounds out and Frank Thomas flies out. Three more putouts, and the Mets can bring this off.

With Roger Craig now pitching, it shouldn't be impossible. He lost twenty-four games last year, but one thing he has is control. In 233 innings he walked only seventy batters. So now he walks two of the first three he sees. With one out, Frank Bolling comes to the plate. He represents the tying run. The count goes to three balls, two strikes. Bolling meets the last pitch sharply. It goes to Neal at third on one big hop. Neal fires to Hunt for the force at second, Hunt pivots, throws— double play.

Craig turns and starts for the clubhouse in center field. He is joined by Gil Hodges and young Hunt. They do not caper or strut. They just trudge off with half their day's work done. In the stands, fans are holding up a banner fashioned in three sections.

"Win or Lose," it reads, "We Love You."

As for the second game, the fourth against Milwaukee—well, once in their happy lives the Mets swept a series. It was a two-game series last May against Chicago. But a four-game series? Who'd believe it?

Big Poison

Paul Glee Waner, 1903–1965

NEW YORK, N.Y., *September 1, 1965*

PAUL WANER had been one of baseball's finest hitters for a dozen years before a chance remark dropped in the dugout disclosed that he couldn't read the advertisements on the outfield walls. He never had been able to read them from the bench and he hadn't given it a thought, for in his philosophy fences were targets, not literature.

Naturally, steps were taken immediately. With his weak eyes, Paul was batting only about .350. It stood to reason that with corrected vision he'd never be put out. So the Pirates had him fitted with glasses and he gave them a try.

He hated them. For the first time in his life, that thing the pitchers were throwing turned out to be a little thing, a spinning, sharply defined missile no bigger than a baseball. He had always seen it as a fuzzy blob the size of a grapefruit.

Nearsighted millions read about the experiment and chuckled in sympathetic appreciation of his disgust. We in the myopia set see the world as a rather pleasant blur where vaguely outlined objects any distance away appear larger than life, like a street lamp in fog.

The point is, Waner had been whacking that indistinct melon in exact dead center ever since he left the town team in Harrah, Oklahoma.

When Paul Waner died, the obituaries cited the statistical proof of his greatness as a ballplayer, mentioned his election to the Hall of Fame in 1952, and, of course, referred to the nicknames he and his kid brother Lloyd bore in the game—Big Poison and Little Poison.

Both were small men physically but Paul, with a batting average of
.333 for twenty big league seasons, was somewhat more poisonous to
pitchers than Lloyd, who hit .316 for eighteen years. Actually, though,
Paul's nickname was neither a tribute from the pitchers' fraternity nor
a reference to his preference in beverages, appropriate though it would
have been in either case.

"Poison" is Brooklynese for "person." A fan in Ebbets Field was supposed to have complained, "Every time you look up those Waner boys
are on base. It's always the little poison on thoid and the big poison on
foist."

Maybe the quote is apocryphal but the facts support it. Between
them, the brothers made 5,611 hits, about four times as many as a
whole team gets in a season. Since Eve threw the first curve to Adam,
only eight men have made more than three thousand hits. Paul's 3,152
put him ahead of some pretty fair batsmen named Rogers Hornsby, Ted
Williams, Lou Gehrig, and Babe Ruth.

By rights the records should credit Paul with 3,153 hits or else there
should be a separate page in the book for him alone. It would read:
"Most Hits Rejected by Batter Lifetime—1, P. Waner, Boston NL, June
17, 1942."

When the second game of a doubleheader started that day, Waner
had 2,999 hits. He had opened the season with 2,955 and had struggled
through fifty-two games toward the shining goal of three thousand.
In twenty-five games he'd been shut out, but now one more hit would
do it.

With Tommy Holmes a base runner on first, the hit-and-run was on.
Holmes broke for second on the pitch and as Eddie Joost, the Cincinnati shortstop, started over to cover the bag, Paul hit toward the spot
Joost had vacated. Joost slammed on the brakes, spun back, and got his
glove on the ball but couldn't hold it.

In the press box the official scorer lifted a forefinger to indicate a
single, which it was. A roar saluted the three-thousandth hit. Beans
Reardon, the umpire, retrieved the ball and trotted to first base with
the souvenir.

Waner was standing on the bag shaking his head emphatically and shouting, "No, no, no!" at the press box. Reluctantly the scorer reversed his decision. Two days later Paul got number three thousand off Rip Sewell, of Pittsburgh, and this was a clean single to center.

Because his hitting overshadowed everything else, Waner's defensive skill is rarely mentioned, but he was a superior outfielder, one of the swiftest runners in the National League with a wonderful arm. One season he threw out thirty-one base runners to lead the league.

"He had to be a very graceful player," Casey Stengel has said, "because he could slide without breaking the bottle on his hip."

Casey was Waner's manager with the Braves and he knew it was a myth that he enjoyed his nips between games. Most of the tales told of him around the ballparks tell how he might show up somewhat bleary after a night of relaxation, strike out three times. then triple the winning runs home on his fourth trip.

The late Bill Cissell, an American League infielder, spent some time with the Waners and their friends in Sarasota one winter. They had a field baited for doves, but not every shot fired there came out of a 12-gauge. In fact, Bill reported—and he was an excellent jug man himself—sometimes the safest place in the county was out in the field with the birds.

Top of the Mad, Mad World

The Mets Amaze the Fates, Not to Mention the Orioles

QUEENS, N.Y., *October 17, 1969*

"IT HAS all been very interesting," a man said before the game, "but what can they do for an encore?"

"They'll think of something," said another, a true believer. He had been watching the Mets ever since they introduced the pratfall to baseball back in 1962. He had faith.

They thought of something. They thought of the most ridiculous, the most preposterous, the most widely improbable absurdities that ever encumbered a World Series match. And now that the foolishness is ended the New York Mets, those golden-hearted clowns of all creation, stand assured forevermore of their place in baseball mythology.

It happened in Shea Stadium yesterday. Shea Stadium was the name of a playpen that used to stand on Flushing Meadow. Two-legged termites took it down piece by piece immediately after the Mets chopped up the Baltimore Orioles for the fourth successive time and won the championship of this dizzily whirling globe, four games to one.

This is how the fates, laughing fit to split, arranged for the Orioles to snatch a 5–3 defeat from the jaws of a 3–0 victory:

In the sixth inning, Cleon Jones led off for New York against Dave McNally, who had allowed three hits up to that point. Jerry Koosman had allowed only five hits, but three of them had come in the third inning in this order: Pop single by Mark Belanger, two-run homer by McNally, of all people, and a drive struck angrily by Frank Robinson that went screaming clear over skeleton bleachers built for this series beyond the fence in left-center.

It was high time the Mets do something if they were to avoid a return to Baltimore for a sixth and possibly a seventh game. But what? "Let's dig up the old Shinola play," somebody up there suggested.

The Shinola play was introduced to World Series competition in 1957 in Milwaukee. Nippy Jones of the Braves howled that a pitch by the Yankees' Tommy Byrne had struck him on the foot but Augie Donatelli, the umpire, wouldn't believe him until he was shown a smudge of shoe polish on the ball. Thanks to his neat grooming, Jones was awarded first base, he scored the winning run, and Milwaukee won the championship.

Lou Dimuro was Thursday's plate umpire. A skeptic like Donatelli, he had coldly rejected Frank Robinson's claim that a pitch by Koosman in the top of the sixth had struck him. Even when Robinson stalked off the field and held up the game five minutes while he applied ice to his bruised thigh, Dimuro stood his ground, embarrassed but obstinate.

So now in the same inning, the umpire was understandably cool to Jones' claim that he'd been nicked on the toe by a McNally pitch. "Shut up and bat," Dimuro was saying, when here came the Mets' manager, Gil Hodges, carrying the ball which had skidded into the Mets' dugout. It bore the telltale smear.

Waved to first base, Jones cantered home ahead of Donn Clendenon when that tall citizen busted his third home run of the series. Now it was a 3–2 ballgame. What could the Mets think of next?

You wouldn't believe this. They thought of Al Weis. Al Weis has played baseball in the major leagues for seven years and in that space he had hit six home runs. So he led off the seventh inning with his seventh. It gave this .215 hitter an average of .500 for the World Series; it gave the Mets a 3–3 tie. Now what?

Having started it all with his elegantly polished booties, Cleon Jones was elected to signal the closing flourish. Leading off in the eighth, he slugged a double against the wall in center. Then with one out, up stepped Ron Swoboda, the archetypal Met. He looks like L'il Abner; he forgets things; he gets lost; he swings a bat with a wild, impassioned dedication.

Eddie Watt was pitching now. With first base open, prudence advised against giving the muscular Swoboda a pitch he could hit. Watt's first delivery was low and outside. His second was higher and not so wide. Swoboda placed it neatly just inside the left-field line for two bases.

In came the winning run, and nothing else mattered. Swoboda scored the fifth run when the Orioles, beaten and aware of it, butchered a play. In the ninth, Koosman held them off at the pass. The last play of 1969 was a fly to Jones. He caught the ball and dropped to his knees in thanksgiving, but Koosman didn't see that. With the crack of the bat, Jerry Grote had rushed out from behind the plate and flung himself on the pitcher's bosom. When it ended, Koosman was wearing his catcher like prayer beads.

"I Do Not Feel That I Am a Piece of Property"

Curt Flood Resists the Reserve Clause

C URT FLOOD was nineteen years old and had made one hit in the major leagues (a home run) when his telephone rang on Dec. 5 of 1957. The call was from the Cincinnati Reds, advising him that he had been traded to the St. Louis Cardinals.

"I knew ballplayers got traded like horses," he said years later, "but I can't tell you how I felt when it happened to me. I was only nineteen, but I made up my mind then it wouldn't ever happen again."

It happened again last October. The Cardinals traded Flood to Philadelphia. "Maybe I won't go," Curt said. Baseball men laughed. Curt makes something like $90,000 a year playing center field, and less than that painting portraits in his studio in Clayton, Mo. "Unless he's better than Rembrandt," one baseball man said, "he'll play."

It was a beautiful comment, superlatively typical of the executive mind, a pluperfect example of baseball's reaction to unrest down in the slave cabins. "You mean," baseball demands incredulously, "that at these prices they want human rights, too?"

Curtis Charles Flood is a man of character and self-respect. Being black, he is more sensitive than most white players about the institution of slavery as it exists in professional baseball. After the trade he went abroad, and when he returned his mind was made up. He confided his decision to the twenty-four club representatives in the Major League Players Association at their convention in San Juan, Puerto Rico.

He told them it was high time somebody in baseball made a stand for human freedom. He said he was determined to make the stand and he asked their support. The players questioned him closely to make sure this was not merely a ploy to squeeze money out of the Phillies. Then, convinced, they voted unanimously to back him up.

Realizing that if Flood lost his case through poor handling they would all be losers, the players arranged—through their executive director, Marvin Miller—to retain Arthur J. Goldberg, former Secretary of Labor, former Justice of the Supreme Court, former United States Ambassador to the United Nations, and the country's most distinguished authority on labor-management relations.

Baseball's so-called reserve clause, which binds the player to his employer through his professional life, had been under fire before. Never has it been attacked by a team like this.

The system is in deep trouble, and yesterday's action by the baseball commissioner, Bowie Kuhn, did nothing to help it out. Because the news was out that Flood was going to take baseball to court, Kuhn released to the press the following correspondence:

"Dear Mr. Kuhn," Flood wrote on Dec. 24, 1969, "after 12 years in the major leagues I do not feel that I am a piece of property to be bought and sold irrespective of my wishes. I believe that any system that produces that result violates my basic rights as a citizen and is inconsistent with the laws of the United States and of the several states.

"It is my desire to play baseball in 1970, and I am capable of playing. I have received a contract offer from the Philadelphia club, but I believe that I have the right to consider offers from other clubs before making any decisions. I, therefore, request that you make known to all the major league clubs my feelings in this matter, and advise them of my availability for the 1970 season."

Kuhn replied:

"Dear Curt: This will acknowledge your letter of Dec. 24, 1969, which I found on returning to my office yesterday.

"I certainly agree with you that you, as a human being, are not a piece of property to be bought and sold. That is fundamental in our society and I think obvious. However, I cannot see its application to the situation at hand.

"You have entered into a current playing contract with the St. Louis club which has the same assignment provisions as those in your annual major league contracts since 1956. Your present playing contract has been assigned in accordance with its provisions by the St. Louis club to the Philadelphia club. The provisions of the playing contract have been negotiated over the years between the clubs and the players, most recently when the present basic agreement was negotiated two years ago between the clubs and the Players Association.

"If you have any specific objections to the propriety of the assignment I would appreciate your specifying the objections. Under the circumstances, and pending any further information from you, I do not see what action I can take, and cannot comply with your request contained in the second paragraph of your letter.

"I am pleased to see your statement that you desire to play baseball in 1970. I take it this puts to rest any thought, as reported earlier in the press, that you were considering retirement."

Thus the commissioner restates baseball's labor policy: "Run along, sonny, you bother me."

Super Stainless
Classic

The All-Star Game Has That Foamy Feeling

DETROIT, MICH., *July 14, 1971*

I N T H E fourth inning Johnny Bench went to bat for the second time. He had already delivered two runs with a thunderous shot into the upper deck, probably fifty feet above the 415-foot mark in right-center field. He had connected with the second pitch Vida Blue threw him, and his hit was the first ever made by a National League player against Oakland's child prodigy.

Bench has been batting .250 for the Reds this summer, getting his share of hits past the human beings who play third base in his league. Now, though, that monster was out there again, crouched, poised to spring, that fiend he'd been seeing in his dreams ever since October.

In John's dreams, the creature was always suspended horizontally in midair, his outstretched glove spearing a line drive that should have been a World Series double or triple.

Bench swung on a pitch by Jim Palmer. The ball was a hummer to the third baseman's left, smoking toward the outfield on one fierce hop. The creature sprang. The ball was already past him, yet the glove seemed to suck it back. Thrown out by forty feet, Bench flung both hands aloft in surrender.

"Won't you for cryin' out loud gimme a break?" he cried.

Brooks Robinson—for it was indeed he—laughed.

That was the moment of pure beauty in the midsummer exhibition between the pick of the two major leagues. The rest of the time it was the Super Stainless Classic, the sorry exercise in huckstering that baseball has allowed its All-Star Game to become.

Ford Frick was commissioner when the St. Louis beer baron, Gussie Busch, bought the Cardinals and wanted to rename the park Budweiser Stadium. "Knock it off," Frick said. Baseball wasn't holding still for such blatant commercialism.

Today the Gillette Co. runs the election of All-Star players as a gigantic campaign to peddle razor blades and shaving cream. As mementos, the commissioner gives the players Linde Star rings, fake sapphires provided by Union Carbide. The customers—there were 53,559 in Tiger Stadium and some paid scalpers $50 a ticket—are subjected to an unutterably dreary charade by moppets in a "pitch, hit, and throw" competition sponsored by Phillips 66.

Then National Broadcasting Co. takes over from Bowie Kuhn and the umpires, and runs the show for the greater glory of the television sponsors.

During the pre-game discussion of ground rules, prop men pick their way over a tangle of TV cables on the playing field and hang lavaliere microphones on the two managers.

In the fifth inning here, Frank Umont, the plate umpire, interrupted the action to order Pete Rose and Ron Santo down off the top step of the Nationals' dugout. "You've gotta be kidding," they said, for a stranger in shirt sleeves was squatting in the playing area at a corner of the Americans' dugout. A TV director. Tardily, Umont waved him away, but the guy was wool-gathering and didn't notice until the Americans' trainer explained that baseball rules older than the commissioner allowed only the manager and trainer on the bench without a uniform.

An inning later, the showman and an accomplice got out of there, but it was later still before another space cadet wearing a headset was ousted from the Nationals' dugout. He finished the game squatting on the playing field beyond the bench, ignored by Umont.

It's an exhibition, a show, an opportunity for the underprivileged clientele in an American League town to enjoy Willie Mays and Hank Aaron. But it isn't baseball because that's not how the game is played.

There was every evidence that Detroit was enjoying all the muscle-bulging that led to the first American League victory in nine years. Vida Blue, the winning pitcher, was twelve years old the last time the Americans made it. Home runs were the agency then, too, but none had the velocity of Reggie Jackson's blast here. It was taking off for Windsor, Ontario, when it smashed against the light tower on the right-field roof, approximately ten stories high.

"Hardest I ever saw," said Al Kaline, who has played here eighteen years. "I'm only sorry it hit something."

Starting with Ted Williams in 1939, only eight players have hit fair balls out of this park. Except for the light standard, Reggie would be the first to hit one out of the country.

The Man Who
Signed the Midget

Robert O. Fishel, Baseball's Publicity Stuntman

NEW YORK, N.Y., *January 21, 1972*

T HE MAN who signed the midget is about to be stuffed and mounted "for long and meritorious service to baseball." After twenty-six years, many good deeds and an occasional venial sin as a baseball man, Robert Oscar Fishel, vice president and public-relations director of the Yankees, has been tapped by the New York baseball writers for the Bill Slocum Award and will receive same at their annual hog-killing.

If the writers had drawn a seine from Pelham Bay Park to the Battery, they couldn't have caught a happier choice. Nor could they have found a talent scout with a higher batting average. Since he got into the game in 1946, Bob Fishel has signed two individuals to baseball contracts—Eddie Gaedel, the greatest midget ever to play in the major leagues, and Harry Brecheen, a crafty and gifted pitcher who became a brilliant coach of pitchers. Thus the Fishel batting average stands at 1.000.

Fishel is not a tall man, and he specialized in signing players of somewhat less than average stature. When he got Brecheen to put his name on a contract as player-coach with the St. Louis Browns of 1953—Bob did the business because all other club officials were away in training camp—Harry was a scrawny 158 pounds. Gaedel weighed 65 pounds and stood three-foot-seven.

The Gaedel caper brightened the season of 1951. Since then, a whole hairy generation has learned to read, perhaps without ever hearing how Bill Veeck traduced, debauched, and desecrated the national game and increased the Browns' attendance from 247,131 to 518,796—more than they had drawn the year they won their only pennant.

Fishel and Veeck had formed a warm friendship in 1946 when, as account executive for a Cleveland advertising agency, Bob put together a radio network for the Indians, whom Veeck had just bought. When Veeck, impelled by a death wish, sold the Indians and bought the Browns, Fishel went along.

"Many critics," John Lardner wrote at the time, "were surprised to know that the Browns could be bought, because they didn't know the Browns were owned."

They soon learned. With the unmitigated Veeck calling the shots, bombs burst in air, beer flowed, bands played, and the Browns lost and lost and lost. Veeck dreamed up a special promotion as a birthday celebration for Falstaff Brewery, the team's radio sponsor. "I'll do something so spectacular it'll get you national publicity," he promised the beer people.

He had no idea what he was going to do, but that never deterred William O. Veeck. He asked a booking agent to deliver a midget for the birthday party, a Sunday when the Detroit Tigers would be in St. Louis for a doubleheader.

"The agent kept trying to send us dwarfs," Fishel recalls now, "grotesque gnomes you couldn't present in a baseball uniform. Veeck held out for his midget and we finally got Eddie Gaedel, a nice-looking little guy. The uniform was no problem. The seven-year-old son of Bill DeWitt, our vice president, had one hanging in the clubhouse. We swiped it and had the number $1/8$ sewn on the back."

In their first interview, Veeck handed the midget a toy bat and had him crouch low. The strike zone is measured from just above the batter's knees to his armpits "when he assumes his natural stance." Since Gaedel was going to bat only once in his life, his natural stance could be whatever Veeck said it was.

"His strike zone was just visible to the naked eye," Veeck relates in his memoirs. "I picked up a ruler and measured it for posterity. It was 1½ inches."

They hid Eddie out in a hotel a few blocks from the ballpark. Fishel drove his old Packard to a nearby street intersection, parked, and the waiting Gaedel climbed in and signed two standard player contracts for $15,400 a season, or $100 a game. One contract was mailed on Friday to the American League office, where it wouldn't be scrutinized until Monday. The other was entrusted to Zack Taylor, the Browns' manager, in case of resistance from the umpire.

By the time the great day arrived, Gaedel had begun to feel like a big league star. Though he had been warned to stay in that crouch and draw a base on balls, he was striding about swinging his toy bat with authority. "We were all terrified," says Fishel, who had smuggled Eddie into the park.

Before the first game, a seven-foot birthday cake was wheeled out, appropriate greetings extended to the sponsor, and the tiny Brownie popped out of the cake. "I should have been fired right then," Fishel remembers. "I was so nervous I forgot to alert the photographers to stay around. By the time the second game started, only the United Press cameraman was still around."

Gaedel led off in the second game as a pinch batter. "What the hell!" said Ed Hurley, the plate umpire, but Taylor showed him the signed contract and the roster of players.

Bob Swift, the Detroit catcher, got down on his knees to offer Bob Cain, his pitcher, some sort of target. Weak with laughter, Cain couldn't find the strike zone even though Gaedel stood almost erect. The midget walked and gave place to a pinch runner, who was left on base. The Browns lost, 6–2.

Like Old Times, Sort Of

Yankees–Red Sox Rivalry Is Life Blood of the Game

BRONX, N.Y., *September 15, 1972*

THIS WAS how it used to be when excitement was New York's daily bread. There was a time when the town wouldn't have seemed the same without the Yankees and Red Sox at the top of the league, going for the jugular.

Ralph Houk would remember Sept. 26, 1949. In Yankee Stadium that day, Johnny Pesky slid home on a squeeze play, Willie Grieve called him safe, and Boston took over first place with one week to go. Houk, the Yankees' catcher, was sure he had tagged Pesky out and he told Grieve so in the cool, measured accents of a homicidal maniac. Frothing delicately at the lips, Casey Stengel, the Yankees' manager, bumped bellies with the umpire. Joe Page, the Yankees' great relief pitcher, hurled his glove away in a fashion tending to incite to riot. Nevertheless, the Red Sox left town that Sunday night with a one-game lead.

They brought it back six days later, needing one victory in their last two games. On Saturday Johnny Lindell's home run won the game and Page's relief pitching kept it won. John Lindell was known to take a drink now and then; Page was known to take two. In the press room below decks, the baseball scholar Garry Schumacher lifted a glass. "What I liked about this game," he said, "the rogues win it."

On Sunday the Yankees' Vic Raschi protected a 1–0 lead for eight innings. In their last turn at bat, the Yankees scored four runs. In theirs, the Red Sox got three. There had been 72 recorded injuries on the Yankee team that year. When Tommy Henrich caught a foul for the season's last putout, Bill Dickey, a coach, sprang from the bench and split his head on the dugout roof. No. 73.

It was in Boston that the 1948 Yankees had lost the pennant and their manager, Bucky Harris. They were back in the Bronx for a double-header on Sept. 28, 1951, with the Yankees two games away from another championship. With two Red Sox out in the ninth inning of the first game, Allie Reynolds had an 8–0 lead and his second no-hitter of the season. But the man at bat was Ted Williams.

Williams hit a towering foul behind the plate. Yogi Berra circled under the ball, lunged for it, and missed. Yogi wanted to die, but Reynolds helped him to his feet, patted his bottom, and went back to the mound. Williams hit another foul, a twister toward the first base side. Chasing it blindly, Berra was a step from the dugout. "Plenty of room!" Tom Henrich bawled. Yogi clutched the ball and Reynolds clutched Yogi. While the pitcher savored his second no-hitter, the Yankees won the second game and the pennant.

That's how it used to be. There was a time when you thought it would always be that way. Then came a time when it wasn't that way at all. One year the Red Sox won a pennant but no excitement rubbed off on the Yankees, who were ninth. For eight years nothing that was good rubbed off on the Yankees.

Now, at long last, it seemed like old times. The Red Sox were in town with a half-game lead in the American League East, a half-game over the Yankees and Baltimore. To be sure, in these days of divisional play a pennant race is a race for only half a pennant, but such as it is, this is the only race the Yankees have enjoyed in eight years.

At the end of a showery day, the crowd was under sixteen thousand but the Beautiful People were there. Mrs. Charles Shipman Payson, a lifelong National League fan who married a Red Sox fan before she brought the New York Mets into the world, sat near the Boston dugout and her husband wore his old Red Sox cap. In an anguish of divided loyalties, M. Donald Grant split away from his boss and sat on the Yankees' side as a proper New Yorker should. Bowie Kühn, the supreme being of baseball, sat downstairs robed in majesty. Pete Rozelle, supreme being of professional football, sat upstairs with Lee MacPhail, the Yankees' supreme being once removed. In a gathering of such brilliance, only a great game could have shone.

This one was shiny only in the early stages. Rob Gardner, who pitched for the Mets one summer but repented, gave the Yankees four perfect innings, though three of his pitches in the fourth were struck with cruel ferocity. Tommy Harper hit one into the bleachers but Roy White flung himself halfway over the wall and picked off the home run. A line drive by Luis Aparicio was caught on the dead run by Bobby Murcer. Carl Yastrzemski smashed a putout to deepest left.

Getting nowhere with this heavy artillery, the Sox brought out pop-guns in the fifth. They bunted, they chopped, they poked at the ball, and got four runs with an attack that sent only one hit skipping through the infield. With large Lynn McGlothen throwing hard for Boston, subsequent developments were of no consequence.

In his office, Ralph Houk set fire to a ten-inch cigar. His troops had won four straight games and lost the one that would have put them in first place. The manager was stained, sweaty, and probably tired, but calm. He spoke highly of Gardner and McGlothen. He said he was delighted with the Yankees' position, a game and a half out with the Orioles coming in for three games. Somebody said he seemed oddly cheerful in defeat, and Houk did a double take.

"Should I lie down and cry with Baltimore coming in in two days?" he said. "Because we lost a ballgame? I never heard of anybody winning them all. I hope my players don't lie down and cry."

"I don't think they will, Ralph," a man said.

The Company Way

The Players vs. the Commissioner's Office

W NEW YORK, N.Y., February 23, 1973
HATEVER GAINS are achieved, or damage done, in the current contract dispute between the baseball players and the men who own them, there has already been at least one result. Any misconceptions about the role of the commissioner that may have lingered in the minds of fans have been eliminated. On two or three occasions since the haggling began, Bowie Kuhn has abandoned the pretense of neutrality and has issued press releases presenting the owners' side to the public. No longer can there be any illusion that the commissioner's office is a court of last appeal or its occupant an impartial magistrate or a house dick riding herd on the bosses to protect the players from exploitation. From here out everyone must accept Kuhn for what he has been ever since he was hired—his employers' mouthpiece, a front man, a figurehead.

During the owners' December convention in Honolulu, Kuhn called a press conference to publicize modifications the bosses had offered to make in the reserve system that gives them ownership of their employees. Although he was aware that the players already had rejected the offer as inadequate, he called it a "spectacular break-through," "historic."

Marvin Miller, executive director of the Players Association, was in the Bahamas at the time and was given ten minutes' notice of Kuhn's announcement. When Miller accused Kuhn of violating an agreement not to argue the dispute in the press, Kuhn replied that the league presidents, Chub Feeney and Joe Cronin, and John Gaherin, the owners' representative in labor talks, had assured him there was no such agreement. He did not say in so many words that Miller and Dick Moss, the players' counsel, and Tom Seaver and Joe Torre were lying when they said there was an agreement.

More recently, Kuhn took it upon himself to issue another statement accusing Miller of trying to mislead the players, the public, and the owners. This time he conceded out loud that he was on the owners' side.

Not that the players needed to hear this admission from him. In 1968, when the owners replaced William D. Eckert with their own lawyer, not one living soul confused the new commissioner with the first commissioner, Kenesaw Mountain Landis. From that day forward, everybody realized, the game would be played the company way. That is why the players fought for and won impartial arbitration of grievances, bypassing the commissioner.

The office of commissioner was created, and Judge Landis lured from the Federal bench to fill it, in order to restore public confidence in baseball after the crooked World Series of 1919. Fifteen of the sixteen frightened owners pledged themselves to acknowledge the commissioner's supreme authority without question or complaint. (Only Phil Ball, owner of the St. Louis Browns, refused and fought Landis as long as Ball lived.)

Landis was a tyrant, and the player's best friend. He told the men who paid his salary how they must behave and he threw the book at any who tried to cheat. When he decided a player had been kept down on the farm too long or otherwise treated unfairly, he declared him a free agent entitled to sell his services to the highest bidder. In a single ruling he would free as many as one hundred farmhands of the Detroit Tigers or St. Louis Cardinals. Players felt no need of a union or a lawyer or agent because the commissioner's door was always open and they were confident he would give them a square shake.

Happy Chandler, who succeeded Landis, posed as the player's friend, too, but he was a posturing politician who sang in public without due process. Once he was called upon to adjudicate a quarrel between a club owner and a man in uniform. He fearlessly threw the man in uniform out of baseball for a year.

Happy left office for reasons of health; that is, the owners got sick of him and moved up Ford Frick from the presidency of the National League. Ford didn't regard the owners as rascals who had to be watched. As he saw it, they were responsible men with the right to make their own rules and it was his job to enforce the rules. He was capable and honest, and farsighted by comparison with his employers, but there were times when a firmer hand at the top would have benefited baseball.

Spike Eckert, the fourth commissioner, was an invisible presence who barely kept the swivel chair warm. The owners played two dirty tricks on him, in 1965 when they hired him and in 1968 when they fired him.

By this time the owners had a fairly clear idea of what they wanted in a commissioner and were dead sure what they didn't want. What they didn't want most was impartiality, so they chose the lawyer who had acted for them in such matters as the sack of Milwaukee.

They have not been disappointed. There has never been a commissioner who stood more erect, wore better clothes, or kept his shoes more meticulously polished than Bowie Kuhn.

The Game They
Invented for Willie

Say Hey But Never Say Sorry

WHEN WILLIE got the hit, Ray Sadecki and Harry Parker were watching on television in the clubhouse of the New York Mets. For a moment there was silence. Then Sadecki, who had pitched an inning and one-third, turned to Parker, who had pitched one inning. "He had to get a hit," Sadecki said. "This game was invented for Willie Mays a hundred years ago."

It was the longest day in the long, long history of World Series competition, and for Willie Mays it was eternity. It was the second match in the struggle with the Oakland A's for the baseball championship of creation. It was the nineteenth such game for Willie in a span of twenty-two years. In the forty-third year of his life, this may have been the final bow for the most exciting player of his time. So he lost the game in the ninth inning, won it in the twelfth, came perilously close to losing it again—and walked away from disaster grinning.

Never another like him. Never in this world.

"Yesterday," a man told him, "you said you were going to let the kids win it the rest of the way. What do you say about the old folks now?"

Willie took a sip from a can of Coke. He lounged on a platform behind a microphone, one leg slung over a television receiving set. His jaw worked rhythmically on a cud of gum.

"What old folks you talkin' about?" he asked.

Strictly speaking, Willie never lost the game and never won it. It only seemed that way. When the Mets had the decision in hand, 6–4, in the last of the ninth, Mays fell down chasing a drive by Deron Johnson and the two-base hit that resulted started a rally that tied the score.

Willie had gone into the game as a pinch runner and had fallen down rounding second, but that had been only an embarrassment without effect on the score. For the most spectacular outfielder of an era, though, that pratfall in center was catastrophic.

"I didn't see the ball," he said, and he wasn't the only one dazzled in the sun field of Oakland-Alameda County Stadium. "I tried to dive for it the last second. We had a two-run lead and I shoulda played it safe."

His chance for redemption came in the twelfth with the score still tied, two out and two Mets on the bases. The game had already gone on longer than any World Series match before, longer than the one between the Cubs and Tigers that consumed three hours twenty-eight minutes in 1945.

Rollie Fingers, fifth of the six pitchers who worked for Oakland, threw a strike and Willie slashed at it, missing. Fingers threw another and Willie slapped it straight back, a bounder that hopped high over the pitcher's head and skipped on into center field, sending Bud Harrelson home with the run that put New York ahead.

"I think it was a fastball, up," Willie said. "I'd seen Fingers a lot on television and he likes to work inside and outside, up and down. Yesterday was the test. He threw me a fastball, then gave me a breaking pitch and came back with a fastball, so I knew he'd feed me 80 percent fastballs."

Waxed mustache twitching angrily, Fingers flipped his glove away in disgust. One play later the Oakland manager, Dick Williams, sent Fingers away, too, but more in sorrow than in anger. By that time Cleon Jones had singled to load the bases, and errors soon would let in three more runs.

With New York in front, 10–6, Reggie Jackson opened the rebuttal. He drove a mighty shot high and deep toward the wall in center. Willie went back to the fence, set himself, and saw the ball drop in front of him.

"I saw it," he said afterward, "and in a close game I might have had a chance on it, but we had a four-run lead then and I didn't want to kill myself because we got a lot more games to play."

"But Willie," a man said, "you fell down in center field. What happened out there?"

"Two balls come out there," he said. "That's most of it." His voice dropped, took on a comforting tone. "You've seen me play enough. I wasn't out there long today. You know when I play regular. . . . But I'm not a player that makes excuses."

Excuses? Some of those who heard him could remember the catch he made off Cleveland's Vic Wertz in the World Series of 1954, the time he ran down Carl Furillo's drive, spun completely around, and threw out Billy Cox at the plate, the impossible chance he grabbed off Roberto Clemente of Pittsburgh. To be sure, this time Jackson scored and the A's went on to fill the bases. But excuses? Not for Willie, ever.

Henry's Finest Hour—
Bowie's, Too

Aaron Ties Ruth's H.R. Record;
Kuhn Minds the Game's Real Business

CINCINNATI, OHIO, *April 5, 1974*

T HE ONLY way it could have been better would have been for Henry to hit the very first pitch, the one thrown by Gerald Ford.

Of all the contributions Hank Aaron has made to baseball in twenty blameless years, of all his accomplishments as a player and his acts of graciousness, generosity, and loyalty as a person, none was half so valuable as his achievement of yesterday. It isn't only that his 714th home run matched a record that for more than forty years was considered beyond human reach, and it isn't particularly important that this courteous, modest man has at last overtaken Babe Ruth's roistering ghost. What really counts is that when Henry laid the wood on Jack Billingham's fastball, he struck a blow for the integrity of the game and for public faith in the game.

With one stroke he canceled schemes to cheapen his pursuit of the record by making it a carnival attraction staged for the box office alone, and he rendered moot two months of wrangling between the money-changers and the Protectors of the Faith.

Standard-bearer in the latter camp was Bowie Kuhn, whose rare exercise of authority as baseball commissioner brought about Aaron's presence in the lineup. When the game's upright scoutmaster notified the Atlanta Braves that he expected Aaron to play two of three of the team's early games, he brought back to memory an observation made some years ago by the late Tom Meany as toastmaster at a sports dinner in Toots Shor's.

"Ford Frick just reached for the rye bottle," Tom announced between introductions. "It's his first positive move in four years."

This is the sixth season in office for Frick's successor-once-removed, and nothing he did in the first five years was anywhere near as important as his action in this matter. Bill Bartholomay, the Braves' president, meant to keep Aaron on the bench through the first three games in Cincinnati in the hope that crowds would fill the Atlanta park to see Henry go after Ruth's record in eleven-game home stand that opens Monday night.

Kuhn realized that in the view of most fans, leaving the team's cleanup hitter out of the batting order would be tantamount to dumping the games in Cincinnati. He explained to Bartholomay what self-interest should have told the Braves' owner, that it is imperative that every team present its strongest lineup every day in an honest effort to win, and that the customers must believe the strongest lineup is being used for that purpose.

When Bartholomay persisted in his determination to dragoon the living Aaron and the dead Ruth as shills to sell tickets in Atlanta, the commissioner laid down the law. With a man like Henry swinging for him, that's all he had to do.

Thanks to Mrs. Herbert Aaron's muscular son, 2:40 P.M., April 4, 1974, will stand until further notice as Bowie Kuhn's finest hour. That was the time of day when Henry hit the ball, and although his 715th home run will mean more to him because it will advance him into a class all by himself, it was his finest hour, too.

To be sure, he didn't realize that beforehand. While the controversy that Bartholomay started was going on, Henry said some foolish things. He talked about protecting the Atlanta box office and about the rights of Atlanta's dwindling body of customers. He said it didn't matter whether he played or not because the Braves weren't going anywhere this year.

When they said, "Suppose the commissioner orders the Braves

to play you," he said that in that event he guessed the commissioner would have to make out Cincinnati's batting order, too. This smart-aleck line must have been fed to him, for Henry isn't a smart aleck.

Had he given it any thought he would have realized that there was no need for Kuhn to worry about the Cincinnati batting order because nobody in the Reds' organization was playing tricks for box-office pur-poses. Kuhn knew he could rely on Sparky Anderson to start the team he considered most likely to win. If he could have placed the same reliance in the Braves' brass, he would never have set a precedent by pre-empting the manager's responsibility.

As it turned out, there was nothing contrived about the locale or the timing of the event. It happened in the first inning on Henry's first time at bat and the hit produced the first runs of the season.

It was witnessed by a standing-room-only crowd of 52,154 who weren't lured in by Aaron but rather by the local tradition that dictates that every ambulatory citizen of Cincinnati must attend the opening game even if he doesn't show up again all summer. It wasn't even post-poned till tomorrow, when the box office could use a special attraction and the game will be on national television.

The way Henry did it removed all taint of commercialism. For this day, at least, the business of baseball made way for sport.

The Terrible-
Tempered Mr. Grove

Robert Moses "Lefty" Grove, 1900–1975

LEFTY GROVE was a pitcher who, in the classic words of Bugs Baer, "could throw a lamb chop past a wolf." One day in Yankee Stadium he threw them past three wolves named Babe Ruth, Lou Gehrig, and Bob Meusel. The Philadelphia Athletics were leading, 1–0, when Mark Koenig led off the Yankees' ninth inning with a triple. Grove threw three pitches to Ruth, three to Gehrig, and three to Meusel, all strikes. Meusel hit one of them foul. Another time Grove relieved Jack Quinn with the bases full of Yankees. That day it required ten pitches to strike out Ruth, Gehrig, and Tony Lazzeri, who hit two fouls. In still another game he relieved Roy Mahaffey in Chicago with runners on second and third and nobody out. Again he struck out the side on ten pitches. When Don Honig's book *Baseball When the Grass Was Real* comes out, it will include George Pipgras' account of batting against Walter Johnson for the first time. He took two strikes, stepped out of the box and said to Muddy Ruel, Johnson's catcher, "Muddy, I never saw those pitches."

"Don't let it worry you," Muddy said. "He's thrown a few that Cobb and Speaker are still looking for."

Grove's fastball was like that, but he didn't have Johnson's comforting control. (One season when Johnson won thirty-four games he gave up only thirty-eight bases on balls; batters could oppose this gentleman confident that they wouldn't be hit in the head by accident or design.) Along with his blinding swift, Grove had the quality that Uncle Wilbert Robinson described as "pleasingly wild."

"But Groves wasn't a pitcher in those days," Connie Mack once said. "He was a thrower until after we sold him to Boston and he hurt his arm. Then he learned to pitch, and he got so he just knew, somehow, when the batter was going to swing."

It was typical of Connie Mack that he could pay an all-time record of $100,600 for a man—$600 more than the Yankees gave the Red Sox for Ruth—manage the guy for nine years, win three pennants and two world championships with him, and never learn to pronounce his name. To Connie, Lefty was always "Groves," Lou Boudreau was "Mr. Bordeer," and Zeke Bonura and Babe Barna were both "Bernair."

Robert Moses Grove was a tall, genial gentleman of seventy-five with a head of lustrous white hair who loved to sit around at baseball gatherings cutting up old touches. Lefty Grove, who threw bullets past Ruth and Gehrig and the rest, stood six-foot-three and wore an expression of sulky anger stuck on top of a long, thin neck.

He was a fierce competitor who made little effort to subdue a hair-trigger temper. His natural speed had dazzled and overpowered minor league hitters, and he wasn't accustomed to adversity when he got to the American League. When things went bad he raged blindly, blaming anybody who was handy.

One team that drove him wild was the Washington Senators. Before reaching the majors he had worked against them in an exhibition game. He was wild and they combed him over without mercy. When Clark Griffith heard about his old friend Connie paying all that money for Grove he said it would be a cold day in August before that busher ever beat his club, or words to that effect. Chances are some thoughtful soul relayed the remark to Grove. At any rate, the Senators whipped him the first seventeen times he worked against them.

Lefty threw his most memorable tantrum in St. Louis on August 23, 1931. He had won sixteen straight, tying the American League record shared by Smoky Joe Wood and Walter Johnson, and was going for his seventeenth against the tractable St. Louis Browns. While Dick

Coffman was pitching a shutout, Goose Goslin got a bloop single off Grove and ran home when Jimmy Moore, a substitute for the injured Al Simmons in left field, misjudged an ordinary liner by Jack Burns. Beaten, 1–0, Grove took the visitors' clubhouse apart locker by locker, cursing Moore, Coffman, Goslin, Burns, and especially Simmons, who was home in Milwaukee consulting his doctor.

The press found Grove surly and laconic and put him away as a grouch, although it wouldn't have been hard to discover what made him the way he was. A product of the bituminous fields of the western Maryland mountains, he had little experience with strangers and no exposure to social graces. People who had more schooling than he or had traveled more widely made him uneasy. Retreating into a shell, he became one of the great lobby-sitters of his time, a graven image shrouded in cigar smoke.

On the mound he was poetry. He would rock back until the knuckles of his left hand almost brushed the earth behind him, then come up and over with the perfect follow-through. He was the only three-hundred-game winner between Grover Alexander and Warren Spahn, a span of thirty-seven years. He had the lowest earned-run average in the league nine different years, and nobody else ever did that more than five times. If the old records can be trusted, Alexander, Christy Mathewson, Johnson, and Sandy Koufax each won five ERA titles. Some men would say these were the best pitchers that ever lived. Are the records trying to tell us Old Man Mose was twice as good as any of them?

Grove held at least one record that doesn't appear in the books. In 1920 Martinsburg, West Virginia, got a franchise in the Blue Ridge League and hired Grove at $125 a month. Martinsburg had no ballparks but the team opened on the road and a little jerrybuilt grandstand was flung up before the first home game. There was no money for a fence, however, so Grove was sold to Jack Dunn's Baltimore team for $3,000. That makes Old Mose the only player ever traded for an outfield fence.

The Men Who
Run Baseball

Owners, Players, and the Ties That Bind

"**B**ASEBALL MUST be a great game," a wise man wrote many years
NEW YORK, N.Y., *October 26, 1975*
ago. "It survives the men who run it." The men who were running baseball then are all gone today, but the breed is not diminished. Somehow
the game continues to attract a familiar type—upright, God-fearing
men, more or less law-abiding, with few noticeable flaws except self-
ishness, arrogance, insensitivity, and bullheaded obstinacy.

It is a pity so few of the men who own baseball attended the World
Series. They probably would have enjoyed it and they might have
learned something about the product they have for sale. It is a measure
of their dedication to the sport that most of them found something
else to do.

Still, it would be a mistake to conclude that they are not dedicated
men. They are piously dedicated to the status quo, and never is this
more evident than when they dabble in an exercise which they refer
to as "collective bargaining." This is a relatively new term in their
vocabulary, which they learned to use in testifying before judges,
Congressional committees, and similar audiences. "These are matters
for collective bargaining," says Bowie Kuhn, their hired mouthpiece,
when authorities inquire into the reserve system, blacklists, boycotts,
and other practices of questionable legality.

Then their representatives meet with the players' representatives to discuss the reserve system, blacklists, and boycotts. They bring no ideas to these meetings, make no proposals, suggestions, or counter-proposals. When the players have made their pitch, the owners say, "We like things the way they are." Suggest that this performance doesn't fit the dictionary definition of collective bargaining, and they are aggrieved. "We listened, didn't we?" they say.

This pattern has been observed in the five "collective bargaining" sessions held this year on the pension plan and the basic agreement covering working conditions, both of which expire before the 1976 season opens. Naturally, no progress has been made, but Nov. 21 will bring a test case with a direct bearing on some of the issues.

Grievances filed by Andy Messersmith of the Los Angeles Dodgers and Dave McNally of Montreal come up for arbitration on that date. They go directly to the heart of the reserve system.

Messersmith, a pitcher who has been a twenty-game winner in both leagues, and McNally, who didn't know at the time that he had left his future behind in Baltimore, declined to sign contracts last spring and their employers exercised the option of renewing their contracts uni-laterally for the season of 1975. Now that the season is over, the players are asking Peter Seitz, the arbitrator, to declare them free agents.

The standard one-year player contract always gives the owner an option on the man's services for another year. If they don't agree on a new contract—containing an option for still another year—the employer has the right to renew the expired contract "for a period of one year on the same terms." When a player in the National Foot-ball League has completed his option year he becomes a free agent, although the NFL has other rules that limit his freedom. The baseball people have never recognized this escape hatch. Their position is that "on the same terms" means "with another one-year option."

This dubious contention has not been tested in any formal pro-ceeding. Several players have started down this route but they always turned off this side of a showdown. They refused to sign because they didn't like the terms offered, and if they were stubborn long enough, they finally got what they wanted. Sparky Lyle, for example, played to the last day of the season before the Yankees came through and signed him for the year that was ending and a year to come.

With McNally and Messersmith there is more than money involved. Traded from Baltimore where he had been a twenty-game winner four times, McNally couldn't win in Montreal and left the club. He finished the season on the disqualified list. He doesn't expect to play again and he isn't asking for anything. He is simply saying: "I accepted disqualification for this year. You cannot make it for life." The Expos could make his case moot by giving him his release.

Messersmith wanted a no-trade clause in his contract. "Andy," the Dodgers told him, "we wouldn't dream of trading you but we can't make it official by putting it in your contract because that would set a bad precedent. All the fellows would want a no-trade contract."

Messersmith thought about that. The longer he thought, the more it sounded like an employer saying: "Andy, you're worth $100,000 but we can't pay you what you're worth because if we did, all the others would want the same."

So he didn't sign. He has now fulfilled all the terms of the last contract he did sign. In any business in the world outside of professional team sports, he would be free to work where he pleased. Does a contract he never signed renew itself annually as long as he lives? That wouldn't be a contract. It would be a set of leg irons.

Celluloid Series

67 Innings in 30 Flickering Minutes

NEW YORK, N.Y., *January 11, 1976*
I T TOOK the Cincinnati Reds sixty-seven innings of sweaty effort over a span of twelve days to beat the Boston Red Sox last October, four games to three, for the baseball championship of the United States. By putting Jack the Ripper to work in the cutting room, Major League Baseball Films has achieved the same results in thirty minutes. It is no knock on the movie to say that the original production was a better show than the celluloid version. The 1975 World Series transcended the art of David Wark Griffith, Federico Fellini, and Ingmar Bergman. With that kind of material, filmed highlights of the competition should be the best production of its kind since Lew Fonseca started recording these events for the magic lantern long ago. It is.

Not that it is without flaw. When the film had its premiere Friday in the offices of the baseball commissioner, the audience spotted a few minor mistakes, like a dubbed-in shot of Cincinnati's Alex Grammas in the coach's box in Boston wearing his white home uniform. But there were errors on the field, too, eight of them.

Appropriately, because it remains the most happily debated incident in the series, the opening shot shows the bunt by the Reds' Ed Armbrister and his collision with Carlton Fisk, the Boston catcher, who is shown an instant later screaming "Interference!" through a massive cud of eating tobacco. The play put César Gerónimo in position to score the winning run in the ten-inning third game, and brought a death threat to Larry Barnett, the umpire who rejected Fisk's claim that he had been illegally impeded trying to field the bunt.

For the record, it looked like interference last Oct. 14 and looks like interference on the film. Though the hierarchy closed ranks to support the umpire, the rule book still says that it is interference when the batter or runner "fails to avoid a fielder who is attempting to field a batted ball."

After that opening shot, the film goes back to the beginning and skims the high spots game by game. There are wonderful pictures of the whirling dervish delivery of "Louise" Tiant, as Joe Garagiola identifies Boston's winning pitcher in the first game. Louise, Joe observes on the sound track, is all elbows, fingernails, and kneecaps, and no matter where you sit in Fenway Park there'll be a moment when he looks you straight in the eye.

Equally captivating is a shot of Tiant's father laughing while his bearded son feels his way around the bases like a blind man deserted by his seeing-eye dog and totters home with the first run of the series.

The managers and some players wore battery-powered microphones under their shirts, and there were recorders in each dugout to pick up conversation. Thus the film audience hears what Sparky Anderson and Darrell Johnson have to say to relief pitchers—usually it's "men on first and second nobody out let's go"—and the sound track delivers an expurgated version of Johnson's remarks immediately after the Armbrister bunt.

In the unforgettable sixth game the brilliant rookie Fred Lynn hits the wall leaping for a drive by Ken Griffey. Charlie Moss, the Red Sox trainer, administers to him, and at length Lynn gets to his feet. "I'll be O.K.," he says faintly. "Sure?" Moss asks.

A little later the camera focuses on right field for Dwight Evans' spectacular catch of a smash off Joe Morgan's bat. It was the eleventh inning with Griffey on base, and it appeared that night that the ball was headed for the seats. A slow-motion shot from center field shows that Evans made his leaping catch several steps from the wall, and perhaps the ball would not have gone over. It was, nevertheless, an extraordinary save with the ballgame in the balance. Instinctively, Evans threw toward first. Then he resumed his position and a moment passed before he realized that he had doubled Griffey off base, retiring the side.

Then comes The Moment. Leading off the home twelfth, Fisk pulls a high, hard shot to left. He stands watching, writhing, laying on the body-English as the wind pushes the ball toward the foul line. When it clears the wall fair, he takes flight.

"It was a crucial game for us," he says, "and maybe a crucial game for baseball itself. It showed people how the game of baseball should be played."

Bowl for Catfish

The New Yankee Stadium Welcomes All Worshippers

Bronx, N.Y., *March 1, 1976*

W HAT WITH lawsuits, glacial contract talks, and padlocked training camps, there is no telling when the game of baseball will get under way this year, but the business of baseball opens today in the Bronx. Starting this morning, tickets will be on sale at the Yankee Stadium box office for a game with the Minnesota Twins on Thursday afternoon, April 15, the first athletic contest scheduled for the rebuilt playpen. Maybe the players won't be ready by then, or the owners ready to pay them, but the ballpark will be. That brings up a point that hasn't been mentioned out loud: What about the clubs' leases on municipal stadiums? From San Francisco Bay to Long Island, most of the teams play in publicly owned parks. In the improbable event that the owners made good their implied threat to call off the whole season, could their landlords still hold them responsible for a summer's rent?

However, this piece is about the new playpen at 161st Street and River Avenue, which is, as of today, better prepared than the team for the opening of the season. Fifty-three years ago Colonel Jacob Ruppert and Colonel Tillinghast L'Hommedieu Huston spent $2.5 million on a showcase for Babe Ruth. How much the taxpayers are spending to fix it over for Catfish Hunter is a question whose answer depends on who is doing the figuring. It is difficult to calculate the cost at less than $65 million, easy to show where $100 million is being spent, though not all of that comes directly from the local taxpayers' pockets.

In any event, when you consider that William H. Seward picked up

Alaska for $7.2 million, the stadium figures are impressive. So is the stadium.

The House That You Built is roomier, handsomer, more comfortable and convenient than the House That Ruth Built, yet it is still Yankee Stadium. It is still the park where Don Larsen pitched that perfect World Series game, without a windup and without sleep; where Ruth hit his sixtieth home run of the 1927 season off Tom Zachary, and Roger Maris hit his sixty-first in 1961 off Tracy Stallard; where Yogi Berra fell under the pop foul that should have completed Allie Reynolds' second no-hitter of 1951, whereupon Reynolds threw the same pitch to Ted Williams for another foul that Yogi caught. It is still the Home of Champions, the home of Joe DiMaggio and Mickey Mantle, or Miller Huggins, Joe McCarthy, and Casey Stengel, the place where Max Schmeling knocked out Joe Louis and Louis knocked out Schmeling.

There were 65,010 seats in the old stadium, and not every one was behind a pillar. There are 54,200 plastic pews in the rebuilt stands, all wider than the old wooden ones, and there isn't a post in the joint.

A decade has passed since freeloaders gathered in numbers to watch games from the elevated station platform of the subway and the roofs of nearby apartment buildings. Even if the Yankees get good, those crowds won't be back, for that view is cut off by a scoreboard costing between $2.5 million and $3 million. It has a message board that can show instant replays, carry advertisements, and wish the umpire a happy birthday.

If and when there are customers, color-coded escalators will carry them to the proper seat level. About three hundred can graze at one time in a cafeteria, the first public restaurant in any New York park, and the Stadium Club will accommodate around five hundred. The Stadium Club has two levels. The upper, which can be entered directly from the mall outside, is the bar; food is served below ground, and an elevator carries Beautiful People to sixteen luxury boxes with heat, air-conditioning, television, and facilities for snacking and snorting.

Features most fans won't see include a private dining room for management, a television studio, the home clubhouse where the Yankees' lockers are done in red, white, and blue, a sauna, a gymnasium, and a trainer's room equipped to cure anything short of a broken leg or lead in the bustle. There are air-conditioning vents in the home dugout.

The two questions most frequently asked about Yankee Stadium are "Did anybody ever hit a fair ball out of the park?" and "Which players are buried in center field?" The answers are "no" and "none." The monuments that stood in center field as memorials to Ruth, Huggins, and Lou Gehrig now occupy a grassy little court between the bullpens in left, just beyond the low wall that bounds the outfield.

Ruth, Huggins, and Gehrig. They made a ballpark into a shrine. Indeed, it was so nearly a place of worship for some that more than one fan requested in his will that his ashes be scattered over the field.

Management never approved, sharing the views of Mrs. Ann Clare, who used to be track superintendent at Saratoga. When a horseplayer from Gloversville, New York, left a request that his ashes be scattered over the homestretch, Mrs. Clare said positively no.

Next morning she asked, "What is that white stuff over near the rail?"

"Might be frost, Mrs. Clare," one of the track crew said. "It was pretty cold last night."

"In August? Here, you with the shovel and you with that broom, gather that up and bring it here."

They brought her a shovelful of pale dust with bits of bone and knuckle. She had them dig a hole in the infield, and as they smoothed fresh earth over the contents of the shovel, she said a silent Hail Mary.

"At least some of the poor man had a decent burial," she said later.

The Game's
Greatest Day

A Lump in the Throat at the Baseball Hall of Fame

A COOPERSTOWN, N.Y., *August 9, 1977*
LL WEEKEND, the Otesaga Hotel and the shaded streets had
crawled with autograph buffs in assorted sizes. Monday morning was
hot and sultry, but long before ten o'clock every chair on the lawn of
Cooper Park was occupied and so was every foot of standing room
behind the Baseball Hall of Fame. The folding chairs and the crowds
behind them faced a platform of new lumber with a corral behind the
stage where whippers-in were herding demigods into two meandering queues. At a signal, the living legends filed up to take their seats
on the platform. Cheering started with the first arrival. It went on
and on, swelling in volume as the stage filled. Cheers used to be meat
and drink to the men in the queues, but Burleigh Grimes doesn't hear
much applause these days in Holcombe, Wis., nor Fred Lindstrom in
New Port Richey, Fla.

"This day in the year of baseball," Bowie Kuhn would tell the crowd,
"is the greatest day we have." And for once, not even Charlie Finley
would have disagreed. It was the thirty-eighth annual Hall of Fame Day
in this jewel of a village, this charming settlement beside Lake Otsego
where Abner Doubleday almost surely did not lay out the first baseball
diamond in the dust of Farmer Phinney's pasture.

On the baseball calendar there are many holidays—the day the
season opens and the day it ends, the day the World Series starts and
the moment it is won, the day Lou Brock steals another base, the day

Pete Rose makes another hit, the day Rod Carew wins another batting championship, the day George Steinbrenner issues another ultimatum.

All are memorable, but this is the day that gives the game continuity. The simple ceremony inducting new members into the Hall of Fame—this is how baseball pauses to look back on its honored past, to savor its lively present before stepping into its predictable future.

Al Lopez will be sixty-nine years old in less than a fortnight. He was the most skillful of catchers for nine different teams in the majors and minors over twenty-four seasons. He played 1,950 big league games and put in twenty years as manager in three cities. He is a grown man, yet it was all he could do to control his voice when he thanked the players, fans, and press for helping him win a niche in the brick shrine on Main Street.

It was easy to appreciate what he felt. Very few players get to the majors unless baseball means a good deal to them, and none becomes a candidate for the Hall of Fame unless he is wholly dedicated to the game. To be installed in the pantheon reserved for the finest that ever lived—that is knowing success as few are privileged to know it.

A toad would be moved.

Three of the six enshrined this year made it posthumously. They were Martín Dihigo and Pop Lloyd, whose color barred them from the organized leagues, and Amos Rusie whose fastball fathered the cliché, "You can't hit 'em if you can't see 'em."

The other three were on their feet. And the cheers out front weren't the only applause they heard as the commissioner presented them. There was also a welcome from the men behind them, the elite whose company they were joining.

That was a company, indeed—Charlie Gehringer, Bill Terry, Joe Cronin, Bob Feller, Luke Appling, Burleigh Grimes, Red Ruffing, Lloyd Waner, Roy Campanella, Stan Coveleski, Stan Musial, Rube Marquard, Buck Leonard, Monty Irvin, George Kelly, Cool Papa Bell, Whitey Ford, Earl Averill, Billy Herman, Fred Lindstrom, Judy Johnson, Robin Roberts, and the former umpires Cal Hubbard and Jocko

Conlan. At today's prices, all the OPEC countries and Steinbrenner's partners couldn't pay their salaries.

Still, you wouldn't call them expensive. When Lopez was a sixteen-year-old in Ybor City, the Spanish section of Tampa, Fla., he was catching Walter Johnson and his colleagues on the Senators and would have been happy to do it free. However, the Senators' owner, Clark Griffith, was generous to a fault. He paid Al $5 a day, $35 a week.

"It was 1924," Al said, "Bucky Harris' first year as manager. The Washington club trained in Tampa and Donie Bush, the manager before Bucky, had a Cuban guy catching batting practice but the Cuban was gone in '24. A Tampa sportswriter who knew me from sandlot ball got me the job. Years later when we were good friends Donie would say, 'How old do you claim you are? You're a few years older than that because you caught batting practice for me in Tampa.' I'd say, 'No, Donie, that was some other Cuban.'

"Anyway, Bucky liked me and got Griff to offer me a contract but I had signed the day before with the Tampa Smokers of the Florida State League. Griff said he'd buy me and the Smokers said O.K., $5,000. 'What!' Griff said. 'I'll give you $1,000.' But it was no deal.

"A few years later when I was with the Brooklyn club the Senators trained in Biloxi, Miss., our manager, Max Carey, called me over to the bleachers where he was sitting with Griff. I said, 'Hello, Mr. Griffith.'

"'I know that boy,' Griff told Carey. 'He caught batting practice for me and I could have had him for $1,000.'"

The Moving Finger Writes, Etc.

One, Two, Three for Reggie Jackson

Bronx, N.Y., October 19, 1977
I T HAD to happen this way. It had been predestined since November 29, 1976, when Reginald Martinez Jackson sat down on a gilded chair in New York's Americana Hotel and wrote his name on a Yankee contract. That day he became an instant millionaire, the big honcho on the best team money could buy, the richest, least inhibited, most glamorous exhibit in Billy Martin's pin-striped zoo. That day the plot was written for last night—the bizarre scenario Reggie Jackson played out by hitting three home runs, clubbing the Los Angeles Dodgers into submission, and carrying his supporting players with him to the baseball championship of North America. His was the most lurid performance in seventy-four World Series, for although Babe Ruth hit three home runs in a game in 1926 and again in 1928, not even that demigod smashed three in a row.

Reggie's first broke a tie and put the Yankees in front, 4–3. His second fattened the advantage to 7–3. His third completed arrangements for a final score of 8–4, wrapping up the championship in six games.

Yet that was merely the final act of an implausible one-man show. Jackson had made a home run last Saturday in Los Angeles and another on his last time at bat in that earthly paradise on Sunday. On his first appearance at the plate last night he walked, getting no official time at bat, so in his last four official turns he hit four home runs.

In his last nine times at bat, this Hamlet in double-knits scored seven runs, made six hits and five home runs, and batted in six runs for a batting average of .667 compiled by day and by night on two sea-coasts three thousand miles and three time zones apart. Shakespeare wouldn't attempt a curtain scene like that if he was plastered.

This was a drama that consumed seven months, for ever since the Yankees went to training camp last March, Jackson had lived in the eye of the hurricane. All summer long as the spike-shod capitalists bickered and quarreled, contending with their manager, defying their owner, Reggie was the most controversial, the most articulate, the most flamboyant.

Part philosopher, part preacher, and part outfielder, he carried this rancorous company with his bat in the season's last fifty games, leading them to the East championship in the American League and into the World Series. He knocked in the winning run in the twelve-inning first game, drove in a run and scored two in the third, furnished the winning margin in the fourth, and delivered the final run in the fifth.

Thus the stage was set when he went to the plate in last night's second inning with the Dodgers leading, 2–0. Sedately, he led off with a walk. Serenely, he circled the bases on a home run by Chris Chambliss. The score was tied.

Los Angeles had moved out front, 3–2, when the man reappeared in the fourth inning with Thurman Munson on base. He hit the first pitch on a line into the seats beyond right field. Circling the bases for the second time, he went into his home-run glide—head high, chest out. The Yankees led, 4–3. In the dugout, Yankees fell upon him. Billy Martin, the manager, who tried to slug him last June, patted his cheek lovingly. The dugout phone rang and Reggie accepted the call graciously.

His first home run knocked the Dodgers' starting pitcher, Burt Hooton, out of the game. His second disposed of Elias Sosa, Hooton's successor. Before Sosa's first pitch in the fifth inning, Reggie had strolled the length of the dugout to pluck a bat from the rack, even though three men would precede him to the plate. He was confident he would get his turn. When he did, there was a runner on base again, and again he hit the first pitch. Again it reached the seats in right.

When the last jubilant playmate had been peeled off his neck, Reggie took a seat near the first-base end of the bench. The crowd was still bawling for him and comrades urged him to take a curtain call but he replied with a gesture that said, "Aw, fellows, cut it out!" He did unbend enough to hold up two fingers for photographers in a V-for-victory sign.

Jackson was the leadoff batter in the eighth. By that time, Martin would have replaced him in an ordinary game, sending Paul Blair to right field to help protect the Yankees' lead. But did they ever bench Edwin Booth in the last act?

For the third time, Reggie hit the first pitch but this one didn't take the shortest distance between two points. Straight out from the plate the ball streaked, not toward the neighborly stands in right but on a soaring arc toward the unoccupied bleachers in dead center, where the seats are blacked out to give batters a background. Up the white speck climbed, dwindling, diminishing, until it settled at last halfway up those empty stands, probably four hundred fifty feet away.

This time he could not disappoint his public. He stepped out of the dugout and faced the multitude, two fists and one cap uplifted. Not only the customers applauded.

"I must admit," said Steve Garvey, the Dodgers' first baseman, "when Reggie Jackson hit his third home run and I was sure nobody was listening, I applauded into my glove."

The Ever-Renewing Promise of Spring

Season Opener at Yankee Stadium

★ ★ ★

Bronx, N.Y., *April 6, 1979*

IN THE press box somebody asked who had been the last man to pitch a no-hitter on opening day. There had been only one, the guy was told, Bob Feller. Nobody knew for sure just when that had happened, but there would be time to look it up. It was still only the sixth inning. "Well," someone else said, "this will be the first by a left-hander. And the first perfect game ever on opening day."

There were 52,719 cash customers in Yankee Stadium yesterday, and many of them must have been talking in the same vein, for every time Ron Guidry threw the ball the crowd responded with wild-animal cries. The young man who was the best pitcher in baseball last year had got the warmest greeting by far when Bob Shepard, the announcer, introduced individuals on the Yankees and Milwaukee Brewers in the half-hour ritual before the game. His public had howled with pleasure as Guidry retired batter after batter through the first, second, third, and fourth innings and the Yankees took a lead of 1–0.

There was a standing ovation when Sal Bando became Guidry's fifteenth consecutive victim. Five innings were gone and no Brewer had reached base by any means. Robin Yount led off the sixth, and cheers rolled in thunderous waves as the count went to three balls, two strikes. There was a foul tip that Thurman Munson couldn't hold, then Yount lined out to Bucky Dent at shortstop. Sixteen batters, sixteen outs.

The count went to three and two on Gorman Thomas, Milwaukee's center fielder. There is an old superstition that when a pitcher is working on a no-hitter, nobody should distract him by mentioning it, but if Guidry were stone-deaf he still could have heard the fans telling him about it. If he were in Westchester County, he would have heard.

Thomas singled smartly to left. The cheers turned to boos, then whistles. And then Guidry's public rose en masse, roaring, beating palms together, howling. The ovation went on and on, swelling in ardor while Charlie Moore waited to bat. So all right, the no-hitter was gone, the perfect game no longer perfect, but there was sunshine on the grass, a big pennant proclaiming the Yankees champions of the world flapped lazily from the flagpole in center field, the home team was still in front, and baseball was back in the big town. The thermometer registered only 53 degrees, but the voice of the turtle could be heard in the land.

Minutes later, Guidry was gone, his shutout was gone, and the Yankees' lead was gone and so was the game. The Brewers, whom many expect to be New York's strongest challengers in the American League East, scored four runs in that sixth inning and were on their way to a 5–1 victory. For the eighth time in ten years, the Yankees were losing their opening game.

As opening days go, this was a standard product. The weather wasn't as cold as some opening days past, but the men who own baseball will take care of that in the future. Since the turn of the century, they have encountered rain, sleet, snow, and ice in April, so each year they start the season a little earlier. This was the earliest opening on record, but there is no reason to believe the record will stand more than a year. If there was nothing unusual about the Yankees' dropping their opener, the entertainment did have one uncommon aspect. They played this one without American League umpires because fifty of the fifty-two regular umpires in the big leagues are on strike. Behind the plate was Al Forman, a liquor salesman; Fred Spenn, a professional umpire employed last year by the American Association, was at first base.

Jimmy Dunne, who sells cargo containers on the docks, was at second. The man at third was Richie Lazar, a New Jersey caterer.

They were dressed like umpires, three in blue, with Lazar in a red blazer. As a matter of fact, all of them are umpires or have been. Spenn, Dunne, and Lazar officiate games in the Eastern College Athletic Conference.

Forman umpired in the National League from 1961 to 1965. One winter he worked winter ball in Nicaragua. He was a minor league umpire then and was sent down as chief of staff because he could speak Spanish. Since the National League let him go he has been selling booze, but when the call came to fill in for the regular umpires who are on strike, he had only to reach in the closet for his shiny blue serge.

Crouching behind the plate, Al Forman was a living object lesson for all who cared to learn: Don't give your old clothes to the Salvation Army, they may still come in handy.

Strangers though they were, the umpires got through nine innings with only one awkward moment. In the seventh inning Yount hit back to Dick Tidrow, Guidry's successor on the mound, and Tidrow bobbled the ball, then threw it past Chris Chambliss at first base.

Spenn waved Yount to second base and Yankee debaters sprang into action. As umpire-in-chief, Forman reversed his colleague, ruling that a fan in a front-row seat had reached out and touched the ball after it had eluded Chambliss.

The double-decision had no effect on the score. Yount returned to first base, took second on a sacrifice bunt, and brought in the game's last run on a single by Thomas.

When it was all over, somebody checked. It was 1946 when Feller pitched that no-hitter. It didn't seem to matter much.

The Grass Turns
Brown on
Boston Common

It's Yaz's Year But Not the Sox'

Boston, Mass., *September 8, 1979*

I T'S WORSE here than in most places. There are twenty-two teams in the major leagues that won't make the divisional playoffs, twenty-four that won't win a pennant, twenty-five that will miss out on the baseball championship of North America. In other towns these disappointments come with the franchise. You can't win 'em all, as the St. Louis Browns used to remind themselves unnecessarily. In Boston, it is disaster.

The Red Sox don't always die on Labor Day. They won a pennant in 1975 after an eight-year famine. They won a pennant in 1946 and in 1918 they won a World Series. So the season doesn't always end when August does. It just seems that way. The grass in Boston Common turns brown in September. The zinnias wither in the Public Gardens. And the crowds keep coming—to pray, to boo, to weep.

When the Sox engaged the Baltimore Orioles today, it was the forty-fourth time this season that more than thirty thousand customers bought their way into a playground that seats 33,538. One would conclude from this that Red Sox fans are the most tolerant in the world. One would be mistaken. Mike Barnicle is a Red Sox fan. He writes a column in the *Boston Globe*, not on the sports pages.

"What has 18 legs and no arms?" he wrote the other day. "What turns pale yellow in the fall? What folds easier than toilet paper? What baseball team can impersonate the main course at a Thanksgiving Day dinner?

"The Red Sox could qualify for a group rate on a heart transplant. For more than a month now they have looked like accordions or folding chairs. They are an absolute, bottom line disgrace.

"They are an embarrassment. They are a collection of dressing room fighters. They are pathetic. They are a team without character."

If this is how fans feel about their team, why do they keep on laying out $3 for general admission, $7 for rooftop seats? The dimensions of Fenway Park have something to do with it. If the Red Sox are successful in April and May, the customers tell themselves that maybe, just possibly, if Butch and Pudge and Yaz and the Rooster stay healthy and the crick don't rise, this could be one of those rare years when September games mean something. Afraid to wait lest they be shut out of those games, they buy up tickets months in advance.

A month ago, the Sox had the second-best record in baseball. They had won thirty games more than they had lost and were sitting second, poised for a charge at the Orioles. Starting last Monday in New York, they would play three games with the Yankees, then four here with the Orioles, three in Fenway with the Yankees, and three with the Orioles in Baltimore. Those thirteen games could decide the championship in the American League East.

They may indeed decide the race, but the Red Sox aren't in it. A month ago they forgot how to play baseball and there isn't any race. They can't even play the role of spoilers, for the Orioles had twelve defeats fewer than the Milwaukee Brewers this morning and nothing that the Sox might do from here out would seriously impair Baltimore's prospects.

In the desolation of September, the immediate future held one enchanting promise. Sometime soon Yaz would make the three thousandth hit of his illustrious career. It didn't happen today when the Sox lost again, 3–2, but it could be tomorrow or Monday. Since man first learned to earn his victuals swinging a club, fourteen players have made three thousand hits. Bereft of hope for the team, New England waits today to welcome Carl Michael Yastrzemski into that company.

Capt. Carl took a long step toward the goal last night in the opening game of the series. When he went to the plate to lead off the second inning against Jim Palmer, 33,322 constituents arose and saluted him. He singled to right and there was ecstasy in the stands. Four more hits to go.

Reaching first base, Yaz discarded his spiked shoes and pulled on sneakers. After 2,852 games in nineteen seasons, his feet give him constant pain. He was retired at second base in a double play.

A home run by Jim Rice had tied the score at 1–all when Yaz next went to bat, with two out in the fourth inning. Again he singled to right, again he changed shoes, again the inning ended when Bob Watson flied out. Yaz went out on an infield grounder on his third time up.

Then it was the ninth inning, Baltimore leading, 2–1, and Sammy Stewart pitching for the Orioles. You don't see many 2–1 games in Fenway, and precious few witnesses have seen the Red Sox playing well enough to preserve a score like that lately. Leading off again, Yaz sliced a drive against the wall in left—a hit that usually goes for two bases unless the outfielder handles the rebound swiftly and throws accurately.

Head down, feet torturing him, Yaz rounded first. Ken Singleton's perfect throw beat him to second by the length of a long, despairing sigh. He had 2,998 hits but he was out, and the Red Sox never got the run Yaz would have scored when Watson, next up, hit a double.

"If this were 1969," a man said to Earl Weaver hours after the game, "he would have gone into second standing up and Watson's hit would have tied the score."

"And we'd still be out there," the Baltimore manager said, "because I've got that kind of pitching."

"Haven't you had any tough defeats this year?" he was asked.

"Forty-six of them," Earl Weaver said.

Mr. Yastrzemski, Please Hold for the President

Patience, Endurance, and Hit No. 3,000

BOSTON, MASS., *September 14, 1979*

I N BOSTON somebody said Carl Yastrzemski had made his first hit when John F. Kennedy was President and might not make his three thousandth until Teddy was. However, after a delay that was beginning to make everyone's teeth hurt, Yaz did the deed in time to be congratulated by President Carter. "Give me a number," a member of the White House staff had said several days ago to Bill Crowley, the Red Sox vice president for public relations, "and we'll call within twenty minutes after the game ends." "I can't keep the Boston press waiting twenty minutes," Crowley had said. "They're more important to me than you are."

When Cap Anson reached three thousand hits in 1897, there was no congratulatory phone call from President McKinley, who was preoccupied getting a protective tariff through Congress. When Ty Cobb made it in 1921, news accounts of the game mentioned his achievement in the twelfth or fourteenth paragraph. When Sam Rice retired in 1934 with 2,987 hits, it didn't occur to him that maybe he should stick around for thirteen more.

In those days, Media was where the Medes and Persians came from. Many years ago a wise man wrote that baseball was the game of professional athletes and amateur statisticians. Today it sometimes seems that statistics are bigger than the game or the players, in the eyes of the "media," at least.

Carl Yastrzemski has been playing professional ball for twenty-one years. He has made hits in All-Star Games, in pennant playoffs, and in World Series, yet not one of them commanded such attention or stirred such emotions as his ground single to right field off the Yankees' Jim Beattie Wednesday night in the eighth inning of a game the Red Sox had already won.

If it weren't for press and television and radio, nobody would be willing to pay $10,000 for Yaz's footprints in plaster. If the three thousandth hit had not become a "media event" it wouldn't have cost Yaz $600 a day to keep twenty-six visiting relatives in Boston to see history made, and his kids wouldn't be overdue in school in Florida.

When Anson made his three thousandth hit, nobody realized that the number would attain significance. Nobody knew Anson was founding a club so exclusive that eighty-two years later it would have only fifteen members. When Cobb reached that plateau, he was en route to 4,191 hits and he hardly noticed the milestone as he passed. The first time in memory that there was any special commotion over somebody joining the 3,000 Club was in 1958 when Stan Musial made it, and there were special circumstances then.

The Cardinals were on the road when Stan hit No. 2,999 and Fred Hutchinson, the manager, announced he would hold Musial out of their last game in Chicago so he could get the big one at home. This was understandable. Given his choice, Musial would prefer that the event take place before a friendly crowd, and the prospect of seeing it happen would attract additional customers in St. Louis, as it did for the last week in Fenway Park.

It was only mid-May, though, and nobody knew the Cardinals were destined to finish in a tie for fifth place. With his team in the pennant race, a victory in May would count as much as a victory in September. In the circumstances, it was felt that Hutch had no right to sheathe his principal offensive weapon.

Defying his critics, Hutchinson did leave Musial out of the starting batting order, but in the sixth inning he saw a chance to win and called on Stan. Musial ripped a double for No. 3,000, rousing spectators to silence.

To say that there was a time when the three thousandth hit didn't alter the course of the stars in their flight is not to disparage the hitter's achievement. Babe Ruth's sixtieth home run in 1927 caused no wild excitement, either; he was only breaking his own record of fifty-nine and there was no reason to doubt that he would hit sixty-one in another year. But Babe never made three thousand hits and neither did Lou Gehrig or Rogers Hornsby or Joe DiMaggio or Ted Williams.

"I haven't had the greatest ability in the world," Yaz said. "I'm not a big, strong guy. I've made nine million adjustments, nine million changes. I've worked hard over the wintertime. I've paid the price. And God gave me a tremendous incentive and body to excel and that desire inside of me."

That's what it takes—the willingness to pay the price—and keep paying it year in and year out, summer and winter. Along with the willingness, there must be the opportunity, for nobody has made his three thousandth hit earlier than his sixteenth season, and only a tiny minority can stay in the majors that long.

This is Yaz's nineteenth season with Boston. His forty-year-old Achilles tendons punish him day and night. When he made No. 3,000 he was wearing a spiked shoe on his left foot and a sneaker on his right. He is ready for carpet slippers but instead he runs all winter and now he means to get Nautilus exercising equipment because, "If it can help Freddie Lynn get thirty-seven homers, I'm going to pump it."

D.H.

The Loathsome Ploy to End the Nine-Man Game

The outlook wasn't brilliant for the Mudville ten that day;
The score stood four to two with but one inning more to play . . .

NEW YORK, N.Y., *August 18, 1980*

CHANCES ARE Ernest L. Thayer, who created the mighty Casey, and
DeWolf Hopper, whose recitations immortalized him, have got beyond
the stage of whirling in their graves. The game they knew as baseball,
the nine-man game, is played only in the National League and Japan's
Central League today, and it came perilously close to eradication from
the National League the other day. By the narrowest of margins, the
league voted against adopting the loathsome designated-hitter rule in
slavish imitation of the American League.

As Bill Lee, the thinking man's pitcher, pointed out several years
ago, the designated hitter serves one useful purpose. It relieves the
manager of all responsibility except to post the lineup card on the
dugout wall and make sure everybody gets to the airport on time.

Once there was a theory that devising strategy, dictating and alter-
ing tactics, matching wits with the licensed genius across the way were
part of the manager's job and that his degree of success in these areas
accounted for his ranking in his profession. In the ten-man game,
most decisions are made for the manager automatically. If he wants
to phone his bookmaker in the third inning, there is seldom anything
else demanding his attention.

The only excuse anybody gives for adopting the d.h. rule is that
baseball is in a rut and cries aloud for some change, any change. The

fact is, baseball has had longer to test and polish its rules than any other team game in the country, and this process of evolution has produced a code that seldom demands change because it is beautiful in its fairness and balance. If you don't know a rule governing a certain situation, give it some thought; when you have arrived at a decision that is fair to both sides, you will have the rule as it is written.

Tested, altered, and adjusted over a century, the rules for nine-man baseball became a triumph of checks and balances. There are moves the manager can make in the interest of offense, but he must pay for them. When to remove the pitcher used to be, and in the National League still is, one of the major decisions up to a manager. Suppose the pitcher allowed a run in the first inning and none since. It is now the eighth inning, it is his turn to bat, and the team is still trailing, 1–0. The pitcher is strong enough to work at least a couple more innings but he can't win without a run and he isn't likely to contribute much to the offense.

If you take him out for a pinch batter, you lose his services and must rely on the bullpen, and that's the way it should be. This charming balance is a major factor in the attraction of the game.

With the corruption called designated hitter, the balance is destroyed, the challenge to the manager eliminated. He pinch-hits for the pitcher every time around, and it costs him nothing. National League managers have to think; American Leaguers don't, and maybe that helps explain the result of the annual All-Star Game.

A designated hitter has added a few points to the team batting average and presumably added a few runs to the season's score. The men who own baseball have long had the notion that more hitting and scoring produces more business, but there is no proof of that. The d.h. rule is in its eighth year now, and as yet nobody has been overheard saying, "Let's go out and watch the designated hitter."

By the winter of 1972 the governing intellects in the American League were in a panic. For more than a decade A.L. attendance had run substantially behind business in the National League. One year the N.L. had drawn 17,324,857, a tidy 5,456,297 more than the American.

"So what can we do about it?" the Americans asked one another.

"My cook says the public wants more hitting and scoring," one replied.

"Well," said another, "suppose we pinch-hit for the pitcher every time up but let the pitcher stay in the game. Think that might add some pizzazz?"

"Can't hurt to try," said still another. "Sure, it changes the whole game but who cares? Alexander Cartwright is dead."

So it came about, and the changes were immediately reflected at the box office. That is, the American League and its ten-man game continued to run behind the National League every year, millions behind, until 1977, when it added franchises in Seattle and Toronto, expanding to fourteen clubs while the Nationals remained at twelve.

Then A.L. figures inched up, edging past the other league for the first time in many years. In the American League press guide, the 1979 attendance of 22,371,979 is marked with two asterisks denoting "major league and professional sports league record." Broken down on a team-by-team basis, the American League average was 1,597,999 and the Nationals? 1,764,468. And still those chumps almost went for the d.h.

Stee-rike!

The Long, Hot, Empty Summer of No Baseball

NEW YORK, N.Y., *July 26, 1981*

J ACQUES BARZUN wrote—and if he isn't sick of re-reading it, he has a strong stomach—that "whoever wants to know the heart and mind of America had better learn baseball."

Thomas Wolfe celebrated the "velvet and unalterable geometry of the playing field," and Bill Stern, the most inventive sports broadcaster since Baron von Munchausen, solemnly assured us that when President Lincoln lay dying, the man he called to his bedside was not Andrew Johnson, his Vice President, or Gen. Ulysses S. Grant, who had just accepted Lee's surrender at Appomattox Court House, but Gen. Abner Doubleday.

"General Doubleday, don't let baseball die," the President whispered, and breathed his last. The summer game has always had a formidable body of supporters. Yet, in spite of them, the feeling grows that Baseball 1981 is dead. Representatives of the players on the twenty-six teams will meet tomorrow to decide what they can do about salvaging the last two months of the season, but there is no visible reason for optimism.

To bring the strike to an end and get back on the field for August and September, the players would have to give up a significant part of the freedom they and their predecessors fought for through most of a century.

For the employers to achieve peace on their own initiative, they would have to concede defeat in a calculated and costly campaign to clamp a lid on the free agent market.

Though this situation, like an Amtrak timetable, is subject to change without notice, it does not now appear that either side is ready to give in. The chances are that for anyone who wants to know the heart and mind of America, the textbook will remain closed for the rest of this year.

It goes without saying that baseball will be back eventually. It is the most beautiful of games, with deeper roots in America than any other sport can show. Like the Winged Victory, it can be mutilated but it will survive.

The question is, if baseball is resumed next April, how mutilated will it be? Its hold on public interest almost surely has been loosened already. Will public disenchantment be reflected at the box office and among television sponsors in the immediate future?

Have the club owners, by provoking and prolonging a costly strike, seriously damaged their own product? They are capable of it. A poll shows that almost half the population doesn't miss baseball. That shouldn't surprise anyone. Nowhere near half the population ever buys a ticket, and if there is no baseball on the tube tonight, viewers can still watch "The Dukes of Hazzard."

However, those who are interested in the game have strong feelings about the strike. While there is no great unanimity among them, most seem angry at the owners, and that is a significant switch.

In past labor-management disputes, 95 percent of the press sided with management. In this quarrel, at least 70 percent of the press, perhaps a good deal more, has been pro-players and anti-management. Why? Because of the transparent union-baiting tactics of the owners' representatives, their intransigence, their undisguised determination to score a victory at whatever cost.

Chances are the press view is the public view, and the fans have swung over to the players' side. The owners keep insisting that the last thing in the world they want is to bust the union. Without the players association, they say, baseball would be overrun by agents trying to use the game for their own selfish purposes, and all would be chaos.

This may be true, but the owners' conduct leaves no room for doubt that they are determined to emasculate the union, to weaken it and recapture some of the power they wielded when, as feudal lords, they owned their employees outright.

To achieve this, they seem willing to take the monumental losses of a season without income and risk defacing their product in the public view. "Another such victory over the Romans," King Pyrrhus said after a costly battle, "and we are undone."

Envoi

Red Smith's Final Column

New Canaan, Conn., *January 11, 1982*
U p t o now, the pieces under my byline have run on Sunday, Monday, Wednesday, and Friday. Starting this week, it will be Sunday, Monday, and Thursday—three columns instead of four. We shall have to wait and see whether the quality improves.

Visiting our freshman daughter (freshwoman or freshperson would be preferred by feminists though heaven knows she was fresh) we sat chatting with perhaps a dozen of her classmates. Somehow my job got into the discussion. A lovely blonde was appalled.

"A theme a day!" she murmured. The figure was not altogether accurate. At the time it was six themes a week. It had been seven and when it dropped to six that looked like roller coaster's end. However, it finally went to five, to three and back to four, where it has remained for years.

First time I ever encountered John S. Knight, the publisher, we were bellying up to Marje Everett's bar at Arlington Park. He did not acknowledge the introduction. Instead, he said: "Nobody can write six good columns a week. Why don't you write three? Want me to fix it up?"

"Look, Mr. Knight," I said. "Suppose I wrote three stinkers. I wouldn't have the rest of the week to recover." One of the beauties of this job is that there's always tomorrow. Tomorrow things will be better.

Now that the quota is back to three, will things be better day after tomorrow?

The comely college freshman wasn't told of the years when a daily column meant seven a week. Between those jousts with the mother tongue, there was always a fight or football match or ballgame or horse race that had to be covered after the column was done. I loved it.

The seven-a-week routine was in Philadelphia, which reminds me of the late heavyweight champion, Sonny Liston. Before his second bout with Muhammad Ali was run out of Boston, Liston trained in a motel in Dedham.

I was chatting about old Philadelphia days with the trainer, Willie Reddish, remembered from his time as a heavyweight boxer in Philadelphia.

"Oh," Willie said apropos of some event in the past, "were you there then?"

"Willie," I said, "I did ten years hard in Philadelphia."

There had been no sign that Liston was listening, but at this he swung around. "Hard?" he said. "No good time?"

From that moment on, Sonny and I were buddies, though it wasn't easy accepting him as a sterling citizen of lofty moral standards.

On this job two questions are inevitably asked: "Of all those you have met, who was the best athlete?" and "Which one did you like best?"

Both questions are unanswerable but on either count Bill Shoemaker, the jockey, would have to stand high. This little guy weighed 96 pounds as an apprentice rider thirty-two years ago. He still weighs 96 pounds and he will beat your pants off at golf, tennis, and any other game where you're foolish enough to challenge him.

There were, of course, many others, not necessarily great. Indeed, there was a longish period when my rapport with some who were less than great made me nervous. Maybe I was stuck on bad ballplayers. I told myself not to worry. Some day there would be another Joe DiMaggio.

Afterword

"Give us this day our daily plinth," my father, Red Smith, and his pal Joe Palmer, the racing columnist, would pray, one with a scotch and soda in hand, the other bourbon and branch water, as they convened in Palmer's book-lined study at the end of a day. It was their private joke—a plinth is the base of a column—but the prayer was fervent. My father's search for his plinth was unending.

In my memory, Pop was always writing a column, in a press box at the ballpark or racetrack, in his basement office at home, in a plane or train, or in the family car on summer vacation trips to Wisconsin. He would balance his Olivetti portable on his knees in the passenger seat, typing as my mother drove, shushing my sister, Kit, and me in the back seat. Once, when we moved into our house in Connecticut, he had the movers set up a table and chair beneath a tree and wrote a column there. It was moving day, but his deadline was looming, as always.

The columns, including those so ably collected in this volume, were his métier, although he would have sneered at that word. The form suited him. He was good at capturing an event or a thought or a story in 800 words or so, often with an elegant phrase or a snatch of dialogue or the perfect anecdote. He was good at it and he knew it. He demurred repeatedly when people urged him to write a full-length book about sports or anything else. "I'd rather go to the dentist," he'd say.

Later in life, the suggestion of a biography or, worse yet, an autobiography was dismissed out of hand. "To be written about, is to be written off," he told me more than once. That's not true, of course, but it revealed his lifelong anxiety about being passed over or forgotten.

The column was his contract with life. As long as he was writing it, he felt he was in the center of things, that he still mattered. That's why he kept at it until the week he died. As long as he was writing, he was part of the world he had lived and loved.

The annual sports calendar provided his material and often established our family's rituals: spring training in Florida, the Kentucky Derby on the first Saturday in May, then the Preakness in Baltimore, the Belmont in New York, Saratoga in August, baseball through the summer, the World Series and college football in the fall, heavyweight championship fights and, every four years, the Olympic Games. It made for an intoxicating mix.

Curiously, for all the pleasure he took in it, he was an accidental sportswriter. As he told the story, he was a junior man on the news copy desk at *The St. Louis Star*, making about forty dollars a week, when the editor, the redoubtable Frank Taylor, discovered that half his six-man sports staff was on the take from a local fight promoter and fired them. Looking around for a replacement, he called my father over and supposedly the following conversation ensued:

TAYLOR: Do you know anything about sports, Smith?

SMITH: Just what the average fan knows, sir.

TAYLOR: They tell me you're very good on football.

SMITH: Well, if you say so.

TAYLOR: Are you honest?

SMITH: I hope so, sir.

TAYLOR: What if a fight promoter offered you $10, would you take it?

SMITH (*long pause*): $10 is a lot of money, sir.

TAYLOR: Report to the sports editor Monday.

Once he got into it, he relished writing sports and thought it was as good a vehicle as any to shed some light on the human condition. "I never felt any prodding need to solve the problems of the world," he said in an interview years later. "I feel that keeping the public informed in any area is a perfectly worthwhile way to spend your life. Sports constitute a valid part of our culture, our civilization, and keeping the public informed and, if possible, a little entertained about sports is not an entirely useless thing."

But during World War II, when he was the father of two and 4-F because of his eyesight and covering "games children play" for *The Philadelphia Record* while others were at the front, he admitted to a "desperate feeling of being useless."

"I was traveling with the last-place Philadelphia Athletics," he recalled, "and more than once, I thought, 'What the hell am I doing here?'" He comforted himself with the published report that FDR thought sports were important for morale. Readers, he said, could read the war news first and then turn to sports to get updated on what he described as "matters of major inconsequence."

Pop roamed off the sports beat occasionally, covering the national political conventions in 1956 and 1968, but when invited to expand his column to politics and world affairs, as James "Scotty" Reston and others had done before him, he declined. Same answer when he was asked to become the sports editor of the *New York Herald Tribune*. No, he said, the column was his thing, the one thing he did best. He'd stick with it.

He defined himself as a newspaperman, not a sportswriter or columnist. "I'd like to be remembered as a good reporter," he said in more than one interview, and he meant it. The much-advertised romance of journalism was real to him, as real in his seventies as it was when he left Green Bay, Wisconsin, for Notre Dame and a string of newspaper jobs. Until he reached *The New York Times*, already at normal retirement age, he had always worked for the second newspaper in a city. "I killed 'em all," he used to say with a smile.

He was often described as modest and unassuming, and he did adopt an aw-shucks diffidence in the face of prizes and praise. It wasn't exactly an act; he thought he was lucky to have had the chance to do all that he did. But he worked devilishly hard, took his writing, if not himself, seriously, constantly sought to be better, and bathed in the admiration he received, especially from colleagues. As Daniel Okrent notes earlier in this volume, he was stung when Arthur Daley won the Pulitzer before he did, and he often dismissed the prize as a sop given by the journalistic old-boy network to its favorites on the establishment papers.

Until he won his own Pulitzer, that is, on May 3, 1976, at age seventy.

I was the *New York Times* correspondent in Israel at the time. When I reached him on the phone in the midst of a newsroom celebration, champagne corks popping in the background, I dead-panned: "You'll refuse it, of course." He lowered his voice and growled into the mouthpiece: "Not on your life!" We both laughed our heads off. I was enormously pleased, and so was he.

Pop enjoyed great good health for all but the last few of his seventy-six years. Again, he was lucky, given all the late nights, booze, and decades of unfiltered Camels. His idea of a good time was to sit late at Toots Shor's saloon, trading stories with the parade of writers, ballplayers, fighters, mobsters, politicians, and hacks that would come by his table during the course of a night. He was successful financially, but his real definition of economic well-being was to have enough money to be able to grab the check for the table at Shor's on occasion and not break the bank in the process.

He loved his life, had two kids and two good marriages, and lived long enough to know his six grandchildren and two of his great-grandchildren and to take my son, Chris, fishing for the first time in his life. They laughed together and Chris caught a fish. That sunny day on Martha's Vineyard became grist for a column, of course, his plinth for the day.

When his health was failing near the end, he struggled to overcome the congestive heart failure and kidney disease that would take his life. He wanted to get better, he said, the Super Bowl was coming up and he wanted to cover it, to write another column, a good column, and then another after that, and make that one better. Spring training was not that far away.

But if he didn't get better, he told me, he had no complaints.

"I've had a great run," he said.

And he did.

Terence Smith, January 2, 2013, Shady Side, Maryland

Sources

For each of the Red Smith columns included in this volume, the text is taken either from one of several collections of Smith's columns or from the column's original periodical publication. Smith's columns for *The Philadelphia Record*, the *New York Herald Tribune*, and *The New York Times* were often interlarded with subheadings that have been omitted in the present volume, as they were in previous collections of Smith columns such as *Out of the Red* (1950) and *Views of Sport* (1954). The subtitles that accompany each column have been added for this edition, and several columns have been given new titles (the titles of Smith's columns were composed by his editors, and many of his regular "Views of Sport" columns for the *Herald Tribune* were untitled). Occasionally the original column provided a dateline that is different than the date of publication, usually by a day or so; in this volume the columns are dated according to its dateline (when given) rather than the date of publication. The place-names appearing before the date at the beginning of each column have sometimes been added or changed.

The list below gives the source text for each column. Recurring sources are as abbreviated as follows:

NYHT   *New York Herald Tribune*
NYT   *The New York Times*
OR   Red Smith, *Out of the Red* (New York: Knopf, 1950).
PR   *The Philadelphia Record*
RSB   *Red Smith on Baseball* (Chicago: Ivan R. Dee, 2000).
RSR   *The Red Smith Reader*, ed. Dave Anderson (New York: Random House, 1982).
SA   *Red Smith's Sports Annual 1961*, ed. Verna Reamer (New York: Crown, 1961).
SW   Red Smith, *Strawberries in the Wintertime* (New York: Quadrangle/ The New York Times Book Co., 1974).
TAF   Red Smith, *To Absent Friends* (New York: Atheneum, 1982).
VS   Red Smith, *Views of Sport* (New York: Knopf, 1954).

Prologue: My Press-Box Memoirs: *Esquire*, October 1975.

BASEBALL 1934–1951

Dizzy Dean's Day: RSR.

It Wasn't the Hits: *PR*, Oct. 2, 1938, as "Note to Charley Fisher, Who Wonders at Lack of Interest in Greenberg—It Wasn't Hits They Cheered in 1927 but the Man—Ruth."

A Toast to Coach Wagner: *PR*, Apr. 1, 1940, as "This Boyhood Hero Wasn't Forgotten by Ex-Worshiper."

Winning by Striking Out: *RSR*.

Big Man for His Size: *PR*, Oct. 22, 1943, as "Griffiths Big Man for Size."

Spit Is a Horrid Word: *OR*.

Plagiarists from the Polo Grounds: *RSB*.

It's All Genuine, Although Synthetic: *RSB*.

Silvertooth Mike Is Right Again: *RSB*.

The Big Train, Westbound: *TAF*, as "The Big Train and His Buddies."

Next to Godliness: *OR*.

Pitching Takes Brains: *OR*.

Young Old Master: *OR*.

They Let George Do It: *OR*.

Jim Crow's Playmates: *OR*.

The Babe: *TAF*, as "News Aboard Ship."

They Played It by Radio: *RSB*.

A Nation of Hams: *NYHT*, Aug. 31, 1949, untitled (column's second subheading provides title here).

One Vote for Will Harridge: *OR*.

The Vacant Chair: *RSB*.

Off the High Board: *VS*.

New Year's Baby: *RSB*, as "Opening Day, Yankee Stadium."

American Indian Day: *VS*.

Miracle of Coogan's Bluff: *VS*.

The Real Amateur: *RSB*.

SPORTS IN THE FORTIES

Gaelic Disaster: *Best Sports Stories of 1944*, ed. Irving T. Marsh and Edward Ehre (New York: E. P. Dutton, 1945).

The Lost Cause: *OR*.
The Most Important Thing: *OR*.
A Whole Troop of Calverley: *OR*, as "A Case of Malnutrition."
Falling Off Mountains: *OR*.
The Strongest Lady in the World: *OR*.
Boxing's Elder Statesman: *OR*.
The Pure in Heart: *OR*.
You Get a Funny Feeling: *OR*.
They Trut Him Good: *OR*.
So Long, Joe: *OR*.
Water-Fed Panther: *OR*.
Videots: *OR*.
Rendezvous with Danger: *OR*.
The Old Man Earned His Pension: *PR*, Mar. 8, 1940, as "Coast Fans
    Still Debate Merits of Biscuit and Kayak."
Death of "The Iceman": *TAF*.
Love Story: *OR*.
Belmont of the Backwoods: *OR*.
A Day of Beauty: *OR*, as "Beauty's Day."
A Horse You Had to Like: *TAF*.
Derby Day, Southern Fried: *OR*.
A Very Pious Story: *OR*.
Super: *NYHT*, Sept. 8, 1949, untitled.
Missouri Mortician: *OR*.
Kings Get in Free: *OR*.

FISHING FOR TROUT
Opening Day: *VS*.
The Rills of Home: *VS*.
Young Man with Fly Rod: *VS*.
Somewhat Like Poetry: *VS*.
No Orchestral Din: *OR*.
Rainbow in the Dust: *VS*.
The Brakes Got Drunk: *VS*.
Laughing River: *NYHT*, June 16, 1958.

SPORTS IN THE FIFTIES

Grimacing Greyhound: *VS*, as "Czech and Double Czech."

Airborne Parson, *NYHT*, Feb. 6, 1956, untitled (first subheading provides the title here). Three paragraphs at the end of this column about another event at the Millrose Games have been omitted.

Golf Is a Gentleman's Game, *NYHT*, Dec. 22, 1955, untitled.

Basketball in a Cage, *VS*.

Biological Urge, *VS*.

Pattern of Violence: *VS*.

Night for Joe Louis, *VS*, as "Now It Was Night."

Still Life: *VS*.

Cheap at Half the Price: *VS*.

The Fight Club Upstairs: *NYHT*, Jan. 27, 1954, untitled.

Relentless Defender: *NYHT*, Sept. 22, 1955, untitled.

Two Champs on the Ropes: *NYHT*, Mar. 27, 1958, as "Basilio Walks Away—Robinson Takes to Bed."

Patterson's Man: *NYHT*, June 4, 1958, as "Portrait of a Fight Manager."

That Old Mary Ann: *TAF*, as "Max Baer."

Circus on Ice, *NYHT*, Jan. 13, 1956, untitled.

Top Dogs, *NYHT*, Feb. 9, 1954, untitled.

One Red Rose: *VS*.

A Gold Cup: *VS*.

The Swiftest Halfwit: *TAF*.

Great, Glittering, Gilded Fleshpot: *NYHT*, Sept. 15, 1959, as "Home of the Brave."

Sportsmen of the Fifties: *NYHT*, Dec. 17, 1959, as "Feverish Fifties."

BASEBALL 1952–1961

The Mother Tongue: *VS*.

A Chapter Closes: *RSB*.

Dept. of Emotional Reactions: *RSB*.

A Bus Named Adolphus: *VS*.

A Real Rough, Lovely Guy: *RSB*.

Like Rooting for U.S. Steel: *RSB*, as "Martin's Hit in 9th Wins Yanks 5th Series in a Row."

"And Take d'Batboy Witcha!": *NYHT*, Apr. 27, 1954, untitled.

The Color of Money: *NYHT*, Dec. 16, 1954, untitled.

Knothole of Memory: *NYHT*, Jan. 19, 1955, untitled (first subheading provides the title here).

Straws in the Pasture: *RSB*.

All Guys Finish at Last: *RSB*.

Curtain Call: *RSB*.

Connie, As Ever Was: *TAF*.

The Name Is Averill: *NYHT*, Apr. 5, 1956, untitled (first subheading provides the title here).

Connoisseur of Bottles: *NYHT*, Apr. 25, 1956, untitled (first subheading provides the title here).

Ted Williams Spits: *RSR*.

Perfection: *RSB*, as "Larsen's Feat a First in Any Series."

Wake for a Ball Club: *TAF*.

East Goes West and League Goes South: *RSB*, as "Nice Guys Finish."

Man You Listen To: *NYHT*, May 14, 1958, untitled.

Hutch and The Man: *RSR*.

Pity the Poor Umpire: *NYHT*, June 10, 1958, as "The Head Hunters."

A Demigod of Picturesque Grace: *TAF*, as "Napoleon Lajoie."

His Last Bow?: *RSB*.

59 Homers and Counting: *NYHT*, Sept. 21, 1961, as "Babe's Home Town."

SPORTS IN THE SIXTIES

Bike Ride: *SA*.

Who Broke the Tape?: *SA*, as "Who Win?"

Subway Alumni: *NYHT*, Nov. 28, 1963, as "For Subway Alumni, A Homecoming."

The Hessians: *SA*.

One Drunk, Unarmed: *RSR*.

Skinning the Sacred Bear: *NYHT*, Dec. 28, 1961, as "The North Country."

Fight Night New York: *NYHT*, Oct. 21, 1966, as "Fight Night, Past Tense."

Most Alone: *SA*.

The Road Back to Göteborg: *SA*, as "The Fight."

Death of a Welterweight: *RSR*.

"I'm the Greatest": *RSR*.

The Patrioteers: *NYHT*, Feb. 23, 1966.

Greaseniks: *SA.*
A Yank at Ascot: *SA.*
Dead Sea Downs: *RSR.*
A Not-So-Typical Day at the Races: *NYHT*, Aug. 17, 1962, as "Jump Race."
The Daddy of 'Em All: Publishers-Hall Syndicate column, Aug. 1, 1967.
Biting the Hand of the Masters: Publishers-Hall Syndicate column,
     Apr. 21, 1968.
The Black Berets: *RSR.*

FISHING FOR BASS
On Kangaroo Lake: *NYHT*, Aug. 2, 1955, as "The Pale Bass of Kangaroo."
The Mysteries of Europe: *NYHT*, Aug. 1, 1957, as "Around Europe in
     Three Hours."
Matted with Bass: *OR.*
Island Derby: *VS.*
Right Little, Tight Little Isle: *VS.*
You Give Up: *VS.*

SPORTS IN THE SEVENTIES
Constant Reader: *TAF.*
The Big Fight: *SW.*
It Takes Two: *NYT*, as "It Takes Two to Make a Fight."
Homecoming in the Slammer: *RSR.*
Massacre in Munich: *SW*, as part of "Avery's Adventures in Wonderland,"
     a longer essay combining several columns about the 1972 Munich
     Olympics.
The Round Jack Nicklaus Forgot: *RSR.*
Pound for Pound, Our Greatest Living Athlete: *RSR*, as "Willie Shoemaker."
A Little Greedy, and Exactly Right: *NYT*, June 11, 1973.
The Frenchman's Rare Day in June: *NYT*, June 12, 1977.
"I'm Always Ready to Lose": *NYT*, June 10, 1979.
Undefeatable: *SW*, as "Auld Lang Syne."
Ambush at Fort Duquesne: *SW.*
Super-Sloppy Football: *NYT*, January 15, 1978, as "Nobody Will Be
     Arrested."

BASEBALL 1962–1981

A Character and a Constant: *NYHT*, June 12, 1962, as "Age of Yogi."

Vexed Vigilantes: *NYHT*, Oct. 18, 1962, as "The Vigilantes."

Gotham's Urchins: *NYHT*, Apr. 22, 1963, as "Paradise Lost."

Big Poison: *TAF*.

Top of the Mad, Mad World: *RSB*, as "The Most Ridiculous."

"I Do Not Feel That I Am a Piece of Property": *RSB*, as "Curt Flood's
13th Amendment."

Super Stainless Classic: *SW*.

The Man Who Signed the Midget: *SW*.

Like Old Times, Sort Of: *SW*.

The Company Way: *SW*.

The Game They Invented for Willie: *RSR*.

Henry's Finest Hour—Bowie's, Too: *RSR*, as "Henry Aaron's Finest Hour."

The Terrible-Tempered Mr. Grove: *TAF*.

The Men Who Run Baseball: *NYT*, Oct. 26, 1975.

Celluloid Series: *NYT*, Jan. 11, 1976, as "With an All-Star Cast."

Bowl for Catfish: *TAF*.

The Game's Greatest Day: *NYT*, Aug. 10, 1977.

The Moving Finger Writes, Etc.: *RSR*, as "Reggie Jackson's Three Homers."

The Ever-Renewing Promise of Spring: *NYT*, Apr. 6, 1979, as "Don't Throw
Your Old Suits Away."

The Grass Turns Brown on Boston Common: *NYT*, Sept. 9, 1979, as "Grass
Turns Brown."

Mr. Yastrzemski, Please Hold for the President: *NYT*, Sept. 14, 1979,
as "A Call from Jimmy."

D.H.: *RSR*, as "Loathsome Ploy: The D.H."

Stee-rike!: *NYT*, July 26, 1981, as "The Long, Hot, Empty Summer of
No Baseball."

Envoi: Red Smith's Final Column: *NYT*, Jan. 11, 1982, as "Write Less—
And Better?"

Index